*Governance in the Americas*

RECENT TITLES FROM THE HELEN KELLOGG INSTITUTE FOR
INTERNATIONAL STUDIES

Scott Mainwaring, *general editor*

The University of Notre Dame Press gratefully thanks the Helen Kellogg Institute for
International Studies for its support in the publication of titles in this series.

Alberto Spektorowski
*The Origins of Argentina's Revolution of the Right* (2003)

Caroline C. Beer
*Electoral Competition and Institutional Change in Mexico* (2003)

Yemile Mizrahi
*From Martyrdom to Power: The Partido Acción Nacional in Mexico* (2003)

Charles D. Kenney
*Fujimori's Coup and the Breakdown of Democracy in Latin America* (2004)

Alfred P. Montero and David J. Samuels, eds.
*Decentralization and Democracy in Latin America* (2004)

Katherine Hite and Paola Cesarini, eds.
*Authoritarian Legacies and Democracy in Latin America and Southern Europe* (2004)

Robert S. Pelton, C.S.C., ed.
*Monsignor Romero: A Bishop for the Third Millennium* (2004)

Guillermo O'Donnell, Jorge Vargas Cullell, and Osvaldo M. Iazzetta, eds.
*The Quality of Democracy: Theory and Applications* (2004)

Arie M. Kacowicz
*The Impact of Norms in International Society: The Latin American Experience, 1881–2001*
(2005)

Roberto DaMatta and Elena Soárez
*Eagles, Donkeys, and Butterflies: An Anthropological Study of Brazil's "Animal Game"*
(2006)

Kenneth P. Serbin
*Needs of the Heart: A Social and Cultural History of Brazil's Clergy and Seminaries*
(2006)

Christopher Welna and Gustavo Gallón, eds.
*Peace, Democracy, and Human Rights in Colombia* (2007)

Guillermo O'Donnell
*Dissonances: Democratic Critiques of Democracy* (2007)

Marifel Pérez-Stable, ed.
*Looking Forward: Comparative Perspectives on Cuba's Transition* (2007)

For a complete list of titles from the Helen Kellogg Institute for International Studies,
see http://www.undpress.nd.edu

# GOVERNANCE
## *in the* AMERICAS

*Decentralization, Democracy, and Subnational Government in Brazil, Mexico, and the USA*

*by*

## Robert H. Wilson, Peter M. Ward, Peter K. Spink, and Victoria E. Rodríguez

*In collaboration with*

Marta Ferreira Santos Farah, Lawrence S. Graham, Pedro Jacobi, and Allison M. Rowland

*University of Notre Dame Press*     *Notre Dame, Indiana*

*Library of Congress Cataloging-in-Publication Data*

Governance in the Americas : decentralization, democracy, and subnational
government in Brazil, Mexico, and the USA / Robert R. Wilson . . . [et al.] ;
in collaboration with Marta Ferreira Santos Farah . . . [et al.].
    p.   cm. — (From the Helen Kellogg Institute for International Studies)
Includes bibliographical references and index.
ISBN-13: 978-0-268-04411-4 (pbk. : alk. paper)
ISBN-10: 0-268-04411-2 (pbk. : alk. paper)
1. Decentralization in government—Brazil. 2. Federal government—Brazil.
3. Decentralization in government—Mexico. 4. Federal government—Mexico.
5. Decentralization in government—United States. 6. Federal government—
United States. I. Wilson, Robert Hines. II. Farah, Marta Ferreira Santos.
JL2420.S8G68   2008
320.8098—dc22
2008000408

# Contents

# Tables and Figures

# Acknowledgments

This book is the result of an international collaboration of a network of scholars at the University of Texas at Austin (Lyndon B. Johnson School of Public Affairs and the Teresa Lozano Long Institute of Latin American Studies [LLILAS]), the Escola de Administração de Empresas (EAESP) of the Fundação Getulio Vargas in São Paulo (FGVSP), and the Centro de Investigación y Docencia Económicas (CIDE) in Mexico City. In addition, Dr. Enrique Cabrero Mendoza, now director general of CIDE, and Dr. Tonatiuh Guillén López (now president of the Colegio de la Frontera Norte, COLEF) both collaborated in our initial meetings, and while their ongoing commitments took them away from full participation, we are grateful for their early input and support.

Indeed, this work is the product of a research network initiated in 2000, and we wish to warmly acknowledge the support provided by our home institutions for this ambitious and long-term project. (The formation of the team and the research strategy are described more fully in chapter 1.) In particular, we would like to acknowledge the following programs for their financial support: at the University of Texas at Austin's LLILAS, we thank the Mexican Center and the Brazil Center; at the Lyndon B. Johnson School of Public Affairs, we thank the Inter-American Policy Studies Program funded by the William and Flora Hewlett Foundation, the International Program of the Policy Research Institute and the Mike Hogg Professorship of Urban Policy; and at the College of Liberal Arts and the Graduate School respectively, we acknowledge the support of the C. B. Smith Sr. Centennial Chair (#2) in U.S.-Mexico Relations and the Ashbel Smith Professorship. At the FGVSP, we are indebted to the

Ford Foundation, the William and Flora Hewlett Foundation, and the Nucleo de Pesquisa e Publicação, EAESP-FGVSP.

The research groups have also benefited from the input of several very able graduate students, including Yael Cohen, Hector Robles Pereiro, and Pamela Rogers, and by the professional administrative support provided by Jayashree Vijalapuram, Gary Moberg, and Martha Harrison, all at the University of Texas, as well as Marco Antonio Teixeira and Roberta Clemente from the Center for Public Administration and Government, EAESP-FGVSP.

We also wish to thank our numerous colleagues for their collegiality and for offering multiple commentary and critique over the years of the project, as well as two anonymous readers for their detailed and critical reading of the manuscript in its early stages. Naturally, the authors are responsible for any remaining errors and interpretation.

Robert Wilson, Peter Ward, Peter Spink, and Victoria Rodríguez
Austin and São Paulo

# Abbreviations

AARP
American Association of Retired Persons

ABONG
Associação Brasileira de Organizações Não Governamentais (Brazilian Association of NGOs)

ACIR
Advisory Commission on Intergovernmental Relations

ALCA/FTAA
Área de Libre Comercio de las Américas/Free Trade Area of the Americas

APPO
Asamblea Popular del Pueblo de Oaxaca (Popular Assembly of the People of Oaxaca)

CEPAM
Centro de Estudos e Pesquisas em Administração Municipal

CNC
Confederación Nacional de Campesinos (National Confederation of Farmworkers)

CONAGO
Conferencia Nacional de Gobernadores (National Conference of Governors)

CTM
Confederación de Trabajadores de México (Confederation of Mexican Workers)

CUT
Central Único dos Trabalhadores (Unified Workers' Central)

**EAESP**
Escola de Administração de Empresas, São Paulo

**FAFM**
Fondo de Aportaciones de Fortalecimiento Municipal (Municipal Strengthening Support Fund)

**FAISM**
Fondo de Aportaciones para Infraestructura Social (Fund for Municipal Social Infrastructure)

**FGVSP**
Fundação Getulio Vargas (Getulio Vargas Foundation), São Paulo

**FUNDEF**
Fundo de Manutenção e Desenvolvimento do Ensino Fundamental e de Valorização do Magistério (Fund for Decentralizing Basic Education)

**IADB**
Inter-American Development Bank

**IBGE**
Instituto Brasileiro de Geografia e Estatística (Brazilian Institute of Geography and Statistics

**INEGI**
Instituto Nacional de Estadística Geografía e Informática (National Institute of Statistics, Geography, and Data Processing)

**LCF**
Ley de Coordinación Fiscal (Fiscal Coordination Law)

**LLILAS**
Teresa Lozano Long Institute of Latin American Studies

**MERCOSUR**
Mercado Común del Sur

**MST**
Movimento dos Trabalhadores Rurais Sem Terra (Landless Rural Workers' Movement)

**NAFTA**
North American Free Trade Agreement

**NGA**
National Governors' Association

NGO
nongovernmental organization

OP
*orçamento participativo* (participative budgeting)

PAN
Partido Acción Nacional (National Action Party)

PRD
Partido de la Revolución Democrática (Party of the Democratic Revolution)

PRI
Partido Revolucionario Institucional (Institutional Revolutionary Party)

PROGRESA
Programa de Educación Salud y Alimentación (Program for Education, Health Care, and Nutrition)

PSD
Partido Social Democrático (Social Democratic Party

PT
Partido dos Trabalhadores (Workers' Party)

PTB
Partido Trabalhista Brasileiro (Brazilian Labor Party)

SEDESOL
Secretaría de Desarrollo Social (Ministry of Social Development)

SNCF
Sistema Nacional de Coordinación Fiscal (National System of Fiscal Coordination)

SNPD
Sistema Nacional de Planeación Democrática (National System of Democratic Planning)

SUS
Sistema Único de Saúde (decentralized health care system)

# Decentralization and the Subnational State

Peter K. Spink, Victoria E. Rodríguez,
Peter M. Ward, and Robert H. Wilson

Why study governance *and* subnational governments? After many years of being ignored, or at least relegated to the shadows of academic research, subnational governments have become a prominent topic. The deepening of democratic practice and decentralization in the Americas over the past two decades, together with emerging plurality of parties in government at the state and local levels, has encouraged many researchers to redirect their attention from the national polity and policy arenas to that of the subnational level. From different disciplinary perspectives and in a range of national contexts, the authors of this book have played an active part in this process and have come together in this study with the objective of adding depth and breadth to previous contributions through the methods of comparative debate. In doing so, we seek to introduce a number of innovations that we have found helpful in examining the complexity of the subnational arena.

First, we concentrate on the issues of "doing" government and formulating public policy at the subnational level: that is, on the midrange perspective of a polity in action. Second, we have chosen to focus upon three of the hemisphere's federal countries—Brazil, Mexico, and the USA—

which are bounded by the commonality of a fairly similar constitutional structure even though their federal arrangements operate in very different ways. The restriction of the scope of our analysis to the federalist framework is a conscious one, setting limits to our conclusions but also allowing us to have a closer look at this institutional innovation, designed from the outset to recognize the different demands of the national and the local, and featuring challenges that were well set out by Woodrow Wilson in his classical paper ([1887] 1941): "Our duty is, to supply the best possible life to a *federal* organization, to systems within systems; to make town, city, county, state, and federal governments live with a like strength and an equally assured healthfulness, keeping each unquestionably its own master and yet making all interdependent and co-operative, combining independence with mutual helpfulness. The task is great and important enough to attract the best minds" (505).

Third, we have sought to include the USA as a comparative case rather than as a benchmark. Many political scientists are rightly critical of U.S. exceptionalism and of the view that the U.S. federalist model is the one to follow or that it offers a baseline from which to assess governmental institutional practice elsewhere. We share that skepticism and hope that in rigorously treating the USA as a comparative case we may achieve greater analytical purchase upon what is happening in all three case study countries. Moreover, we expect that our analysis of federalist practices in recently democratizing subnational governments such as Brazil and Mexico will shed light on some of the tensions and practices of federalism in the contemporary USA. Succinctly put, what can we learn from Mexico and Brazil about governance in the USA?

Fourth, while consciously restricting our possible conclusions initially to federal systems, within our approach of analyzing subnational politics and the institutions in the policy-making environment, we have sought to bring into a single theoretical framework decentralization's "vertical" and "horizontal" dimensions. We will examine political devolution up and down the administrative hierarchy (federal to state to local intergovernmental relations), as well as laterally, by which we mean the opening of the political space between the various branches of governments. This entails not only the separation of powers and the exercise of checks and balances and monitoring, but also the collaborative challenge of different government levels and branches of government having to work together, addressing political and ideological tensions and pursuing different policy agendas. In short, our focus is on the business of doing government—what we will refer to in this study as the practice of "co-governance."

Fifth, we will consider the relationship between subnational governments. Do they collaborate or compete with one another? Most studies to date have focused almost exclusively upon vertical relations and bargaining between the national and subnational governments. We will be looking at the multiple arrangements that actually bear upon intergovernmental relations between, and across, the various levels.

## The Dynamics and Pressure for Political Change

Among the various pressures for change in democratic practice and governance structure at the subnational level, several overarching factors appear present in all three countries. The first is economic liberalization and, particularly, the end of the Cold War, the rise of free trade, neoliberalism, and the emergence of new economic blocs such as the North American Free Trade Agreement (NAFTA) and Mercado Común del Sur (MERCOSUR). Leaving aside whether these have delivered the results initially hoped, there is no doubt that globalization as the spirit of the times has created new economic imperatives requiring a qualitative shift in both the direction of government and the efficiency of the conduct of government. More neoliberal tendencies have argued in favor of a reduction in the size of the state or a so-called "rolling back" of government and a concomitant rise in private or mixed public-private governmental relations. But, in a counter-reaction, globalization has also stimulated stronger local government units—such as cities—to push back and seek ways to build new patterns of international relations and collaboration, such as collaboration among different city leagues. A second, and related, feature is that political liberalization—democratization in the cases of Brazil and Mexico—has resulted in increasing alternation of parties in government, and thus to the juxtaposition of different parties at different levels in both the executive and legislative branches—a Latin American version of the French "cohabitation."

A third force leading to decentralization and the recasting of federalist structures has been the apparent upsurge of communitarian principles and of municipalism that has emerged in different ways and to varying degrees in the three countries, yet is creating a common bottom-up pressure for change. The result has been a broadening of governmental experience, new patterns of governance at local and state levels with greater transparency and accountability, new patterns of political recruitment, new political rationales and orthodoxies, new development priorities, and new fiscal regimes—indeed, the emergence of a whole new type of competitiveness and linkage between party performance and electoral success. The fourth has been the coupling of the emergence, in and by themselves, of more effective subnational governments and a growing international orthodoxy in favor of decentralization (albeit for different reasons) alongside an increased willingness on the part of chief executives at all levels (national, state, and local) to embrace a greater sharing of power and responsibilities across a number of policy areas. The result has been the revitalization of federalist pacts or the awareness of their possibilities. In turn, this has generated further changes in the subnational arena and encouraged greater public participation. We do not presume at the outset that decentralization and the broadening of democratic practices are necessarily linked in any causal way to each other (a point underscored by many others before us, such as Samuels and Montero 2004 and Gibson 2004). Indeed, our starting point is to question whether their different effects are cumulative or not: that is, whether the one—either one—provides a supportive climate for the other.

Finally, a fifth defining element is the need for improved security and for greater public safety—the state as protector of its citizens. Many of the judicial reforms that we observe in Mexico and Brazil, especially, have been predicated in large part upon the need to respond to rising violence and crime, which, for a time at least, threatened to overwhelm the emergence of democratic governance at the national and subnational level (Portes and Hoffman 2003; Beato 1999; Landman 2006). Thus the need to overhaul the criminal justice system has driven the reform and modernization of the judiciary in Mexico and is an increasingly important consideration in Brazil. Since September 11, 2001, security concerns have permeated the systems of governance at all levels in the USA, but especially that of the federal level, leading to the creation of the Department of Homeland Security. In the USA especially, national and international security to protect against terrorism has become a major force shaping both the institutional structures and the government process today.

### Principal Research Questions and Major Findings

The core question that we explore is: *How have the efficacy of subnational policy making and its capacity to address issues and concerns of the "moral commonwealth" been affected by decentralization and changes in democratic practice?* By *efficacy* we mean effectiveness, appropriateness, and efficiency; and we reintroduce the idea of a moral commonwealth to reinvoke the belief that governments are there to serve the people for the common good and that in a democracy society determines what constitutes the common good. To address this overarching issue, we wish to examine the principal factors driving these different changes and analyze their impacts. Ultimately, this will allow us to comment about theory relating to governance and policy making at least within the federalist arena, if not beyond.

Chapter 2 takes a historical perspective and asks, *How have the tensions between central and local authorities been addressed in Brazil, Mexico, and the USA during the past two hundred–odd years of their independence, and what does this legacy mean for the present?* We will show that the history of federal systems is far from linear, certainly not evolutionary, and rarely stable. Granted, there is greater institutionalization of federalism and subnational governance in the USA, and greater volatility and underlying weakness in the institutional structures of Brazil and Mexico, where democratic practices are still under consolidation. However, all three countries have tensions that create pressures and lead to what we describe as pendulum-like shifts between decentralization and centralization. Similarly, we find that among our three systems, locally embedded control and exercise of governance are unique to the USA, both by design and, more specifically, as an outcome of years of evolution and experience. In both Brazil and Mexico, local autonomy, though also prescribed in the federalist design, in effect remains largely incipient. Today, in those two latter countries the federalist pact is still very much an idea that has emerged after rather than before the federation, whereas in the USA it is more consolidated; but there also it is subject to pressures, change, and fine-tuning. Partly because of different judicial traditions, the concept of judicial review (the constitutional monitoring of actions) at the subnational level is also largely associated with the USA, but in Brazil and more recently Mexico, states are beginning to develop similar functions. Above all, taking account of the *longue durée,* we find significant differences in formal constitutional theory and practice across the three countries.

In chapter 3 we begin to explore the impact of decentralization and broadening of democratic practice on the exercise of the separation of powers and on the relations between the executive, legislative, and judicial branches of government at all levels in each country: what we will call intragovernmental relations, these being the relations between the branches of government. We also explore the role of mechanisms developed for citizens and nongovernmental participation within state and local governance. Specifically, our research question here is: *What is the impact of changes in democratic practice and decentralization in activating and shaping intragovernmental relations and institutional capacity at the state and local levels?* To answer this, we must examine the nature of co-governance practices and how these are evolving. In addition, we analyze the efficacy of co-governance arrangements as measured by (a) relations and relative powers exercised by the branches; (b) the modernization of institutional capacity, readiness, and accountability across the branches; and (c) the expectations and opportunities for citizen participation in formal governance through mechanisms such as plebiscites, referenda, single-issue voting, statutory councils, consultative councils, and lobbying.

Our findings show that both Brazil and Mexico are actively engaged in consolidating their democratic structures by assigning greater institutional and functional weight to the branches and by seeking to ensure their modernization and greater technical capacity. However, we also show that the extent to which increased and more genuine participation of the legislature and judiciary translates into more effective policy making remains mixed. In this regard, Mexico, in particular, seems to be experiencing gridlock as it seeks to develop experience in the legislative and executive branches working together. And in Brazil, although at face value the judiciary seems to be empowered, it remains relatively weak. Here, the factor of note is the subtle change taking place in the reinterpretation of the role of the public prosecutor *(ministério público).* Nevertheless, both Brazil and Mexico are actively opening up the political spaces of participation of these two branches relative to the traditional dominance of the executive, thereby moving the theory of federalist provisions closer to actual political practice. In the USA, where the framers of the Constitution prescribed an effective space and functions between the three respective powers, ratified through a series of judicial decisions taken in following decades that would offer checks and balances over the executive, intragovernmental relations have worked reasonably effectively both in the federal government and in subnational governments, although the latter vary markedly according to local constructions. Local government jurisdictions generally enjoy a relatively high degree of autonomy. Here, however, the downside is that power is often so divided, and government so heavily bureaucratized, that a huge industry of lobbyists is required to guide specific interests through the complexity of government.

Important, too, is that all three countries today emphasize the need for effective public engagement in governance: this has been a longtime mandate in the case of the USA but is only a recent expectation and practice in Mexico and Brazil, and one that often remains only incipient, a point that we explore in greater depth in chapter 5. The key point that we underscore in chapter 3 is that co-governance practices are being addressed and worked out according to local traditions and processes in each of the three countries and that there is no single template for how decentralization, federalism, and horizontal relations between the branches can best be achieved. At the same time, we begin to see how the federalist model does allow considerable elasticity for seeking effectiveness in policy and public action.

We address intergovernmental relations in chapter 4 and ask: *What is the impact of decentralization and changes in democratic practice in shaping and recasting intergovernmental relations, both vertically (between the different levels) and horizontally (between governments at the same level)?* We find considerable evidence that decentralization and democratic consolidation affect capacity, but overall federalism appears to work best when the institutional elements at all levels are stronger and more stable. Counterintuitively, perhaps, we find that competition and vying for resources do not appear to lead to a race to the bottom as local governments seek to outbid each other; rather, there is a filling out of subnational spaces that creates greater interdependence and co-responsibility between actors and institutions. Indeed, we find considerable vibrancy of governance at the local level, as well as collaboration between local and state governments, in certain policy-making arenas. And while the state level of government plays important roles in exerting pressure on the federal government and diffusing innovations, states can also be obstructive, resisting local government initiatives and making problematic federal-to-local linkages. Federal roles have also changed markedly, and while they vary for different policy areas, generally the federal government is becoming more engaged in regulation and less engaged operationally in direct service delivery. We also find a growing need to consider additional scales of population centers that are not currently accommodated by federal arrangements—such as large metropolitan areas that often comprise a multitude of lower-level governments.

Today, questions of civil society and of civic responsibility are being increasingly incorporated in discussions of the broader moral commonwealth and of processes of governance. However the assumption that civil society leads to social reform is open to doubt and debate, especially within the Gramscian framework. Therefore in chapter 5 we ask: *Is civil society a leader or a laggard in decentralization? And given decentralization and democratic opening, is subnational civil society consolidating?* Strange questions, one might think, but again, somewhat counterintuitively, with the exception of the USA, where civic participation is generally strong (but electoral participation weak), we find that outside the formally prescribed opportunities outlined in chapter 3, in both Mexico and Brazil civil society organizations are growing in presence but remain, in terms of the polity, generally rather weak. Both countries have compulsory voting in elections, so the relatively high rates of electoral participation must be treated with caution (indeed, the unwarned observer could easily fall into the trap of contrasting the U.S. pattern of high civic participation and low voting with the Brazilian and Mexican pattern of low civic participation and high voting). We argue that civil society is increasing and consolidating its discursive presence but that the space formed by the very different associations and organizations that compose civil society is still by no means consensual and, on the contrary, is the focus of considerable dispute.

In the final chapter we attempt to distill the general findings from our study and offer an overview of the past and present experiences relating to decentralization of federalism and subnational government consolidation, and of decentralization's future. A number of principal conclusions are highlighted and summarized briefly here. First, we are able to identify a number of tensions among contemporary subnational relations, some of which contribute to possibilities for cooperation and others of which are sources of conflict. Because decentralization is not a linear process, we adopt a pendulum metaphor to describe the ways in which the pace and tensions vary across our three nation states, as well as within them among various policy arenas. These shifts back and forth are both temporal and sectoral, as well as political. Globalization adds to the tensions insofar as time-space compression, telecommunications, and the spread of global images and icons have differential impacts nationally, regionally, and locally. To the extent that cities and states are increasingly locked into globalized trading and political relations, this will present a new dimension to intergovernmental relations and institutional development. Subnational governments, while consolidating their intergovernmental relations in the national space, must also stay aware of and remain connected to the world at large. Trading blocs such as NAFTA and MERCOSUR and the likely, albeit postponed, Área de Libre Comercio de las Américas/Free Trade Area of the Americas (ALCA/FTAA) will offer a new supranational tier of governmental and trading relations into which national and subnational governments will need to insert themselves. That is not to suggest convergence toward global baselines: the differences that we detect both between and within the three countries are an important source of experimentation and development potential of best practice from subnational experiences that should be promoted and shared.

A second major conclusion—also pendulum-like in nature—is our observation that intergovernmental relations demonstrate pressures toward decentralization on the one hand and (re)centralization on the other. Decentralization/devolution is rarely a smooth or even process, and within a democracy it is unlikely to proceed unopposed. The nature and level of resistance and contestation were found to vary, depending upon the relative strength of the states, the extent and nature of democratic development, regional characteristics and levels of inequality, and the particular policy and sectoral arenas. Some sectors are easier and make more sense to decentralize than others. Identifying which sectors and determining how quickly to proceed may not be easy, but in all three countries we observe some efforts to recentralize, if only to achieve greater efficiency and economies of scale. The existence of sovereign states and municipal autonomy does not mean local control is fully realized; rather, new forms of insertion into the overall framework of intergovernmental relations are required that will work well for both the federation at large and the subnational space and polity specifically.

Third, we demonstrate that seeking to decentralize and to institutionalize new subnational governance arrangements can also lead to a weakening and a greater fragility and vulnerability of local and regional governments. In short, things may get worse before they get better; and even the latter is not an assured outcome, so that the critics of decentralization are often reinforced in their opposition. Even though the constitutional structures are now in place, they are not always consolidated: the judiciaries vary in their relative strength and effectiveness; legislative bodies at the national and subnational level, at least in Brazil and Mexico, are still trying to wrestle with the art of co-governance, the give-and-take of compromise and negotiation; and in both Brazil and Mexico the parties, their ideological underpinnings, and the ways partisanship translates into effective policy remain poorly understood and weakly articulated. Similarly, all three countries share the problem of how to engage effectively with civil society or, more appropriately perhaps, how to allow for its sustained and effective presence within governance systems.

There are a number of highly practical downsides to decentralization, largely as a result of factors that reduce its potential. Decentralization takes time to achieve, and significant disparities in tax base and in natural resources can accentuate divergence. As diseconomies of scale emerge in some policy arenas, many regions and localities are unprepared for the new challenges, at least in the short term; and, paradoxically, at a time when societies are seeking to democratize and to embrace broader bases of citizen participation, local oligarchs and bosses, far from being excluded from the subnational stage forever, have newfound opportunities to sustain themselves in power. Broadening the reach of public policies does not always guarantee that the priorities of the poor will come first, and decentralizing resources is no automatic guarantee that they will be at the head of the line.

Fourth, and notwithstanding the downsides mentioned above, we conclude our study generally optimistic about the potential of decentralization, not because of any a priori theoretical preference but largely because of the many different ways in which subnational governments have used its discursive effect within the institutional elasticity of the broad federalist model in support of reshaping and improving their policy-making practices and capacities. Indeed, the effectiveness of decentralization of the public sector and the ability of governments to respond to the concerns of the moral commonwealth hinge, in large part, upon developing local government capacity. There is no doubt that, among other things, this will entail more equitable revenue-sharing programs; greater legislative efficiency and effective intra- and intergovernmental relations; the opening of new forms of engagement of civil society; the modernization and upgrading of the administrative and governmental apparatus; trust in the judicial apparatus and the adoption of agreed-upon arbitration and rules of dispute resolution; and a level of career civil service to provide greater continuity in the capacity to implement policies once these have been created by politicians. Given that these do not change from one day to the next, each of these dimensions will continue to present significant challenges for subnational governments and populations for years to come. However, they will also have to compete with other, less positive challenges: threats of new health pandemics, narcotics, and terrorism. Increasingly, subnational governments will be faced with determining how best to collaborate with higher orders of government, sister governments at similar levels, and international organizations in order to ensure that events do not overtake them.

Following our process-oriented and "elastic" federalist point of departure, we speculate about what future federalist institutional architecture will entail: the embracing of new and formerly underrepresented populations such as indigenous groups, greater single-purpose governments; horizontal collaborations and pacts between governments at similar levels; and new so-called "federacy" arrangements built around the spatial patchworks of ethnic, cultural, and linguistic rights that might successfully avoid the centrifugal pressures leading to fragmentation and governmental implosion.[1] In short, federalism will need to develop and grow and at the same time be flexible and elastic in order to accommodate the decentralization and inter- and intragovernmental challenges that lie ahead. If democracy is still in its infancy, with a future of invention ahead of it, the same applies even more to federalism and to federalist democracies.

## Methodology and Case Selection

Our focus is the efficacy of subnational policy making in the context of decentralization and changes in democratic practice. By *efficacy*, we mean the ability of subnational governments to produce positive effects through the design, adoption, and implementation of public policies that respond to the broad demands of the moral commonwealth and are in the public interest. As discussed above, the research on decentralization, at least in Latin America, has focused principally on the factors that led to the decision to decentralize and the changes in governmental authority and incentives for actors in the reformed national-subnational systems. In our case, however, the emphasis is both institutional and vertical.

The countries we examine in depth have presidentialist systems with a constitutionally mandated separation of powers and with some design for checks and balances to operate between the branches (executive, legislative, and judicial). To determine the efficacy of subnational governments, we believe that changes in the powers and actions of all branches in the subnational context and, most importantly, new patterns of co-governance, are crucial developments. Whereas legislative and executive interactions are a priority, the role of the judiciary deserves examination as well. On this particular point, the contrast of the civil code tradition of Mexico and Brazil with the common-law tradition of the USA provides insights into the culture of subnational policy making. A second dimension of our analysis departs from the current literature on decentralization and explores the changes in democratic practice at the subnational level, particularly changes in civil society and their subsequent impacts on citizen participation in subnational policy making.

In choosing to focus on policy-making capacity, we initially considered taking one or two policy arenas and comparing them across the three countries. However, we quickly realized that this would change the principal axis of analysis away from decentralization and changes in subnational government (*qua* government) and toward a comparative sectoral policy analysis, which, while laudable in itself and providing systematic data, would have led us to lose sight of the broader patterns of governance and change. This we did not wish to do, so instead our methodological approach draws upon a range of policy issues, principally from the social policy arena but also from environmental and economic development policy. The contrast across policy arenas and across countries provides the variation needed to capture impacts of various factors. For example, the impact of legal tradition, civil versus common law, becomes more evident when the judiciaries in countries with different traditions are contrasted. As one might anticipate, we found substantial variation in the extent that policy systems have decentralized across countries, even within a single country. In fact, recentralization in some policy arenas can be noted in each of the countries.

Thus this study does not attempt to evaluate outcomes of specific policies. While a worthy research question and one that we acknowledge to be important for future research, it is beyond the scope of this study. For example, understanding the impact of institutional design on education systems and student learning is important, certainly to policy communities in the three countries (Grindle 2004). But that is not our purpose here. Rather, we seek to provide a broad-brush treatment of the efficacy of subnational policy making, and hence we focus on structural changes and incentives for policy actors and citizen engagement in subnational policy making. Furthermore, by focusing on the political and policy-making constraints that subnational governments face, as well as on the powers that a decentralized federal structure has brought to them in these three case studies, our aim is to integrate the subnational level into comparative studies in a more systematic way.

A comparative study such as this offers a perspective that is both theoretically oriented and empirically based. While the countries we are analyzing are vastly different in a number of respects—society, culture, economy, and demography—we expect this combined approach to provide a better understanding of how subnational governments function within a federalist structure. Each country will receive comparable treatment, incorporating examples from several policy areas. Thus our study provides a systematic and detailed exploration of the institutional and political underpinnings of subnational governments.

Returning to the question of choice of cases for this study, the three countries have federalist and presidentialist governmental systems. They are the largest in the hemisphere in terms of population (see table 1.1). They share a common history of decolonization into a regionally fragmented political structure. And although Canada shares several characteristics with the three, including that of a federalist structure and large geographic expanse, its population size and urban system are sufficiently different to suggest that the challenges to subnational governance are likely to be dissimilar in important respects. The other two countries with federalist systems, Argentina and Venezuela, are variants in important respects, lacking a separation of powers at the subnational level. Venezuela until recently did not have a fully fledged system of separation of powers at the subnational level, making it a case of executive and legislative federalism, while Argentina, although it has national and subnational executives, legislatures, and judiciaries, has a constitution that gives the federal government the authority to intervene in the provinces—in any of the three branches (Cameron and Falleti 2005, 266–67). In addition, both have a primate urban system (i.e., one dominated by the national capital), again suggesting to us that the challenges to subnational governance would probably be different from those found in the three countries examined here. In the end, the choice of cases also reflected the belief that the three countries chosen have a great deal to learn from each other.

As one would expect, given the significant differences in the size and productivity of the economies in the three countries, the levels of development and corresponding socioeconomic indicators vary substantially, with Brazil and Mexico trailing the USA significantly (see table 1.1). Brazil's income inequality is among the highest in the world, while that of the USA is among the highest of high-income countries. The three countries have high levels of urbanization, with second-tier cities in each country demonstrating relatively high growth rates. Despite the maturing of the urban system in each country, there are vast geographic differences within each country in terms of population levels and the urban system. Each of the countries has very significant expanses of low population density.

The public sector, as measured by public spending, is much larger in the USA than in the other two countries, as one would expect. Although public spending as a share of gross domestic product is greatest in the USA, it does not vary substantially across the three countries. But on a per capita basis, public spending in the USA is over seven times greater than in Mexico and over ten times greater than in Brazil (see table 1.1).

Each of the countries in our project has, without question, a distinctive brand of federalism. While the general institutional architecture is roughly similar—three levels of government (federal, state, and local), with separation of powers and checks and balances among three branches (executive, legislative, and judicial)—the practices of subnational governments'

Table 1.1 Demographic, Social, and Economic Indicators in Brazil, Mexico, and the USA

A. Geographic and Population Characteristics

| | Size (sq km) | Population (Millions), 2004[1] | Pop. Growth (% per Year), 1985–2000[2] | Number of Municipalities Over 500k | Under 20k |
|---|---|---|---|---|---|
| Brazil | 8,511,965[3] | 178.7 | 1.5 | 30 (0.5%) | 4,019 (73%) |
| Mexico | 1,972,550[4] | 103.8 | 1.8 | 27 (1.1%) | 1,607 (66%) |
| USA | 9,631,418[5] | 293.5 | 0.9 | 29 (.15%)[6] | 18,382 (91%)[7] |

B. Socioeconomic Characteristics

| | GNI/Capita, 2004[8] | Below $1/Day ($ PPP), 1998[9] | Gini Index (in %), 2003[10] | Infant Mortality, 2000 |
|---|---|---|---|---|
| Brazil | 8,020 | 10 | 60.7 | 35[11] |
| Mexico | 9,590 | 8 | 51.9 | 25[12] |
| USA | 39,710 | n.a. | 40.8 | 6.9[13] |

C. Public Sector

| | Governments State | Local | General Government Final Consumption Expenditures as % of GDP (2004) |
|---|---|---|---|
| Brazil | 27* | 5,500 | 14 |
| Mexico | 32* | 2,443 | 11 |
| USA | 50 | 87,525[14] | 15 |

* Including federal district.

[1] World Bank (2006d).
[2] UN Human Settlements Programme (2001).
[3] U.S. Central Intelligence Agency (2006a).
[4] U.S. Central Intelligence Agency (2006b).
[5] U.S. Central Intelligence Agency (2006c).
[6] U.S. Bureau of the Census (2000, Table C-1).
[7] U.S. Bureau of the Census (2002a).
[8] GNI = gross national income. World Bank (2006d).
[9] PPP = purchasing power parity. UN Statistics Division (2006).
[10] The Gini Index measures the extent to which the distribution of income (or consumption) among individuals or households within a country deviates from a perfectly equal distribution. A value of 0 represents perfect equality (when all individuals have the same level of income), and a value of 100 represents total inequality (when one individual or percentile of the population holds all the income). UN Development Programme (2003).
[11] World Bank (2006a).
[12] World Bank (2006b).
[13] World Bank (2006c).
[14] U.S. Bureau of the Census (2002b). The breakdown of 87,525: 3,039 counties; 19,429 municipalities; 16,504 towns and townships; and 48,558 school and special districts.

politics and policy making are quite distinctive and unique. The fragmented nature of local government in the USA is shown by the very large number of government entities: over eighty-five thousand governments, including counties, cities, independent school districts, and special districts (table 1.1). In contrast, Brazil and Mexico have a single type of local government, the municipality. Subnational government expenditures in the USA constitute a much higher share of the nation's public final consumption expenditures than in the other two countries.

As we shall observe in considerable detail, decentralization has also followed distinct paths in the reassignment of responsibilities and changes in institutional design: in the USA the devolution revolution has meant the transfer of a series of responsibilities but also of newfound resources and powers; in Mexico the "new federalism" has been laden with political implications, with state governments becoming the major beneficiaries; and in Brazil, new competencies have been transferred primarily to the municipalities.

### The Research Team and Authorship

The concept of this research effort was first discussed in early 2000. It was determined that a comparative examination of federalism and subnational policy making in the three countries had merit, even though the specific set of research questions would require further reflection. It was also determined that the study must adopt a multidisciplinary approach. It was further decided that the project would utilize previously existing institutional relations that had been developed between the University of Texas at Austin (the Lyndon B. Johnson School of Public Affairs and the Teresa Lozano Long Institute of Latin American Studies), the Center of Public Administration and Government at the Getulio Vargas Foundation (FGVSP) in São Paulo, and the Centro de Investigación y Docencia Económicas (CIDE) in Mexico City. A team of eight senior researchers with training in political science, public administration, geography, social psychology, urban planning, and public policy was assembled, with a working group established for each country. The teams were Larry Graham, Victoria Rodríguez, Peter Ward, and Robert Wilson in the USA; Marta Farah, Pedro Jacobi, and Peter Spink in Brazil; and Allison Rowland in Mexico (and, in the first phase of the project, Tonatiuh Guillén López and Enrique Cabrero Mendoza).

The group met in Austin, Texas, in 2000 to establish a set of specific research questions and a schedule of research tasks. An overall structure was created of the research themes to be addressed, and the broad brush-strokes of a possible book project were established at that time. A member of the country-specific working group was assigned to each chapter and asked to prepare a working paper on the chapter for that country. At the next meeting, in Paraty, Rio de Janeiro, in late 2000, country reports for each chapter were presented and the integration of chapter reports was initiated. One member of each chapter team presented a draft of the chapter at the next meeting, held in San Miguel de Allende, Guanajuato, in 2001. The chapters were discussed first by the researchers contributing to each chapter and then by the larger group. Revisions of individual chapters, incorporating additional authors in some chapters, were undertaken in meetings held in Santa Fe, New Mexico, in 2002 and in Austin, Texas, in 2003. In later meetings, an initial set of conclusions and a chapter outline were developed. A further round of revisions on chapters 1 through 5 was made in São Paulo (January 2005), and a first draft of a complete conclusions chapter was developed. These were reviewed in team meetings in late 2005 and early 2006 after we had received detailed comments from anonymous reviewers selected by the University of Notre Dame Press.[2] A final round of revisions and corrections was made late in 2006, allowing us to take some account of the changes wrought by elections in all three countries during the fall of that year. In all three cases those election results promise some fine-tuning of the processes that have already begun and that we describe more fully in this volume. Specifically, in Mexico the electoral victory of Felipe Calderón for the PAN (Partido Acción Nacional/National Action Party), the significant changes in the composition of Congress, the institutional and extra-institutional challenges mounted by López Obrador and the PRD (Partido de la Revolución Democrática/Party of the Democratic Revolution), and the crisis in the southern state of Oaxaca all have important implications for institutional and constitutional reform and for intergovernmental relations. In Brazil, the reelection of Luiz Inacio Lula da Silva for another four-year term has also highlighted the need for greater cross-party negotiation and consensus building in Congress, and, as in Mexico, the need to address a growing divide between richer and poorer states and its regional manifestation between the north and south of these two countries. Finally, in the USA, the shift of control of Congress from the Republican to the Democratic Party is expected to have important repercussions, not only in arenas of foreign policy and security, but also in relations with Brazil and especially with Mexico.

This has been a remarkable and ongoing collaborative effort, therefore, with multidisciplinary input from all participants. That said, principal responsibility for drafting and integrating each chapter fell to different team members, and this is reflected, by mutual agreement, in the attribution of authorship in each section.[3] In a research program that has covered some five years of analysis, many people have joined in the search for documents and data and have discussed the preliminary findings. Many of these are our students who have followed the arguments and debates and have contributed greatly to the conclusions reached. Others are our close collaborators who have been ready to check assumptions and data sets, helping us test the ideas that have emerged. Marco Antonio Teixeira and Roberta Clemente (in São Paulo), Mona Koerner and Yael Cohen (in Austin), and Hector Robles (in Mexico) have all been key in helping us unravel the many questions that we posed, in checking information, and in identifying voices that needed to be heard. A research program is never an abstract march of ideas; on the contrary, it comprises people and their overarching intellectual and disciplinary concerns.

While our collective scholarly interests in government structures and governance practices in the three countries may have been the starting point, our study comparatively assesses the substantive challenges these governments face as they decentralize and democratize. In short, it seeks to contribute not only to the practice of governance but to the very real and demanding social agendas that our three countries face. In Latin America, social development and the dramatic indicators of inequality in human development have been on the agenda of regional organizations for a number of years. Bernardo Kliksberg (1997, 2001), for example, has constantly drawn attention to the state's role in relation to social issues and poverty. Concerns with effective public policy and the impact on the citizenry were features of the Latin American Council for Administrative Development's policy document (Centro Latinoamericano de Administración para el Desarollo [CLAD] 1998), and many Latin American governments have signed recent international agreements in the areas of human rights, gender, the environment, and other matters. In the USA, despite a shifting of national priorities, poverty, social inequalities and, more broadly, economic growth and quality-of-life issues frequently appear in the country's political discourse. It is in this light that we view the level of responsiveness and responsibility of the subnational level of government. Ultimately, effective decentralization and its impact at the subnational level will be measured not merely in terms of effective government but also in terms of its effect on people and their quality of life.

## Some Key Concepts and Terms Explained

Even though the primary terms used in the book are in common use and can be found in newspapers, reports, and everyday conversations, the versions of these terms that circulate in these spaces are not necessarily the same as the versions that we use in the text. Further, the interdisciplinary nature of our work brings together many different parts of the social sciences whose language repertoires can at times evoke the notion embodied in the phrase of "two peoples divided by the same language." For this reason, in this final section to the opening chapter we seek not so much to define terms definitively, as to explain the positions we take and to offer brief working definitions of the terms that we use. In addition, we will use the final pages of this chapter to engage more substantively with the key themes that underpin this volume: decentralization, democracy, participation, and governance.

First, though, we begin with the terms *presidentialism, federalism*, and *checks and balances*. A presidential regime is one in which the head of state is an elected official with a fixed term of office, as opposed to a parliamentary regime, in which the prime minister is the chief executive, whose accountability is to the parliamentary majority and under whose authority he or she is authorized to form a cabinet for the major positions in government. Regular elections are also mandated in parliamentary systems, but they may also occur if and when the prime minister and the government lose their capacity to mobilize support from Parliament (whether as majority party or as a coalition) and are obliged to call a general election (Cameron and Falleti 2005; Graham 2006). The U.S. system was the first case to adopt a presidential as distinct from a parliamentary regime, and it was constructed within the context of a republic in which there would be a separation and a division of powers between the executive and legislative branches in order to ensure accountability to the people and to limit the powers of the president (executive branch).

In this case, the separation-of-powers principle constrains executive authority by a separately constituted congress and judicial system. In the USA, the Congress became bicameral as a consequence of the "Great Compromise," in which the Senate was to be formed on the basis of two representatives from each state in the republic, while the House of Representatives would be constituted on the basis of numerical majorities. Thus the larger states have more representatives in Congress, in exchange for which the smaller states obtain representation equal to that of the larger states, albeit in a separate body of Congress.

The U.S. federal system incorporates the separation-of-powers principle and organization on a geographic basis, in which power is divided between a national government, whose powers are restricted to specific allocations in the Constitution, and state governments, to whom all powers not specifically assigned to the federal government belong, with the understanding that the balance of power resides in the states, each of which has the power to freely determine the form(s) of subnational governments under state authority. The division-of-powers principle is defined differently across countries, but the constitutionally defined powers of a subnational governmental unit are common to all and distinguish federalist from unitary systems of government. Since the presidential republic of the USA was the first of its kind, the separation and division of powers became identified with how accountability and constraints on power would be determined, and this has been intensely debated throughout the country's history. In *Marbury vs. Madison* (1803), it was determined that the federal courts would have the authority to interpret the Constitution by judicial precedent in a fashion independent of executive and congressional authority. This became crucial in making a federal presidential republic (as defined by the Constitution) function, permitting the courts' interpretation and reinterpretation when clashes of authority occurred that required adjudication. The only break in the principle of adjudication to avoid open conflict was the Civil War.[4]

Thus a system of division of powers and separation of powers—along with its implicit "checks and balances"—is created between levels of government (subnational to national), as well as between the respective branches (powers), to ensure accountability and monitoring and to avoid the excessive accumulation of power in any one of the branches. As we shall observe in detail in later chapters, while Brazil, Mexico, and the USA share these elements in theory, the actual practice of the division and separation of powers varies in each country, as well as over time (see also Mainwaring and Welna 2003).

One dimension of *state reform* not substantially addressed in the literature is the relationship among the branches of government in decentralized systems (O'Donnell 1999). Constitutional reform in Latin America has tended to provide additional powers to the legislative branch, compensating for the historical dominance of the executive in virtually all countries of the region. Even in the USA the development of state legislative competencies was an important concern as early as the 1950s (R. Wilson 1993). But in Latin America the productive exercise of these powers in legislative-executive interactions appears to remain somewhat rare at the subnational level (Gibson 2004).

The research literature on democratization and state reform on subnational policy making in Latin America is also relatively undeveloped. Kent Eaton and Tyler Dickovick's (2004) book addressing institutional design in a historical context focuses on subnational governmental performance, while another major study analyzing decentralization and democracy calls for additional research on policy outcomes in decentralized systems (Montero and Samuels 2004a). But the aspirations of democratization movements for the integration of politically disenfranchised and poor populations into more decentralized regimes, thus producing changes in policy agendas of subnational governments, has received limited attention. A recently developing literature (Campbell 2003; Campbell and Fuhr 2004) is trying to understand the outcomes of decentralization at the local levels and its consequences on local governance (see also Hiskey and Seligson 2003; Moreno 2007). By focusing on the effects of decentralization on politics and policy making at the subnational level in Brazil, Mexico, and the USA, we expect that our study will make a significant contribution to this emerging area of scholarly interest.

We adopt an institutional and organizational-based definition of *government* and use the term interchangeably with *the public sector.* Therefore, government will include all elements of the executive, legislative, and judicial branches. By *governance,* we refer to the relationship between the government and the governed as practiced through its multiple dimensions. This relationship contains formal legal dimensions, such as the protection of human rights, rule of law, and free and fair elections (in the democratic context), as well as informal dimensions including political culture, civic engagement, interest group formation, openness of government to citizen input, public spaces, a free press, and political parties.

By *public policy* we refer to the actions and formulations taken and made by government. Policy includes, as Thomas Dye (1997) argues, not only what governments choose to do but also what they do not choose to do. In all three countries, the latter is as, if not more, important than the former. We take an expansive view of action, including public-sector investments; implementation of social and economic development programs; and operations of governmental institutions, public regulatory systems, and judicial systems: in sum, the range of actions taken by public-sector institutions. In this volume we are concerned with two principal phases of the policy process: the articulation of meaning and the construction of agendas that lead to the definition of policies; and policy implementation, that is, of the actions that result from the policy definition, the allocation of resources and responsibilities. Of course, we recognize from the outset that in many policy arenas the implementation of public policy will rely heavily on nongovernmental actors, whether these are for-profit or nonprofit. In chapter 3, we introduce the term *co-governance* to underscore the respective roles played by the branches and by citizens in the formulation and implementation of public policy.

Both unitary and federalist systems of government face the challenge of balancing governmental power and authority between national and subnational governments. On a different scale, the European Union faces a similar challenge in defining roles and authorities of nations vis-à-vis the EU itself. The relationship between national and subnational governments, referred to here as intergovernmental relations, is not stable over time, especially in geographically large and regionally diverse countries (Montero and Samuels 2004a; Gibson 2004; Eaton and Dickovick 2004).

In such contexts, mismatches between resources and responsibilities can create tensions in the intergovernmental systems and can never be entirely resolved. Regional differences in economic performance will, in fact, redefine these mismatches over time. The relative power of national and subnational political officials can shift as well. These complex systems do not lead to stable patterns, but in recent decades broad support found virtually worldwide for decentralization of governmental authority in national space has emerged. Still, *decentralization* is far from a consensus term, as we shall observe in detail below.

## Decentralization in Theory and Practice

*Decentralization* is usually conceived as a vertical process that devolves resources and decision-making autonomy to the subnational and local tiers of government authority. This breaks or weakens the traditional hierarchical and often rigid pecking order in which one executive level exercises authority over subordinate levels. Decentralization seeks to bring greater responsibility to the lower levels. As a complex phenomenon, various definitions of decentralization exist. Some clear-cut distinctions are made in the literature among political, economic, social, and administrative decentralization; between functional and area decentralization; and among devolution, delegation, and deconcentration.[5] Only when these distinctions are clarified can one begin to draw lines and attach labels that identify systems as "administratively decentralized," "politically centralized," and so on. In essence, though, all types of decentralization are only variations of the same phenomenon: the dispersion of functions and power from the center to the periphery.

As we will observe in chapter 2, the USA adopted a highly decentralized governmental structure, with powers residing largely at the state and local levels. Although the intergovernmental balance has varied over time, the principle has always been one of a highly decentralized federalism, in a comparative sense. In Brazil and Mexico, the process has been less consistent, but with a tendency of urbanization and power to be heavily centralized in one or two cities whose comparative advantage progressively increases to the detriment of other regions. Recent policies of vertical decentralization—whether political or economic—seek to recast that hierarchy and provide greater opportunity for subnational autonomy.

In essence, the fundamental disjuncture between centralization and decentralization is that "some functions of the state are inherently better handled by the center while others are inherently better resolved by a deconcentrated structure" (S. Cohen et al. 1981, 34). At times, this more pragmatic stance of "working better" can also become a principle, as in the concept of subsidiarity, according to which decision making and responsibilities should be accorded to the lowest level possible and the only functions left to the higher levels should be those that cannot reasonably be performed elsewhere.

Once a government decides to decentralize (for whatever reason), the next issue is deciding *what* to decentralize. In an effort to retain as much control as possible, and because most decentralization efforts (at least in the initial stages) tend to be rather tentative and half-hearted, most national governments opt for decentralizing the more *routine* tasks to subordinate units, while the *strategic* tasks remain under the center's control. From both an administrative and a political point of view, deciding which functions are to be handled where, and by whom, constitutes the central issue.[6]

Yet in spite of the perceived advantages of decentralized structures, there are many practical reasons for centralization (see Oates 1990, 2005), and traditionally Latin America has been overarchingly centralized (Borja et al 1989; Graham 1990). Comparative analyses of centralization and development also reveal that as industrialization advanced, governmental control sometimes decreased (giving way, also, to more political decentralization) and led to rapid economic growth. This was the case in Great Britain and Japan, which were much more localist and developed more rapidly than, for instance, France and China, which had inherited strong imperial bureaucracies. The same circumstances favored the development of Germany, which showed higher rates of industrial growth before 1850, when its system was more fragmented (Teune 1982, 98). But as industrial development continued, pressures for change mounted. It became increasingly necessary for the state to intervene to address such issues as cyclical recessions, to stimulate growth, and to solve the social problems caused by capitalist development (Olloqui

1983). Thus governmental centralization evolved into something that was accepted and even desired in most countries, at least until the middle of the twentieth century.

Several factors developed toward the second half of the twentieth century that demanded reconsideration of the apparent advantages of centralization. Demographically, the nature of countries was quickly changing, with rising urbanization and especially the growth of "secondary" cities. Associated with population growth and rapid urbanization were the multiple problems of providing basic infrastructure, full employment opportunities, and adequate services—all away from the central (and often primate) city. Excessive centralization also made decision-making and bureaucratic procedures slower and more rigid, and many countries began to show large regional inequalities because the prevailing system was unable to take effective advantage of the country's resources. Decentralization began to appear more and more as a developmental consensus, something that made sense within an increasingly democratic world order.

In the early postwar period leading up to the early 1960s, decentralization was placed on the high moral ground along with democracy and economic development, serving as a lever for the former and a guarantee of the latter (B. Smith 1988). At the same time, it was also recognized that decentralization was a difficult process. Problems of skills, traditionalist or patrimonialist styles and cultures, local elites, personalist leaders, lack of fiscal competence or structure, and corruption were among the many elements that emerged. Decentralization was seen as de-concentration, that is, the delegation or transference of authority, power and/or services from the center, which could or could not also include the corresponding structures of democratic representation (B. Smith 1985).

Generally speaking, by the 1970s most industrialized countries had adopted policies to harness the decentralization process to their economies and their public administration apparatuses. In fact, during this decade most countries embarked on ambitious decentralization programs of one type or another. It is significant that the majority of these programs were also related to the overall objective of increasing political participation (Teune 1982, 102).

Progress in the communications field also facilitated decentralization, making it increasingly easier to maintain coordination from a distance.

Many industrial nations experienced an important shift in their production patterns under late capitalism. Industrial production became more "footloose" and shifted toward high-amenity areas (e.g., the U.S. Sunbelt) or to lower-labor-cost regions on the national and global peripheries. At the national level this stimulated a process of counterurbanization, with a corresponding decline in the older, established industrial and urban centers. In some developing countries a similar shift has been observed, as their formerly highly concentrated urban patterns allegedly demonstrate a "polarization reversal" (Townroe and Keen 1984).

By the early 1980s, decentralization was beginning to acquire a further layer of meaning as part of the growing debate on economic reform and the fairly widespread adoption of structural adjustment models (Schuurman 1998), and later of market-oriented neoliberal economic policies (Snyder 2001a). National governments were seen as top-heavy and needing to be "downsized" or "rolled back," to use two of the many expressions that circulated during this period. Public services should be decentralized either to the market (outwards) or to the local level (downwards) as a way of guaranteeing a better customer-oriented service. In many Latin American countries, given the lack of an effective local government framework (Nickson 1995), the answer was the various parallel Social and Emergency Investment Funds organizations and structures, which were in effect to assume most, if not all, social policy.

Although the tendency throughout various regions of the world was to move toward decentralization, that process was not straightforward in Latin America. In Latin America, from independence on, political factors tended to support a more centralized state, which could control whatever conflicts arose among local and regional power brokers and bosses *(caciques)*. As Graham (1990) argues, decentralization of power and relaxation of control would have equaled disintegration of those national institutions. Yet this had changed by the 1980s, as externally imposed structural adjustment policies obliged states to downsize both their public bureaucracies and their level of state intervention, often handing off functions to the private sectors and to nongovernmental organizations (NGOs). Equally important, democratization had led to the eclipse of bureaucratic authoritarian regimes; through the ballot box different parties were coming to power, many of them with support that was regionally (and provincially) based. Moreover, the heavy protection formerly associated with the economies (as well as the polities) was shifting toward greater global integration and externally oriented manufacturing growth. To a greater or lesser extent, subnational governments and their associated regions were moving into the frame. The states were being brought "back in." Moreover, the international orthodoxy of the World Bank and other institutions underscored the need to strengthen regional administrative capacity that would be capable of taking on the mantle of devolution of power, resources, and responsibilities. Information exchanges about so-called best-practice experiences in local development and public administration were promoted. And often it became apparent that some level of re-regulation and new institutional development was required to ensure economic efficiency with some level of social justice as countries sought to devolve and decentralize to subnational entities (Snyder 2001b).

Decentralization in Latin America has been described as the "quiet revolution" of the 1990s (Campbell 2003). Certainly most countries have taken major steps to reduce the highly centralized nature of decision making and resources vested in the other major cities—sometimes, as in Brazil, even creating a new federal capital in an attempt to hasten that process. Ultimately, though, decentralization has been fostered by new industrialization imperatives and regimes of accumulation; by democratization and political liberalization; by strong international advocacy from institutions like the World Bank (Hiskey and Seligson 2003); and in some cases, too, by a growing awareness among leading political actors that stability, continuity, and staying in power may best be achieved by relinquishing some of the centralized claims upon power—what one of us has described as retaining power by appearing to give it away (Rodríguez 1997; see also O'Neill 2005). Recent research on decentralization in Latin America has determined that the specific factors leading to the decision to decentralize, including electoral and partisan politics and incentives embedded in governmental and political institutions, vary considerably across countries (Montero and Gibson 2004; Gibson 2004; Campbell 2003; Beer 2001). The decision to decentralize may have been affected by international forces, but the country case studies convincingly argue that country-specific political dynamics are of primary importance in decisions to decentralize governmental structures (O'Neill 2005).

Yet another layer in the multiple meanings attached to decentralization refers to its role in the strengthening of the broader social fabric. Events in eastern Europe (Keane 1998), the earlier recognition of the role played by NGOs (Carroll 1992; Lemaresquier 1980), and the importance attached to participation in rural and urban development planning experiences (Bebbington 1997) brought decentralization back to the social arena as a challenge to the new orthodoxies of privatization. Either decentralization was seen as a strategy for strengthening civil society or, conversely, the strengthening of civil society was itself seen as a requirement for decentralization, thus providing a new and updated version of the decentralization-democracy-economic development triad (Spink, Clemente, and Keppke 1999). As these various meanings were woven through the existing fabric of ideas, the economic or market arena would also be incorporated through the growing emphasis on the role of philanthropic and private (business and commercial) organizations as part of the societal capacity for social policy action, leading to the emergence of the so-called third sector. Moreover, the recent quickening of interest in and assertions of the self-governance rights of many indigenous communities at the subnational level have further increased the saliency of decentralization.

Recent research has attempted to assess the actual impacts of decentralization in federalist structures on democratic practice (Stepan, in Gibson 2004). This research concludes that the conflation of democratization and decentralization is, in fact, mistaken. That is, a decentralized governmental system does not necessarily enhance democracy or civil society. In Bolivia, for example, while a major national commitment to decentralization was found to bolster citizen support for system change at the national level, where the newly empowered local governments proved weak and unable to fulfill their newfound commitments, local populations reacted with negative views of the political system (Hiskey and Seligson 2003). As we have previously mentioned, our study gives considerable attention to this point.

Thus, after a blossoming of theoretical and empirical literature from the mid-1970s onwards, during the mid-1990s some analysts began to express reservations about the widely proclaimed benefits of decentralization, especially in relation to developing countries (Tanzi 1995; Prud'homme 1995). While they were supportive of decentralizing efforts, their criticism focused primarily on the adverse effects of decentralization on the economy, specifically in three areas: threatening macroeconomic stability, exacerbating income inequality, and weakening economic and production efficiency (Moreno 2005). Tanzi argues that decentralization programs in developing countries are characterized by the absence of a clear and thorough contract between the central and the subnational governments and that the negative outcomes are exacerbated because local policy makers have inadequate management systems. Prud'homme argues that a decentralized system exacerbates income inequality, since empirical analyses demonstrate that in a centralized system the wealthier regions subsidize the poorer ones, a point echoed by Hutchcroft (2001), who suggests that devolution can be especially problematic where it strengthens the role and influence of local authoritarian bosses and *caciques*.

With regard to *fiscal decentralization,* which in theory is expected to increase economic efficiency, the critical literature also demonstrates that in developing countries this may not be the case. For a variety of reasons, the infrastructure conducive to the potential efficiency gain is not present—for example, local policy makers are unresponsive and unqualified and often lack the resources and the incentives to improve their performance. The empirical evidence presented in various studies, sometimes sponsored by international organizations such as the World Bank and the International Monetary Fund (see Ter-Minassian 1997; Litvack, Ahmad, and Bird 1998; Bird and Vaillancourt 1998), has led some scholars and analysts to caution policy makers about the design and implementation of decentralization initiatives, or at least to point to variations in a local state's capacity to bounce back from economic shocks that the nation or region has suffered (Hiskey 2005b). In particular, these authors suggest that special attention be given to expenditure responsibilities, assignment of taxes, intergovernmental transfers, and borrowing at the subnational level (Wibbels 2005).

## Democratization and Governance: Theory and Practice

As outlined in the first half of this chapter, our study of subnational government is embedded within a context of both decentralization and, in the case of Brazil and Mexico, democratization. Issues of representation, participation, and civil society are central to each of the core chapters in this volume, so we should probably pause briefly here to discuss democratic theory that shapes our three societies, as well as to clarify some of the specific terms that we propose to use.[7]

Scholars claim that participation in civil society leads to more participation in formal politics and to deepening democracy. A paradox in Mexico and Brazil—and the rest of Latin America, for that matter—is that while citizen groups have been prominently active politically in civil society, they invariably remain marginal players in formal politics. In emerging democracies such as these, this is significant because a lack of fair representation of all social groups could undermine the legitimacy of the new democratic system. Time and again we see references to the fact that it is difficult to label a country as democratic if a large portion of the population is in effect excluded from formal political participation. The exclusion of marginalized groups makes the state less responsive to the needs of its citizens, especially if a group has special interests and needs.

### Representation

In her pivotal theoretical work on the concept of representation, Hanna Pitkin (1967, 1969) traces the evolution of the concept from ancient Greece to the modern period and states, very directly, that "there does not even seem to be any remotely satisfactory agreement on what representation is or means" (Pitkin 1969, 7). The theoretical literature is burdened with persistent and unresolved controversies: some scholars distinguish between representative government and other forms of government; others argue that every government is representative of the people; and still others argue that no government can ever be truly representative. A further strand of controversy in the literature concerns the role and behavior of the representative: Should the representative follow his or her own judgment when making a decision (the "delegative" mode), or should he or she blindly follow the wishes of his or her constituency? These "seemingly irresoluble conflicts and controversies" (Pitkin 1967, 7) continue to be present in contemporary discussions of representation, and thus one of the more fundamental questions for political theorists continues to be how governmental institutions will represent the interests of citizens. In essence, to explore the issue, it is necessary to look at two broad lines of inquiry: what a representative does, that is, what constitutes the activity of representing; and what a representative is, that is, what he or she must be like in order to represent.

In the nineteenth century Jeremy Bentham and James Mill argued for elite representation, where representatives would govern on behalf of their constituents because ordinary people did not have the time, knowledge, or wisdom to make the best decisions. In short, consultation with the public was not required. Interestingly, it was within this concept of elite representation that Mill's son, John Stuart Mill, wrote one of the more radical pieces of his time. In his *Considerations on Representative Government* ([1861] 1958), he boldly argued that every section of the population, including minorities, should be proportionally represented in government. Theorists concerned with this so-called "mirror" representation argue that representatives should be reflective of the society they govern. In the founding era of the United States, for example, John Adams believed that in the young nation the newly created legislature "should be an exact portrait, in miniature, of the people at large, as it should think, feel, reason, and act like them" ("Letter to John Penn," in Adams 2000, 493). As noted earlier, the compromise reached in the USA in 1776 between those arguing for "mirror" representation and those arguing for "delegate" representation was to have a bicameral legislature where both interests could be represented. The Senate would serve and represent the interests of the elite, while the House would come closer to reflecting the general population.

Thus the theoretical literature concerning the concept of representation is rich in controversy and debate, so much so that, Hanna Pitkin (1969) tells us, we are almost tempted to conclude that "representation has nothing to do with freedom, democracy, self-government, or the public interest. In short, one might conclude that our conventional democratic ideal of representation is a myth, a delusion, impossible of realization in practice. In practice, representation is tyranny" (9). However, the controversies and debates on the different types of representation (the independent representative versus the representative that has a mandate from the constituency) and what representatives should look like ("mirror" representatives of their constituency versus "superior men and women" who are chosen for their "talent and wisdom") not only continue but have paved the way for more contemporary views of democracy and representation.

## Participation

Participatory democracy theorists argue that participation is the key to effective governance. Rousseau's view is that nonparticipatory systems make freedom impossible. In his discussion of the general will and the social contract, where "laws, not men, should rule," Rousseau makes two fundamental points: first, that participation is necessary for making good decisions and ensures good government; and second, that representative government protects private interests. John Stuart Mill (1962) expanded on the importance of representation and, like Rousseau, stressed the educative function of participation. One learns democracy through participation (especially at the local level): "We do not learn to read or write, to ride or swim, by being merely told how to do it, but by doing it, so it is only by practicing popular government on a limited scale that the people will ever learn how to exercise it on a larger one" (168). In addition to stressing the importance of citizen participation for effective government, Mills' father, James Mill, emphasized the importance of educating the electorate into socially responsible voting.

Participation, in effect, is often considered almost synonymous with voting, although the concept evokes different things for different people. In various analyses, participation ranges from marching in a protest demonstration to writing a letter to a public official. Parry and Moyser (1994), for example, identify five principal modes of participation—voting, contacting, campaigning, group action, and protest—but their overall focus seems to be on elections and voting. In the wider democracy literature, participation in elections occupies a prominent place. Robert Dahl's modern form of democracy—polyarchy, or the rule of multiple minorities—for example, is a political order with high levels of civic involvement where citizens have the ability to oppose and remove the leaders of government. Of the seven characteristics he sees as a condition for a polyarchy—elected officials; free and fair elections; inclusive suffrage; right to run for office; freedom of expression; alternative information; and associational autonomy—four are directly related to elections and voting (see Dahl 1989, 221). In contrast to the Madisonian (minority-rule) and Populist (majority-rule) democracies he critiques, Dahl proposes his polyarchy as an alternative model where elections are central because they provide the mechanism through which citizens can exert control over their leaders. This offers an alternative to both "the mischiefs of faction" that preoccupied Madison and the "tyranny of the majority" associated with populist (majority-rule) democracies. In a polyarchy, elections are central because they provide the mechanism through which citizens exercise control over their leaders. While minorities still rule, the competition among them for the votes of the people makes them responsive and accountable to the electorate.

Indeed, most thinking on participation as a key element in a democracy equates participation with the selection of rulers and the ability to vote them out of office.[8] The protective feature of participation in a democracy from the individual citizen's perspective is seen in an entirely different light by theorists concerned with protecting the stability of the system. In essence, their concern is that too much participation is dangerous to the state and that therefore protective mechanisms for the state must be in place. This concern was particularly felt in the mid–twentieth century, as mass participation was manipulated first in the service of fascism and then, after World War II, in the service of totalitarian regimes.

In the view of the theorists of the 1940s and 1950s, the only means of participation available to the citizenry is voting. Joseph Schumpeter, for example, in his influential *Capitalism, Socialism and Democracy* (1943), bases his theory of democracy on an elite minority who act as leaders. The distinctive feature of his notion of democracy is competition for leadership among the elite. The role assigned to the people is simply that enough of them vote so that they keep the political machinery running, but all governing decisions are made exclusively by the elite. After all, "the electoral mass," he tells us, "is incapable of action other than a stampede" (283). In *Democratic Theory* (1962), Giovanni Sartori advances Schumpeter's theory by positing not only that elites must rule in a democracy but that there must be competition among the elites. Citizens must limit their participation to voting, and indeed he considers a high degree of political apathy among the people to be healthy for the system. The fear that the active participation of the people in the political process leads straight to totalitarianism is almost palpable in Sartori's arguments. Indeed, he openly tells us that once a democratic system has been established, the participatory ideal must be minimized. Harry Eckstein further argues in "A Theory of Stable Democracy" (1966) that for a democracy to remain stable it must include a healthy dose of authoritarianism. Robert Dahl, too, perceives the dangers inherent in the participation of the average man. In *A Preface to Democratic Theory* (1956) he argues that apathy is not necessarily a bad thing because the lower socioeconomic groups tend to be less active politically and it is among these groups that authoritarian personalities tend to develop. Thus increased levels of their participation could threaten the stability of the system.

Classical theories of democracy tend to be overly normative, but contemporary theories tend to be much more empirical. Indeed, while voting and elections clearly are an integral component of any type of democratic system and continue to play a critical role, more contemporary analyses have moved on to argue, on the basis of empirical research, that democracy entails much more than elections (see, for example, Linz and Stepan 1996; Schmitter and Karl 1993; Huntington 1996). As we will see below, a whole corpus of literature developed in the 1990s that deals with the issue of mass mobilization and its impact on, and value for, a system's transition from authoritarianism to democracy. This literature recognizes that organized participation is good; the danger is in nonorganized participation. Finally, there is the view that more participation is conducive to better public policies. Quite simply, "[T]he higher the level of participation, the greater the potential for generating policy choices that reflect the needs and interests of ordinary citizens" (Robinson 1998, 156–57).

### Civil Society

While the theoretical pedigree of civil society can be traced back to Adam Ferguson's *Essay on the History of Civil Society* ([1767] 1969), the concept's relevance to our three countries can best be traced to the later essays of Alexis de Tocqueville, who was struck by the propensity of Americans to participate voluntarily in all forms of associations, and to Jean-Jacques Rousseau, who romanticized "the people." The powerful images evoked in their works of a collective people actively participating in the act of governing have colored much of both the theoretical and the empirical work on the relation between the state and civil society. As Larry Diamond (1996, 227) comments, "What could be more moving than the stories of brave bands of students, writers, artists, pastors, teachers, laborers, and mothers challenging the duplicity, corruption, and brutal domination of authoritarian states?"

Much of the classic democracy literature has not been especially encouraging about the prospect of generating an engaged civil society, as witnessed in the work of Schumpeter, Sartori, and Dahl discussed above, but the contemporary discussion on participatory democracy has redefined democracies to include a much stronger and active civil society. In their much-cited work, Juan Linz and Alfred Stepan (1996) and others like Robert Putnam (1993, 2000) have led this discussion and catalyzed a large amount of ensuing work. Putnam's study of Italy (1993), for example, found that civic participation leads to stronger institutions and more effective governance and that this, in turn, strengthens democracy. But how does that participation originate? Is a civic culture a result of many years of association, or can social capital, to use a contemporary phrase, be stimulated by social engagement? Either way, scholarly and popular discussions and debates have made *civil society* a fashionable term that implies both destructive and constructive functions. The view of civil society as a destructive force developed during the Cold War, when civil society was seen strictly in terms of opposition to authoritarian or totalitarian regimes, with the goal of their overthrow. A large body of literature developed around the concept of civil society as the nemesis of the state. The second view, of civil society as a constructive force, focuses on how civil society can monitor and restrain the exercise of power by the state and democratize authoritarian states (Diamond 1996, 230). Here civil society plays a more direct role in the process of governing, in the form of citizens' participation in civil society organizations and formal politics.

### Democratization

Worldwide, the ratio of individuals living in a democracy rose from one-third to two-thirds in the ten years or so from 1985 (Jaquette and Wolchik 1991, 1), generating an ever-growing literature on democratic transitions and consolidations. In this new and somewhat crowded field, the work of Linz and Stepan (1996) is key. They argue that five elements are necessary for a country to move from transition to consolidation: a free and lively civil society; a relatively autonomous and valued political society; a rule of law to provide guarantees for citizens' freedom and associations; a state bureaucracy; and an institutionalized economic society (7). But even where these five conditions of polyarchy are established, there is often only a minimal commitment to what O'Donnell (1999, 39) has described as "horizontal accountability," where institutions and state agencies are authorized and empowered to oversee, control, redress, and sanction unlawful actions of other state agencies. As O'Donnell notes, horizontal accountability is an extension of the well-known theme of the division of powers and its associated system of checks and balances between the executive, legislative, and judicial branches, but in contemporary polyarchies it extends to various overseeing agencies, ombudsmen, accounting offices, *controlerías,* and so forth. O'Donnell (1999, 43–45) further argues that to enhance this horizontal accountability a number of conditions are desirable, including the allowance of some role for opposition parties in monitoring government agency performance and investigating corruption *(fiscalías);* the creation of modernized formal accounting agencies *(controlerías);* the development of a professionalized and independent judiciary; sound, reliable, and transparent information-gathering systems; public participation; and investigative media. The point here is to create a level of modernization and participation that will improve governance.

The comparative literature on democratization has grown rapidly and shifted its attention from issues of democratic transition to the challenges of democratic consolidation, even developing a full typology of consolidation. Indeed, the literature is expanding so quickly that Andreas Schedler (1998), somewhat tongue-in-cheek, refers to it as "the aspiring subdiscipline of 'consolidology'" (92). Following Huntington, Schedler argues that the minimal criteria for consolidation are two sets of elections, power changing hands, and no threat of a democratic breakdown. Linz and Stepan (1996) suggest that "[a] democratic transition is complete when sufficient agreement has been reached about political procedures to produce an elected government, when a government comes to power that is the direct result of a free and popular vote, when this government *de facto* has the authority to generate new policies, and when the executive, legislative, and judicial power generated by the new democracy does not have to share power with other bodies de jure" (3).

However, as Linz and Stepan (1996) remind us, there is a difference between liberalization and consolidation. Some governments just plateau at the transition stage and never reach consolidation. Moreover, one important point in Linz and Stepan's analysis is that a transition to democracy and the shape a new democracy will take are heavily conditioned by existing political structures. What a regime transitions *to* will be determined to a large extent by what the regime is transitioning *from*. This was true for America in 1776, for Brazil's transition from bureaucratic authoritarianism, and for Mexico's electoral overthrow of an "inclusionary authoritarian" regime dominated by over seventy years of one-party rule. Each of these transitions shapes the nature, pace, and depth of democratic consolidation.

In reviewing democratic transitions and consolidations in Latin America, Peter Smith (2005, 342) concludes that present-day democracy remains rather shallow (see also Domínguez and Shifter 2003). Electoral democracy has taken root, but it is not a very deep democracy—especially if one also takes account of the "horizontal accountability" criteria espoused by O'Donnell. In part this is because democratic change across the continent has been recent enough to afford relatively insufficient time for Samuel Huntington's (1991, 266–67) "two turnover" test to apply in many nations, although there are several countries where this has occurred—including Brazil. But this is at the macro, national level. As we will see in this volume, conceiving and institutionalizing democracy—measured across the dimensions of representation, participation, and civil society outlined above—is one thing, but implementing, developing, and consolidating it is quite another. And if this assertion applies to national systems, then it is equally germane at the subnational and local levels. Here, more often than not, checks and balances are few, representative institutions are weak and untested, and freedoms and rights are restricted—in practice if not in principle (Domínguez and Shifter 2003). Thus our study will complement the small number of other recent analyses that have sought to examine the broadening and deepening of democracy into the subnational sphere. O'Donnell (1994) coined the term *brown zones* for those regions or subregions where the state's writ is weak or nonexistent, and non- or limited democratic governance exists across regions as well as within nations. Thus an important part of our task in the following chapters is to assess whether, and to what extent, decentralization and the forging of new intergovernmental relations assist or make more fragile the process of democratic transition and consolidation.

# TWO

# Two Centuries of Federalism in Brazil, Mexico, and the USA

## Lawrence S. Graham and Allison M. Rowland

The central question for this chapter is how the tensions between central and local authorities have been addressed in Brazil, Mexico, and the USA during the two hundred–odd years of their existence as independent nations. It is intended both to orient the discussions in the following chapters and to enrich them with an understanding of how and why each of these nations finds itself in its current position at the beginning of the twenty-first century.

Federalism has been studied more extensively in the USA than in any other country, and researchers have argued that its practice can be considered in terms of three alternatives: an inclusive-authority model, in which hierarchical relations prevail; a coordinate-authority model, in which national and state authorities are coequal and autonomous; and an overlapping-authority model, in which bargaining relations predominate (Graham 1990, 40; Wright 1982, 9–10). All of these have been present at some time or other in the USA. Brazil and Mexico have contributed to broadening the federalism debate by adding a third level of government to these discussions. The concept of the free and autonomous *municipio* has been a powerful idea cutting across the centuries, embedded in Brazilian and Mexican constitutions through the explicit recognition of three levels of governance, as opposed to the two present in U.S. federalism.

In both Brazil and Mexico, effective federalism is also seen as a part of the struggle to consolidate democratic practices. Historians have called attention to the relevance of the Cortes of Cadiz, since democratization in Iberia was curtailed by political realities in ways similar to major portions of Latin America. Today regional autonomy models of governance in Spain and Portugal have entered the discourse. Thus it should come as no surprise to find in the Brazilian transition of the 1980s and in the Mexican transition of the 1990s a resurgence of interest in securing autonomy for their states and in decentralizing power to reinforce the role of state and local governments, as well as citizen groups operating within those arenas.

Recent efforts to implement effective democratic federalism in Brazil and Mexico have drawn on both U.S. and European experience. In the redesign of social policy, Brazilians have looked to Europe, while their legal scholars have expanded their analysis and understanding of juridical concepts of federalism developed through the U.S. court system and have incorporated case-based legal precedents into their civil-law system. Meanwhile, with the increase in bilateral exchange of all kinds since the signing of NAFTA, large numbers of Mexicans involved in state and municipal government have begun to study and visit their counterparts in the USA (and elsewhere) with hopes of being able to imitate their variety and vitality.

Economic globalization and the emergence of new regional political accords that transcend the boundaries of individual nations have sparked new interest in comparisons among types of federalism. Several federal formulas have begun to emerge on a *supra*national level (for example, the European Union) as reformers have looked for more appropriate governmental frameworks through which to coordinate economic and social policy, while respecting the sovereignty of individual states. Federal arrangements take as a given two or more autonomous spheres of sovereignty within the confines of a single governmental framework.

The origins of federalism can be characterized as bottom-up, as in the decision by the colonies of the future USA to join together to form a national government. Alternative federal models, in which federalism is constructed from the top down, also exist and have recently begun to be considered in a new light. Brazilian and Mexican experience with federalism has followed this top-down pattern, except on one very important issue: rather than incorporate parliamentary forms of government, their federalist constitutions establish strong executive authority and couple federalism with the establishment of presidential republics, incorporating the division and separation of powers inherent in the U.S. Constitution. In the Brazilian case, federalism emerged at the end of the nineteenth century as a legal construct that ratified the de facto existence of two distinct levels of authority, the one national and the other regional or local. Earlier cycles of centralization had always attempted to suppress or to deny the existence of a distinct level of subnational power that in turn always resisted attempts to centralize. Similarly, in Mexico, the difficulties in constructing a national state throughout the nineteenth century were due in part to attempts to deny the importance of regional and local governments, in spite of a series of federalist constitutions. Only the strongly centralizing, authoritarian governments of Porfirio Díaz and later the PRI (Partido Revolucionario Institucional/Institutional Revolutionary Party) managed to impose a truly national government, by suppressing local and regional autonomy.

This chapter considers the shifting balances of power between national and subnational actors over nearly five centuries. Despite considerable variance within each country's experience, we argue that each faced similar problems during five distinct eras and that the way in which each country tackled—or ignored—these problems helps explain the current issues of federalism that each faces today.

We begin our discussion at the point of nation formation, during which the key issues were the definition of new national communities and the arrangements established to govern each, in the context of legacies left by the colonial powers. Next, we examine the nineteenth century from the perspective of nation building, with particular emphasis on the challenges to federalism and the establishment of a tenuous division of powers between levels of government in the last quarter of that century. The subsequent section addresses the recentralizing backlash by the national governments, which began in each country during the 1930s, partly in response to economic upheaval caused by the Great Depression but also for domestic political reasons. Then we consider divergent patterns of federalism in the three countries during the period between the end of World War II and the 1980s. We close with a discussion of the profound transformations in each country during the 1980s, in response to political and economic changes in the wider world.

## Nation and State Formation

The formation of independent nations from European colonies in the Americas started much earlier than in Africa or Asia, with the Revolution in what eventually became the United States of America in 1776. Mexico, Brazil, and most of the rest of Latin America followed suit during the next half-century, mostly in response to instability and political change among the European colonial powers. Once freed of colonial structures, each of these countries faced the task of forming a new, independent government and defining a national identity. This task was facilitated or impeded in part by the political, social, and economic heritage that their respective colonial masters had left in place, as well as the practices and philosophy of the European immigrants (and their descendants) who dominated the political life of each country.

### Colonial Legacies

The withdrawal of the European colonial powers from the Americas left substantially distinct legacies in each country. These legacies affected both the stability of the federal pact eventually established and the extent to which federal principles aided in meeting the challenges of subsequent decades and centuries.

*In Mexico*, the formation of autonomous local governments *(municipios)* began in 1519 with the founding of La Villa Rica de la Vera Cruz by Hernán Cortés. This pattern is reflected in the constitutional status of municipal government since the days of Mexican independence. However, Cortés had no vision of the inherent goodness of local government; rather, he was following Spanish tradition, which allowed him, as captain-general of the *ayuntamiento* (town council), to shake off the authority of Spanish government in Cuba, under whom he had originally sailed. As time went on, the Spanish crown, suffering from a lack of resources to pay for official government expeditions, began to grant private individuals the right to explore and claim land in the new territory, in exchange for recognition of Spanish sovereignty and one-fifth of the profits gained. As historian Alejandra Moreno (1995, 48) notes, this system made the *conquistadores* anxious to recoup their private expenses, usually at the expense of the indigenous peoples living on the lands they claimed for Spain. Given the structure of the preexisting societies in what was to become Mexico, this system also led to full-scale military confrontations rather than scattered battles over land.

As the Spanish crown grew in power during the second half of the sixteenth century, it also began to bring New Spain under more centralized control. In addition, from 1555 on, the conversion of indigenous people to Christianity and the forced abandonment of their languages in favor of Spanish became a function of the state (Moreno 1995, 52). This further centralized what had been a land of many distinct empires. Economic forces pointed in the same direction: mining provided the basic source of tax revenues for the colony's administrative expenses, and all of the products were shipped through Mexico City on to Spain. The *haciendas* (basically, large plantations) established during the colony served mostly the domestic market for foodstuffs, since infrequent rains and the lack of artificial irrigation made reliable large-scale production more difficult (Moreno 1995, 57). At the same time, dramatic decreases in population (caused mostly by plagues of smallpox and venereal disease, against which the Indians had no resistance) made labor scarce for the haciendas and resulted in feudal systems, enslavement of indigenous people, and the eventual importation of slaves from Africa. Mexico City, the administrative center of the country, became increasingly important as an economic and demographic center as well, a pattern that would continue to the present day.

*In Brazil*, unlike Mexico, colonial power was never exercised with the same degree of central control. This was largely because sixteenth-century Portugal had acquired more territory in Asia, Africa, and the Americas than it was able to administer directly. The riches produced by its trade in Asia and the extensive system of forts it had to develop to secure the safety of its commerce with the Orient, around the horn of Africa, and across the Indian Ocean meant that the vast and mostly unmapped territory it ostensibly ruled in South America was largely left to govern itself under the nominal jurisdiction of the captain-generals and, later, governors sent from Lisbon in the name of the Portuguese crown.

The sugar boom of the 1530s and 1540s was decisive in its impact on Brazilian culture through the assimilation of thousands of Africans imported through the slave trade with Portugal's African territories. The outcome of this was a distinctive Afro-Brazilian regional culture that has ever since left a mark on northeastern Brazil.

In this regard, the history of the Portuguese colonial empire is markedly different from that of Spain (Collis 1943). The incorporation of Portugal into the Spanish Empire between 1580 and 1640, as a consequence of dynastic politics, led largely to the abandonment of Portugal's overseas territories. After 1640, recognizing that little could be done to recapture their position in Asia, the Portuguese reestablished control of northeastern Brazil and made Salvador, in the province of Bahia, the capital of Portuguese America.

The second major period of economic growth and development was in the 1730s, when gold was discovered and some six hundred thousand Portuguese immigrated into what is today the center of Brazil. Accordingly, from the 1700s until independence in 1822, the wealth produced by Brazil was more than sufficient to trigger Portugal's economic recovery, its autonomy, and the establishment of its American colonies as the new center of its empire. The discovery of precious minerals south of Bahia in the province of Minas Gerais (the "general mines") and the desire of the crown to secure its monopoly of the gold and precious stones produced by these mines were instrumental in the decision to move the capital southward to the port of Rio de Janeiro.

From the 1700s until independence in 1822, while the crown asserted its hegemony over Brazil, it was never able to completely abrogate the traditions of local rule embodied in the municipal governments of each of the provincial capitals. Underlying this later development of national authority was the earlier, autonomous development of a Portuguese American presence by Portuguese nationals who assimilated themselves into the New World and colonized without central direction. The Portuguese originally laid claim to their American territories through their division into sometimes spectacularly large *capitanías*, whose administration was essentially privatized and feudal. The legacy of this pattern of colonization was a weak central government, dependence on private individuals, and de facto decentralization. The leaders of regional "oligarchies" were named by, and reported directly to, the king, but their power lay with their large land holdings and slave labor. The regions were only nominally linked to one another (Murilo de Carvalho 1993, 54). While the *capitanías* were formally disbanded in favor of a general government by

1750, the pattern established in this era endured for centuries afterward. This point is important because from the beginning Portuguese America, unlike Spanish America, developed by necessity considerable tolerance for two distinct levels of governance.

*In the USA*, in contrast to Mexico and Brazil, immigration and colonization were not carried out by groups of single men in search of gold or other riches to send back to their homelands (indeed, there was little to be found in the eastern half of the future country). Instead, entire families came, usually as parts of religious or political groups in search of freedom to practice their beliefs, something they were not afforded in England or other parts of northern Europe. The results of this pattern of settlement were profound, both in terms of the types of government established and in terms of the relations with the previous inhabitants of these territories.

The first permanent settlement of the future USA established a system of government that ruled by the explicit consent of the governed from the early days of the colony. The Mayflower Compact laid the foundation for a form of self-government never before seen on a large scale. In the decades that followed, small communities whose members owned and worked on family farms became the dominant form of settlement of the new territories. As time went on, larger plantations and cities sprang up to serve export markets for raw materials and agricultural goods, especially in the South. The colonies formed under this system (which later became the states of the new republic) were small, internally homogeneous, and governed through direct contact with the English crown. Only later did issues of mutual defense lead to the banding together of these colonies into a single nation. As the population expanded, more land was demanded for agricultural use, which resulted in increasing hostility both from indigenous groups with prior claims to the land and from other imperial powers that had more recent designs on the territories. Questions of the treatment of the colonies by the English crown also became more important, particularly the taxes and tariffs imposed on trade. But control of these colonies by England did not end the way it did for Mexico and Brazil, whose independence arose in large part from the domestic problems of their imperial masters. In the future United States of America, the process involved first negotiation with England and later a Revolutionary War that served to galvanize the proponents of a union (McCullough 2001).

### Defining the National Community: Maintaining National Cohesion in the Face of Regional Diversity

At independence, all three of the new countries had to confront the question of how to establish a national identity across spatially vast territories and diverse regional cultures.

*In Mexico*, the problem of establishing a shared national identity troubled leaders throughout the nineteenth century. The loss first of modern-day Central America in the 1820s, followed only a few decades later by Texas and parts of today's southwestern USA, emphasized the difficulty of creating a coherent Mexican nation. At various points during this period, Guadalajara, Yucatán, and Zacatecas all were considered serious risks for secession as well, an issue that helps explain the constant struggle between the sovereignty of states and the desire to centralize power that characterized the country. In addition, in spite of *mestizaje* (the "mixing" of Spanish and indigenous people, the former mostly men and the latter mostly women), approximately one million residents of the new country—members of at least thirty distinct indigenous groups—were not integrated into political life and did not even speak the same language as the dominant groups.

*The USA*, in contrast to a shrinking Mexico, continued to add substantially more territory right up to the Civil War of the 1860s, as well as afterward. Indeed, it appears that the gradual process of independence from England, which culminated in the intense struggle of the Revolutionary War, served to commit the states to a united country The failures of the Articles of Confederation to provide a viable format for governing the former colonies when issues of common concern to all of them emerged (such as the need for a single currency) convinced reformers of the need for a stronger union. The outcome of this was the Constitution of 1787, which provided for a federal form of government that established strong central authority in instances linked to the survival of the new nation but at the same time guaranteed the states their rights and liberties.

Once the question of the right to secede was laid to rest in the Civil War of the 1860s, the continental aspirations of the USA were encapsulated in the doctrine of Manifest Destiny, which opened the door to successive waves of westward migration by European immigrants and their descendants. A comparatively small indigenous population, with which the European settlers hardly mixed, combined with a plantation-based economy in the South to make the importation of African slave labor attractive in the USA. Indigenous peoples were exterminated or pushed west and north ahead of the white settlers, and their limited numbers represented little threat to the newly dominant immigrants.

*In Brazil*, the threat to unification came less from foreign powers (although there were persistent border skirmishes in the South and West) than from the internal lack of cohesion. There was no single defining event in Brazil, such as occurred in the USA with the Revolutionary War and the Continental Congresses, which mobilized the public throughout the North American colonies against continued British rule. Indeed, at the time of Brazil's independence, the idea of creating a single country was not obvious to the political representatives of the regions, who identified themselves in the Portuguese Cortes through their provincial identities (e.g., *paulistas* or *gaúchos*) rather than as Brazilians. The unity of the country was based more on interest in the continued existence of the established economic system, including but not limited to slavery, than on more noble ideas about how to form an ideal government (Murilo de Carvalho 1993, 58).

On the other hand, as in the USA and in contrast to Spanish American experience, a strong cultural identity, which Charles Wagley (1964) has called "Luso-Brazilian," did emerge to provide a unifying force that transcended the weakness of formal political institutions. As a result, there was no decisive movement leading to the disintegration of Brazil and the formation of independent successor states, each with its own newly formed government, as occurred in Spanish America, once the legitimacy of monarchy was challenged. There were separatist movements at various points in Bahia and the southernmost state of Rio Grande do Sul, but at no time did this degenerate into national conflict on the scale of the U.S. Civil War. Instead, steadily and assuredly, a distinctive cultural identity emerged and was projected over the space inherited at independence.

At the outset, the Portuguese king served as an important symbol of unity to the new nation. At the same time, the dependence of the most profitable aspects of the economy on the labor of black slaves, who made up as much as one-third of the total population in the late nineteenth century, continued to limit the possibilities of their developing an identity as

Brazilian citizens. Meanwhile, large numbers of indigenous people had been killed through slavery or disease, and the half-million or so who remained were pushed west and further marginalized by the dominant Luso-Brazilian culture on the coast. Still, in the original core of Brazil in the Northeast, there was a great deal of assimilation and blending of Europeans of Portuguese ancestry with the Indian and African population (E. Cunha 1957). What occurred in the Brazilian central and southern regions, as the frontier was pushed westward, was very different from the formation of the Northeast and the movement of its population westward over time, into the interior of the country (Moog 1983).

### New Governmental Arrangements

One of the concrete results of the process of independence for each country was a constitution, which can be seen as the outcome of negotiations among the various factions with power to influence national political life. However, while the U.S. Constitution of 1787 has endured nearly intact for over two centuries, Mexico made substantial changes to its constitution on at least three occasions, and current national debate includes proposals for revamping the entire document. Meanwhile, Brazil moved more dramatically, over the course of its independent existence, from constitutional monarchy to federal republic in the nineteenth century; in the twentieth, the country also has had several different constitutions, authoritarian as well as democratic.

*In the USA,* the basic tenets of its federal system—strong subnational units and relatively weak central authority led to well-defined spheres of competence for two distinct levels of government. This emphasis on dual sovereignty, with the basis for a common national government derived from powers transferred from the states upward, arose quite naturally from the thirteen original colonies, each with distinct economic bases and semiautonomous, self-governed towns and villages. It is important to remember, though, that there was considerable controversy over the form of union to be established in the aftermath of independence. The original charter of government, the Articles of Confederation of 1776–77, was soon replaced by the Constitution precisely because of the recognition that some form of central authority was necessary to support state governments faced with local rebellions.

The constitution that emerged from these debates is a relatively brief and general document that essentially divides the federal government into three branches and defines a separate but sovereign sphere of action for the states. Local governments (called counties and cities in most states) are defined not in the federal constitution but in individual state constitutions. The federal charter focuses explicitly on limiting the scope of government at all levels and clearly reserves for the states those powers not granted to the federal government. Even so, defenders of individual rights saw it necessary to amend the Constitution shortly afterward with the Bill of Rights, which essentially elaborates on the provisions designed to counteract government tyranny and to protect the rights and liberties of individual citizens.

*In Mexico*, although the Spanish Empire collapsed in 1808, its leaders were slow to react to the opportunity for independence, even though discontent with the colonial system had been growing for some time. Finally, in 1810, a rogue priest named Miguel Hidalgo y Costilla gave what has become known as the *grito* (cry) of independence in front of parishioners in the village of Dolores, Guanajuato, sparking widespread regional revolts against viceregal power. The Spanish government, which had recovered by 1811, managed to suppress unrest but was forced by events in Mexico and elsewhere to hold a convention at Cadiz to determine the outlines of the empire's new constitutional monarchy.

While the Constitution of Cadiz (1812) met many of the demands of the Mexican delegation in attendance at the convention, it remained in force for less than a year before a hard-line viceroy in Mexico returned government to its previous practices. However, events in Spain once again drove changes in Mexico: liberal power in the Cortes threatened to do away with privileges enjoyed by the church. Wealthy Spaniards and Creoles in Mexico reacted to this menace by turning to Colonel Agustín Iturbide to crush remaining rebel forces within the territory and to negotiate an agreement with Spain through which independence was finally declared in 1821. Thus, ironically, the Wars of Independence in Mexico were eventually won not by republicans but by monarchists. Neither the basic conception of government nor the membership of the political and governmental elite changed. However, the new governing document, the Plan de Iguala (1821), laid out a constitutional, rather than absolute, monarchy with continued respect for the provincial governments established by the Cortes de Cadiz, a detail that helped lay the foundation for the country's first federal constitution (Guillén López 2000).

Iturbide was elected emperor by a hastily called Assembly in 1822 and managed to maintain a unified country by gaining the loyalty of the only truly nationwide institution, the Catholic Church. Both the church and the military were used to counterbalance continued provincial restiveness, and they remained supporters of Iturbide's government in large part because of the Plan de Iguala's guarantee of *fueros,* the privilege of trying legal matters in their own courts (Barrón 2001). Thus an enduring pattern emerged in which a centralized government was identified with the conservative political and economic elite of the capital, while liberals and radicals in the provinces preferred decentralized federalism (Guillén López 2000). This trend only deepened the ideological content of the debates.

The governing compromise, expressed in the federal Constitution of 1824, reflects the influence of Montesquieu and other European thinkers, as well as the neighboring U.S. Constitution, in its separation of federal power into executive, legislative, and judicial branches and the creation of states with a similar separation of powers. However, this constitution also reveals the importance of the Constitution of Cadiz, particularly in the provision of representative government and political independence for each province (Benson 1992).

As ideological debates over the form of government for the new country dragged on, the two immediate concerns of Mexican government were the state of public finances and the territorial integrity of the former colony. Financial problems emerged not only from the large public debt inherited from the colony but also from expenditures necessary to support a large army. In addition, economic disruption from continued unrest implied lower revenues for central government, as did the abolition of the head tax on Indians (González y González 1995, 84–85). Yet the military was constantly on the move to address threats of secession by the former viceroyalties of Guadalajara and Zacatecas, as well as in the Yucatán, which remained dissatisfied even after the establishment of federalism in the new constitution. Already by 1822, the Central American provinces had declared their independence from Mexico, and incursions by Spain and France in the following years, as well as designs on Texas by the USA, contributed to a country in recurrent crisis.

The Mexican Constitution of 1824 can be described as merely a *model* of national government, or a statement of purpose, since the institutional apparatus necessary to govern the country still did not exist (Guillén López 2000; Merino 1998). Indeed, while federal states existed (significantly, with their own sources of income), there was no nationwide federal government. Somewhat tragically, even contemporaries saw the ineffectiveness of the Constitution of 1824 in laying a real foundation for government as an example of the futility of importing basic agreements on government from other political and social contexts (Tocqueville [1835] 1969; Brazilian senators cited in Murilo de Carvalho 1993, 60).

*Brazil*'s experience was very different from Mexico's. Even before the French invasion of the Iberian Peninsula, the relationship between Brazil and Portugal contrasted substantially with the relationship that Mexico and the USA had with their respective imperial powers. Indeed, in Brazil and Portugal there was serious debate over whether *either* could survive as an independent country without the other. For this reason, the temporary solution to problems in Europe in 1807 was for the entire Court of Dom João VI to resettle in Rio de Janeiro, where the governmental system continued essentially as it had before, with a weak central administration nominally overseeing the activities of private landowners across Brazilian territory. Only after Napoleon's defeat in 1814, when the Portuguese Court returned to Lisbon, did the question of an independent Brazil become more salient. At first the two countries formed a united kingdom, but in 1820 liberals in Portugal revolted and succeeded in establishing their own Cortes, which included a system of elected representatives from the colonies. However, sending deputies from the Brazilian regions to discuss issues of government in Lisbon proved unsatisfactory. Indeed, the majority of those governing the united country appeared more interested in reestablishing the former colonial relationship than in developing a new, more balanced one.

The question of how to form a new country from the former colony, however, was problematic. To many residents, especially the large landholders, the idea of unifying the regions into a single *Brazil* was not obvious. At the time there was little economic or political interaction among the regions, and the relations of each region with Portugal typically had been conducted directly with the king rather than through the viceroy in Rio de Janeiro (Murilo de Carvalho 1993). Trade patterns linked each province directly with external markets, and there was little domestic commerce among provinces. Nor were Brazilian elites interested in changing the prevailing social or economic order, since it was a system from which they benefited (Fausto 1999, 78).

This led many to conclude that constitutional monarchy was the answer to the need of the newly independent nation to take control of a vast territory and to avoid fragmentation. In addition, the fairly homogeneous Brazilian elite (most of whom had administrative experience in other colonies and had studied together in Portugal) were concerned that without a strong central government they might follow the example of the former Spanish colonies, which at the time were engaged in protracted and bloody civil conflicts (Murilo de Carvalho 1993, 57). While the reigning monarch, Dom João VI, favored constitutional monarchy for both Portugal and Brazil, it was essential that he return to Portugal to secure his throne and his political agenda. The solution for Dom João was to leave his son, Dom Pedro, in Rio as regent and heir to the Brazilian throne. Once the court had returned to Lisbon and it became clear that he was likely to be removed as regent, Dom Pedro joined with local forces and declared Brazil's independence in 1822 (Payne 1973, 518–19).

The installation of a constitutional monarchy turned out to be complex, in part because it implied consolidation of a more centralized system than that to which the regional powers had become accustomed (Murilo de Carvalho 1993, 58). Indeed, apart from the king, there were few political or economic bonds among the regions that could serve to unite the new country once the Portuguese court left Rio. The limits on imperial powers were made clear when Pedro I dissolved the Constituent Assembly in 1824 and imposed a constitution of his own design. To declare the existence of a unified empire was one thing, but to govern effectively was another.

This first Brazilian constitution, which was imposed by a monarch rather than discussed and ratified by "the people," began a pattern in which regimes were established by fiat, even though effective governance required that the country's rulers accommodate regional interests. Still, this document did manage to organize the jurisdictions of the branches of government, allocate powers among them, and guarantee individual rights for citizens (who, of course, made up only a very small fraction of the population at that time, the rest being women, slaves, and those free men whose incomes were not judged to be high enough) (Fausto 1999, 79–80). The Brazilian political system was defined as monarchical, hereditary, and constitutional. A bicameral legislative branch was organized, with a Chamber of Deputies (elected indirectly) and a Senate, whose members were essentially appointees of the crown and who held their posts for life. The emperor could dissolve the Chamber with the approval of the Poder Moderador (a sort of fourth power established in the Constitution) and could also veto decisions of the legislature. Finally, the Constitution divided the country into provinces, which were headed by appointed presidents.

In protest against the dissolution of the Constituent Assembly by Pedro I, the five northeastern provinces, led by Pernambuco, immediately declared their independence and proclaimed the formation of the Confederation of Ecuador. The rebel provinces were subdued in short order, but later military failures along the border with Argentina exacerbated the financial problems of the empire and its residents and created a rift between the army and the king (Fausto 1999, 83–85). In 1831, the king was forced to abdicate to his infant son.

## Nineteenth-Century Efforts at State and Nation Building

Once independence and a constitution were established in the three countries, there was still much to decide in terms of governing structures and practices. Indeed, independence seemed to be nearly the only issue upon which political factions in these countries could agree. Each country underwent profound changes and protracted struggles during the nineteenth century, as a result both of ongoing ideological conflict over the shape of the new nations and of rapid social and economic changes, which in turn undermined the collection of public revenue. Each country also was shaped by its need to hold the new nation together in the face of internal dissent and continued imperial jockeying. Another element of instability during the nineteenth century in all three countries resulted from ongoing tensions in the relationship between the states or provinces and their central governments and the absence of agreement on how to resolve these differences, short of war or secession. Underlying these problems was a more basic struggle over the future form of government in each.

*The USA* entered the nineteenth century in relatively good shape, since the foundations for independent government had been established with the approval of the Constitution and the Bill of Rights, tested during war and peacetime, and essentially ratified by the political elite in the previous decades. The Constitution of 1787, and the practices of government in the intervening years, provided a stable framework upon which to balance the demands of the states for independence in most issues of government against the need for some central coordination in issues like the coinage of money or international affairs. This system was essentially "dual federalism," under which each of the two levels of government agreed to limit itself to a clearly defined sphere of action and responsibility, with little or no overlap. However, under the leadership of Chief Justice John Marshall (1801–35), the Supreme Court made it clear in its broad interpretation of the commerce clause (clause 3, sec. 8, art. 1) that Congress had the power over and above the states to regulate all forms of commerce (Janda, Berry, and Goldman 1989, 120), thereby ensuring the development of a single national market. This power of judicial review introduced into U.S. federalism a distinctive dimension that was not present in either Brazil or Mexico and that has proven to be essential in resolving partisan issues in the USA concerning the proper relationship between the national and state governments.

The bloody Civil War at midcentury represented a dramatic breakdown of this consensus, especially over the issue of slavery in the South and the question of citizenship rights for African Americans. But it also reflected a conflict among the states about the correct assignment of the functions of the two levels of government, rather than the complete collapse of the legitimacy of the governing compact or of the Constitution itself. This helps explain why the original constitution and the system of dual federalism survived almost intact after the war and the years of federal occupation of former rebel states. In this regard, the great compromise after the Civil War, which permitted the reincorporation of the southern states into effective national political participation, was to leave to the states control over voting in local as well as national elections.

In contrast, in both Brazil and Mexico, the tensions between monarchists and republicans involved the very form of government. *In Brazil,* the constitutional crisis provoked by Pedro I led to economic chaos, military discontent, and the succession to the throne of Pedro II, who was still a child. The next seventeen years, under regents acting in the new emperor's name, were difficult times for the new nation, as the balance of power between central and local authorities, as well as consensus over the need for a unifying central government, was never sustainable for long. The constitutional reform of 1834, which provided for provincial assemblies and a division of fiscal resources between the center and the provinces, did lay the foundation for what some have called the "Republican Era of the Empire," but this was not sufficiently attractive to several regions to avert continued threats to national unity.

A centralized monarchy, under the adolescent Dom Pedro II, and with the support of conservative dominance of the legislature, finally brought some stability to the country from 1841 to 1888 (Murilo de Carvalho 1993, 63). Limits were again placed on the powers of the provinces, and municipalities officially remained mere administrative organs, without executive powers, thus leaving little margin for the development of self-government. Provincial governors were named from the center, and the systems of justice and police were controlled from Rio de Janeiro as well. Guerrilla warfare was constantly waged by indigenous groups, escaped black slaves, and urban workers, while powerful landholders established de facto control over the municipios within their jurisdictions, to the chagrin of those controlling the provincial capitals.

Nevertheless, administrative and governmental centralization in Brazil under the constitutional monarchy of Dom Pedro II was successful for nearly half a century in unifying the formerly fragmented nation and acting as arbiter in conflicts among elites. The Conservative and Liberal parties alternated frequently as the majority in the Chamber of Deputies. Stability also helped maintain the economic and social status quo, and the boom in coffee exports in turn emphasized the role of Rio de Janeiro as the political and economic center of the country.

This system was radically altered in 1889, when a military coup d'état deposed Pedro II and declared a republican government. Ironically, the success of centralized government since the 1840s in stabilizing the country led to the downfall of this system, as states once again had become more ambitious about expanding their powers through decentralization (Murilo de Carvalho 1993, 63). Equally important was the destruction by the monarchy of its own conservative support through the Edict of Emancipation, which ended slavery and undercut the forced labor upon which the sugarcane plantations of the Northeast depended. Indeed, the very slogan of the national system was reversed, and rather than centralization being the key to unity, *decentralization* was argued necessary to maintain Brazil as a unified nation (Love 1993, 186). In addition, forces in favor of the formation of a republic had expanded in response to economic and demographic change. With the growth of cities came increases in the number of urban professionals—generally liberal in their outlook—as well as changes in the makeup of the military elite, which no longer was composed of members of the landowning aristocracy. However, the military was not liberal: it preferred order and progress, and left to its own devices it would probably have established a dictatorship (Fausto 1999, 149).

As it was, the country's first republican constitution was ratified in 1891. It was inspired by the U.S. model and was both liberal and federal in its design. The national president would be elected for a four-year term, and senators (three per state) were now limited to nine-year terms, while deputies (elected in proportion to state populations) would serve three-year terms. Direct, universal suffrage was established for everyone but women, beggars, illiterates, and enlisted men, while church and state were formally separated. States were granted wider fiscal powers, including the taxation of exports and access to foreign loans, and were also charged with their own courts and allowed to form militias.

The central government maintained control over import taxes and coinage, attempted to attract foreign investment, and paid the national debt (much of which dated from the imperial period but some of which was related to the republic's military expenditures) Awareness of Brazil's weakness in the War of the Triple Alliance (1865–70), in which Brazil joined Argentina and Uruguay to defeat Paraguay, convinced the army of the need to guarantee sufficient resources to defend Brazil's borders, especially in remote areas. The center also served as a proponent of national integration, an arbiter among regional interests, and the guarantor of internal stability through the use of armed forces, which it used to restore order in the states whenever necessary (Fausto 1999, 165). However, no mechanism to promote regional redistribution from richer to poorer states was established (Love 1993, 187), and the states of the North and Northeast continued to stagnate.

During this period of relative state autonomy, regional oligarchies flourished once again. Indeed, one historian argues that federalism in

Brazil's highly unequal social structure necessarily implied reinforcing these structures (Murilo de Carvalho 1993, 75). The *coronéis* (colonels) were rural landowners who accumulated power through use of political patronage and control of tax revenues. These also banded together to form Republican parties in each of the states, although few of these parties ever achieved a permanent national presence. Indeed, the parties were clientelist machines based at the state and municipal levels, with little ideological or even pragmatic foundation. This meant that politics itself remained a local matter (Love 1993, 181). To this day, a decentralized party structure characterizes the country, forcing national presidential candidates to form alliances among regional groups. During the First Republic, the oligarchies of the most prosperous states, São Paulo and Minas Gerais, basically rotated the presidency among themselves, with Rio Grande do Sul being the only other state with sufficient power to register an effective dissenting voice. Indeed, it was Rio Grande do Sul's attempt to break this system of rotation in 1930 once and for all that led to the overthrow of the First Republic.

In spite of the struggles in Brazil and the USA in the nineteenth century, both were more successful in establishing and maintaining a national government than was Mexico. *In Mexico*, the constitution adopted in 1824 laid the foundation for a federal system, although, significantly, it maintained the *fueros* for the church and the army and did not consider the individual and social rights that were adopted in later constitutions. During the years after 1824, conservatives were able to limit the real degree of decentralization of power through the deployment of armed forces to meet various military threats, and liberals ended up accepting the formation of a military structure of government that ran parallel to the state governments. In short order, the central government began to take advantage of the military presence in the states to manipulate local elections and interfere in state sovereignty, a precedent that survived through most of the twentieth century. The system proved unstable not only in the states but also at the national level, where one government after another was installed and removed. From 1821 to 1850, there were *fifty* federal executives, most of which were installed through military coups, and some of which were headed by the same individual on several occasions (González y González 1995, 91).

The problem was that the central government abided by the 1824 Constitution for only a short period before security concerns led to a de facto centralized military government. In response to the generalized political chaos and continued ideological struggles during the first decade of the new constitution, the so-called "Seven Laws of 1835" were approved by Congress. The 1824 document was formally superseded, and a centralized, unitary government was created. Under these new arrangements, the state governors were now appointed by the president rather than elected, and these governors appointed municipal prefects. This put an end to the first attempt at Mexican federalism and established a strongly centralized, unitary government in its place.

The secession of Texas in 1836 made clear that this form of centralization was ineffective for defending territorial integrity (Vásquez 1993). A decade later, full-fledged war broke out between the USA and Mexico. The defeat of Mexico culminated in 1848 in the Treaty of Guadalupe, by which the country lost more than half its territory to its rival. The country bordered on collapse for the next two decades as a series of governments rose and fell, including a second attempt at monarchy, under Maximiliano (1864–67). Finally, in 1867, liberal forces managed to reestablish the federal Constitution of 1857, and Benito Juárez was elected president.

This time, the federal system remained in place for fifty years, at least on paper. But as in Brazil, limitations on the powers of subnational governments were introduced that led to persistent problems later on. Most important was the establishment of the Senate in 1874. Paradoxically, rather than representing the interests of the states in the formation of national policy, this body served as a mechanism for central government intervention into state affairs, since senators were more closely linked to the president than to state governments and had the power to replace state governors who displeased the federal executive. Thus an ostensibly decentralizing effort became an instrument of centralization (Carmagnani 1993; Marván 1997), and this was fully exploited later on by the dictatorship of Porfirio Díaz.

Díaz established an increasingly centralist regime that lasted from 1876 to 1880, and then again from 1884 to 1910. Federal institutions were weakened, but this was the first time that a truly national Mexican state was established, by suppressing regional political elites and developing a certain degree of centralized administrative organization (Guillén López 2000). During this period, governors and other political officers were closely supervised by the center, although the principle of elections was always upheld. In addition, through a constitutional amendment during his first term, Díaz was able to secure his own reelection by a docile Senate for six successive terms of office. Ironically, while this administration made notable progress in attracting foreign investment in physical infrastructure, it was apparently not particularly adept at public finance. From 1890 to 1910, the Mexican central government spent only one-half of the amount per capita that Brazil did (Topik 1988, cited in Love 1993, 215).

In all three countries, adjustments became necessary in the legal framework as the end of the century approached. In the USA, the Supreme Court often decided in favor of the states during the nineteenth and early twentieth centuries, and there were attempts to restrict the commerce power of national government. However, the Court prohibited the states from erecting barriers to the free flow of trade across state borders. Throughout the period, the concept of dual federalism was reinforced by the acceptance of distinct spheres of fiscal responsibility between the federal and state governments, although the supremacy of the national government in questions of commerce was sustained in an important ruling in 1918 regarding child labor (Janda, Berry, and Goldman 1989, 125).

In Brazil, the military revolt of 1889 signaled dissatisfaction with the distribution of power between the national government and the provinces. It was resolved in the Constitution of 1891, which adopted federalism as the more appropriate legal framework within which to recognize the dual level of authority that had always been present. Under this framework, financial resources that had been concentrated in the hands of the national government under Pedro II were shifted to the state governments. Such was the degree of this decentralization that the Republic of 1891 bordered at times on being simply a confederation of states.

In Mexico, throughout the nineteenth century, the discord over an appropriate legal framework was never resolved. The federal Constitution of 1824 was quickly suppressed in the name of national unity, and the 1857 Constitution did not begin to be respected until a decade later. However, the latter's attempt to reestablish a system of power sharing among levels of government, as well as its protection of individual rights, eventually endured for more than half a century. Indeed, it was not overthrown but essentially subverted once Díaz began to recentralize power. This pattern would be repeated in the following century by the PRI regime, which, in spite of the federalist provisions of the Constitution of 1917, also reconcentrated power in the hands of the national government while scrupulously upholding constitutionalism. Meanwhile, the battle over fiscal resources in Mexico resembled U.S. experience more than Brazilian, since throughout much of the nineteenth century financial resources were concentrated in the state or provincial governments. Thus much intergovernmental dispute centered on how to secure a solid fiscal base for the central government to allow it to meet external threats.

### The Recentralization of Power

The 1930s mark a turning point in all three countries, with the reestablishment of stronger central control after decades of either factional struggle or complacent decline in national government activity. The political crises provoked by the Great Depression gave credence to economic theories that suggested that a firm hand—that of the federal executive—was necessary to secure economic stability and to maintain national unity and integrity, especially in the face of threats from Germany and Japan as the decade went on. International pressures generated by the coming of World War II, however, varied greatly in terms of impact. They were of fundamental importance in changing the balance of power in U.S. federalism because of the need for a strong presidency to prepare the country for the realities of international politics as Hitler became dominant in Europe. They were of some consequence in Brazil because of the flirtation of Vargas with the initial successes in Germany and Italy and, later, his about-face to support the Allied effort. Ironically, the decision to send troops to join the USA in the Italian campaign proved to be his undoing domestically, since returning military officers joined with the civilian opposition to overthrow his regime. International pressures were of less importance in Mexico, where the centralization of power internally was more closely related to securing PRI control and offsetting the influence of the USA and Great Britain on internal affairs.

*In Mexico*, the era of relatively balanced federalism during the nineteenth century was much shorter than in the USA or Brazil. Still, the centralizing dictatorship of Porfirio Díaz from the mid-1880s on was an old-style, oligarchic regime that in spite of its rhetoric of modernization lacked the mass base and nationalistic orientation of twentieth-century governments in Mexico and other countries (Hernández Chávez 1993). The orientation of the *porfiriato*'s high-level politicians to the interests of the central government rather than to society, where crushing poverty was the norm, allowed the political situation to deteriorate to a point at which the actual overthrow of Díaz and his cronies at the beginning of the 1910 Revolution was a rather simple exercise. The difficulties began with the attempts to form a new government.

The revolutionary movement in Mexico consisted of the intersection of various regional groups, which converged almost exclusively on the need to rid the country of Díaz. The philosophies and interests of each faction, however, were substantially distinct, and nearly a decade of disorder, coups, and countercoups followed as the victors disputed the division of the spoils. The separation of political groups into regional alliances, each with little confidence in the others, also explains the unanimous ratification of federalism in the 1917 Constitution, much as occurred for the 1857 Constitution (Hernández Chávez 1993). The new constitution respected the bicameral design of the national congress, and the structure of sovereign states and *municipios libres* (free municipalities), as elements that would ensure a more decentralized government, based on the autonomy of the states.

However, in short order, the creation of a hegemonic party system and the return to extraconstitutional practices rendered ineffective the formal institutional design and neutralized the system of checks and balances set out by the Constitution of 1917. While the tenure of any national president was limited by the establishment of six-year terms with no reelection, once the PRI was consolidated in the 1930s the presidency eventually gained direct control not only over the legislative and judicial branches but also over the governments of states and municipalities, through its dual leadership of state and party.

The process of recentralization was relatively quick, though never debated as such. The expansion of federal government at the expense of the sovereignty of the states began in the 1920s. Proposals for the country's physical and economic reconstruction after the decade-long war represented an opportunity for the national government to intervene in the development of the states. In addition, military leaders held the country's most important public offices until the 1940s, dominating political life. Furthermore, the task of making good on the new "social guarantees" established in the 1917 Constitution (including education, labor, and land redistribution) was assumed by the central government, and the presidents used their powers in these areas to manipulate the relationships with states and their residents (Hernández Chávez 1993). Another push toward centralization arose from the development of the idea of *mexicanidad*, a nationalism that flourished after the war, celebrating the uniqueness of the *mestizo* and of Mexican history, especially in the arts. Mexican muralists, architects, and classical composers gained international fame for their depictions of the nation's supposed essence and its role in world history, but enduring regional differences tended to be glossed over.

Immersed as Mexico was in domestic political intrigue, as well as economic and physical reconstruction, the effect of the Great Depression there was less dramatic than in many other countries. Export and import markets had already been disrupted by a decade-long war, which had also caused the physical and occupational dislocation of millions of residents. President Lázaro Cárdenas (1934–40) took advantage of the opportunity to centralize the government even more, extending the scope of *presidencialismo* through the application of the national economic development theories that were in favor throughout most of the world until the 1980s. These theories suggested that the administration of a nation's scarce resources should be planned, organized, programmed, and implemented by the central government.

Under this rationale, the government nationalized the petroleum and electricity industries. This period also marked the emergence of the two most important unions, the Confederation of Mexican Workers (Confederación de Trabajadores de México, CTM) and the National Confederation of Farmworkers (Confederación Nacional de Campesinos, CNC), both of which were directly linked to the federal executive. States and municipalities were relegated to minor roles: in fact, Mexican states spent less as a percentage of total public revenue during this era of supposed federalism than did Brazilian states under the Estado Novo dictatorship, whose leader emphasized the nonfederal character of his rule (Love 1993, 209). Thus, without changes in the federal Constitution of 1917, Mexico entered the 1940s with a political and administrative system that was much more centralized than the Constituent Assembly had intended.

*In the USA*, in contrast, the interim between post–Civil War Reconstruction in the 1860s and the 1930s was marked by an increasingly complex set of intergovernmental relations. In some spheres, a laissez-faire approach to government at the federal level resulted in a de facto decentralization to state and local levels. But as a national market became the central economic project, the states lost a degree of autonomy and the federal government assumed new regulatory roles, led by railroad regulation and, later, banking (R. Wilson 1993, 69–73). During the same period, massive immigration from Europe (and on the West Coast, also from Asia) combined with increased international trade and adventurism, and technological innovations, to bring the country unprecedented prosperity, especially after the 1890s. But this newfound wealth was concentrated in a few hands, and radical political parties and labor unions fought bitterly against shabby and unsanitary housing, low wages, unsafe working conditions, and ruthless strikebreaking by business owners, who were supported in many cases by the police forces of the states.

The precipitous rise in the stock market beginning in the 1920s proved too good to last. In 1929, the country plunged into the Great Depression and quickly dragged much of the rest of the world down as well. Banks failed, taking customer deposits with them, and millions of people were thrown out of work. To make matters worse, a long drought in the Midwest and West caused crop failures, and many farmers lost their land through repossession by creditors.

President Franklin D. Roosevelt, elected in 1932, had run on a platform that promised massive federal programs to help lift the country out of the Depression. His New Deal attempted to create employment through central government programs, which ranged from agriculture to photography and centered on massive construction of physical infrastructure: highways, public buildings, irrigation and flood control projects, bridges, waterworks, and more. With a broad popular mandate for such actions, the federal government not only took on tasks previously considered beyond its scope but also gained enormous power relative to the states and local governments. Later, as the country increased industrial production to support the Allies in World War II and then entered the war, the power of the federal government expanded even more, from managing factories to rationing the use of materials such as rubber and nylon, as well as food supplies, among the general population.

The new power of the federal government was concentrated in the president, in his role as promoter of New Deal programs and as commander in chief of the armed forces. The judiciary eventually supported Roosevelt's strong presidential role, but only after a major national debate and the executive's efforts to change the makeup of the Supreme Court by appointing judges more in accord with his concept of federal executive power. As a consequence, from the 1930s through the 1960s, the Court supported the expansion of federal regulatory powers; broadened the definition of citizenship to include all Americans, regardless of gender, race, or condition; and assumed an activist role in adjusting the Constitution to the realities of twentieth-century America.

*In Brazil*'s First Republic (1889–1930), the balance of power lay with the state governments, but the dominance of national politics by the oligarchies of Minas Gerais, São Paulo, and Rio Grande do Sul ensured that the country was still governed in accordance with the interests of a limited number of sectors, particularly rural landowners and the "coffee bourgeoisie." However, from 1910 on, revolts among midlevel military officers, the rise of radical political parties, and urban unrest suggested challenges to this form of government. Even among the more privileged classes, reformers lobbied for free and secret ballots, reduced fraud, and expanded rolls of eligible voters.

Brazil was more severely affected by the crash of international financial markets than was Mexico, in large part because of its higher degree of dependence on exports, particularly coffee. Indeed, Brazil's financial troubles actually preceded the Great Depression, since several federal administrations during the 1920s had aggressively printed money to help stabilize coffee prices. This led to high inflation, falling exchange rates, and rising foreign debt, all of which had effects on the country's living standards and prospects for economic development.

In 1929, the collapse of the international financial system, combined with the unwillingness of President Washington Luis to approve special economic aid to the hard-hit coffee and cattle sectors, provoked rebellion among discontented politicians and soldiers from Minas Gerais and Rio Grande do Sul, led by the latter's governor, Getúlio Vargas. The national military deposed the president before Vargas's band of rebels reached Rio de Janeiro, but faced with popular demonstrations the military eventually ceded the provisional presidency to Vargas.

The ascension of Getúlio Vargas to broader political power transformed the national state into a centralizing force in politics and economics. Industrialization and modernization were promoted by the national government, urban workers were wooed into and then dominated by corporatist labor unions with direct ties to the chief executive, and the national military achieved a new importance in both industry and the maintenance of internal order. Vargas sidelined traditional regional oligarchies by dissolving Congress and limiting the autonomy of states, dismissing elected governors and directly appointing their replacements (the *interventores*), closing state and municipal legislatures, taking over public education, and reducing the power and financial resources of state militias (Fausto 1999, 199).

By 1934, when Vargas's provisional presidency should have been drawing to a close, he convoked a Constituent Assembly to ratify his changes in the governing system. Thus, in contrast to the extraconstitutional mechanisms used to centralize government authority in Mexico and the USA, a new legal framework supported changes in Brazil's government. The same Constituent Assembly also established an indirect election designed to extend Vargas's mandate until 1938, when his successor was to be chosen by popular vote. However, supposed and real conspiracies by communists in the following years provided ready pretexts for Vargas to expand his authoritarianism and repression of dissent. These threats, exaggerated by the government itself, also led directly to a new coup in 1937, through which Vargas installed himself as dictator under the Estado Novo.

The Estado Novo did not mark a major break from the previous administration, but it did involve an additional degree of centralization, with Vargas proclaiming the end of federalism and liberal democracy in Brazil. The states were reduced to administrative organs of the central government, and the *coronéis* became irrelevant in local politics, since the elections that they aimed to control were no longer held (Love 1993, 209–13). Congress was again disbanded, and a "Constitutional Charter" was imposed to allow Vargas more freedom of action to overcome supposedly destructive partisan politics. Civilian and military bureaucrats focused their efforts on promoting "national independence" through industrialization and modernization, including the establishment of import substitution policies.

## Divergence in Governance after 1945

Peace on the international front after World War II made it possible for all three countries to focus on domestic matters. In responding to internal issues, the federalism practiced in Brazil, Mexico, and the USA diverged dramatically: it became nearly unrecognizable in centralized, authoritarian Mexico, while in Brazil the balance of power between levels of government oscillated between eras of decentralization and centralization, depending in part on whether the national regime was more or less democratic. In contrast, in a context of expanding suffrage, the main issue in the USA became how power was to be shared between federal and state authorities and the proper balance between national and local authority. Because of this diversity, this section treats each country in turn at some length.

*The USA* entered the postwar world with a strong national government centered on the presidency. Still, this dominance of national government did not go uncontested: a debate on intergovernmental relations, with a focus primarily on federal-state relations, began in the USA in the 1950s, much earlier than in Brazil and Mexico, and continued over the decades (Council of State Governments 1949; Commission of Intergovernmental Relations 1955; Joint Federal-State Action Committee 1960).

Nevertheless, wartime powers, concentrated in the federal executive to ensure coordination in military action abroad and economic policy at home, quickly evolved into what became known as the imperial presidency under the impact of the Cold War. Competition with the Soviet Union for hegemony throughout the globe required the continuation of coordinated security policy and economic policy, and this was facilitated by bipartisan cooperation in Congress. On domestic issues, the consensus built by Roosevelt, with its emphasis on the role of the federal government in advancing economic and social policy, continued until the 1960s. The high point was the inauguration of the Kennedy administration and its vision of an America that would be all-inclusive domestically and hegemonic abroad in its benevolent use of power.

To make cooperative federalism work, from the 1940s through the 1970s the activist Supreme Court took a liberal approach to the Constitution and reinterpreted it to fit the times. Symbolic of this image of the

Court was the decision in *Brown vs. Board of Education*, in 1954, which ended legal separation of the races in public schools as legally practiced in some states and placed the federal courts solidly behind equal rights for all.

The assassination of Kennedy in 1963 and the escalation of the Vietnam conflict provoked a realignment of political and social forces in the country. The troubled presidency of Lyndon Baines Johnson (November 1963–69) reflected the increasing divisions within American society over the role of the federal government as an agent of social change, as well as the national debate over security policy and the commitment of the USA to the Vietnam War. Protests against the war in Vietnam and internal divisions over President Johnson's vision of the Great Society at home were key factors in his decision not to run for a second full term of office.

Over the years, the mechanisms and forms of cooperative federalism changed as political forces shifted. For example, Johnson's controversial War on Poverty (1964–68) took as a given that the federal government would lead other levels in social policy. The Johnson administration set guidelines and parameters designed to end poverty in the USA, while state and local authorities were expected to cooperate with the regional and local branches of the federal bureaucracy as they implemented new programs, such as the Job Corps for unemployed young people and the Head Start program for the children of working mothers. But in undertaking programs designed to deal with urban problems through the empowerment of the disadvantaged, federal bureaucrats found themselves in direct conflict with some state and local authorities, whose existing power bases were threatened by this mobilization.

The succession of Richard Nixon (1969–74) became identified with the redefinition of presidential leadership and the readjustment of economic and social policy by way of changes in the relationship between the federal government and the states. Nixon is perhaps most remembered for his abuse of the extensive powers of the presidency during his campaign for a second term, which culminated in the Watergate affair and his subsequent resignation from office. However, his impact on reversing the balance of power in the federal system by returning power to the states under the New Federalism of his first term served as a catalyst for an eventual realignment in American politics. Its significance was overshadowed at the time by the national debate over how to curtail the potential for abuse of the informal powers and practices that had made the president supreme in American politics.

During this period, the vision of a Great Society held by Johnson and his supporters, in which activist federal social policy would attack the sources of inequity and injustice in American society, gave way to a more conservative vision of America. Nixon's New Federalism was designed to supersede the conflict engendered by the activist social policy of the Johnson administration. Following an alternative construct of cooperative federalism, the Nixon administration sought to decentralize government, especially the ability of state and local authorities to take the initiative on policy issues.

State governments, in turn, were charged with responsibility for distributing the funds to local authorities, according to local preferences. The key mechanisms for accomplishing this were block grants to the state governments in exchange for their acceptance of the conditions imposed. At the same time, a growing percentage of the federal budget came to be consumed by "entitlements," such as Social Security, Medicare, and Medicaid, which were mandated by the national legislature; the states had little or no voice in these decisions. The federal government also expanded its use of regulatory strategies to induce the cooperation of state and local governments in implementing its policy (Advisory Commission on Intergovernmental Relations [ACIR] 1984), but in fields such as environmental protection, education, and health and safety, federal regulatory strategies were gradually expanded and became a source of contention as financial burdens were placed on state and local governments (Derthick 1987; ACIR 1984).

Nevertheless, transfers to the states began to restore the balance in the federal system by increasing the fiscal capacity of states and the municipalities under their jurisdiction to meet needs in education, health, and transportation according to their own priorities. Whereas Johnson's War on Poverty program generated controversy, opposition, and demonstrations, the sharing of resources between national, state, and local governments was the glue that made cooperative federalism work from 1968 into the 1980s.

*In Mexico*, national presidents continued to expand their powers from the 1940s to the 1980s. This pattern stands in stark contrast to the debates in the USA from the 1960s onward over the role of the state in society and the economy and the relative power of subnational governments. Through the establishment of a corporatist political and economic strategy begun under Lázaro Cárdenas (1934–40), the national president came to dominate not only relations among the national government powers (Congress and the judiciary) but also the political processes within every state and municipality in the country. Still, in spite of one-party rule, strict adherence to the revolutionary doctrine of no reelection ensured that no single individual came to dominate Mexican political life in the postwar period in the style of Roosevelt in the USA and Vargas in Brazil.

The disadvantages of this centralized, single-party arrangement would eventually become clear, but its lasting contribution was to bring a measure of political stability to Mexico that it had not enjoyed in all of the previous century, with the exception of the *porfiriato*. This stability allowed for the "Mexican economic miracle" of the 1940s to the 1970s. In contrast to economic growth under the Díaz regime, this period brought benefits to broad sections of the population and, ironically, contributed eventually to growing demands for democratization and decentralization.

Meanwhile, stability in politics from the 1940s to the 1970s was built on the hegemony of the PRI and was reflected in the regime's identification with the Constitution of 1917 and the goals of the revolution. While politics was authoritarian in terms of control over the state, society, and the economy, such principles as regular elections were assiduously respected in the determination of executive officials at the federal, state, and local levels. Formal structures were deceptive, however: the Mexican state was designed as a federation, but the reality was a centralized and hierarchical regime, in terms of the locus of government in Mexico City, the primacy of the presidency of the republic over other elements of the government, and the ruling party that supported this system.

Likewise, while lip service was paid to the concept of an independent congress and judiciary, the checks and balances written into the Constitution were inoperative during this period (Carpizo 1978; Marván 1997). As chief executive and head of the party, the president exerted extraofficial influence over the behavior of public officials, while the recourse to fraud at the ballot box ensured the victory of preselected candidates.

Similar processes operated in each of the states, with governors dominating legislative and judicial branches through their control of candidate selection and nominations, respectively. At the municipal level, there
was no judiciary, and the local council *(cabildo)* was not formally en-
dowed with legislative powers, although in some areas their members
came to demand these. In the meantime, the absence of a formal division
of powers led to strong *presidencialismo* at this level as well (Guillén
López 1996).

Since the formalities of the constitution were carefully followed, the
PRI could claim that Mexico was a democracy, albeit a controlled or "im-
perfect" one. However, dissenting voices emphasized that there was no
effective alternative to the PRI monopoly on government and to the organizations that it set up to control its three major mass constituencies:
the peasantry, the workers, and the middle sectors of Mexican society
(school teachers, bureaucrats, and small tradespeople).

The first sign of widespread opposition appeared in the political crises
of the late 1960s, especially in the rapidly growing cities. Broad swaths of
urban residents found themselves outside the corporatist structure that
had been developed by the postrevolutionary regime, and the system ap
peared incapable of integrating this new middle class into its fold, in spite
of the populist presidential strategies of the time. Thus many Mexican
scholars (González Casanova 1981; Pereyra 1990) argue that the student
protests of 1968 and their violent suppression by government mark the
beginning of movement toward the opening of the Mexican political sys
tem, although this process would not be consolidated until decades later.

Indeed, in 1968 the PRI was not yet willing to cede power, and opposition forces were not in a position to demand it. Around this time, the
discovery of petroleum reserves of even greater magnitude than formerly
suspected allowed the party to reassert control through the strategic distribution of the income generated by these resources among disgruntled
sectors of the population. However, a decade later, the fall of oil prices,
massive *peso* devaluation, and the debt crisis of 1984 marked the end of
rapid economic growth, which in turn contributed to a widespread disil-
lusionment with the existing political system and eventually led to serious
questioning of the dominance of the president and his party (Hernández
Chávez 1993).

In response to these manifestations of rising domestic discontent and later to the pressures exerted by the international agencies that had stabilized the economy after near-collapse in 1982, a series of federal executives embarked on initiatives to make government more effective and efficient. From 1970 to 1982, these can be summarized as a focus within the state on administrative reform that recognized the need to deconcentrate a limited sphere of decision making in order to restore confidence in government and the one-party system. Federal government initiatives such as Integrated Programs for Rural Development (Programa de Inversiones Para el Desarrollo Rural, PIDER), the state-based economic development committees (Comités Promotores del Desarrollo Económico, COPRODEs), and the CUC (Coordination Agreements, Convenios Únicos de Coordinación]) during the José López Portillo *sexenio* (1976–82) were instrumental in the development of administrative arrangements that began to recognize the diversity of the country's regions and their needs.

These programs also began a trend toward incorporating professionally trained specialists into policy areas, especially in such fields as rural development and public health, rather than relying on generalist politicians and narrowly trained technicians. In addition, reflecting worldwide trends at the time, planning was elevated to constitutional status in 1982, and the National System of Democratic Planning (Sistema Nacional de Planeación Democrática, SNPD) laid out a framework for coordination among local, state, and national executives and representatives to set the course for development. Because of the continued dominance of the PRI in the political system, the SNPD was almost entirely ignored for the first decades of its existence, but it did set a legal precedent for decentralized planning, which some states and municipalities were beginning to employ by the 1990s, albeit to limited effect (Cabrero 1996, 1998; Rowland 2001).

Thus, while the USA adjusted its federal formulas to reduce the hegemony of Washington, in Mexico the political centralization characteristic of the consolidated PRI regime was reflected in sustained economic growth nationally, but with little fiscal benefit to state and local governments. A physical expression of this political centralization was the spectacular demographic growth of Mexico City, which became the largest city in the world during this period. By the end of the 1970s, the PRI elite could take satisfaction in forty years of sustained state-led economic growth, but beneath this rosy macroeconomic picture were found increased internal inequities, with marked discrepancies between rich and poor individuals, as well as between affluent and marginalized regions. The oil boom that began in the 1970s increased expectations that these inequities could be addressed through central government policies, but inflation and the collapse of oil prices in 1982 put an end to the bonanza and spurred a new round of economic and political reforms.

*In Brazil,* the disintegration of the centralized Vargas regime, an unsuccessful attempt to reinstall democracy, and the recourse to authoritarian rule combined to heighten the tensions between those favoring centralization and decentralization. While the 1940s to the 1980s was a period of consolidation of the PRI regime in Mexico, these years were marked in Brazil by two distinct cycles of centralized, authoritarian rule (1930–45, 1965–87) and decentralized, democratic rule (1946–64, 1988–present). Vargas's Estado Novo concentrated power in the hands of the central government to an extent previously unknown and laid the foundations for Brazil's economic modernization. But his external realignment in support of the Allied wartime effort made the pressure to democratize unavoidable. In 1945, the democratic opposition, the National Democratic Union (União Democrática Nacional, UDN), outmaneuvered Vargas, thanks to the alliance of military officers returning from the war in Italy with the civilian opposition. Presidential and congressional elections in December of that year gave a decisive mandate to democratic forces to form a new government.

Under the new president, Congress wrote a new charter, the Constitution of 1946. But, as was to be the case a little more than forty years later in a second constitution (1988), conservative forces exercised sufficient voice to limit the extent of democratization. The underrepresentation of voters from large urban areas in elections for representatives to the Chamber of Deputies, combined with the adoption of the U.S. model for guaranteeing each state the same number of representatives in the Senate, allowed conservative political forces to capture sufficient representation at the federal level to defend their interests.

With the pro-Vargas alliance dominant in Congress, the PSD (Partido Social Democrático/Social Democratic Party) and the PTB (Partido Trabalhista Brasileiro/Brazilian Workers' Party) established a pattern of control over the public agenda that remained intact throughout these years. By August 1961, however, public sentiment shifted to Vice President João

Goulart of the PTB. Fearful of Goulart's left-populist support, conservatives attempted to change the rules of the game governing presidential power by legislating into existence a semiparliamentary system. When the electorate refused to ratify this change through a popular referendum, a political and economic crisis ensued. The regime finally collapsed in March 1964, and a reluctant military intervened at the request of conservatives and moderates who were fearful that Goulart would radically alter the prevailing political and economic order. The new governing military and civilian alliance resorted to authoritarian controls, including its first authoritarian decree, an Institutional Act that abolished all the existing political parties.

Without ever officially declaring a new authoritarian regime, the military and their civilian allies so rewrote the 1946 Constitution with Institutional Acts that in 1967 they codified these changes in a new constitution de jure. More radical yet was the 1969 amendment to this new document, written by the military ministers while Congress was in recess, which concentrated powers in the national government. Through these alterations, military control of the presidency and hence of the republic was ensured. With de jure and de facto power to build a new ruling coalition, senior military officials identified those in civil society, essentially of middle- and upper-class background, who supported the new order as a political and economic necessity. This military-civilian alliance shared a vision: the purging of corrupt, patronage-oriented politicians and the ending of the acute inflationary spiral that Brazil had become locked into during sustained political crisis, in order to achieve state-controlled economic growth and the development of Brazil's internal market.

By 1970, the installation of an authoritarian regime was complete, and the political and economic crisis was over. With political order reestablished, the technocrats in the Ministry of Finance and the National Planning Ministry took control of fiscal policy, reduced inflation dramatically, and revived the economy through direct support to domestic firms and intervention in domestic markets. The result was the "Brazilian Economic Miracle": from 1968 to 1972 growth rates averaged 10 percent per year and foreign investments and loans poured into the country. Brazilians experienced an economic boom, only to discover in their first oil shock in 1973 just how vulnerable they were to international market fluctuations.

The end of the economic miracle coincided with increased control over dissidents. In turn, as opposition was repressed on an ever-expanding basis, more demonstrations and strikes broke out. Finally, the failure of the economic model and the lack of legitimacy of the military-technocratic government led to increased demands for a return to democratic government. From 1974 until 1985, a protracted transition began as the government and its supporters realized that their national project had failed and looked for a suitable means of exiting from power without losing their ability to influence who would govern in the aftermath.

Meanwhile, the opposition mobilized groups outside government to an extent never before seen in Brazil, until finally the two sides agreed upon an exit strategy for the military, which centered on permitting a conservative opposition leader, Tancredo Neves, to be selected as president by a congress elected under rules set by the outgoing regime.

Uncertainty continued long afterward, for on the eve of assuming power in March 1985 Tancredo Neves died. Under the newly agreed-upon rules, his vice president, José Sarney, a conservative politician identified with the groups that had supported the authoritarian regime, became president of Brazil. Democratic rule thus returned to Brazil in the midst of troubling conditions: sustained economic crisis and control of the presidency by those who had collaborated with the departing regime.

In this protracted struggle between democratic and authoritarian forces, as well as an extended national debate over how to modernize the country, centralization prevailed and the issue of how to manage core-periphery tensions in a large and diverse nation was lost. It was revived only in the 1980s as regional and local political forces reasserted themselves and made use of the new fiscal resources passed to them from the federal government under the 1988 Constitution.

### Increased External Pressures and Adjustments in Governmental Structure: The 1980s and 1990s

In the 1980s, Brazil, Mexico, and the USA all made major adjustments in the practice of federalism and intergovernmental relations in response to momentous changes in politics and economics at home and abroad. Once again, the precise timing of these changes varied in each of the three countries, but as a result state and local governments gained power and importance relative to national levels. The path was indirect in Brazil and Mexico, where certain government practices hitherto considered to be the domain of national authority came under increased international scrutiny and control. On the one hand, efforts by multilateral agencies (especially the International Monetary Fund and World Bank) to provoke changes in the management of these economies exerted pressure to cut public spending and reform public administration. These agencies also began to show greater willingness to consider intervention in domestic political and governmental practices that previously had been considered off limits to them. On the other hand, more attention came to be devoted internationally to human rights, questionable electoral practices, and police or military abuses. These changes were intimately linked with new technologies that made it easier for residents of Brazil and Mexico to compare their situations with those in other countries and to exert pressure on their governments for change. Activists outside government also began to find wider audiences domestically and internationally for their protests and new strength in their ability to organize citizens.

In the USA, the processes of internationalization or globalization in the 1980s initially provoked rapid economic transformation (expressed in changes in urban form and the distribution of income) as well as the immigration of millions of new residents from around the world. These changes took place in a context of an aging population of voters, the majority of whom preferred to reduce public spending on social programs and have the money go toward a military buildup instead, while continuing to search for tax relief for themselves. Thus U.S. federal government also faced pressures to cut spending, balance its budget, and leave more margin for decision making to the state and local levels.

One consequence of these changes in political practices and legal structures in Brazil, Mexico, and the USA was the devolution of fiscal resources to state and local government, accompanied by cuts in expenditures by central governments. This led initially to a major reduction in central deficits and to some downsizing of the central bureaucracy. Accompanying these changes was growth in public sector employment at the state and local level as responsibility for an increasing range of services was transferred to subnational levels of government.

*In the USA*, the major political developments during the 1980s were divided government and the resurgence of coordinate-authority federalism. In the immediate postwar period the prevailing image of politics in this country was that significant differences between the two parties were nonexistent, but fifty years later the opposite was true. Partisan differences had become so great as to make compromise difficult on nearly all major issues facing the country. The conventional wisdom that the pull to the center was sufficient to isolate the extremes and encourage legislative bargaining and compromise cutting across political party lines no longer held during the last two decades of the twentieth century. Each party now felt it essential to secure its bases in the electorate rather than to engage in national-level processes of compromise. The stakes became higher for legislative programs, especially when one party controlled the White House and the other, one or both of the houses of Congress. Thus, critics noted, partisan divisions became so great that little could be accomplished in domestic politics.

The extended period during which the Republicans controlled the White House (1980–92), under Ronald Reagan and George H. W. Bush, also made it possible to change the balance of power within the Supreme Court. Presidential nomination of more conservative justices, confirmed by the Senate after bitter partisan fights, resulted eventually in a narrow margin among the justices in favor of strict interpretations of the Constitution during the 1990s. This moved the federal government out of its hitherto dominant role in social policy, reducing the regulatory powers of the executive branch and granting to the states increased power to determine their own policy. While the activist stance of the Court had appeared reasonable to those identified with earlier Democratic administrations (Roosevelt, Truman, Kennedy, and Johnson), the implementation of progressive social policy, in particular, provoked increasing hostility from major sectors of American society. One consequence was the determination of Republican political leaders to limit the Court to a strict interpretation of the Constitution, thereby reversing changes in the distribution of power they found unacceptable.

At the time of Ronald Reagan's first presidential victory in 1980, realignment in American politics and government was much discussed, but there was little consensus about how to characterize the process. In hindsight, we can appreciate a major readjustment since the postwar era in both the separation of powers and the division of powers between the federal and state governments. These are expressed, respectively, in the resurgence of congressional power relative to the presidency and in the devolution to the states of substantial amounts of control over policy. As a consequence, both the Republicans and Democrats who held office after Reagan governed under very different circumstances than their predecessors.

In this setting, governors assumed a new importance in U.S. politics, since issues that could not be resolved at the national level were transferred to the states. Governors expanded their roles, pushing for further decentralization to enhance their powers and widening the policy domains in which state governments could make decisions that directly affected the lives of their residents. Thus, as the USA entered the twenty-first century, it returned to a coordinate-authority model of federalism, ratified by a strict-constructionist Supreme Court, in which national and state authorities had become once again coequal and autonomous.

Under the Reagan administration, decentralization of decision making and reductions in intergovernmental transfers were pursued aggressively. In a sharp departure from the administrative decentralization and efficiency concerns of the Nixon period, Reagan's stated purpose was to reduce the size and scope of government intervention at all levels (Conlan 1988). It was argued that this retrenched system of government would improve the relative position of states, since their resources would be reduced less than those of the federal government. The administration succeeded in shifting principal responsibilities for administering federal aid programs to the states, to the detriment of local governments. New block grant programs were federal-state in nature, and the share of federal aid bypassing states and going directly to local governments declined (Walker 1991). Some of Reagan's proposals to reduce the role of the federal government were curtailed by Congress, but in many areas—health, economic development, water development, environmental policy, and telecommunications—the federal government retreated from its leadership role in policy development and funding (Bowman and Pagano 1990).

The administration of George H. W. Bush (1988–92) maintained the spirit of devolution, but with a more pragmatic tone. As the 1980s wore on, the debate on the appropriate division of responsibilities and relative autonomy of states began to be overshadowed by the growing federal debt. The rapid increase in federal military expenditures and the inability to increase federal revenue (in no small part the result of the 1981 federal tax reduction) placed severe constraints on federal aid to state and local governments. Federal decisions on aid were subject to poor fiscal conditions as well as to strong political forces encouraging administrative decentralization. The reduction in aid placed new pressures on state and local policy making. However, the administrative decentralization of preceding decades helped prepare states for the challenges of the decentralization of policy making (R. Wilson 1993).

Under Bush, the Republican-controlled presidency found progress on major policy issues extremely difficult to negotiate with a Democratic-controlled Congress. Policy stalemate continued when the party roles were reversed during the Clinton presidencies. The one area where agreement occurred, the need for a balanced budget, resulted in reduced opportunities for states and localities to acquire financial assistance from national government.

The changes in intergovernmental relations in the USA during the 1980s and 1990s cannot be characterized as an orderly decentralization of responsibilities. Rather, they created opportunities and needs for state and local governments to take action to fill a vacuum. The basic structure of intergovernmental relations remained centered on the national government, particularly in terms of federal regulation and supportive judicial decisions, but states had new opportunities to initiate action and design programs in various policy areas (Walker 1991; Elazar 1987a). By the end of the 1990s, devolution had been broadly accepted, and congressional delegations of both political parties tended to support decentralized decision making and greater state and local responsibility.

*In Mexico*, new roles for subnational governments came as an unintended result of incremental reforms to the broader political and economic framework, implemented by national elites beginning in the 1980s. Political changes in the Mexican system were equal in scale to those of the USA, if very different in context, during the last two decades of the twentieth century. The shift was from one-party hegemony under the PRI to a competitive multiparty system based on three main parties: the PAN, the PRD, and the PRI. Since the late 1960s, the PRI had responded to pressure from domestic opposition groups in favor of political liberalization with piecemeal reforms in political processes. However, recurring challenges to the legitimacy of the system, as well as external pressures beginning in 1985 to reduce public expenditures, made the decentralization of administration and policy making an attractive possibility for a party reluctant to relinquish its hold on government.

The first wave of significant administrative reforms occurred during the *sexenio* of Miguel de la Madrid (1982–88). Particularly important were the creation of a National System of Fiscal Coordination (Sistema Nacional de Coordinación Fiscal, SNCF) in 1980 and the constitutional reform of 1983, which was designed to strengthen municipalities. The ostensible goal of the SNCF was to increase efficiency in administration and collections and grant greater liberty to states and municipalities in spending their share of federal transfers. In practice, however, significant decentralization of public revenue was not achieved through the SNCF because the total amount transferred to the states and municipalities—although around three times greater than the level in 1980—still had not surpassed 30 percent of total public spending by the year 2000 (Rodríguez 1997). States and municipalities of all sizes continued to depend far more on central government transfers than on local sources of finance. Until recently, the amount of these transfers was determined arbitrarily by the president and the governors under unclear rules that made local planning and budgeting nearly impossible. Thus fiscal issues remained a key point of contention in intergovernmental relations in Mexico.

To the extent that some shift toward decentralization in the distribution of public finances was evident in national-level statistics during this period, it was mainly the result of increased collections of the property tax and local services fees by a handful of urban municipalities, rather than an outcome of central government policies (Cabrero 1996, 1998). However, like the earlier planning legislation, these formal changes finally began to be reflected in changes in practice years later, when the capacity of local officials in some municipalities had improved substantially (Cabrero 1996, 1998).

The rise of electoral competition at the local level also changed the incentives for local officials from subordination to state and central government to increased attention to local interest groups and their demands. In spite of continuing limitations, electoral competition represented an important spur to action on the part of subnational governments, including those municipalities and states ruled by the PRI. By the 1990s, even party hard-liners had come to see the usefulness at election time of sufficient subnational political autonomy to publicly challenge the policies and practices of higher levels of government. State governors took on greater importance in political debates, even if their actual sphere of action was limited. Unfortunately, claims of electoral fraud remained common, especially at the state and municipal levels, where elections were overseen not by the highly regarded national federal electoral institute but by its (decentralized) state counterparts.

In sum, until well into the 1990s, the Mexican system was characterized by the absence of constraints on presidential and, within more limited spheres, gubernatorial power. In spite of official public discourse promoting decentralization in administration and government, the political system remained highly centralized (Graham 1990; Rodríguez 1997; Ward and Rodríguez 1999). In addition, the history of administrative incapacity and institutional weakness of municipalities, combined with bureaucratic practices and traditional politics fostered by a hegemonic party system, remained formidable obstacles to the decentralization of power (Rowland 2001). Despite all the changes in government, the three major political parties remained centered in Mexico City and directed from the top down, in stark contrast to their counterparts in the USA and Brazil. Even in a plural Congress (as of 1997), none of these parties showed interest in facilitating the creation of regional parties to reflect increasing political and economic differentiation within the country. Laws governing the registration of new parties continue to make regional political parties nearly impossible, and nonpartisan candidates are not permitted to run for office.

Still, enormous political, economic, and social changes took place in Mexico during these years, and in this sense efforts to maintain centralized, one-party control were ultimately doomed. On the one hand, the country moved from a state-dominated economy to a market-based system more compatible with world trends and more open to international influences. Close on the heels of these changes, political liberalization, beginning with the relaxation of electoral controls at the municipal level, led to competitive politics in many localities, as well as a new level of pluralism in Congress. This process culminated in 2000 with the recognition by outgoing PRI President Ernesto Zedillo that the PAN's candidate, Vicente Fox, had won the election and the right to become the first non-PRI national president in nearly seven decades.

Significantly, Fox's political party began its transition to national political importance with a series of electoral victories in northern municipalities in the mid-1980s. As voters gained confidence in the potential for non-PRI parties to govern (and to be allowed to govern), the PAN's victories spread to important cities nationwide, as well as to state governors and the national congress. Nevertheless, throughout this period, the majority of municipalities and states continued to be ruled by the PRI, albeit often as a result of disputed elections, especially up until 2000. Even after the PRI was eclipsed into third place in the 2006 elections, the party still governed in over half of the states. This series of events suggests that—even beyond federal policies—the interests and practices that favor centralization have lost power relative to those that favor decentralization.

Finally, it is worth emphasizing that the dramatic changes in intergovernmental relations in Mexico came about with nothing more than changes in practice and piecemeal reforms to specific articles of the 1917 Constitution. Whether a complete rewriting of the legal framework for government is necessary to foster more democratic and more effective government remains a question of political debate.

*In Brazil*, politics during the last decades of the twentieth century was marked by a resurgence of subnational governments, economic crisis, and economic restabilization under Cardoso, first as finance minister, then as president. Decentralization and the revitalization of federalism through the creation of distinct political arenas at the national, state, and local levels played an important role in opening the political space necessary for competitive politics to emerge and allowed for the hold of traditional clientelist politics to be challenged effectively for the first time. While the prevailing literature bemoans the dominance of clientelist politics in the Brazilian political system during this period, new political space was opening up at the state and local levels, and there reformist politicians were able to begin to restructure political and social relationships. This latter development was very weak at the outset, with reformist politics appearing only in some midsize towns during the 1980s. But the trend spread by the beginning of the 1990s to Porto Alegre, Vitória, Belo Horizonte, Recife, and the São Paulo industrial belt, and by the end of the decade reformist politicians began to organize and compete in other venues, while reformist political alliances became more likely to appear at the state and local levels (Graham and Jacobi 2002; Setzler 2002; Wampler 2000).

The fact that Brazil democratized *before* engaging in economic restructuring produced a different set of economic and political outcomes than in Mexico. This sequence of events strengthened federalism as a structure within which competitive politics could function. No single individual or group was able to dominate politics at all three levels of government, and the new political framework made economic restructuring more difficult to achieve because it required participants from all three levels to engage in bargaining and compromise. Much as in the USA from 1960 to 1980, an overlapping-authority model of federalism began to emerge in Brazil during the 1980s and 1990s.

The Constitution of 1988 establishes a legal framework for an expanded democratic regime, beyond the limited democracy enshrined in the 1946 Constitution. At the same time, there are marked similarities between the two documents in terms of the constraints implied by the underrepresentation of urban areas and the overrepresentation of rural ones. Nevertheless, the adoption of the 1988 Constitution represented a dramatic turning point and established the institutional framework of a decentralized government. It strengthened the role of subnational governments, both states and municipalities, confirming a process that had begun some years before. It attributed new competencies to subnational governments, mainly to the municipalities, reflecting the decentralizing demands from the social movements that had been fighting against dictatorship since the 1970s. Indeed, the new constitution establishes a very decentralized federal model; its definition of the municipality as an entity of the federation *ente federado*—makes it a singular case in the international context (Kugelmas and Sola 1999, 69).

For years after the return to elections and open political competition, however, Brazil could be classified as a low-level democracy. Saddled by a state-dominated economy and governmental practices that embodied the symbiotic relationship between government and the business community (the original basis for economic modernization), Brazil did not embrace meaningful economic reform until the election of Fernando Henrique Cardoso (1994–2002). In fact, Cardoso's initial presidential victory was a consequence in large part of his success as finance minister under the previous president. In his second term, after successfully stabilizing the national economy, Cardoso ran into severe obstacles as he tackled administrative reform. In attempting to modernize the Brazilian state, he faced broad conservative opposition, since these reforms touched their bases of political power and threatened the long-established and well-ingrained practices of clientelist politics. Despite this political opposition in his second term, Cardoso continued to push ahead with economic reform and democratic practices. Accepting competitive politics and engaging in the bargaining made necessary by the division and separation of powers, Cardoso more than any other Brazilian president had to deal with the realities of presidential federalism.

Under the 1988 Constitution, Brazil has experienced devolution of power to the states to a degree not seen since the First Republic. A key component of this decentralization has been the revival of the role of state governors as major players in national politics (Abrucio 1998). At the same time, Brazil has changed dramatically since the First Republic in terms of economic, political, and social structures. This renewed importance of gubernatorial politics speaks to a new reality in Brazilian governance: the establishment of a federal system in which power is divided between federal, state, and local authorities in such a way that there is an effective interplay between state and national political arenas.

In practice, Brazil's long-standing tradition of fiscal federalism reveals both advantages and disadvantages. For example, a key prerogative of the state governments was to borrow abroad without seeking approval of the federal government; this was a practice that states such as Minas Gerais continued to use during authoritarian military-technocratic centralized rule in the 1970s (Graham 1990). Yet another was the capacity of the state governments to engage in deficit financing and then pass the responsibility for repayment to the national government.

The Cardoso government maintained macroeconomic rigor, and the reduction of federal government spending imposed greater responsibility on the states and municipalities. This process, as discussed in chapter 4, was uncoordinated and generated substantial intergovernmental tensions (C. Souza 1996, 2001; Eaton 2004b). President Cardoso significantly curtailed state government spending authority at the outset of his second administration. By imposing fiscal responsibility on the states, he ended the practice of passing on their indebtedness to the federal government when they became unable to fund the programs to which they had committed. While the effects of these reforms vary greatly among states—from privatization, to mixed enterprises, to reformed public banks—they reflect a new reality in which the states have significant powers and constituencies that constrain the actions of central government. The accomplishments in promoting economic reform in the direction of consolidating markets and public sector fiscal responsibility should not be minimized, but they also highlight the delicate balance between local fiscal discretion and the national need to maintain macroeconomic stability.

In this sense, political space was opened at multiple levels in the 1990s. This permitted multiple outcomes in politics, including both traditional, clientelist alliances and programmatic, reformist alliances. Thus if on the one hand Cardoso had to confront a conservative clientelist alliance in the federal congress in his second term, on the other hand reformist candidates and political organizations could find ample space in which to gain governmental experience at the state and local levels. Furthermore, the political bargaining and compromise that Cardoso engaged in at the federal level had the effect of consolidating his economic reforms, so that markets could be expanded and fiscal federalism enshrined in practice for the first time in Brazil's national experience. Simultaneously, local governments and citizen groups found the political space they needed to attend to pressing issues in social policy. The election of Luiz Inacio (Lula) da Silva in 2002 and 2006 underlines the gains in terms of democratic practices, but his moderation in office also suggests that the scope for leveraging economic and social reform remains limited by the need to sustain a working majority, not just in Congress but in the electorate at large.

### Conclusions

This institutional-historical view of intergovernmental relations in Brazil, Mexico, and the USA establishes that the relationship between national and subnational governments in all three countries has been marked by tensions and has never remained stable for long. It also shows that the relative level of centralization and decentralization in the practice of federalism is related to the way that these intergovernmental tensions are resolved. The USA has institutionalized its federal system and sustained decentralized practices long enough to ensure the vitality of state and local governments, despite all the conflict embedded in this complex system. In part, this is because the fundamental basis of the system—the representation of diverse interests through periodic elections—has maintained its legitimacy for broad sectors of the population throughout history.

In contrast, federalism and decentralization remain constrained to a great extent in Mexico and to a lesser extent in Brazil by the absence of a sustained experience with democratic rule and the consolidation of representative government. These combined legacies—linked to authoritarian governmental practices, social and electoral exclusion, and poverty—continue to place constraints on making federalism work and giving content to decentralized policy initiatives. This is not to minimize the very real political, social, and economic transformations that Brazil and Mexico have undergone over the last two decades, but it does call attention to what has become obvious for recent leaders of these nations: it is a daunting task to simultaneously consolidate democratic rule and establish an economic system capable of sustained growth that also benefits wide sectors of the population.

This finding stands in contrast to the contemporary comparative literature on federalism, which tends to focus on the difference between strongly institutionalized and weakly institutionalized systems. The discussion of the three cases in this chapter emphasizes instead that the institutionalization of federalism is closely tied to the fate of democratic initiatives. In the USA, the longevity of a federal presidential republic is inseparable from the institutionalization of the system of checks and balances, as well as the division of powers inherent in its federalism. This contrasts with the periodic collapse of presidential regimes elsewhere in the Americas. Brazil's moderate success in making federalism work corresponds to the successes and failures in liberalizing its political system from the end of the nineteenth century to the present. Similarly, Mexico's weakly institutionalized federal system and continued resistance to decentralization are directly correlated with the delays until the 1990s in liberalizing and democratizing its presidential republic. In both Brazil and Mexico, the repeated recourse to authoritarianism has placed serious constraints on the development of federalist practices that could reaffirm the vitality of state and local governments.

Thus we draw three main conclusions from this chapter. First, local control has been, and remains, an important and virtually undisputed political value since the founding of the USA, even though the municipal level of government does not enjoy constitutional protection. In this case, the history of federalism from its inception has been bottom-up, not top-down, and U.S. federalism has long been unique in the sense that the states existed as independent units of government prior to the creation of a common national government. In Brazil and Mexico, the constitutional protection of municipal prerogatives, as well as those of the states, has been breached more often than not. Autonomy for subnational governments remains a goal rather than a shared political value—as has been the case with many other constitutional guarantees in these countries.

Second, the review of federalism and intergovernmental relations in these three countries suggests that as democratization in Brazil and Mexico moves forward it is almost certain to give rise to new variants of federalism, responding to the desire for increased regional and local autonomy. In this context the regional autonomy model, derived from Iberian experience and closely linked with the democratization of Spain and Portugal in the 1970s, merits attention. In all four cases the long repression of regionalism and localism, the imposition of central controls, and the removal of nondemocratic constraints have provoked a lively debate over how to decentralize in response to regional and local political interests. In each system, whether federal or unitary, securing regional autonomy and promoting the vitality of regional identities remains an important part of the struggle to limit the power and control of central government authorities. Under recent arrangements, autonomous regions in Spain and autonomous statutes in Portugal for governing the Azores and Madeira are, in a sense, de facto federal arrangements. These constitutional provisions give subnational units of government the power to control nearly all issues of significance to them, apart from the conduct of foreign policy, controls over the military, and limits on the taxing authority of the central government.

The appearance of the European Union has also changed the common ways of thinking about federalism. With its nascent federal structures built around the principle of *subsidiarity*, in which decision-making authority is vested in elected and appointed government officials at the lowest level (local authorities), it is the only instance apart from the USA of a federal system being built from the bottom up, through the transfer of powers from its constituent members to a higher level of governance. Issues that cannot be resolved within the lowest level of government are bumped up to the next level (regional authorities) for consideration and if necessary from them to national authorities. Those issues of importance to the European Community as a whole, and beyond the scope of individual member governments, are then dealt with in the European Commission (Brussels) and/or the European Assembly (Strasbourg).

The European Union's experimentation with multiple levels of governance is relatively recent, and it is not at all clear whether its members see this as a form of federalism. Nevertheless, the process of constructing a larger union, along with the transitions in Spain and Portugal, has stimulated renewed interest in the development of three-tiered models of government. These experiences have served to refocus attention on the importance of autonomy at the subnational level and the differing arrangements possible in designing an appropriate framework for processing regional and local interests. In large, complex governmental systems, federalism can be an important bulwark in sustaining democratic practices, especially when it is coupled with the principle of judicial review as the mechanism for arbitrating disputes between national and subnational authorities.

Our third conclusion is that the failure of political systems to resolve internal tensions arising from regional demands for a voice in local affairs has often facilitated the recourse to extraconstitutional solutions. The practice of centralization and decentralization in political and fiscal spheres has, consequently, often followed patterns of political power that can negate constitutional allocations of authority. Narrowing the gap between the formal attribution of power under federalism and the realities of how power is actually distributed is a perennial challenge. Whether extraconstitutional measures become a problem or form part of a solution lies at the heart of continual movement in intergovernmental relations in all three cases.

This dilemma cannot be reduced to a general argument in favor of centralization or decentralization. Rather, the question concerns the appropriate mix in designing and implementing policies and programs that can work under the federal pact at the national, regional, and local levels at any particular moment in time. As a consequence of this ongoing debate, cycles of greater centralization or decentralization accompany the changing balance of power in the practice of federalism; they range from hierarchical inclusive-authority federalism to coordinate-authority arrangements with co-equal federal units and extend to overlapping-authority patterns focused on bargaining among federal units.

Our review of the history of these three countries emphasizes the importance of broader social change in placing new challenges before governments and transforming intergovernmental relations and the role of subnational governments. In politics, the centralized, hierarchical structures of the past are inappropriate for today's mass democracies, in which all people are considered equal before the law. In economics, older systems for the extraction of wealth for the benefit of national governments are regarded as too cumbersome to serve quickly changing global markets. Technological advances like the Internet and global positioning systems, which put more information into more hands, change both what citizens know about governments and what governments may know about citizens.

Still, it is impossible to ignore the fact that large segments of the population in all three countries have been left out of discussions about the form of their government, as well as specific decisions of that government. While the general trend has been one of greater and more effective inclusion, all three countries have failed often, and in a variety of ways, to ensure all their citizens equal and effective protection and treatment under the law and meaningful participation in the processes of government. This complex issue warrants separate discussion. But what is clear here is that the legitimacy of governing arrangements remains grounded in constitutions that provide for the consent of the governed and limit government through the separation and division of power. Thus, in these three cases, federalism has become an integral part of the struggle to establish and maintain democratic practices in all three societies. These concepts have proven over time to be difficult to implement, yet they are essential to the continuation of this system of government and to the structuring of viable alternatives for democratic regimes and democratic practices.

# THREE

# The Changing Institutional Capacity of Subnational Government

*Toward Effective Co-governance*

## Victoria E. Rodríguez, Peter K. Spink, and Peter M. Ward

Until relatively recently most analyses of federalism and decentralization in Latin American countries focused almost exclusively upon relations between the various levels of government, looking up and down the levels of government from central to local, with a particular emphasis upon the central and highest level. It is equally true that in most of these studies the term *government* is associated almost exclusively with the executive branch, especially in heavily centralized federal and presidentialist systems. Although the other branches are also institutionalized, they have been largely invisible in the discussion—except for their legitimating functions for the national polity and, in the case of the judiciary, for their day-to-day work in civil, contractual, and criminal justice affairs.

### Horizontal versus Vertical Decentralization and the Separation of Powers

The central aim of this chapter is to assess the impact of changes in democratic practice and decentralization on intragovernmental institutional development and performance at the subnational level. We use the term *intragovernmental relations* to differentiate these relations from *intergovernmental relations,* a term most widely used to refer to relations *between* different levels or, occasionally, to relations among governments at the same level—the latter being the focus of chapter 4. Breaking down this question further, we propose to examine the efficacy of these co-governance arrangements measured in three ways. First, we examine the relative powers exercised by the principal branches of government and the changes that are taking place in the three countries with regard to the balance of governmental power. Second, we explore the modernization of institutional capacity and readiness across those branches. And third, we analyze the expectations and opportunities for citizen participation and engagement in formal governance through such mechanisms as plebiscites, referenda, and single-issue voting procedures. Other aspects of citizen participation, such as interest groups, consultative councils, forums, and lobbying, will be discussed in chapters 4 and 5.

As we outlined in chapter 1, centralization and decentralization are usually understood to describe a vertical structure and process in which resources and decision-making authority are organized and transferred between the central (federal) government and subnational and local tiers of government. However, a second dimension of decentralization that is studied less systematically also opens up the political space. This is *horizontal decentralization,* which embraces the political space of the roles, activities, and powers between the three *branches* (or powers) of government (Rodríguez 1997), as well as institutional changes in the ways citizens may exercise their individual or collective authority.[1] Under federalist structures these powers are separated by design. As Ackerman (2000) points out, while this constitutional design may create a structure of more or less equal powers, it can also weight effective power in favor of either the executive or the legislative branch. However, in countries experiencing democratization, the "separation of powers" is a question not merely of prior design but of a deliberate process to "loosen and separate" previously compacted institutional relationships, and this results in a recasting of the roles played by each branch and level of government at both the national and the subnational level.

In the USA the Founding Fathers, after the experience with the Articles of Confederation, fashioned a bottom-up federalist system of a union of states in which the relative power of the national executive was highly constrained vis-à-vis the legislature and the judiciary. As Ackerman (2000) and others before him have amply explained, the U.S. model gives the president very substantial powers over the executive branch and the federal bureaucracy but also gives the predominant power for lawmaking to a lower house of representatives that is elected nationally and a strong upper house representing the states, each of which sends two (locally) elected senators to Washington. Although the balance of power varies depending upon the party composition of the respective houses and their relative alignment with the policy orientation of the president, this presidentialist system of federal government creates structural impediments to the efficacy of policy making and accentuates the possibilities of gridlock.[2] This separation of powers is replicated at the subnational state level, where the effective powers of the state executive (the governor) are similarly circumscribed, though to varying degrees in each state.[3]

In contrast, in our other two federalist systems, the executive branch has until recently ruled supreme, broadly speaking, at least operationally if not institutionally. As we saw in chapter 2, in Brazil this executive dominance was deliberately imposed through the top-down federalist structure adopted from the republic's outset coupled with a highly centralized control and distribution of public funds. In Mexico, while the government was closely modeled on the U.S. structure and sought to provide "sovereignty and freedom" to the states, as well as "freedom and autonomy" to the municipalities, the overarching hegemony of the executive branch evolved over a long period. A history of dominant individual presidents during the nineteenth century, and then almost total control by a single-party system in the twentieth, effectively sublimated other institutional powers to those of the national president. Such executive dominance and centralization were achieved through the exercise of what are referred to as "metaconstitutional" powers derived from the almost absolute power and influence of the executive himself, who controlled the distribution of the spoils and could cajole, suborn, and orchestrate Congress and the judiciary to do his bidding—in effect making the other balancing powers almost entirely ineffective.

In this study, instead of using the more traditional term *separation of powers*, we would like to introduce the idea of *co-governance* in order to emphasize and refocus the challenge that faces countries like Brazil and Mexico to create a genuinely effective institutional interaction between the executive, legislative, and judicial branches within their constitutionally defined federalist pact. While *separation of powers* helps us to describe differences and focus on institutional checks and balances, *co-governance* helps us understand performance and the consequences of effective institutional positioning and roles played out in subnational policy making. Effective policy making and, more importantly, implementation will be seen to frequently incorporate more than a single branch of government, as well as different legislated mechanisms for citizen engagement and participation. In looking at the different institutions in action, we seek to draw attention to the way government is a result of their combined efforts.

## Separation of Powers in Comparative Perspective: The Different National Theories

We initiate this discussion with a shorthand description of the structures of co-governance by branch and by level in each country, including how the various key posts are filled. In terms of democratic theory, table 3.1 depicts the structures of democratic representation and participation. To expedite the discussion, no attempt is made here to rehearse the contents of the table; instead, the reader is invited to delve into the detail as appropriate, while we provide an overview of the broad differences and points of comparison between the three countries.

Although the three countries are formally similar in terms of the structure of the branches at the federal and state levels, albeit with key differences, they diverge considerably at the substate (local) level. Overall, five broad differences across the three countries seem worthy of mention. First, *the USA is decentralized in a much more heterogeneous way*, with a large raft of local and sublocal governments that are often accorded high levels of individual autonomy (cities or townships with home rule charters, for example). There are also independent school districts, municipal utility districts, and so on, all with highly specific functions at the sublocal level. Such a patchwork of overlapping local governments and areas of jurisdiction does not exist in either Brazil or Mexico, where a singular notion of municipality forms the primary tier of government.

Table 3.1  Federal and Subnational Arenas in Brazil, Mexico, and the USA

| COUNTRY & BRANCH | FEDERAL | SUBNATIONAL ARENA | | |
| --- | --- | --- | --- | --- |
| | | STATE | LOCAL | SUB/SUPRALOCAL |
| **BRAZIL** | | | | |
| *Executive* | *President*, and *Vice President* on single slate, elected at large, majority vote; second round if no one wins more than 50% of votes, partisan, 1 reelection permitted, 4 year-term. | 26 states and DF. *Governor and Vice Governor*, elected at large, majority vote: second round if no one wins more than 50% of votes, partisan, 1 reelection permitted, 4-year term. | 5592 municipalities *Prefeito* and *Vice Prefeito* on single slate; second round if no one wins more than 50% in munici-palities with more than 200,000, and by simple majority in those of less than 200,000. Elected at large, partisan, 4 year term, with 1 reelection. | Inter-municipal Consortia (agreements between municipalities on topics of common interest). Depends largely upon negotiated interests and funding. Some metropolitan regions, but not elected (created by state's congress). |
| *Legislative* | Bicameral: *Chamber of Deputies*, 513 members proportional to population by state but with a minimum of 8 and maximum of 70; 4-year terms, elected by population by state, open list proportional representation. Partisan; reelection allowed. *Senate*, 81 members, 3 for each state and Federal District, 8 year terms elected by population by state; open list proportional rep-resentation, partisan and reelection allowed. One third and two thirds renewed every alternate four years. | *Legislative Assembly:* Size determined by federal constitution and based on the number of federal deputies (three times the number of federal deputies for the state up to 36 plus the same number of federal deputies over 12); 4-year terms, open-list proportional representation, partisan, reelection allowed. | *Chamber of Vereadores:* Size determined by Federal Constitution and varies from 9–21 in municipalities up to 1 million, 33–41 in municipalities of 1–5 million, and 42–55 in more than 5 million; 4-year terms, open list proportional representation, partisan, reelection allowed. | Ad hoc arrangements decided locally. |

*Judiciary*

*Supreme Federal Tribunal*, 11 ministers, presidential appointment, senate confirmation by absolute majority, age 33–65 with strong legal reputation, compulsory retirement at 70 (*expulsório*) or voluntary retirement after 30 years with at least 5 in judiciary.

Higher Court of Justice (*Superior Tribunal de Justiça*) 33 ministers, presidential nomination, senate confirmation drawn from different areas of the federal and state judiciaries, lawyers and public prosecutors.

Higher Labor Court (*Tribunal Superior do Trabalho*), 27 ministers, presidential nomination, senate confirmation, widely drawn.

Higher Electoral Court (*Tribunal Superior Eleitoral*), 7 ministers (3 voted by STF, 2 by STJ and 2 nominated by President).

National Accounting Office (*Tribunal de Contas da União*), 9 ministers, one-third president, two-thirds congress.

Court of Justice (Tribunal de Justiça). Number of *desembargadores* varies in accordance with state constitution.

State Accounting Office (*Tribunal de Contas Estaduais*): own legislation but follows the norms of National Accounting Office in terms of organization, composition and control.

Regional courts of the federal system (Justice, Labor and Electoral)

Art. 31 of the Constitution prohibits the creation of new municipal-level accounting offices (*Tribunal de Contas Municipais*). A few remain (São Paulo, Rio, Goiás) as also are a few state-level accounting offices solely for municipalities (for example, Tribunal de Contas dos Municípios de Ceará, Goiás). In the remainder, the supervision and control of municipal accounts is provided by the State Accounting Office.

Table 3.1 Federal and Subnational Arenas in Brazil, Mexico, and the USA (*cont.*)

| COUNTRY & BRANCH | FEDERAL | SUBNATIONAL ARENA | | |
| --- | --- | --- | --- | --- |
| | | STATE | LOCAL | SUB/SUPRALOCAL |
| **MEXICO** | | | | |
| *Executive* | *President*, elected at large, majority vote, partisan, no reelection, 6-year term. (No vice president.) A few positions are appointed, requiring ratification by the Senate (e.g., the Attorney General). | 31 state *governors* and 1 *jefe de gobierno* (governor equivalent) for the Federal District, elected at large, majority vote, partisan, no reelection, 6-year term. All other positions appointed, some with confirmation by state congress. | *Ayuntamiento*[1] headed by *municipal president* elected at large, majority vote, partisan, no reelection, 3-year term. Other positions often require approval. Also, occasionally by *usos y costumbres* in some indigenous communities. "Elected" by local indigenous population, based upon traditions, informal 1- to 3-year terms, nonpartisan. | Auxiliary authorities (of different forms); whether elected or appointed varies by state. Usually nonpartisan; no reappointment/reelection. Functions are to represent/promote interests of communities and sometimes to deliver services. |
| *Legislative* | Bicameral: *Chamber of Deputies*, 300 by elected vote (population districts); 200 by proportional representation, 5 regions); 3-year terms, partisan, no immediate reelection. *Senate*: 4 per state, 2 elected by majority; 1 for runner-up. 32 additional senators allocated by proportional representation from a national list. 6-year terms, partisan, no reelection. | Unicameral: *Chamber of Deputies*. Number varies by state (population districts); some by elected vote (population districts); some by proportional representation, 3-year terms, partisan, no immediate reelection. | *Ayuntamiento*. Pseudo-legislature/ city council (in *cabildo* session), elected on mayor's slate, some proportional representation, partisan. | |

| Judiciary (Civil Code) | | |
|---|---|---|

*Supreme Court*, 11 ministers, by presidential nomination appointment and Senate confirmation, nonpartisan, 15 years maximum.

*Electoral Tribunal, Collegiate and Unitary Tribunals,* and *District Judges* (all positions of which are regulated by a federal judicial council of the Supreme Court); for 6-year terms and can be reratified for an additional term(s).

*Tribunal Superior de Justicia del Edo*, varying number proposed by governor or the Tribunal Superior de Justicia with state legislative confirmation, for 6 years with possibility of one additional term. Other state judicial powers include a variety of judgeships, justices of the peace, etc., regulated by a state judicial council.

Very occasionally receive delegated functions for resolution of day-to-day matters relating to community issues. But for the most part state courts have jurisdiction. Recent federal innovation also allows for the creation of a judicial panel to review administrative conflicts between the *ayuntamiento* and citizens.

**Table 3.1** Federal and Subnational Arenas in Brazil, Mexico, and the USA (*cont.*)

| COUNTRY & BRANCH | FEDERAL | SUBNATIONAL ARENA | | |
| --- | --- | --- | --- | --- |
| | | STATE | LOCAL | SUB/SUPRALOCAL |
| **USA** | | | | |
| *Executive* | *President* and *vice president* on single slate, electoral college, partisan, 4-year term, two terms max. Other positions appointed, some with confirmation by Congress. | 50 states, *governor* elected by majority vote, partisan, 4-year terms, varying reelection possibilities. Other executive positions often elected (*lieutenant governor, attorney general, treasurer, commissioners,* etc.), usually partisan. | *Counties, parishes, boroughs, townships,* home rule (*cities*), *municipalities,* etc. Varying structures but usually nonpartisan (*mayor, commissioner, city manager, sheriff, tax assessor,* etc.). Varying election and appointment mix, terms (usually 2–4 years). | Multiple *functional special districts* (educational, solid waste, water supply, etc.) *Independent school districts* (ISDs). Usually elected, some appointment, usually nonpartisan. |
| *Legislative* | Bicameral: *House of Reps.* 2-year terms, elected by population districts, partisan. *Senate*: elected, partisan, 6-year terms, two per state. | Bicameral (except Nebraska) *Senate* (4 years) and *House* (2 years), elected by majority for state-determined population districts, partisan, varying term limits and reelection opportunities. | *City councils*: elected by majority, at large or by district, or mix, 2 years, nonpartisan. | |

| Judiciary (Roman/ Common Law, except Louisiana) | Supreme Court (9 justices, appointed by president, confirmed by Senate, for life). 11 U.S. circuit courts (3 judges in each, by presidential appointment). | U.S. district courts (for federal questions) State Courts: (for state law, single judge usually, elected, nonpartisan). (1) trial courts; (2) intermediate courts of appeal; (3) court of last resort (varying names in each state). Local courts for minor criminal and civil matters (varying names), single judge, elected. |
| --- | --- | --- |

Note: This table does not detail the often special arrangements pertaining in federal capitals (DC, DF, Brasilia).
[1] The ayuntamiento comprises two sets of functions: (1) an executive role undertaken almost exclusively by the municipal president, who has sole responsibility for administration; (2) a legislative and oversight role articulated by its members through a collegial body called the cabildo.

The Brazilian municipality carries the distinction of being a federal entity, since the federation was formally constituted by the association of states and municipalities in the 1988 Constitution, without, however, having any direct territorially based representation in Congress. In Brazil and Mexico *submunicipal* organizational structures are institutionally weak, comprising delegated authority from the mayor to outlying municipal districts (in Mexico) or various ad hoc arrangements such as regional administrations or local districts in Brazil.

The second major difference to emerge from table 3.1 is *the absence of proportional representation within the legislative electoral processes of the USA,* with elections being won by the candidate who has achieved the largest plurality. In contrast to Brazil, there are no runoff elections in the USA or Mexico for elections to the executive branch. (U.S. city and other generally nonpartisan elections are the exception, where runoff elections are normal to ensure an absolute majority.) A second difference is that most local elections in the USA are nonpartisan, being based upon the perceived qualities of the individual candidate rather than his or her affiliation to a political party. In Mexico, by contrast, all politics is party politics, while in Brazil it is a blend of party and personalistic criteria, set within a maze of competing (and often small) parties where regional factors play an important role. Proportional representation is important, either to allocate places on the basis of the overall vote, as is the case in Brazil, or to ensure some level of minority-party involvement in governance through the mixed direct/proportional representation system that exists in Mexico. And although there is some discussion of their merits, runoff elections are not part of the Mexican tradition. In both Mexico and Brazil proportional representation, in some guise or other, has been an important mechanism for ensuring plurality (often for legitimacy-building purposes). In the USA, where districts are won on a basis of simple majority, plurality is guaranteed through the variety of districts, the presence of two strong parties, and voting traditions that have enabled alternation between them.

A third feature across the three case studies is variation in *the opportunity for direct reelection to the executive and legislative branches.* This is highly constrained in Mexico, where there are strict term limits, back-to-back reelection is not possible, and personal incumbency is not an issue. Brazil and the USA are more similar in this respect, although

Brazilian legislation is more recent and more extensive. It applies the two-term rule to the executive at all levels and allows for multiple reelection to the legislature. However, as Samuels (1998) and others (Pereira, Leoni, and Rennó 2004) have pointed out, incumbency is much lower in Brazil than might otherwise be expected, with an election turnover in the Chamber of Deputies of around 50 percent (with about two-thirds of incumbents running for reelection, of whom two-thirds win, accounting for the 50 percent turnover). Two factors appear to be at play here. First, in the proportional representation list model there is less direct incumbency advantage than in a single-member district (Carey, Niemi, and Powell 2000)—unless, that is, deputies seek to identify themselves with a specific self-defined geographical area or strong interest group. Party loyalty is another identifier, although there are no sanctions on party change and much movement can take place within the career of a single legislator (Desposato and Samuels 2003). Second, Brazilian political career paths are much more mobile, with movement backwards and forwards, upwards and downwards, and between the executive and legislative branches (including a considerable number of public agencies). In this sense the mobility is similar to that of Mexico, where back-to-back reelection is not allowed. Samuels (2003) has pointed out how the national congress is perceived as a stepping-stone to the subnational executive arenas that control resources and facilitate career cultivation. Indeed, he argues that the fact that seats are won at large under a proportional representation system and directly overlap with political jurisdictions (states) makes for close ties to the state government apparatus. (U.S. representatives often serve areas and interest groups that are not vested in spatial jurisdictions that correspond to a particular city or county.)

In the USA, the two-term rule was introduced in the 1950s and applies to the presidency, with variation for executive office at the state and municipal levels, while for the legislative branch a few states have introduced rules restricting reelection. Thus constituency interests often predominate, overriding partisanship, and make for prolonged terms in office by the same individual, with lower incentives to move into different career paths. The profound advantages of incumbency, greater governance experience, strict hierarchical systems of seniority in the legislative branch, and some level of autonomy and authority vis-à-vis the party contribute to further strengthening the checks and balances between the branches.

In Mexico reelection remains largely anathema throughout the system (although since 2001 it has been discussed, without much enthusiasm, for the legislative branch), and this has made for a weak legislative role, a lack of constituency politics, poor institutional memory, high levels of systematic turnover, strong party influence, and gridlock. Interestingly, although the restrictions on immediate reelection do generate apparent mobility, they do not appear to lead to a significant change in the overall pool of political actors.

A fourth difference between the systems is that *only in the USA do bicameral arrangements exist at the state government level* (in most states at least). This, too, strengthens the legislative role vis-à-vis the executive branch and the judiciary and in many respects replicates the checks-and-balances opportunities that exist at the federal level. However, although it does not follow automatically that the lack of an upper house at the subnational level in Brazil and Mexico makes for weaker local congresses, certainly in the USA the combination of lower and upper houses strengthens the legislative powers (Ackerman 2000).

Fifth, there are also *important differences in the judiciary* between the three countries. Mexico and Brazil both were strongly influenced by the Civil (Napoleonic) Code, which gives greater weight to the letter of law as it is written, taking each case on its own merits without reference to previous case law and to precedent. Thus both national and especially state-level courts in these two countries do not play such a strong formative or judicial review role in constitutional questions as is the case in the USA, where interpretation and jurisprudence are cumulatively built around case law. In Mexico so-called constitutional controversies or challenges are passed up to the national Supreme Court; and although in Brazil the state courts do have some relatively minor role in relation to the states' constitutions, they are themselves highly dependent upon the national constitution (Rodrigues 2002, 13–54). In marked contrast, U.S. state judiciaries are paramount and will resolve major constitutional controversies or challenges against the state government unless the matter relates to a federal "question" or has been appealed to the higher (Supreme Court) level. This was shown dramatically in 2000 when the State of Florida polling results for the presidential election were contested; the Supreme Court sought to argue that the conduct of the election was a state matter and that therefore no federal intervention on its part was required. Ultimately the Supreme Court ruled by a majority decision to recognize the Florida result, and President Bush won the Florida electoral college votes, even though his opponent, (then Vice President) Gore, had polled a slightly higher proportion of the popular vote. In short, the national and subnational judiciary is an important constitutional branch of government in the USA, but it has much less weight as an independent constitutional institution in Brazil and virtually none in Mexico.

Each of the three countries under study has a number of different arrangements to cater to sub- or supralocal jurisdictions, not all of which are institutionalized. Examples are the various original indigenous peoples and their territories in each country: the independent tribal territories in the USA; the tribal peoples' own councils and those of the former fugitive slave *quilombos* in Brazil; and in Mexico the recently recognized *usos y costumbres*, which offer local alternatives for indigenous and non-indigenous populations alike, as does the Agrarian Law, which provides for submunicipal government in *ejido* communities for *campesinos*. The same applies for supralocal (sometimes cross-jurisdictional) entities such as tribal territories and, in large metropolitan areas, municipal consortia, regional consultative groups, and *mancomunidad* (commonwealth) models that allow for governmental collaboration. As in the USA, municipal and governor associations have also begun to be important in Mexico and Brazil, but their consultative roles and/or operational responsibilities complement, rather than substitute for, existing executive and legislative powers. These sub- and supralevel dimensions of governance are discussed in more detail in chapter 4.

These five broad dimensions of comparison offer a "snapshot" overview that does not take into consideration the changes being made in the different branches of government. Thus in figures 3.1 to 3.3 we try to provide a more dynamic overview of the different patterns in order to show both the relative influence of the respective branches and the directionality of change along a low-to-high continuum at each of the three levels of government. Although highly generalized, the picture that emerges shows that the USA has developed a broad basis of effective governance and civics (i.e., it is heavily weighted toward the right-hand side of the diagram), with Mexico at the weaker end (left-hand side) of the spectrum and Brazil falling somewhere in the middle. Only in the executive branch does Mexico appear to be weighted toward the strong-government end of the continuum. The trends and nature of these arrangements are discussed in more detail below.

Figure 3.1  Relative Powers of Governmental Branches and Directionality of Change: Federal Level (1990s–Present)

| | LOW | | | | | HIGH |
|---|---|---|---|---|---|---|
| **A. Relative Powers of the Executive** | | | | | | |
| *Institutional* | | | USA⇒⇒BRZ MEX | | | |
| *Operational* | | | USA⇒⇒ | BRZ | ◄◄MEX | |
| **B. Relative Powers of the Judiciary** | | | | | | |
| *Institutional* | | | MEX | BRZ | USA | |
| *Operational* | | MEX→→ | BRZ⇒ | USA | | |
| **C. Relative Powers of the Legislative Branch** | | | | | | |
| *Institutional* | | | | BRZ/MEX | | USA |
| *Operational* | | BRZ→ | | ⇐⇐USA⇒⇒ | | |
| | | MEX→→ | | | | |
| **D. Opportunities for Active Democratic Participation** | | | | | | |
| *Institutional* | USA | | | BRZ/MEX | | |
| *Operational* | USA/BRZ/MEX | | | | | |
| *Interest groups, etc.* | BRZ/MEX | | | USA | | |
| **E. Modernization (Apparatus of Government)** | | | | | | |
| *Executive* | | | | BRZ/MEX | | USA |
| *Congress* | | BRZ→ | | | USA | |
| | | MEX→ | | | | |
| *Judiciary* | BRZ→ | | | | USA | |
| | MEX→ | | | | | |
| **F. Professionalization (Careers, Etc.)** | | | | | | |
| *Executive* | | | | | BRZ/MEX | USA |
| *Congress* | | MEX→ | BRZ ⇒ | | USA | |
| *Judiciary* | | | MEX→ | | | BRZ⇒USA |

→ Filled-in arrows indicate a current change in direction from the country's placement on the continuum, whereas the open arrows indicate a possible range of starting positions.

⇒ Open arrows indicate a spectrum depending on state/local constitutions.

→→/⇒ Double versus single arrows in figures 3.1–3.3 indicate a wider spread on the continuum.

Figure 3.2 Relative Powers of Governmental Branches and Directionality of Change: State Level (1990s–Present)

| | LOW | | | | | HIGH |
|---|---|---|---|---|---|---|
| **A. Relative Powers of the Executive** | | | | | | |
| *Institutional* | | | | | BRZ ⇐⇐USA⇒⇒ | ◄MEX |
| *Operational* | | MEX | BRZ | USA→ | | |
| **B. Relative Powers of the Judiciary** | | | | | | |
| *Institutional* | MEX | | BRZ | | USA | |
| *Operational* | | MEX | BRZ | | | USA |
| **C. Relative Powers of the Legislative Branch** | | | | | | |
| *Institutional* | | | MEX | BRZ ⇐⇐USA⇒⇒ | | |
| *Operational* | | BRZ→ MEX→ | | | USA | |
| **D. Opportunities for Active Democratic Participation** | | | | | | |
| *Institutional* | MEX | BRZ | | | | USA |
| *Operational* | | MEX | BRZ | | | ⇐⇐USA⇒⇒ |
| *Interest groups, etc.* | | MEX | BRZ | | | USA |
| **E. Modernization (Apparatus of Government)** | | | | | | |
| *Executive* | | | | | BRZ/MEX/USA | |
| *Congress* | | BRZ→ MEX→ | | | USA | |
| *Judiciary* | BRZ→ MEX→ | | | | USA | |
| **F. Professionalization (Careers, Etc.)** | | | | | | |
| *Executive* | | | | | BRZ/MEX | USA |
| *Congress* | | | MEX/BRZ | ⇐⇐USA⇒⇒ | | |
| *Judiciary* | | MEX→ | | | BRZ⇒USA | |

→ Filled-in arrows indicate a current change in direction from the country's placement on the continuum.

⇒ Open arrows indicate a spectrum depending on state/local constitutions.

Figure 3.3   Relative Powers of Governmental Branches and Directionality of Change: Local Level (1990s–Present)

| | LOW | | HIGH |
|---|---|---|---|
| **A. Relative Powers of the Executive** | | | |
| *Institutional* | ⇐⇐USA⇒⇒ | ←MEX   BRZ→ | |
| *Operational* | | ⇐⇐USA/MEX⇒⇒ BRZ | |
| **B. Relative Powers of the Judiciary** | | | |
| *Institutional* | NO SEPARATE LEGAL INSTITUTIONS BRZ/MEX† | | ⇐⇐USA⇒⇒ |
| *Operational* | NOT APPLICABLE BRZ/MEX†** | | ⇐⇐USA⇒⇒ |
| **C. Relative Powers of the Legislative Branch** | | | |
| *Institutional* | MEX*** | BRZ | ⇐⇐USA⇒⇒ |
| *Operational* | | MEX   BRZ | ⇐⇐USA⇒⇒ |
| **D. Opportunities for Active Democratic Participation** | | | |
| *Institutional* | MEX | BRZ | USA |
| *Operational* | MEX→ | BRZ | USA |
| *Interest groups, etc.* | MEX | BRZ | USA |
| **E. Modernization (Apparatus of Government)** | | | |
| *Executive* | | BRZ/MEX | ⇐⇐USA⇒⇒ |
| *Congress* | BRZ   MEX*** | ⇐⇐USA⇒⇒ | |
| *Judiciary* | NOT APPLICABLE BRZ/MEX†** | ⇐⇐USA⇒⇒ | |
| **F. Professionalization (Careers, etc.)** | | | |
| *Executive* | MEX   BRZ | | USA |
| *Congress* | MEX***→   BRZ | | USA |
| *Judiciary* | NOT APPLICABLE BRZ/MEX†**   USA | | |

→ Filled-in arrows indicate a current change in direction from the country's placement on the continuum.

⇒ Open arrows indicate a spectrum depending on state/local constitutions.

† Not including indigenous and/or tribal legal systems (e.g., *usos y costumbres*).

** Not applicable—no constitutional or administrative oversight.

*** *Cabildo* not empowered as a legislative organ but has limited similar functions.

### The Practice of Intragovernmental Relations:
### The Emergence of Checks and Balances between the
### Executive, Legislative, and Judicial Powers

#### The Spectrum of Federalist Practices

While all three countries have a long history of federalism, the actual institutional models of Brazil and Mexico are quite recent in origin. Contemporary federalism in Brazil dates largely to the 1988 Constitution, while in Mexico so-called "authentic federalism" is arguably even more recent—most would point to the mid-1990s definitive electoral reforms and decentralization initiatives as the turning point—but here too the rates and profoundness of change vary temporally and spatially. As we described in chapter 1, a number of factors drive these changes at the macro level and intersect and accentuate the drive toward political opening. However, a recent factor—that of the need for improved public security—may be working in the opposite direction by closing down public spaces, reducing liberalization, and strengthening the federal executive branch, as is arguably the case in the USA today.

There is a large literature on the relative strengths of executive and legislative branches at the national level (Carey and Shugart 1998; Montero and Samuels 2004a; Mainwaring and Shugart 1997), and similar analyses are now emerging for the subnational level (Beer 2003, 2004; Nickson 1995). Specifically in Brazil, federalist powers have been analyzed by David Samuels and Scott Mainwaring (2004), who portray various dimensions of a weak-to-strong continuum. A strong federalist structure emerges, the authors argue, where one or both of the following conditions prevail: first, the Constitution affords firm powers to subnational institutions (branches and parties), and these are not undermined by the "metaconstitutional" powers of the national executive; second, subnational actors exercise major influence and can effectively undermine or distort the national executive's policy agendas. Samuels and Mainwaring adopt Tsebelis's (1995) ideas of veto players and analyze how the relative weights of these two arenas of veto have shifted in Brazil since 1964. On the institutional side, they argue that four principal variables are important in shaping the degree to which federalism constrains the initiative of the executive (the national president in the case of Brazil): (1) fiscal resource allocation and share, and the capacity of subnational governments to increase their resources; (2) power of the local executives (governors primarily); (3) the level of symmetry (balance of political powers) in bicameral powers at the national level, such that relative symmetry between the two chambers strengthens the subnational government's capacity to constrain and veto the central government; and (4) the range and levels of functions attributed to subnational government both in theory (constitution) and in practice.

These lines of analysis provide a broad model that can also be used to assess change within each country and provide a basis for contrast between them. Just as the aforementioned study examines the levels of effective autonomy and room for maneuver between federal and subnational governments, so we too can begin to analyze the relative powers of the three branches at the state and local level and evaluate the extent to which they offer a series of constitutional checks and balances over each other. Specifically, we can assess the degree to which each of these branches (or sets of actors) significantly exercises influence and aegis over budgeting, policy making, and policy implementation.

Figures 3.1 to 3.3 describe broadly what is taking place in the three countries in relation to the relative powers of the three branches and also in relation to the degree of active democratic participation present, the level of modernization of the government apparatus, and the professionalization of personnel within government. In the first four sets of vectors (rows) on the diagram, we distinguish between what might be termed "institutional" and "operational" weight and influence. Generally speaking, "institutional" influence refers to where that branch of government or activity falls on the continuum in theory, as it is designed in constitutional and related rules, while "operational" influence refers to actual practice and implementation. Wherever important movements and shifts appear to be taking place, we use arrows to indicate the direction of those shifts. To give an example of how the diagram should be read, the executive branch in Mexico is accorded low to moderate institutional powers under the Constitution, yet under the PRI the *actual* powers in practice were overarching, and since 1995 under both the PRI and the PAN they are moving back toward the middle ground (figure 3.1).

Each diagram depicts a single level of government—federal, state, and local—and should be read against the detailed descriptions in table 3.1.

The general position of each country is located on the continuum, and only where there is widespread variation of actual position in any single polity do we indicate that spread with open (non-filled-in arrows)—see figure 3.2 for the U.S. executive branch, which reflects the variation between "strong" and "weak" governor systems in that country. Significantly, perhaps, one observes such variation only in the USA; in both Brazil and Mexico it was less difficult to determine where to place the country for the whole polity. This implies not only that governmental decentralization may be greater in the USA but that the space for state and local variation is much greater also. It must be emphasized that figures 3.1 to 3.3 are qualitative assessments; the precise locations that we offer are based upon our understanding of the particular parts of national and subnational government and are likely to be debated. But we hope that our attempt at an overview will prove helpful.

If these diagrams were to be superimposed one on top of each other for any one level, two clear broad patterns would emerge. First, the USA invariably stands out on the right-hand side of the diagram, showing a strong relative mix of powers and the most robust co-governance practices. Generally speaking, Brazil falls in the middle range, while Mexico appears to have an incipient separation of powers that has been dominated by the executive branch. Second, most of the arrows reflect important strides in horizontal decentralization of government in Mexico (especially) and Brazil, such that in these countries practice is beginning to catch up with theory. In the next section the broad driving forces and principal directions of these changes in the three countries will be examined.

### Commonalities and Divergences within the Branches

*Executive Supremacy: Changing Traditions?*

Any model of government constructed around the principle of a balance of powers depends on that balance of power. A balance can result from respect for differences and institutional roles or from the fact that, fundamentally, power is in balance. To have strong legislatures to face strong executives it is necessary to have clear party groupings that can act consistently in relation to each other in order to provide what the elegant phrase of the Westminster (parliamentary) model refers to as the "loyal opposition."

In both Brazil and Mexico, while the institutional powers of the executive are theoretically well balanced by the constitutional design, operationally those powers are much higher and the executive generally shows very little respect for the "loyalty" (i.e., good-faith participation) of the opposition—and vice versa (see figures 3.1–3.3). In Mexico, at least until the middle to late 1990s, the widely described "metaconstitutional" powers gave the president influence and room for political maneuvering that went far beyond the constitutional and formally delimited powers. For example, within his own party he could effectively ensure the resignation of an elected governor, even though it was beyond his constitutional purview to do so. For six years, at least, his influence and power was almost absolute, a situation that began to change only as opposition parties that were not exposed to the same orthodoxy and internal discipline began to win power from 1989 onwards (Camp 2006; Rodríguez and Ward 1994). To the extent that any significant checks existed at all, they came primarily from two sources: First, the need, among executives at lower levels, to avoid falling foul of the executive at the higher level (the national president or the state governor);[4] and second, the no-reelection rule, which provided a useful safety valve in that incompetent or corrupt leaders could be dropped at the end of three or six years. This began to change when opposition parties came to the fore from the late 1980s onwards, since they owed no loyalty to their traditional (PRI) superiors and were able to break ranks and no longer follow the orthodox rules of behavior. Second, legislatures—plural or not—have begun to be empowered and to exercise greater authority in co-governance. Possible impeachment by Congress and committee oversight by the legislative branch are now having a greater impact.[5] In fairness, too, executives are much smarter, recognizing that co-governance is a two-way venture and that, while their room for maneuver is constrained, co-governance with the other branches offers the distinct advantage of sharing and diffusing responsibility (particularly for actions that are unlikely to be popular), as well as enhanced legitimacy and often better government.

In Brazil, although the legislature has the power to impeach executive leaders at all levels, it does not have the power to institute criminal or civil proceedings. This power is assigned to the independent prosecutor's office (Ministerio Público), which will have to decide if it thinks there is a case to be made. The legislature has the power to institute "parliamentary commissions of inquiry" (Comissão Parlamentar de Inquerito, CPIs), which have powers of investigation equivalent to those of the judicial authorities (art. 58VI-3 of the Constitution), yet their effectiveness lies more in making matters public than in following through with effective punishment of identified (mal)practices. They have become a regular feature of the federal legislature—as in the inquiries that took place in 2005–6 on various highly charged questions, including the corruption of public officials—and they attract considerable public attention. Specific cases of corruption within the legislature are treated by its internal ethical committee and the institutional sanction of a vote of censure for the lack of "proper behavior." The results—in terms of checks and balances—at times can be unpredictable, as in the case of the various charges of vote rigging and the purchase of loyalty from small parties that surrounded the PT (Partido dos Trabalhadores/Workers' Party) in the same period. On paper the laws are in place, but the judicial process has been often slow in responding. More recently, a new generation of younger and enthusiastic public prosecuting attorneys in the Ministerio Público (similar in part to the Office of the U.S. District Attorney)[6] has shown that alternative postures are possible. Cases have been taken up throughout the public arena, and different levels of government are beginning to be taken to task either for not fulfilling constitutional requirements or for not following through local decisions. This role as a "societal representative" (Stein et al. 2006) in a pioneering study (Arantes 2002) has been shown to be a result both of a largely endogenous and "extraordinary process of institutional reconstruction" and of a discursive broadening of the public prosecutor's role to assume the constitutional directive to defend social interests (art. 127) and to assume the defense of society as a whole in relation to diffuse and collective rights (for example, in relation to the environment, consumers, public property, and even social rights).

Brazil, despite two successive center-left governments with a declared aim of effectiveness and transparency, continues to offer considerable space for executive leaders to engage in negotiation and bargaining through patronage and or "personalism," and in both the executive and legislative branches there is still plenty of scope for patronage and spoils politics. In the judiciary patronage has largely been a question of nepotism through the employment of parents in different administrative posts. This practice has recently been outlawed by the country's new external supervisory body for the judiciary, the National Justice Council (Conselho Nacional de Justiça). In Mexico, similar sorts of *caudillismo* are less pronounced today than in the distant past and remain heavily constrained by the restriction on constituency-based politics that the no re-election rule brings.

In the USA the framers of the Constitution deliberately sought to constrain the power of the executive branch relative to the legislative branch in particular, as well as to empower each state with an equal "reach" into government through the Senate. Thus the president has limited power and is subordinated to the Congress. Although the president has some leeway to act on issues of foreign affairs, he is especially weak when it comes to domestic affairs, and his powers are articulated primarily through his influence over the federal bureaucracy and appointments of public officials to leadership positions within it. In fact, less than 20 percent of legislation proposed by the executive branch is approved. An individual president's effectiveness in domestic policy is related to his ability to negotiate, bargain, and influence key members of Congress. Another way that a president can have a lasting effect on policy well beyond his term in office is through appointments to the federal courts, especially the Supreme Court.

In the USA there is significant variation between "strong" and "weak" governors relative to the local state congresses. Like the president, governors are able to exercise considerable statewide influence through their powers of appointments—to boards, commissions, task forces, and so on—that may extend beyond their mandate. The modernization of state governments has frequently enhanced the relative power of governors, but in a few states there are several separately elected top officials whom the governor cannot remove or control, including the lieutenant governor, the state treasurer, the secretary of state, the state auditor, the attorney general, and the superintendent of public instruction. Although the power of the office of the governor varies widely among the states, and notwithstanding a broad pattern of strengthening of the office observed in recent years, the model in the USA makes for relatively weak government compared to the state executive (governor) system in Brazil and Mexico.

Not surprisingly, control over the budget is the key, and in the USA the state executive is especially constrained in those states where the budget has to be approved in its entirety or not at all: that is, where line-item vetoes are prohibited. However, most executives retain some kind of line-item veto on budgets as well as an overall power of veto or the power not to sign a piece of legislation.[7] To the extent that blockages and gridlock are overcome, in the USA this is achieved through negotiation and horse trading rather than by skilled debate. Control over agenda setting and the committee process itself provides opportunities to kill or cramp the passage of legislation, as does a filibuster; in the case of the Texas Democrats in 2003, physically decamping to an adjacent state removed the quorum required for business to proceed. But such extreme measures are usually unnecessary. The threat of gridlock generally obliges partisans to work with each other and for the legislative and executive branches to build compromise, if not consensus. At the local level, however, the institutional separation of functions among executive, legislative, and judicial branches is much more blurred, so that the functions sometimes overlap and are generally less constrained by partisanship.

In both Brazil and Mexico there is no tradition of multiple elected officials (treasurer, government secretary, police chief, etc.), and executives can usually bypass and overrule their legislatures in a number of ways, with some notable exceptions and differences in the two cases. In Brazil the powers of the legislative branch were in general stronger in the earlier years of the republic, then waned over the following hundred years, and began to recover again in recent years. For example, at the state government level, recent historical studies are suggesting that there has been a major loss of legislative power over the last hundred years, with major gains for state governors (Clemente 2000). In Mexico the opposite is true: traditionally weak legislatures have only in the last decade begun to challenge the executive branch to any significant extent. Recent research suggests that such challenges and institutional developments in Mexico are enhanced where legislatures are composed of a plurality (Solt 2004; see also Beer 2003).

In Brazil, even if the proposed budget is not voted up, the executive can still authorize a monthly expenditure up to one-half of the previous year's budget according to its previous programmatic structure. The executive can also introduce budget measures that allow for the real-location and management of budget funds between categories, but this previously widespread practice (at all levels) has been greatly reduced at the subnational level by formal requirements for a fixed-percentage expenditure in certain areas, as will be discussed later. In both state and municipal assemblies there are mechanisms whereby mayors and governors can require urgency or reduce the assembly's influence on budget matters. At the national level, a similar example is set by the presidential use of so-called "provisional measures" authority *(medidas provisorios)* introduced in the 1988 Constitution; such measures come into immediate effect pending congressional approval and can be reissued at will. Former President Fernando Henrique Cardoso, for example, a leading democrat, introduced and revised more provisional measures in the first five months of his first government than in the three governments before him (setting a record of 6.8 provisional measures a month). Moves were made to restrict the reissuing of measures, but Luiz Inácio Lula da Silva's first administration continued the trend, issuing some 4.8 provisional measures a month. Some states have adopted the same practice, but this is not by any means widespread.

To the extent that traditions of executive performance are changing across the three countries, it is Mexico where the most movement can be observed, this being in the direction of a sharp decline in executive operational authority, mostly relative to the legislative branch. Elsewhere, at federal and state levels especially, and in Brazilian local government as well, executives continue, much as before, to find ways either to circumvent the legislative branch, as in Brazil, or to "work" with it, as in the USA.

### Congresses, Assemblies, and Local Councils: A Revival of Legislative Powers?

It follows as a partial corollary of the previous discussion that in both Brazil and Mexico the legislative branch lags in its adjustment to imbalances between the three powers. Important changes are under way in both countries, especially at the state level in Mexico and at the municipal level in Brazil. In Brazil, Fiscal Responsibility Law No. 101, enacted on May 4, 2000, requires the union, the states, the federal district and municipalities, the other powers (legislative and judiciary), and all public agencies and accounting tribunals to attend to, monitor, and comply with certain norms of public finance and fiscal management. It imposes heavy penalties on budget deficits and incorporates a number of different spending requirements and limits—for example, on salaries (Khair and Vignoli 2001; Vignoli 2002). Because of its focus on the responsible use of public funds, the law serves also as a control mechanism for a number of limits imposed by different federal programs and also constitutional spending requirements—for example, in the area of education.

However, providing the legislature with access to impeachment mechanisms is not in itself a guarantee of increased democracy. It can also lead to situations in which progressive leaders can find themselves hostage to a hostile and conservative state or local assembly. The rules are there to be used, but there are no guarantees that newly empowered legislatures will act responsibly and work constructively with the executive branch— as has already become apparent in Mexico (Ward and Rodríguez 1999; Camp 2006).

In the USA the legislative branch is empowered to react to executive initiatives, as well as to closely monitor and control the bureaucracy (Huber and Shipan 2002, 2004); it also actively promotes legislation and lawmaking in its own right. In both Mexico and Brazil, the various assemblies and local councils are generally at the reactive end of the governance process: they can approve, negotiate, and confront budgetary questions; can act on tributes and taxes and on development plans; and are required to approve or disapprove changes in the organization of the public sector. Although assemblies and local councils may propose legislation, unless the executive branch is also actively interested in pursuing a piece of legislation and is willing to provide some support, such legislative-initiated proposals are unlikely to prosper.

In Brazil, the power of the legislature is also weakened by a lack of restrictions on party loyalty: once elected, representatives, if they so choose, can and do move from one party to another. There are a few exceptions to this practice, one of which is the PT, which has been able to build a reasonable degree of internal loyalty over some twenty-five years, although here a number of internal crises—mixing ideology and campaign financing—have led to concern with its capacity to sustain this position. The open-list voting model means that votes are often linked to a person rather than a party, and if the representative "pays attention" to a self-defining constituency, shifts away from the party line or indeed from the party itself, this is usually not seen as problematic; they are part of the game and one that the political elites manage with efficiency and effectiveness. The number of parties, for example, in the national congress jumped from five in 1982 to ten in 1986 and eighteen in 1994 (Nicolau

1995; Panizza, 2000). In the 1998 elections some twenty-five parties were in some way or another represented.[8] Few, if any, political parties can be said to be truly national, with regional differences being quite considerable. In consequence, at the state and municipal levels the variety can be extraordinary. Panizza's (2000) conclusions, while designed for the national level, are a good guide to the situation as a whole:

> Brazil's moderately institutionalized party system is characterized by most of the political shortcomings typical of unstable party systems rather than by the rigidity and polarizing effects of over institutionalized systems. Personalism, lack of internal discipline, large-scale party switching, poor accountability, high legislative turnover and unreliable parliamentary majorities are among the most common criticisms leveled at the country's party system. But institutional rules do not determine political outcomes; they only set the framework in which politics takes place. (521)

In Brazil legislatures at all levels are nearly always proto-coalitions[9] that depend on the articulating capacity of leaders to build a platform of support for government. This in itself leads to further movement from one party to another as elected officials search power bases from within which they can provide services to their electorate. Parties are organized on a municipal, state, and national level, with each level being relatively autonomous in the way it carries out its affairs. Thus some may require runoffs and others may resort to more traditional "conversations," and incumbents do not necessarily require approval of their party higher-ups to run for reelection (Samuels 2003).[10]

In the USA and Mexico the party structure is more straightforward: a basically two-party system in the USA and a three-plus system in Mexico, with three main parties and a small number of lesser parties, of which only one is significant (PVEM or the "Green Party"). Independents are not allowed in Mexico; all candidates must run on party tickets, leading in some cases (most notably with the PRD, especially in the past) to a weakening in party ideological coherence and mixed or weak loyalties (Bruhn 1997, 1999). The lesser degree of personalism and higher propensity for party loyalty means that legislative performance is more party based. In Mexico, state legislatures are increasingly competitive. In September 2003, for example, in fourteen of the thirty-two legislative assemblies no single party had an absolute majority, and in a further three cases the government was divided: that is, the party with an absolute majority was different from the party holding the governorship (Morales Barud 2003). To date, however, these legislative patterns and their co-governance and policy-making outcomes have been little studied in Mexico, or even elsewhere (Morgenstern 2002).

In the USA, state legislative politics is firmly party based, but a lack of term limits in most states, as well as incumbency politics, makes for both strong partisanship and a diversity of constituency interests that must be accommodated. Moreover, the dual chamber at national and at most state levels makes for clearly defined roles and responsibilities in the legislative process and intensive oversight. Seniority (years in office), too, is an important feature of the U.S. system, particularly when it comes to committee assignments. The extent to which parties are represented in legislatures in the USA, or the extent to which there is a juxtaposition of parties in the two branches (or across the two chambers), is likely to shape patterns of governance in any single governmental session. Large majorities are likely to make bold legislation easier to pass, while competitive relations will almost certainly induce a greater level of caution and less highly differentiated policies. Similarly, partisanship might be accentuated in highly divided governments as parties try to outmaneuver and veto the influence of the other(s).[11]

In the USA it is noteworthy that relations between the branches have become more complex as the degree of competitive partisan politics has increased in recent years. An analysis of party control of state legislatures in the USA since 1960 reveals a major narrowing in recent years of the control that any one party is able to exercise in state legislatures.[12] Since 1995 control over the state legislature has been almost equally divided between the Democratic and Republican parties. Similarly, the number of states with "divided" governments has risen from the upper teens to the upper twenties over the past forty years.

In Mexico, "divided governments" are a recent phenomenon of the late 1980s onwards but are now an important feature of the subnational (and national) landscape. However, there is no doubt that Mexico's legislative institutions are weaker for both structural and historical reasons, since seventy years of almost total PRI executive rule made for acquiescent legislatures—little more than rubber-stamping bodies. Greater pluralism is leading to more active legislatures, but structural weaknesses remain: most notably the lack of experience resulting from the no-reelection rule; the short terms; the different routes to election (direct versus *plurinominal* or proportional representation); the relative weakness of ideology to underpin party loyalty and policy making; and the apparent incapacity to compromise and negotiate with the executive branch, itself in part a product of the lack of constituency interest and the no-reelection rule. Committee oversight functions are traditionally poorly developed, and there is nothing like the level of accountability and public scrutiny common in the USA.

That said, in both Brazil and Mexico subnational legislative committees are becoming more critical and demanding greater accountability, partly following the lead set by the federal legislative branch.[13] Public scrutiny, especially through investigative journalism, is becoming more serious and is feeding legislative scrutiny; and legislatures themselves are being modernized and strengthened (Rodríguez and Ward 1999; Beer 2003; Lawson 2002; Hughes 2006). However, at the state level in both countries, the lack of a second chamber, while in some ways a democratic luxury that society can ill afford, does carry opportunity costs in terms of lesser overall congressional power. Also, in Mexico, now that direct electoral competition is leading to alternation and high levels of pluralism in state and national assemblies, the original rationale of segmented proportional representation to ensure some significant (but constrained) participation of "opposition" parties is less compelling. In Mexico particularly, legislatures are beginning to exercise their powers and are being taken seriously—hence the bold arrow toward the center ground in figures 3.1 and 3.2—but the process remains recent, and Mexican legislatures still have much to learn about responsible co-governance, as do their Brazilian counterparts, albeit for different reasons.

In the USA at the local level (figure 3.3) other forms of legislative authority such as councils, school boards, and municipal districts boards vary hugely in nature but tend to be nonpartisan. Moreover, as mentioned above, their executive and deliberative functions are often blurred—in essence engaging in both. Thus, while their role may be that of oversight, they will often have policy-making functions as well, especially where they instruct an appointed manager and associated staff concerning the broad policy lines that should be followed. In Brazil, the single model of local government—the municipality—makes for clearer legislative functions, albeit in an often highly partisan setting. In Mexico, by contrast, the co-governance role of the *cabildo* (council) is heavily circumscribed. This is not because of traditional structural constraints or party weakness but simply because the *cabildo* is not directly and separately elected. Voting takes place for the municipal president, and this choice implies the acceptance of a pretabled slate of councilors *(regidores)* who are included along with other councilors from the opposing slates in a (varying) proportion to the overall vote. Thus the choice of the municipal president (executive) and the choice of the council (a quasi-legislative branch in this case) are firmly linked. That said, one should not assume that council members blindly follow the party whip—they often have personal loyalties that place them at odds with the municipal executive and may act (out) accordingly. Despite their quasi-legislative status, in figure 3.3 we consider them to be the equivalent legislative bodies at the local level—at least for the purposes of comparison in this chapter.

### The Judiciary: A Branch or a Twig?

Figures 3.1 and 3.2 give an immediate impression of the relative strength and thickness of the judicial "branch" across the three countries. In the USA, while originally conceived as "the least dangerous branch," charged with no greater responsibility than to interpret the laws that Congress made, the judicial branch is "thick" and plays a weighty role in both national and state governance. In Brazil, while the traditional institutional role of the judiciary is strong, it has been weakened operationally by its own internal administrative inefficiencies and a number of charges of "sentence fixing." In Mexico it is relatively weak, although there has been substantial invigoration at the national (Supreme Court) level since 1994 and its role is becoming important. However, at the subnational state level it plays a small and insignificant role relative to the other two branches; indeed, it plays no effective constitutional role in state government (González Oropeza 2003).

The structure of the U.S. judicial branch is decentralized such that federal and state courts operate side by side. Dual hierarchies characterize the American court system (Vago 1991). Both federal and state courts exist in each state but are separate from each other. State courts settle most of the nation's legal actions under the provisions of state law and in this sense therefore often play a defining role in constitutional questions and challenges to state government decisions, practices, or alleged breaches of state law. Federal courts deal only with decisions that involve a "federal question": that is, cases involving the (national) Constitution or federal laws. In Texas, for example, the constitutionality of the school finance system was determined to be a matter for the state court system, even though federal courts may intercede in state and local school systems to review possible violation of the rights of individual students. The organization and structure of state court systems vary widely. State court systems may have three levels of courts: the trial courts, intermediate courts of appeal, and a court of last resort (Vago 1991). The lowest courts in the judicial hierarchy are courts of limited jurisdiction. These courts handle minor civil and criminal cases.

In each state there is also a U.S. district court with federal jurisdiction only. A single judge presides over these cases, and juries are used in about half the cases decided. Above the district courts in the federal hierarchy are eleven U.S. courts of appeal or circuit courts. The nation is divided into eleven geographic jurisdictions called circuits. The circuit courts hear appeals from district courts within their jurisdiction or circuit. A panel of three judges decides cases in the circuit courts. The court of last resort at the federal level is the U.S. Supreme Court, which is presided over by nine justices.

Positions on these courts are appointed by the executive, with Senate approval, rather like the Supreme Court. The process of nomination and appointment to the appellate courts has changed over the years but has increasingly been encumbered by partisanship.[14] In many states judges, especially local ones, are elected: "Judicial selection is a highly political process that affects very directly the interests of the most powerful partisan forces in states and communities" (Saffell 1987, 177). Judges run for office on a regular slate, and in many states they must attach party labels to themselves.[15] But the point to underscore here is that in the USA the structure of the judiciary is well developed vertically as well as horizontally and that it can, and does, play an important role as one of the branches of subnational co-governance.

In Mexico and Brazil the judiciary is less well fleshed out (table 3.1), and its constitutional review role is weaker. Nevertheless, changes are taking place. In both countries—and throughout the region—there is arguably an important "judicialization of politics" afoot (Sieder, Schjolden, and Angell 2005) in which the judiciary is playing a greater role in ensuring the democratic (horizontal) accountability of other branches and of the bureaucracy (O'Donnell 2003) and in which its own, more vertical "societal accountability" is ensured by the citizenry, who exercise "watchdog" functions over the judicial branch itself (Smulovitz and Peruzzotti 2003).

In the recent Inter-American Development Bank (IADB) report *The Politics of Policies* (Stein et al. 2006), Brazil's judiciary was generally rated positively in terms of its independence, and some evidence was presented of its role as a veto player in constitutional terms. Indeed, reform is very much a current topic of concern (Rodrigues et al. 2002; Sadek 2000, 2001; Renault 2005), and the acceptance, albeit reluctant, that there should be external control through the new National Justice Council is recognition of its necessity. The changes are beginning to take place to ensure the greater capacity and credibility of the judicial process, as well as very elementary rights. For example, the "citizenship project" of the Justice Tribunal of the State of Acre (Veronese 2002) has been active in assisting people with legal documents and certificates, in providing on-the-spot help with minor legal problems, and in offering a number of community justice outreach programs. Similarly, the judiciary's prison supervision has extended to aid work placement and rehabilitation through supervisory judges working with civil society organizations in the states of São Paulo and Minas Gerais. In relation to constitutional issues and executive action, although the development is very recent, members of the Federal Supreme Court have both individually and collectively entered the arena of discussion, and as a result, at the subnational and local levels, the judiciary is beginning to accept legislative challenges to executive action. Equally, the higher electoral court has been active in setting the framework for elections and has moved to place restrictions on campaign financing and accounting practices.

What seems to be taking place is a process of reform in practice that moves from the more specialist agencies within the judiciary into the judiciary as a whole, and the agencies within the judiciary, such as the state-level accounting tribunals *(tribunais de contas),* are now having greater effect on government performance and policy implementation. In a number of cases, data on municipal and state budget performance have been made available online, and in the state of Pernambuco the tribunal has introduced a very innovative program of public education—using local cultural forms and music—to convince people of the importance of assuming a more active role in monitoring public action. A recent study by Arantes, Abrucio, and Teixeira (2005) pointed to the growing interest by the Public Prosecutor's Office (Ministerio Público) in creating partnerships with the tribunals in order to strengthen overall accountability within the subnational public sector (see also Arantes 2005). Perhaps we could say that in Brazil the judiciary, while not yet a fully developed "branch" of co-governance, is at least learning how to bear fruit.

In Mexico reform of the judiciary has progressed far less than that of the legislative branch; while adjustments and reforms have been made in all states to emulate that of the federal level, thus far these appear to have had relatively little impact upon government performance. President Zedillo's 1994 initiative for reforming the judiciary was primarily targeted at reforming the criminal justice system and had little to do with a new federalism agenda and the constitutional resolution of intergovernmental or intragovernmental controversies. Nevertheless, such reforms are expected to have important spillover effects for new federalism and for state government. Traditionally the judiciary—even more than the legislature—has been dominated directly by the executive and by political interference and considerations (González Oropeza 2003). Until the 1994 reform there was little independence of the national Supreme Court or its statewide equivalents. This reform amended twenty-seven provisions of the Constitution that, among other things, transformed the nature and size of the Supreme Court and added a new administrative judicial agency (Council of the Federal Judiciary) whose main functions are to appoint and oversee the circuit and district courts, approve the federal judicial branch budget, and undertake training for the federal bench. From 1995 onwards, the Supreme Court was to comprise eleven judges (reduced from twenty-six) appointed for fifteen years (i.e., no longer lifetime sinecures), each one to be selected by the Senate with a two-thirds majority vote from three candidates offered by the president. There were also significant attempts to ensure that Supreme Court judges would be impartial and would enjoy no other salaries or remuneration, so that the positions would be less likely to attract senior politicians "in transit" (i.e., between political appointments) and more likely to attract candidates who would be career and distinguished judges (González Oropeza 1996b). The new law also sought to strengthen the principal appellate legal tools against government in Mexico that have existed since the nineteenth century: namely individual citizen claims through injunction *(amparo)* and the resolution of conflicting claims between government jurisdictions, called constitutional controversies *(controversias constitucionales;* see Berruecos 2002). The reform was an important first step in establishing the credibility of the judiciary as an independent and impartial system of justice and empowering the third branch of government under new federalism (Domingo 2005).

Most states have set about reforming their judiciaries along similar lines—namely a Tribunal Superior de Justicia that can operate in plenary session of all judges or individually with court hearings *(salas)* presided over by a single *magistrado*. These *salas* mostly cover penal suits, with additional courts for family and civil hearings. But at the state level there is no constitutional role, and any controversies are considered a federal question to be settled through the Supreme Court. The Court's involvement in federalist issues increased during the Zedillo presidency (1994–2000), mostly through consideration of constitutional controversies. But as Domingo (2005) remarks, "[T]he judicialization of politics in the upper echelons of the judicial branch has not directly translated into better lower level justice administration (although reform processes are taking place at the state level)" (40).

In short, things are beginning to happen in both Brazil and Mexico that may have important repercussions for the emergence of a genuine third branch in co-governance. But the Napoleonic law tradition in both Brazil and (especially) Mexico has meant that only at the national level does the judiciary really serve as a significant check on the executive (and legislative power); states have an almost exclusive role in civil and criminal law, although there are moves recently for state superior courts to exercise local constitutional review functions as well, emulating the national level. We expect this to intensify as subnational governments in these two countries begin to come of age and as state lawmakers begin to develop (and codify) state laws that will be adjudicated at that level.

## Modernization and Professionalization: Strengthening Co-governance and Institutional Capacity

Our discussion and analysis in the following section will focus mostly upon Brazil and Mexico. As figures 3.1 through 3.3 amply show, the USA has a solid tradition of a civil service that is modern and professionalized, having abandoned the spoils system and moved to a career model during the first half of the twentieth century. However, it was not until the 1950s that the different state congresses began to significantly modernize and improve their institutional capacity (R. Wilson 1993, 80–81). This helped all three branches to better fulfill their roles. In the USA the civil service tradition is not only institutionalized within the administration as a whole but fairly transparent and accountable. Transparency, efficiency, and professionalism are not, however, watchwords that are immediately associated with administration in Brazil and Mexico, and here we propose to explore what changes are under way in improving administrative and governmental capacity and their ability to fulfill their co-governmental roles. Specifically, how far is modernization occurring across the three branches, and is it improving governmental capacity and efficacy? Finally, we briefly explore the extent to which there are expanding opportunities for citizens to participate in governance.

### Gender and the Representation and Participation of Women in the Different Branches of Government

In examining human resource development and the process of modernization, we pause, briefly, to comment on one area in which the three countries are quite similar, namely the marked underrepresentation of women's participation in the aforementioned three branches of government. In all three countries men dominate in governmental positions, even though women constitute more than half the electorate. We ask, where are the women, and to what extent are they becoming more represented (Avelar 2001; Rodríguez 2003)? This is, after all, an important dimension of both modernization and human resource development.

Table 3.2 offers an overview of the gender balance using several different data sources. It should be seen more as a qualitative approximation than as an accurate or "hard" data description. At first sight many readers would probably not be surprised at the relatively low level of female participation in institutional politics in Latin America, but they would probably expect some greater participation in the noninstitutionalized arena of social action. Craske (1998, 46) presents data for women's representation in congresses throughout Latin America over extended periods and shows that the average varies between 3 percent and 25 percent (Cuba), but the mode is lower single digits and has only begun to show some change since the 1990s. In the three countries analyzed here in 2003 women are also poorly underrepresented in national congresses: in the lower houses, women held 8.2 percent of the seats in Brazil, 23 percent in Mexico, and 13.6 percent in the USA, nor were the proportions much different in the respective Senates. To date no woman has yet figured as a serious final-round possibility for the presidency, and while women are moving increasingly into significant positions in the national cabinets, their representation is still limited and they are rarely in top-tier positions (the exceptions that prove the rule being Madeleine Albright and Condoleezza Rice [USA] and Rosario Green [Mexico], all of whom held the secretary of state positions in their respective countries). In the Brazilian judiciary the level of participation has been growing steadily (from 11 percent in 1993 to 22 percent in 2005), reaching 37 percent in the more specialist forums, but women are still a long way away from achieving parity with men. Brazil (1996) and Mexico (2002) have legislation in their electoral codes stipulating the provision of quotas for women candidates on electoral lists, and in Mexico this has resulted in a significant increase in women's representation in the legislative branch (Rodríguez 2003). Moreover, since 1996 women have served as party presidents in two of the parties (twice in the PRD and three times in the PRI). In Brazil the numbers have also increased but are still a long way from parity. In terms of internal party organization primarily the left-wing parties have a higher percentage of women on their national councils (Avelar 2001).

Three points can be underscored from table 3.2. First, while women are dramatically underrepresented across the board, they are more likely to be included in legislative positions and in the judiciary than to appear as principal elected actors in the executive branch—governors and municipal presidents. In both Brazil and Mexico lower proportions of women are represented in state congresses than in national congresses; in the USA, the reverse is true and the proportion of women in state congresses is almost double that for the national congress. This is important because state offices (in all branches) in the USA are seen as providing a training ground for women to move into higher office. However, the upward trend is noteworthy. In the legislative branch, although no woman has occupied the attorney general's office in Mexico, women have served

Table 3.2 Women's Representation in Different Levels and Branches of Government in the Three Countries

| Women in Each Branch and Level | Brazil | | Mexico | | USA | | |
|---|---|---|---|---|---|---|---|
| *National* | 1990–92 | 2002/04[1] | 1988 | 2003 | 1977 | 1991 | 2003 |
| Congress (lower house), % | 5.5 | **8.2** | 12 | **23** | 4.0 | 6.1 | **13.6** |
| Congress (Senate), % | 2.5 | **12.5** | 19 | **16** | 0 | 2 | **14** |
| Supreme Court, number (of total) | — | **1** (12) | | **1** (11) | | | **2** (9) |
| *Subnational* | | | | | | | |
| Governors, number (of total) | | **2** (27) | 0 (31) | **0** (32) | 2 (50) | 6 (50) | **7**[2] (50) |
| State congress, % (U.S. includes both houses) | 5.6 | **12.6** | 10 (1999) | **17** | 9.2 | 18.3 | **22.3** |
| State judiciaries,[3] % | 11 | 22.4 | | | 1.8 | | |
| *Local* | | | | | | | |
| Number of top ten largest cities with female mayor | 1 | 2 | | 0 | | | 1 (Dallas) |
| Municipal presidents/mayors, % | 3.7 | **7.3** | 2.1 | **3.7** | 4.7[4] | | **17.5**[5] |
| Local councils, % | 8 | **12.6** | | | | | |

*Sources:* For U.S. data, Rodríguez (2003) and Center for American Women and Politics (2007). For Mexican and Brazilian data, various sources, including Centro Feminista de Estudos e Assessoria (2007) and the Web site of Instituto Brasileiro de Administração Municipal, www.ibam.org.br.
Figures in bold indicate most recent comparative data sets.
[1] There is a gap of two years between municipal elections and state and federal elections in Brazil. Sources: Instituto Universitário de Pesquisas do Rio de Janeiro (2006); Centro Feminista de Estudos e Assessoria (2007).
[2] Eight if we include Puerto Rico.
[3] Taken to include the subnational level of action, Brazil data for 1993 and 2005.
[4] Mayors, townships and councils.
[5] Cities of 30,000 or more.

on the Supreme Court and occasionally held an attorney general position for a state entity. In Mexico women accounted for 7.3 percent of the top officials in the judicial branch in 1984 and 12.4 percent in 1992. Today the number is approximately 41 percent. Generally women are represented in the judiciary in Mexico, but the numbers and proportions rise as one goes *down* the hierarchy and *within* it to more secretarial and clerical positions (Rodríguez 2003, 221). In 1994 women made up 19 percent of Supreme Court justices, 15 percent of federal magistrates, and 24 percent of judges (Camp 1998, 168). In the USA until 1981 the Supreme Court was exclusively a male preserve, and even now there have been only two female associate justices. In Brazil, where the current head of the Supreme Court is a woman, there is a similar pattern, with, again, more women appearing as one moves down the judicial hierarchy.

The second point revealed by the data in relation to elected executive office positions is startling. In Mexico even as late as 2005 only five women had *ever* held the position of governor (if we also include the Federal District), and only three of these were elected into office (the other two being interim replacements).[16] This is truly remarkable when one considers that there are thirty-one states and a federal district and that the "modern period" spans more than seventy years (fifty years since women were admitted to suffrage). Brazil and the USA, while not quite as extreme, are also laggards in the representation of women in top executive offices. In the USA some twenty-five women have served as governors in twenty of the fifty states (sixteen of them elected in their own right), and the current number in office seven is a record number at any one time (and rises to eight if Puerto Rico is included). In Brazil, women governors are also the exception rather than the rule; in the current (2002–6) period only two of the twenty-seven governors are women, and both are the spouses of previous governors.

At the local level (municipal presidents or their equivalents), women appear to achieve a somewhat higher profile, but in all three countries even here they are more likely to serve in the smaller and less important cities and municipalities. This leads to a further and closely related feature: women are less likely than men to hold important executive positions—top governorships in major cities, or ranking ministerial posts. In Mexico in 2003, of the ninety-one women mayors (3.7 percent of 2,412) only seven were in municipalities of two hundred thousand or more (and

none of these was in the top ten largest cities), while 75 percent of all female mayors headed municipalities with a population of thirty thousand
or less. In the USA it is quite common for women to hold local municipal
office, and in June 2003 there were no less than 183 female mayors in cities with a population of more than thirty thousand. However, these were
rarely ranking cities in each state: only eight had populations of more
than four hundred thousand, only one was a top-ten city (Dallas), and 80
percent had populations of less than one hundred thousand. In Brazil
after the 2000 elections there were 317 women mayors in the 5,560 municipalities: still low, but a significant rise from the 176 mayors for 4,762
municipalities in 1992. In 2004, this rose to 418. In Brazil the party that
has done most to encourage women to lead in larger cities is the leftist PT
(Borba, Faria, and Godinho 1998), while in Mexico, somewhat surprisingly, it is the conservative PAN (all seven of the aforementioned cities
were PANista *and* led by a woman).

Third, although the data show that women are woefully underrepresented—especially considering the discussions taking place in other countries in the developing and developed world (Staudt 1998) and the very
equal gender balance that the three countries have in relation to university access—the trend does appear to be slowly moving upward. Hope-
fully, the 2006 election of Michelle Bachelet as South America's first
woman president in the modern period and her appointment of a fifty-
fifty gender distribution in the cabinet will set an example for the rest of
the region. Although still a long way off, there appears to be a distinct
possibility that 2012 will see female presidential candidates in both the
U.S. and Mexican presidential elections.

### Modernization and Upgrading of Administrative Capacity

At all levels of government a shift toward greater modernization and
professionalization appears to be taking place in Brazil and Mexico, and
this is replicated to a lesser extent in all three branches of power at each
level. At the federal level in Brazil, modernization has come through the
widespread attempts at state reform, initiated by the Cardoso government[17] and continued (though after much deliberation) after the election
changes of 2002 that brought the PT and Luiz Inácio Lula da Silva to the
presidency. The primary original stimulus, in addition to the govern-

ment's genuine interest and wish to improve public service and to achieve major public sector reform, was the wide set of economic reforms adopted as elements of the stability plan *(plano real)*. In this modernization process, a number of related management changes were introduced in general civil service organization and personnel. There was a conscious shift to create an elite corps of competitively selected and well-paid senior civil servants who could be responsible for the government's new interministerial program coordination structure. While overall progress and results were not as extensive as expected (Marcelino 2003), this effort did serve to reshape the federal administrative agenda, placing greater emphasis on regulation and policy formation and, as a result, reinforcing the action role of subnational governments (Levy and Drago 2005).

At the state and municipal level there have been several advances. Decentralization often involves a significant renegotiation of roles and responsibilities, and despite some privatization of state enterprise at the state government level, states and local governments have in general expanded their roles, either through direct service provision or through various forms of contractual or concessionary arrangements. Such changes automatically generate pressure for organization and administration, especially when, as in Brazil since the 1998 federal and state elections and the 2000 mayoral elections, a second consecutive period in office is permitted for executive positions. In a country beginning to shake itself free of clientelism and the dominance of traditional local elites, the possibility of back-to-back reelection helped provide greater incentives for effective and improved subnational governance. As a result, improving administration has been a pragmatic necessity to deliver services to people and people to services, rather than a response to an overall discussion about the role and shape of institutions.[18]

Within the Brazilian legislative and judiciary branches, the situation is less positive. The lack of administrative competence and the associated low level of modernization of many legislative assemblies and municipal councils is itself a consequence of their less-than-active role in relation to the executive. There are notable exceptions, but these tend to be linked to the concerns of individual assembly and council presidents rather than to reflect an institutional trend. Within the judiciary, the strong positivist legal tradition through which law automatically produces action has also led to a considerable degree of administrative inefficiency. Judges, who are also required to be managers, have difficulty reconciling the two sets of skills and recognizing that organizational change rarely takes place through decree. Again there are innovations, for example in the use of quality management techniques to look at the flow of judicial processes, but they tend to be linked to specific periods of office. There is some impact of investments in information technology, but in general both still have a long way to go, and for the great majority of Brazilians are still not seen as providing much of a guarantee for daily security.[19]

Mexico shows many similar advances, although here the initial driving force appears to have derived from the alternations of parties in government, and in particular the new teams coming to power who have different (less political) backgrounds, are often trained in the private sector, and are grounded in new techniques (Rodríguez and Ward 1995; Mizrahi 1994b, 2003). Moreover, under Mexican law and after the 1983 reform of article 115, Mexican municipalities have enjoyed considerable autonomy, having control over major servicing and urban development programs. The problem, traditionally, has been one of a lack of resources, but even here Mexican municipalities in general, and cities particularly, in addition to having access to a federal revenue-sharing program, control their own fate insofar as they can raise internal resources, principally from property taxes. State governments, more than municipal ones, have found themselves fettered in their (in)capacity to raise local state revenues. This began to change after 2004 as the alliance of state governors achieved some success in pressing for fiscal reform and a larger share of value-added tax revenues (Díaz Cayeros 2006).

Overall, from the late 1970s onwards there has been a technocratization of the political bureaucracy (Centeno 1994), which increased under Salinas in the early 1990s, some would say with dire effects. Under the Fox administration, while efforts to create sector coordinators or "czars" of economic policy, security, and social development failed, comprehensive administrative reform and modernization programs are in place. Specifically, following the Managerial Administrative Reform initiatives that have been circulating internationally since the 1980s, the Mexican Government Innovation Program is being applied in a number of sectors (Apud 2003). In 2003 a Career Civil Service Law *(Ley de Servicio Profesional de Carrera)* was also passed that, although still incipient in its implementation and impact, should do much to improve the quality and continuity of policy implementation (Arrellano Gault 2004).

Within this modernization the main effort has been to enhance transparency on two principal fronts. First has been the improvement of public accounting and audit systems to create greater legitimacy and credibility in the probity of public officials. Although it is far from complete, Mexico appears to be making major advances in reducing corruption, scrutinizing public expenditure, and ensuring fiscal accountability. The second arena of transparency that has become an important feature of modernization in Mexico concerns freedom of information. Democratization in Mexico has partially hinged upon freeing the media from government interference and control, to the extent that some analysts view the media as a "Fourth Estate" or a kind of fourth branch or power in the governmental structure (Lawson 2002). And even though we are not treating it as such in this volume, there is little doubt that in Mexico, at least, this opening and drive toward greater freedom of investigative journalism is having a profound effect upon consolidating the modernization and professionalization of public sector performance. A landmark step in this process has been the Freedom of Information Law that came into effect in 2003, institutionalized in the Federal Institution of Access to Public Information (Instituto Federal de Acceso a la Información, IFAI). Although it is still a relatively young institution that has jurisdiction only over federal government, more than half of the states have passed state information access statutes. In combination with the growing institutionalization of human rights organizations and the enhanced opportunities for public scrutiny and accountability at all levels and across all branches, there is room for considerable confidence that Mexico can move to the next level in the modernization of its administrative and governmental structures.

These improvements notwithstanding, Mexico remains somewhat behind the USA and Brazil in terms of modernization of the three branches of government. However, the Mexican experience demonstrates three features. First, modernization tends to affect federal, state, and municipal government in that order, although some municipalities (especially larger cities) are often showing an impressive capacity to retool and gear up to meet the governance challenges that they face. Second, modernization (through computerization, greater professional support, data analysis, quality control techniques and monitoring, etc.) occurs first and foremost in the executive branch and only later filters down to the other two branches. Third, within the executive branch, certain sectors have been in the vanguard of these changes—almost always those of finance, the Treasury, and governmental accounting (Ward and Rodríguez 1999). Following these comes the education sector, which, after rapid decentralization to the states in 1993, required a dramatic upgrading in each state's capacity to deliver adequate education services (Robles 2006). In short, modernization has proceeded apace in those areas where it has been impelled to do so, while other areas have lagged far behind. Similarly, within the legislative branch rapid advances can be observed in the committee responsible for fiscal oversight, and many states are now seeking to provide computer and professional assistance to legislators, create institutes for legislative studies, provide library and bibliographic resources, and so on. But until recently the lack of a civil service and the continuing prohibition on direct reelection have inevitably greatly weakened the impact of institutional reforms.

### Moving beyond Representative Democracy: Raising Capacities and Opportunities for Citizen Engagement in Co-governance

Democratization is not just about free and open systems of voting—the essence of representative democracy. It also requires the active participation of citizens in the process of government, or what Carole Pateman (1970) and others call participatory democracy. As democratization has unfolded in Latin America and representative democracy has begun to come of age, the arena of participatory democracy has come to ultimately present the greater challenge. The main issue is how to achieve genuine citizen involvement and participation within each of the branches, and in this final section we explore some of the more formal mechanisms for participation in subnational and local governance. Later (in chapter 5) we will take up the broader issue of an extended political and civic culture, which will take us into the area of citizen participation as everyday practice and the role of associations and NGOs.

Such opportunities have originated almost exclusively in the executive branch—especially in relation to budgeting, planning, and service provision—and, to a lesser extent, in the legislative branch. In the USA the multitude of local government arrangements, from the strong mayor to the town meeting, automatically generates a variety of forms of interaction and citizen presence within the legislative part of the co-governance arena, but in Mexico and Brazil, with their relatively homogeneous models of local government polity, the emphasis has been more on extending mechanisms of consultation through the executive and broadening the interaction between local electors and their representatives in relation to the legislative branch. The executive, however, shows clear leadership in this area. Within the judiciary, apart from some minor citizen involvement through service on juries in Brazil, only the USA has institutionalized civic participation through the courts of limited jurisdiction that handle minor civil and criminal cases, where citizens may be involved as elected judges, civilians, or appointees. Indeed, among the three countries under study, only the USA has made citizen participation a constant, founding, and integral part of subnational government, especially given Jefferson's antifederalist stance and his determination to give power to the local community. For that reason, our discussion of the U.S. case is more extensive here. In the USA the opportunity and expectation of participation in governance activities are both broad and deep, and governing tends to be an open process at the state and local levels.

An early example can be found in the Urban Renewal Program of the 1954 Housing Act, which marked an important change in citizens' role in the implementation of federal policy. The program, which provided for a citizen review of projects, responded to complaints of the so-called bulldozer model of urban renewal (Cole 1974, 12–14). While participation was originally formulated to imply blue ribbon commissions and consequently was fairly elitist, later revisions required the participation of local residents (Rosenbaum 1978, 84). Following this, the Community Action Program (CAP) of the Economic Opportunity Act of 1964 required the maximum feasible participation of residents in program implementation, often leading to direct political action by community residents. And although the Model Cities program of the Demonstration Cities and Metropolitan Development Act of 1966 relied more heavily on implementation through local government and marked something of a retreat from the earlier participation requirements (Cole 1974, 14), in some cities community participation in the program did lead to neighborhood government, whereby communities actually assumed responsibility for implementing programs.

Following federal leadership, state and local governments have also adopted a variety of mechanisms that promote transparency and openness in government. Citizen participation and review is now a standard practice in state and local government. Citizens have demanded more openness, and many states have adopted open meetings and open records laws (Hedge 1998, 41–42), thereby creating more opportunities for citizens and community organizations to participate, furthered in the 1990s through the "reinventing government" movement. Citizen participation is, however, far from uniform, and empirical analysis by Eric Oliver (2001, ch. 3) indicates that levels of participation in local governance are highest in middle-income communities. (To the extent that participation requires resources and some level of sophistication to be effective, the poor and unorganized will receive less benefit from opportunities for participation, a point to which we return in chapter 5.)

Other formal mechanisms to encourage public participation in local governance in the USA include open-records and open-meeting acts, passed in many states, which require all meetings held for public purposes to be open to the public. These acts require that public notice of the meeting place, time, and topics to be discussed be given for a specific period of time prior to the meeting. Citizens may observe all meetings of the legislature and legislative committees as well as board meetings of special districts and school districts. Meeting procedures usually allow citizens to address the members with concerns, and individuals or representatives of special interest groups may request time on the agenda to address the members or the board. In most cases, minutes of all meetings are kept and are available to any citizen that may request them. Citizens may also send written statements to officeholders and elected officials with their concerns. Generally, any documents produced by government are available for review by citizens. In addition, if the government plans to undertake any project or program using federal funds, it is generally required to hold a series of public meetings to inform the public of its plans and to give citizens the opportunity to comment on those plans. Equally, state and local governments must demonstrate to the federal administrative agency that citizens have had the opportunity to comment and that those comments have been considered in designing the program or project utilizing federal resources.

There are ample opportunities for citizens to participate in government at the subnational level. Often state representatives are business or community leaders rather than career politicians, and as such the positions are not well compensated financially, requiring that representatives have additional private sector positions. (While laudable in some respects, this also reduces the likelihood of representation from among low-income populations, single parents, etc.) In addition, the first duty facing the executive when he or she takes office is to appoint individuals to the multitude of public positions in the jurisdiction, and indeed there are often more positions than the executive can find persons to fill. The result is that in the USA there are a variety of opportunities to take a direct part in the policy-making process, for example through neighborhood associations or parent/teacher associations (PTAs); indeed, anyone interested in serving on a public board or other appointed position in small or rural jurisdictions will generally have no problem being appointed.

Plebiscites, referenda, voter propositions, and statute initiatives *(iniciativas de ley)* offer important formal institutional opportunities for political involvement and exist to a greater or lesser extent in all three countries. Suffice it to mention here that such initiatives and opportunities are relatively new to the political scene in both Mexico and Brazil and are themselves dimensions of the new political culture in those countries. They also mark a major difference between the three countries under study in the way government and society relate. In the USA, it is perfectly normal for a number of key state and local government questions to be placed on the ballot for either consultation or decision at election times (Saffell 1987), in marked contrast with Brazil and Mexico.

In the USA a substantial expansion has taken place in the use of citizen initiatives and referendum provisions of state law, now available in about half the states (Weber and Brace 1999, 16). For example, during the forty years between 1940 and 1980, some 248 initiatives appeared on statewide ballots, while the decade 1981 to 1992 saw some 346 initiatives. In 1996 alone, 94 initiatives appeared in twenty states (Hedge 1998, 33). This phenomenon certainly represents heightened citizen involvement, but it has been argued that initiative and referendum are being overused, with inappropriate and sometimes frivolous issues being raised. Also, the outcomes of these elections can marginalize legitimate legislative processes, as was the case with the tax revolt in California in the 1970s.

Mexico and Brazil have seen important changes in strengthening the role of local governance and in changing civil society participation from primarily a consultative process to one that more genuinely welcomes citizens' active participation in governance. For example, *cabildos* in Mexico are integrated on a slate and have, until recently, been largely watchdog sounding boards (at best). In Mexico City itself, since the early 1930s a consultative council has been written into its Organic Law, but it consists of only a council of nominees from various sectors of (middle-class) society whose role is to pass opinions on executive branch initiatives. Also, because it would have been potentially a political threat to the PRI and to the national president, Mexico City was anomalous insofar as it had no form of elected council until the early 1990s and no genuine legislative assembly until 1994; nor was the mayor (now *jefe de gobierno*) elected until 1997 (Ward 1998). The point here is that citizen participation was to be almost entirely *consultative* (and therefore nominal), even in *cabildos,* which, though charged with a quasi-legislative authority, were in fact largely consultative or ignored altogether.

All this changed, of course, with the rise of opposition parties, electoral reform, and the growing presence of non-PRI parties in subnational governments, especially from 1989 onwards. The new electoral landscape gave greater space to citizen participation through access to council and legislative meetings, more open media, and the fact that one no longer needed to be a career politician to seek public office (Rodríguez and Ward 1995; Mizrahi 1994b, 2003). But until the late 1980s the calculus of Mexican politics was to minimize active participation in the decision-making process and circumscribe social mobilization where it might pose a threat. Once the PAN and PRD won power at local and state levels, new avenues opened for participation that broke the former pattern of circumscribed participation. More importantly, civil society broke the barriers to representative and participatory democracy. On the latter front, states at all levels of government began to provide legal frameworks for plebiscites, referenda, and public consultation (Guillén López 1995, 1996).

Nevertheless, although national and state congresses are beginning to come of age in Mexico and local *cabildos* are exercising greater representational influence, Mexico has not yet made the link between civil society and legislative bodies. People remain suspicious and cynical about the role of national and state congresses and have a poor understanding of what they do and how they articulate civil society's interests in relation to the executive branch (Camp 2006). Although Web sites now abound and the Congress has its own open television channel, the linkage between this organ of co-governance and society at large remains vague and poorly articulated.

In Brazil, also, while provisions exist in the Constitution for the national congress to hold plebiscites and referenda (what Benevides [1991] has referred to in a more restricted way as direct democracy), these are very rarely used—normally only when municipalities or states are to be divided. One of Brazil's most famous plebiscites in recent years was that of the 1988 Constitution, which required the electorate (actually on September 7, 1993) to define the form (republic or constitutional monarchy) and the system (parliamentary or presidential) of the country's government. Despite strong moves by both monarchists and parliamentary republicans, only a few people really understood what the discussion was all about, and things remained as they were. More recently, the population was consulted on the question of arms control and a very similar process took place. The Constitution also allows for draft laws to be submitted to Congress by the population, providing that they are supported by at least 1 percent of the electorate, distributed across at least five states. This, however, guarantees only that a draft law is submitted; it does not guarantee success in the law's long and tortuous process of getting approved.

In figure 3.3 along the "Interest Groups" vector, only the USA shows formal, institutional lobbying as a major dimension of participation—usually vested in interest groups. These have proliferated and represent an expanding range of interests and political perspectives (Cigler and Loomis 2002). On the ideological spectrum, one finds extremely well-organized groups from the political right (such as Christian Conservatives and the National Rifle Association) to the left (such as the American Association of Retired Persons [AARP]). Such groups have increasingly assumed the role of political intermediaries and have proven successful in influencing elections; to this extent they are decreasingly institutional in form and tend more to occupy the space opened up by social movements and NGOs. By bringing to bear strong technical analysis of issues, they also influence policy decisions and rulemaking (Furlong 1997, 325–48).

But although these multiple opportunities for direct institutional presence within co-governance in the USA give the impression of genuine breadth and depth, the extent to which people exercise those rights and obligations on a widespread basis is often limited. In the USA the challenge is not to create institutional opportunities for participation but instead to raise the level of active participation and involvement within the many existing options. Unfortunately, unless motivated by a major cause célèbre, most citizens tend toward noninvolvement—not least in the formal dimensions of institutional participation in local elections, bond elections, and referenda. This opens the space for participation and influence peddling by interest groups, the outcome of which usually favors the more powerful, well organized, and better off.

The extensive opportunities and expectations of public participation in government in the USA contrast markedly with the traditions and practices in Mexico, even though the past decade has seen important strides in opening up participation as part and parcel of the democratic and modernization processes analyzed above. Statutory formal participation has been the exception rather than the rule. Exceptions include agrarian *ejido*[20] communities, in which the maximum body has been the general assembly of *ejido* members governed by a steering committee *(comisariado ejidal)* and monitored by a "watchdog committee" *(comité de vigilancia)*. Another example is the tradition of *usos y costumbres,* which allows rural (indigenous) communities to select their leaders and engage in municipal self-government. This form of participation is traditionally anchored in the *cargo* system of rural (male) leaders undertaking honorific positions in local government and has widely been adopted as a mainstream form of local government in several states, especially Oaxaca, where over 400 of its more than 570 municipalities are governed in this way. However, neither can be said to be truly examples of citizen participation in governance; both are really parallel mechanisms of local government delegated to citizens—in this case *ejidatarios* and indigenous men.

Elsewhere in the country the strong executive tradition, opacity of decision making, weak press, and lack of public information have been strong constraints on public involvement, let alone public monitoring. For good or ill, decisions have gotten made, projects have been implemented (often speedily), and consultation, if it has occurred at all, has tended to be political—taking soundings from the principal private interest lobbies and chambers—but even here little could be done once a decision was taken. Within public education, too, there has been no strong tradition for parents to become involved in school board governance; even for head teachers and the unions, parental involvement has been anathema (Grindle 2004; Robles 2006).

An important step forward in improving public participation grew out of President Salinas's Solidarity Program (1989–94), which made the formation of Solidarity Committees composed of local leaders and citizens a prerequisite for receiving funding for local projects (Contreras and Bennett 1994). Although similarly targeted social funding programs (PROGRESA and Opportunidades) since the mid-1990s have not required the same level of institutionalized local involvement, other dimensions of participation have opened up for citizens in general. As non-PRI parties began to win power at the state and local level, so, too, did they seek to make governance more transparent and to involve—or at least consult with—local groups and open up city hall (especially) to individuals and to groups (Cabrero 1996; Ward and Rodríguez 1999). As the calls for democratization increased, civic groups proliferated and demanded greater local involvement. In Mexico much of emerging citizen participation has been local and is now increasingly sought through lobbies (see figure 3.3), but institutional channels for the most part remain rather weakly articulated. Some states have enacted participation laws to ensure the possibility of referenda and plebiscites, but statutory councils, especially those with "teeth," remain relatively rare in Mexico. Mexico has yet to fully develop institutional opportunities for a continuous citizen presence within a more active democracy, and it seems more satisfied at this stage to consolidate the representational democratic arena.

In Brazil, there have been a number of institutional and quasi-institutional developments, very much influenced directly or by the spirit of the 1988 Constitution, which the leader of the Constitutional Assembly called the "Citizens' Constitution." It allowed those who were considered illiterate to vote, thus undoing nearly one hundred years of exclusion, and set out many different rights and corresponding state duties and responsibilities. It also established very specific mechanisms for consultation and control by civil society, which were consolidated in subsequent legislation. As a result, in many areas, the theme of institutional participation has been very much on the agenda.

Three types of mechanisms can be found: those that are required by law to be present in all municipalities or states, the so-called statutory councils; those that are required as part of a specific central government program;[21] and those that, while consultative, serve as general sounding boards for civil society opinion on particular themes and can be quite influential. Most significant are the new statutory councils, such as the Council for Child and Adolescent Rights (law 8.069, 1990), State and Municipal Health Councils (law 8.142, 1990), the Council for Social Service (law 8.742, 1993), and the Council for the Aged (law 8.842, 1994). States too have their own initiatives: São Paulo, for example, has a number of Councils for Public Security, which, since the 1980s, have brought together citizen groups and the police. Recent legislation requires that all municipalities of over twenty thousand inhabitants institute participative master plans *(planos diretores participativos)* for urban development by the end of 2006.

The big and very open question that applies to these new institutional mechanisms is whether they have, in fact, aided inclusion or whether they have reproduced existing patterns of exclusion. On this, the research and evaluation jury seems divided at the moment, and it seems very much a question of considering them on a case-by-case and place-by-place basis (Dagnino 2002). Where local groups are able to articulate their interests and occupy the spaces, and where subnational governments are interested in moving forward with civil society organizations, the success has been considerable. Where one happens without the other, problems emerge, especially when councils are used as a prerequisite for gaining access to federal funds.

These questions are also present regarding Brazil's most recent and already quite famous contribution to the local development toolbox: participative budgeting or *orçamento participativo* (OP, to use its popular form) (Navarro 1998; Avritzer and Navarro 2003). Participative budgeting began at the same time in 1989 in three PT towns: Porto Alegre (Rio Grande do Sul), Ipatinga (Minas Gerais), and Icapuí (Ceará). Under Brazilian local legislation, it is the responsibility of the mayor—as it is of the president and governors—to present the annual budget to the legislative branch. How the mayor goes about this is his or her own choice. Traditionally, budget preparation would be the task of the technical departments generally coordinated by finance or planning. Under OP, budget preparation is shared with the local communities, and while practices vary between municipalities, decisions are jointly made on major investments and civil works, and broad policy priorities are determined for other areas of activity. As the former PT mayor Tarso Genro stated for

Porto Alegre, "The traditional forms of political representation that come from the voting urn would be substituted by direct democracy" (Genro and de Souza 1997, 22–24). In some municipalities, OP has been placed on the statute book as an institutional requirement, but in many others it shares the quasi-institutional space of being a practice legitimated by mayors and by the expectations of communities.

By 2000, it was estimated that there were well over a hundred different OPs around the country,[22] all of which have followed these initial experiences, adapting and changing ideas and practices to fit historical circumstances and local culture. Five state governments have also begun to experiment with OP, including the State of Rio Grande do Sul itself, and while still retaining its progressive label, OP is no longer solely a feature of some PT governments but spans parties and coalitions from the left to the center and center-right of the political spectrum (Teixeira et al. 2002).

The increase in the use of statutory, advisory, and consultative councils in Brazil has extended the quasi-institutional end of the institutional–quasi-institutional continuum in the direction of new alliances, partnerships, and other kinds of linkages between the public sector and civil society organizations operating in a resource-sharing manner, especially at the local level to resolve a variety of urgent social questions (Spink 2002). While not institutional in format, they are nevertheless laying the foundation for a wider approach to thinking about governance.

The growing strength of these different forms of citizen engagement suggests that at least at the everyday institutional level of custom and practice, new and important mechanisms are being crafted. In both Mexico and Brazil there is a general recognition of the need and desirability of greater involvement in subnational governance especially. Increasingly, it is at the local, state, and general subnational levels that people are looking for the more specific territorial-based solutions of economic and social development. Yet with the exception of participatory budgeting, made famous in Brazil, subnational governments in both Brazil and Mexico, and especially in Mexico, appear uncertain about how best to move forward and make effective citizen engagement in co-governance an institutional reality. Even in the USA, where opportunities for citizen participation are mandated, the often-noted general apathy has opened space for more powerful interest groups to exercise greater influence.

## Conclusions: Continuities and Discontinuities in the Strengthening of Co-governance at the Subnational Level

In this chapter we have focused on horizontal decentralization, by which we mean the widening of the space for subnational interaction between the three principal branches of government—the executive, legislature, and judiciary. We have also examined the extent to which new mechanisms to encourage effective public engagement in co-governance alongside the three branches are being created and used.

From the outset, we noted that in Latin America all too often the very word *government* evokes the idea of the executive branch, not least because the other two branches have traditionally been relatively weak in relation to the president, governor, or mayor. Now that Brazil and Mexico are actively seeking to consolidate their democratic structures, we are observing major shifts in the institutional arrangements, patterns, and influence of the branches relative to each other, and part of our task here has been to chart those changes and to assess the respective roles that they play in co-governance. The bottom-line question, therefore, is: What difference (if any) do these observed changes make in generating greater efficacy in policy making, especially at the subnational level? And what is the relationship between politics and co-governance? In the USA, in part because of questions of internal security, the shift in questioning has been in the reverse direction by vesting greater authority in the federal level, and here we ask if, for security reasons, there has been a drift toward a more executive style of politics and policy.

In the USA, ensuring an effective federalism that accorded powers to the subnational level was a construction that the framers of the Constitution sought to lay down from the outset. The aim was to create an effective space between the three respective powers that would offer "checks and balances," in large part to ensure that no one power (especially the executive) would ever become overly dominant. While there has been a constant tension between the relative strength of the levels, federal versus subnational and local, in the USA at least the checks and balances have worked reasonably well, both in the federal government and in subnational governments. Although the power balance has varied over time, if any one power has ever gained an upper hand in the USA it has invariably been the legislative branch, especially since multiple reelection of chief executives was curtailed in the early 1950s. And while there are continuing tensions in the overall federalist architecture and process in the USA (Rodríguez 1997), it can be argued that the USA has taken decentralization and devolution to an extreme. On the positive side, it must be acknowledged that at the national and state levels all three branches are empowered; checks and balances are firmly in place; the judiciary plays a major constitutional review role; and at the local level government jurisdictions generally enjoy a relatively high degree of autonomy. The downside is that power is often so divided, and government so heavily bureaucratized, that a huge industry of lobbyists is required to speak for specific interest groups in order to find ways through the complexity of government. The other side of this coin is that while the U.S. federalist system mandates and institutionalizes public participation in governance, the actual level of effective and genuine participation of citizens tends to be disappointingly low and narrow in its scope.

In Brazil and Mexico, co-governance powers are very much a focus and priority, and important changes are under way. Over the twentieth century both countries evolved strong and highly centralized federal traditions, each with a dominant executive branch. Mexico was especially remarkable in this respect: by the 1970s, after fifty years of uninterrupted one-party rule, the overarching dominant executive branch was becoming ossified, and from the 1980s onward, once democratization processes accelerated, it began to break down. In Brazil, although legislatures and the judiciary were moderately strong in theory, they remained weak in practice. Here too, democratization led to dramatic change articulated through an entirely new constitution in 1988 that represented an important opportunity to recast federalism and to accelerate many of the changes that we have observed in this chapter. While Brazil faced the threat of hijacking by the executive branch in the past, especially at the subnational (state) level, constitutional reform appears to have opened up a new spectrum of co-governance opportunities.

Thus we see the most progress and experimentation in Brazil, followed closely by Mexico, which, as the arrows in figure 3.3 strongly suggest, is moving toward a central position on the spectrum with regard to the balance of powers. As executive operational powers are pared back, and/or as enlightened and canny executives seek to share powers more in keeping with their institutionally sanctioned roles, legislatures are beginning to fill the breach and play a more active role in co-governance through the law and policy-making processes. Along the way, they have to wrestle with issues of partisanship and the need to link party to policy-making behavior—traditionally weakly developed in Latin America (as it is for different reasons in the USA). And while they have a long way to go, our depictions in figures 3.1 to 3.3 clearly indicate that legislative co-governance is beginning to move toward the center ground within the spectrum. In both Latin American countries it seems likely that the extent to which the legislature becomes a truly effective force and a genuine participant in co-governance will depend upon its capacity to better articulate the linkage between party/policy platforms and intralegislative action, as well as to work with the executive branch.

In Brazil, the growing importance of the Ministerio Público and other tribunals that fall within the broad scope of the judiciary, including those dealing with consumer law, in calling attention to the importance of policy decisions may well create an important extra voice in the Praça dos Três Poderes, along with an increasingly investigative press. Sometimes these can also be the decentralized agencies of federal ministries as, for example, the case of subregional offices of the Labor Ministry, which began to apply fines to business firms for not following federal legislation requiring affirmative action in hiring policies toward the physically challenged. Here, the associated prosecutors have been successful in applying fines of some US$200,000 and requiring industries and banks to set clear and measurable objectives.

The path or paths by which this activation may be achieved can only be speculative. Consolidated parties in Brazil may have seemed a direction at one time, but the 2005–6 scandals that surrounded the PT and the apparent acceptance of the wide-scale use of nonregistered funds throughout the political spectrum may have slowed this track considerably. Back-to-back elections could be an important path for Mexico. Perhaps, also, a second (senate) chamber in subnational (state) governments might strengthen the legislative branch, although this would add costs and complexity that many would consider of marginal benefit. However, it seems unlikely that either Mexican or Brazilian legislatures will ever fully approach the strong powers that congresses are accorded in the USA, since both have electoral systems that encourage multiparty pluralities, and both have weak constituency linkages. Moreover, the bicameral arrangements in the USA, the opportunities for multiple reelection, the adherence to seniority in committees, the tightening of competition for congressional control, and the increase of "divided" governments are all factors that make for strong and experienced operationalization of the legislative branch.

That said, although the interparty mobility observed for Brazilian and, to a lesser extent, Mexican legislatures makes unlikely the level of dominance and power found in the strongly two-party model in the USA, the apparent turnover in the legislative branch, with political actors moving in and out of the executive and legislative branches, may be less problematic than is often thought. Now that more viable parties exist and executive reelection is circumscribed, a greater absolute number of political actors are likely to have served in two branches as well as at different levels (federal and subnational) of government. This fact alone, and the fact that there is not the same clearly defined upward "spiralist" track for politicians as in the USA (i.e., local to federal), suggest that both Mexico and Brazil have an opportunity to build upon a growing cadre of politically experienced actors that will emerge over the next two to three generations. Whether such distinctions have significantly affected the bottom line of policy implementation and service delivery is something that we will carry forward to the next chapters.

While it is perhaps an overstatement to suggest that in Mexico and Brazil the judicial branch is more like a twig, it is, nevertheless, the least well developed in co-governance terms of the three branches. In part this derives from the Napoleonic Code tradition in these two judicial systems that makes paramount the legal code as written rather than active jurisprudence (precedent). This means that the legislature codifies laws, and, significantly in both countries, the federal level has clear aegis, so that state judiciaries have an extremely limited role in issues relating to constitutional issues concerning the two other "powers." In the USA, with its "common-law" tradition, both the federal and subnational judiciaries are strong, with important constitutional checks-and-balances roles that make them a genuine and major actor in co-governance. Here too, there are changes in the wind in Brazil and Mexico as the legal implications of constitutional directives begin to be assumed by a new generation of law students and public prosecutors.

Another area where much remains to be done is the arena of public engagement in governance. The USA has a strongly mandated requirement and expectation for citizens to be actively engaged in governance.

Yet while people are generally quite participatory in faith-based organizations and the like (a topic to which we will return in chapter 5), their active participation in local governance is often minimal. Thus the three countries have similar problems, though coming from different directions. Brazil and Mexico are still uncertain about how best to include citizens in the process of co-governance, while in the USA the principal problem is how to reengage citizen populations whose enthusiasm for civic participation has atrophied. Inevitably, co-governance between the branches and encouragement of citizens' active engagement in government make for greater complexity and sometimes more cumbersome government that will periodically call for a "renegotiation" or revitalization of the federal pact. The important point underscored in this chapter is that these challenges are being addressed and worked out according to local traditions and processes in each of the three countries but that there is no single template for how decentralization, federalism, and the cultivation of horizontal relations between the branches should best be accomplished.

# Intergovernmental Relations and the Subnational State

## The Decentralization of Public Policy Making

Marta Ferreira Santos Farah, Pedro Jacobi, Victoria E. Rodríguez, Peter M. Ward, and Robert H. Wilson

The relationship of decentralization and intergovernmental relations to policy making is the focus of this chapter. Federalist systems are considered centralized when the national government has greater weight in the formation and implementation of public policy and in decisions concerning resource allocation than subnational governments. In a decentralized federal system, subnational governments have some degree of autonomy or discretion over policy and resource allocation. And even though national and subnational governments share responsibilities for policy making and implementation, the relative autonomy or independence of action among subnational governments is an important element of the policy-making context. Our goal in this chapter, therefore, is to explore the effectiveness of subnational governments in rising to the new challenges that they face. Specifically we ask: What is the impact of decentralization and changes in shaping and recasting intergovernmental relations both vertically (between the different levels) and horizontally (between governments at the same level)?

This chapter is organized into five sections. The first discusses the effects of reform on federal-subnational relations in terms of policy making. This discussion is then extended in the next section to changes in fiscal federalism—two topics amply addressed in academic and policy literature, although the contrasts that we draw across the three countries make a novel contribution. Third, we assess the performance of these decentralized systems, with particular attention devoted to tensions and conflicts that arise between the federal and subnational governments. The fourth section addresses relationships among state governments and among local governments. Here our focus is upon the reasons why these levels of governments compete and/or collaborate in the three countries, to date a relatively understudied feature of decentralization. The chapter concludes with the findings concerning the performance and challenges of the subnational state in the context of evolving intergovernmental relations and decentralized policy systems.

We will show that decentralization and democratic consolidation do indeed affect capacity but that overall federalism appears to work best when the institutional elements at all levels are stronger and more stable. Counterintuitively, perhaps, we find that competition and vying for resources do not appear to lead to a race to the bottom as local governments seek to outbid each other; rather, there is a consolidation and filling out of the subnational space that creates opportunities for interdependence and co-responsibility between actors and institutions. By and large we find considerable vibrancy of governance at the local level, as well as collaboration between local and state governments—at least in certain policy-making arenas. Sometimes, though, states do pose obstructions and difficulties both up and down the intergovernmental relations system, resisting local government initiatives and making problematic federal-to-local linkages. Federal roles have also changed markedly, and while the situation varies for different policy areas, generally the federal government is becoming more engaged in regulation and less engaged operationally in direct service delivery (J. Zimmerman 2005). Finally, we argue that there is a growing need to consider new institutional arrangements to accommodate new scales of population centers within the architecture of federal arrangements, namely large metropolitan areas that often comprise a raft of lower-level governments.

Our comparative analysis confirms that the policy-making systems have become more decentralized, itself a well-established finding, but we also show how the performance of these systems is subject to inherent federal-subnational tensions that relate to resources, institutions, bureaucratic behavior, and politics. Substantial transfer of authority and responsibility in some policy areas from federal government to state and local governments appears in each of the three countries. In most instances, however, policy making and implementation remain shared responsibilities of federal and subnational governments. In broad terms, in Brazil and Mexico, overall policy formulation remains largely a federal government prerogative but with important roles of implementation in state (Mexico) and especially municipal governments. In the USA, state and local governments tend to have a more significant role in formulation of policy and certainly in implementation. In the three countries, the decentralized systems reflect substantial heterogeneity in the subnational role within each country. The level of resources and capacity available greatly affects the ability and political will of local actors to assume new roles. In each of the three countries, achieving significant change in these very large and complex systems is far from easy.

## Decentralization and Public Policy: The Intergovernmental Context

In the early 1980s, the Brazilian state had a very centralized system of decision making and control of public finance. The federal government possessed an institutional structure adequate to the demands of centralized decision making and implementation. In many instances, federal implementation involved state and local agencies in administrative roles, but with quite limited discretion. With the return to democracy, and under pressure for significant social change, the Constitution of 1988 expanded the importance of state and especially municipal government in terms of new functions and responsibilities. It ratified decentralized policy making by establishing that provision of essential services (education, health, social assistance, and public works) would be principally the responsibility of municipalities, with secondary roles for state government. Only under extreme circumstances would the federal government assume a role, although it did retain a prominent function in the definition of rules and guidelines for subnational policies, as well as control over the transfer of funds.

Even though the new constitution led to an increase in the resources made available to states and municipalities, the intergovernmental distribution of competencies remained poorly defined. The effective transfer of operational attributes and decision-making authority did not accompany the increase in resources available. The lack of clear definition generated inefficiencies; irrational definitions of programs, services, and clients; discontinuities; and a waste of resources. As a result, achieving efficiencies and equity in social policies remained difficult, and high levels of regional inequalities further complicated the challenge (Melo 1996a, 1996b).

This can be seen, for example, in the area of health care, an integrated and decentralized system (Sistema Único de Saúde, SUS) in which each level of government follows broad federal guidelines but defines its own policies and priorities (Arretche 2002). The objectives of SUS include universal coverage and an active community-based preventive health care approach. In Brazil, SUS is perhaps the only federal policy that has been effectively decentralized as a system and, at least in theory, provides for the automatic transfer of federal resources to states and municipalities. Since 1990, a negotiated process has progressively led to a more decentralized system with principal responsibility for service provision in the hands of municipal government, while permitting a differentiated municipal role according to the extent to which the municipalities meet federal requirements. There have also been changes in funding to allow for regional differences and needs (R. Souza 2003). The full municipalization of health services was to occur only upon request from the municipality, yet despite the relative clarity of the rules and the availability of resources, the development of operational capacity in municipalities was varied: many were able to provide basic services (health centers, and in some cases home visits through the growing family doctor program), but few were able to implement what was called "full-service provision," which involved hospitals and other specialist services. In 1996 only 5 percent of municipalities were sufficiently autonomous to have assumed total control in this way *(gestão plena do sistema municipal)*. By 1998, while some 78 percent of municipalities were able to provide the "basic services" level of attention *(gestão plena da atenção básica)*, only 8 percent (460) had achieved full overall management of their local systems. This was to continue to rise in a differential manner such that by 2001 some 90 percent of municipalities were providing basic services, while the proportion of those providing full-service management had increased to 10 percent (563).[1] With the continued slow uptake of full-service provision, the National Health Council was to create a "pact for health" in early 2006 with the objective of providing full services at the local level throughout the country by 2007. Part of the reason for the different rates of policy implementation lay in the distribution of the necessary infrastructure and skilled specialist staff. Even today, outlying municipalities may be able to provide only ambulances to transport patients to state capitals or building facilities that can be used for outpatient treatments. At the same time, as will be seen later in this chapter, some municipalities are finding a different way around these issues by getting together to provide these extra services within innovative forms of intergovernmental collaborative arrangements.

The USA entered the 1980s with "elaborate networks of administrative connections between national and state agencies" created in the 1960s when federal aid programs expanded substantially in number and size (Bowling and Wright 1998). This legacy contributes to the complexity of existing federal-state relations and to the great variation of relations across policy areas. Substantial, if not dramatic, decentralization of authority to states and in some cases local government for the design and implementation of public policy occurred in many fields in the 1980s and 1990s. In some instances, the decentralized policy making was authorized explicitly by Congress, while in others Congress granted to federal implementing agencies the right to grant waivers of federal requirements to qualifying states. In both types of action, federal funding of program initiatives remains significant. During the 1980s Congress offered significant responsibility for environmental regulation to the states. Most states agreed to accept this responsibility, and by 1998 the federal Environmental Protection Agency (EPA) had assigned to individual states the administration of 757 programs (Schram and Weissert 1999, 5). One study concluded that in this form of decentralized implementation success occurs most often when relationships between state and federal officials are based on high trust and extensive interaction (Esler 1998, 263).

But a decentralized and fragmented system remains subject to new challenges. As wildfires have become more widespread and severe, the coordination of multiple federal, state, local, and tribal governments, local fire departments, and other agencies has proven difficult, and new intergovernmental approaches are being encouraged (McDowell 2003). The response to Hurricane Katrina in New Orleans displayed a very poor, if not failed, intergovernmental response (Schneider 2005).

Expanded decision-making authority granted by federal agencies to state agencies for administering federal programs can be found in the U.S. Department of Health and Human Services, which provides waivers for the Medicaid Section 1115 program (Schneider 1997, 89–109) and allows a state a substantial degree of experimentation and innovation in program delivery. With the collapse of federal health reform during the first Clinton administration, states increasingly turned to waivers as a means to respond to extensive change in the health industry. In the Education Flexibility Demonstration Act of 1999, states' prerogatives to waive certain federal requirements and establish their own programs for improving education were expanded (Schram and Weissert 1999, 5). This type of intergovernmental interaction has been described as "discretion seeking" in that states request a suspension or alteration of program requirements, a redefinition of a program as a model of experiment, or greater implementation flexibility in return for higher performance standards (Agranoff and McGuire 1999, 352). Governors find this approach very attractive since, in effect, it avoids having to negotiate with Congress on program design. Nathan (2005) finds in his examination of the evolution of social policy in the USA that states have in fact helped preserve Medicaid during periods of fiscal austerity by taking advantage of the flexibility afforded to states.

Direct congressional action can also lead to decentralized policy making. For example, the Intermodal Surface Transportation Efficiency Act of 1991 received near-universal praise for broadening decision-making authority of local officials in transportation planning. This policy modified long-standing practice by allowing federal funds to be shifted between highway and transit projects by local authorities and offering greater flexibility in satisfying the local finance component, including expanded opportunities for private sector financing of projects. The reauthorization of the act in 1998 contemplated, but did not incorporate, an even more extensive devolution in the form of assigning revenue-raising decisions to state and local government (Innovative Financing of Highways).

The passage of the Personal Responsibility and Work Opportunity Reconciliation Act of 1996 marked a significant change in national policy and a striking example of decentralization of policy making. In a move fostered by a dramatic decline in public support for federal welfare policy, a bipartisan commitment to deficit reduction, and a strong economy, the basic structure of welfare policy was modified and national welfare standards were effectively eliminated. Even though performance requirements continued to condition federal funding, states were delegated responsibility and far-reaching discretion in the design and implementation of welfare policy. States have adopted a wide range of approaches to eligibility, training requirements, time limits, and other issues. A 2000 report by the U.S. General Accounting Office (2000) highlights the difficulties encountered by states in helping families become economically independent but argues that these can best be addressed at the state level in collaboration with local agencies.

In the USA, recent decentralization has been enabled by both congressional and executive branch actions. However, the shift in intergovernmental relations has also depended upon subnational governments taking action on their own. During the national recession of the 1980s, the Reagan government chose not to pursue federal legislation to ameliorate the regional impacts of structural economic change. States in the industrial heartland that were suffering from high rates of unemployment responded by developing their own strategies. Later, even those states better positioned in the new economy adopted economic development strategies. In this field, the state initiatives appear in the context of inaction by the federal government to a pressing national issue (R. Wilson 1993).

In Mexico, decentralization was intended to strengthen municipalities (Reform of art. 115 in 1983) but, in effect, was often negated by the state governments, which sought to block the autonomy that was to have come to municipalities through having more control over their finances: the states quickly found mechanisms to retain control over municipalities. Thus, although well intentioned, in the end the move toward decentralization from the federal government to municipalities actually strengthened the states (Rodríguez 1997; Ward and Rodríguez 1999). Things changed only when opposition parties at the municipal level who were not beholden to the PRI governor and to the party hierarchy (as were their PRI municipal president counterparts) began to exercise the newfound responsibilities with which they were empowered by article 115. However, fearful that their (non-PRI) government would suffer from the withholding of resources, these same administrations sought to raise local internal revenues through more effective taxation and through increased consumer charges for services (Rodríguez 1995; Ward and Rodríguez 1999).

Subsequent attempts at decentralization and devolution during the 1990s went in two directions, sometimes bypassing states almost entirely by the federation, in part to avoid a repetition of what had occurred earlier, and at other times, and increasingly, mandating decentralization to the states, as occurred in the cases of public health and public education. The former pattern was particularly the case with social policy and antipoverty programs such as the highly lauded (though controversial) National Solidarity Program initiated in 1989 by then-President Salinas. In some instances even municipal governments were bypassed as community groups and organizations became beneficiaries of Solidarity projects. However, as Solidarity's success and funding increased, it began to be more formally institutionalized within a "superministry" (Secretaría de Desarrollo Social, SEDESOL), and new mechanisms developed that once again strengthened the hand of the states, though not at the expense of municipalities (at least not as obviously as in the past). For example, in each state a Solidarity "coordinator" was appointed to oversee all Solidarity projects in the state. In some cases these were so powerful and had such plentiful resources that they became almost "parallel" governors. Whereas in the past municipal presidents would seek funding from the governor, now they sought it from the Solidarity coordinator.

In the Zedillo administration, the Program for Education, Health Care, and Nutrition (Programa de Educación Salud y Alimentación, PROGRESA) maintained the local focus of Solidarity, and decentralization efforts incorporated the states. No longer was there the pretense that development funds were directed exclusively at municipalities. A series of fiscal reforms and the creation of new *ramos* (budget lines) were designed to strengthen the hand of the states as they dealt with municipalities. For example, more funds were allocated for municipalities but managed and distributed by the states. Even funds targeted for municipal infrastructure and municipal development (the Fund for Municipal Social Infrastructure [Fondo de Aportaciones para Infraestructura Social, FAISM] and the Municipal Strengthening Support Fund [Fondo de Aportaciones de Fortalecimiento Municipal, FAFM] respectively) were under state and federal control. Under the PAN and President Fox, the program was extended and renamed Opportunidades, with larger allocations of resources from the federal government to the municipalities, including urban ones (that would in principle give them more autonomy), but under control of the state governments.

The second set of decentralization reforms did directly target the states from the outset. From 1983 onwards the public health system began to be decentralized, although many of the earlier initiatives encountered resistance from the powerful state social insurance institutions and by 1987 only fourteen (of thirty-one) states had signed the agreements (Homedes and Ugalde 2006b). President Salinas (1988–94) largely ignored the formal decentralization of the health system in preference to health care assistance through Solidarity, and it was finally implemented a *sexenio* later as part of President Zedillo's "New Federalism" initiative. This brought on board all thirty-one states and the Federal District in the 1996 National Agreement for the Decentralization of Health Services, and by 1999 70.1 percent of federal budget expenditure was managed by the states (up from 23.4 percent funding in 1995). The decentralization continued under President Fox's National Health Plan entitled "Cooperative Federalism" (Homedes and Ugalde 2006a).

The other large slice in this increased share in the national budget that is now managed by states came from the decentralization of public education under the 1993 reform. Here President Salinas saw the clear political advantage of giving the states responsibility for public education in that negotiation with the powerful Teachers' Union would be shifted to each state (Cabrero Mendoza 1996; Pardo 1998; Grindle 2004). Perhaps even more than health care, the decentralization of public education has been a considerable success and was certainly achieved in a relatively short period, although it remains almost entirely state managed, with little input from municipalities (Robles 2006). But in neither program has there (yet) been significant development at the local municipal level.

Thus, in the Mexican case of New Federalism, a clear tendency to strengthen the role of the state vis-à-vis the municipality is observed. Clearly, this does not mean that municipalities have not improved their position at all; they have. But in the end, the winners have been the states, and almost always under close political control of the federation. Indeed, the strengthening of the role of the Congress, which oversees fiscal and intergovernmental transfers, has paradoxically both strengthened the principles of federalism and intensified scrutiny of subnational government performance. At the same time, however, state legislatures are also modernizing and becoming more influential, especially in oversight and authorization of state budgets. Moreover, the rationale for breaking with traditional vertical linkages and working more collaboratively between states led to the very recent creation of a state governors' association, the National Conference of Governors (Conferencia Nacional de Gobernadores [CONAGO]), which is becoming a major player in federal-state relations, as discussed below.

In Mexico administrative decentralization is clearly seen in almost every policy arena; yet there are very few cases or examples where federal government has completely devolved authority. The two most visible cases of decentralization are education and health, both involving state governments. In general, the municipalities have few functions with regard to education, and of those they do have, practically none are compulsory. That is, the execution of these functions is at the discretion of the municipal authority, and few have sought to undertake such functions. Part of the problem in Mexico (as elsewhere) is that the decentralization of specific programs or policies cannot be implemented at the local level because of the lack of human and financial resources.

### Intergovernmental Fiscal Systems

#### Decentralization in Fiscal Structures

The ability of governments to fulfill assigned responsibilities depends critically upon the resource base of these governments. In a federalist system, intergovernmental fiscal relations are defined by several elements. A higher level of government can transfer resources to lower levels. The conditions under which transfers are made—negotiated or automatic—and the extent to which the transfers are restricted to specific purposes affect the level of discretion that lower-level governments have in the utilization of the transfers. Another important dimension of the intergovernmental fiscal system relates to the authority of higher-level governments to limit tax bases and control tax rates utilized by lower-level governments. These latter provisions affect the ability of state and local governments to raise so-called own-source revenues in order to meet the service demands associated with the reallocated competencies (Campbell and Fuhr 2004). As subnational levels of government are expected to raise a larger share of their own revenues, disparities in tax bases become a significant issue in the three countries.

Subnational governments in the three countries have increased shares of total government spending, broadly confirming the decentralization of the public sector in the three countries (see table 4.1). However, the relative shares of subnational government spending are quite different. In Mexico, despite decentralization, local governments (especially rural ones) are highly dependent on intergovernmental transfers; the development of local tax bases has proceeded slowly and is largely restricted to cities where there is greater scope to increase revenues. In Brazil, a more substantial degree of fiscal decentralization has developed, and hard-fought progress in developing local tax bases has been made. In the USA, states and localities have substantial discretion in defining local tax bases and setting rates. In this section the effects of decentralization on financial resources of subnational governments are examined, first, in terms of changes in the structure of these systems and, second, in terms of their adequacy in generating the level of resources necessary to fulfill their assigned functions.

Table 4.1    General Trends in Subnational Fiscal Systems, 1980–2005

|  | BRAZIL | | MEXICO | | USA | |
|---|---|---|---|---|---|---|
|  | *State* | *Local* | *State* | *Local* | *State* | *Local* |
| Change in relative spending | + | ++ | ++ | + | + | + |
| Change in federal transfers | + | ++ | ++ | + | + | - |
| Change in own-source revenue | ++ | + | + | ++ | + | + |
| Autonomy in defining tax base | Limited* | Limited* | Limited | Limited | High | Limited |
| Discretion in setting tax rates | High** | High** | None | High | High | High |
| Autonomy to contract debt | None*** | None*** | Limited | Limited | High | Limited |
| Federal oversight | High/Medium# | High/Medium# | High | High | None | None |
| State oversight | NA | Heterogeneous | NA | High | NA | Limited |

* No autonomy to establish new taxes.
** Limited by local economic conditions.
*** Subnational government had autonomy and ability to contract debt until 2000, when the Fiscal Responsibility Act came into effect.
# According to socioeconomic capacity of subnational unit.
+ Increase.
- Decrease.

In Brazil, the federal government has historically been the primary revenue generator. From the mid-1960s through the mid-1970s, it raised more than 50 percent of total government revenue. Federal revenue was transferred to state and local governments through a process of negotiations, with specific utilization of funds earmarked by the federal government, thereby limiting the ability of state and local government officials to define priorities. These negotiated transfers encouraged the development of relationships with state and local officials based on the exchange of favors, clientelistic in nature, so that subnational officials became largely preoccupied with the transfer of federal funds to the locality. The Constitution of 1988 marked a dramatic shift in the allocation of fiscal resources, first by setting out clearer rules for transfer and second by guaranteeing that a greater share of resources was transferred to states and municipalities (Samuels 2003). Between 1988 and 1995, the transfer to the municipalities increased from 1.76 percent to 3.46 percent of gross domestic product (Afonso, Rodrigues, and Araújo 2000). Between 1980 and 1992, the municipal share of national social spending increased from 11 to 17 percent while the federal share decreased from 65 to 56 percent. More recent municipal data, from 1998, indicate that the municipal share of national spending in education and health was around 30 percent (Afonso, Rodrigues, and Araújo 2000, 36–37).

Despite the rapid increase in own-source revenues, by 197 percent between 1988 and 1998, as anticipated by the Constitution of 1988, data from 1997 show that federal and state transfers still constitute the principal source of revenue for virtually all municipalities (Afonso, Rodrigues, and Araújo 2000, 46). Furthermore, own-source municipal revenue, in 1998, represented only 5.3 percent of total tax revenue in the country. Thus a municipal dependency persists—especially among the small municipalities recently created under the stimulus of the Participation Fund of the Municipalities (Fundo de Participação dos Municípios, FPM)—in relation to federal and state transfers (see table 4.1). This dependence not only results from the constitutionally mandated transfers (e.g., for the education and health sectors) but also is linked to voluntary transfers that remain subject to negotiation, albeit within the scope of federal programs rather than individual relationships. According to Celina Souza and Inaiá Carvalho (1999): "Analyzing the federal government proposal to divide the expense of the minimum income program between the federal government and the municipalities, Lavinas (1998) demonstrates that of the 5,507 municipalities only 251 will receive the expected match" (203). Given the heterogeneity of the now 5,562 municipalities,[2] federal transfers will continue to be critical to the equalization of the expenditure capacity of local government (Eaton 2004b; Haggard and Webb 2004; C. Souza 2002).

Despite successful efforts of some state and local governments to rationalize revenues and expenses, tensions in intergovernmental fiscal relations led to the adoption of the Federal Fiscal Responsibility Law (Complementary Act 101, May 4, 2000). The measure attempts to encourage fiscally sound behavior on the part of subnational governments, reducing dependence on the central government and encouraging fiscal stability in all levels of government (Almeida 2005b). The act establishes limits for expenditures on personnel and public debt and sets goals equilibrating revenues and expenditures (see table 4.1). The states, and especially the municipalities, reacted defensively at first, attempting to delay implementation and seeking more flexibility in the law. However, once it was adopted by Congress, many units of government reacted positively to the new requirements and reformed their fiscal systems. In fact, fiscal health has become a dimension of competition among states for economic development, a stimulus for accountability, and even a factor in reelection success.

The most striking characteristic of subnational finances in Mexico is the dependence on federal funds. Although the situation improved by the start of the new century, in the not too-distant past (1980s) some municipalities—especially the poorer and rural ones—depended almost entirely on the federation for revenues (see table 4.1). The budget of an average municipality showed that federal allocations made up 80 percent of revenue. These allocations (called *participaciones*) are undertaken by formula and distributed in specific funds. Specifically, they take account of total population, level of poverty, and efficiency in that jurisdiction's collection of revenues. Dating from a Fiscal Coordination Law (Ley de Coordinación Fiscal, LCF) of 1980, various revisions have tended to make minor modifications to the latter two criteria. From the 1990s onwards, more than half of the state congresses have developed their own fiscal coordination laws to its near-equivalent and usually based upon the same criteria (Rodríguez 1997; Rodríguez, Rowland, and Ward 2001,

82–90). One of the major changes found in most municipalities is a dramatic increase in funding (see table 4.1). While the transfers under the LCF remained the same or increased in real terms during the 1990s, more aggressive revenue collection at the local level has enabled these local governments to accomplish more through increased spending (Rodríguez and Ward 1995). But small rural municipalities have remained heavily dependent on revenue sharing and special programs like Solidarity and PROGRESA.

In the USA, unlike Brazil and Mexico, subnational governments generate a high proportion of revenue through their own sources (R. Wilson 1993; see table 4.1). The U.S. Constitution and, consequently, Congress place very few limitations on state revenue sources, and state governments define the revenue systems available to local governments (see table 4.1). As a result, subnational governments provide a high share of their revenue through their own sources, but the structures of revenue systems across states and local governments vary considerably. Devolution itself has led to diversification in municipal revenue structures (Krane, Ebdon, and Battle 2004).

Federal transfers to state and local governments have varied significantly over the last several decades. In the mid-1980s, during the Reagan administration, federal aid declined, but in the late 1980s transfers stabilized, and they demonstrated moderate growth again through the 1990s (R. Wilson 1993). From the mid-1970s through the mid-1980s real expenditures by state government held steady. The increase in real state spending after the mid-1980s was based largely on increases in own-source revenue. Furthermore, by the late 1990s, increases in own-source revenues of subnational governments further reduced the relative importance of federal aid. Despite less reliance on federal transfers, state and local governments can be affected by federal policy on their expenditures through the so-called unfunded mandates. In 2003, for example, subnational governments were especially sensitive to the increase in expenditures required by the national policy for enhanced homeland security.

### Impacts of Austerity and Tax Base Disparities on Subnational Fiscal Systems

The adequacy of fiscal systems depends both on the structure of the revenue system and on the productivity of revenue sources. In other words, levels of revenue generation are a function of the size of the tax base and the ability of the tax base to grow. The 1980s was a period of poor economic performance in Brazil and Mexico and only modest growth in the USA. Brazil and Mexico both faced fiscal austerity as a result of modest economic growth and restrictions imposed on revenue generation required to meet national macroeconomic policy objectives. The improved performance in the 1990s, however, did not benefit state and local governments to the extent expected because of macroeconomic policy targets that greatly constrained public sector revenue.

In Brazil in the early 1990s, total resources available to state and local governments actually declined. State governments suffered great fiscal stress due to (1) a recession, (2) increasing budget inflexibility around salaries of public servants, (3) suspended federal investments in the states dating from the mid-1980s, (4) constraints on new borrowing in both national and international markets, and (5) the loss of tax base as firms moved to states offering tax incentives (Abrucio and Costa 1998, 49). To further complicate the financial context, one of the responses of the federal government to the declines in federal revenue in the middle of the decade was to reduce spending by restraining nonconstitutionally guaranteed (i.e., negotiated) transfers to states and municipalities, restricting credit to the states and municipalities, creating taxes, and increasing other revenues not shared with subnational governments (Oliveira and Biasoto 1999, 22). Governors continued to face growing challenges in debt administration even following a recovery of the federal funding capacity for social reform (Arretche and Rodrigues 1999).

The financial capacity of the municipalities was similarly affected by the factors operating nationally. In addition, the initial benefits of the stabilization policy implemented by the federal government were reversed in the second half of the 1990s, with very significant impacts on local spending (Serra and Afonso 1999; Carneiro 2000). The reductions in federal social spending, which repeatedly occurred during the period, affected local initiatives dependent upon these transfers. The municipalities responded to these highly adverse financial conditions in quite diverse ways, reflecting diverse economic conditions across regions and quite varied fiscal capacity among local governments (C. Souza and Carvalho 1999).

Mexico also had serious economic crises throughout the 1980s and into the mid-1990s. The most serious of these were in the early to mid-1980s (starting with the crisis of 1982, which included the nationalization of banks, the world oil crisis, and the 1985 earthquakes that devastated

Mexico City) and then, worse still, the 1994–95 crisis as Ernesto Zedillo took over the presidency. But these are only highlights of extended periods of economic hardship that have been aggravated by the austerity measures imposed by the International Monetary Fund. The belt-tightening measures imposed on government and citizenry had an impact on subnational governments largely by raising the stakes of decentralization and making the shift of resources (and especially responsibilities) a more attractive proposition for the federal government (Rodríguez 1997).

Subnational governments in Mexico responded creatively to austerity measures by seeking ways to develop their own sources of revenue, thus decreasing their dependence on transfers. A case in point is at the municipal level, with updating of the land registry and imposition of property taxes that are more in line with actual property values. This has represented a significant source of revenue, though at a high political cost. No municipal president likes to be remembered as the one who raised taxes, but in the case of one municipality the 70 percent dependence on transfers and 30 percent dependence on own-source revenue were reversed. But innovative practices to improve local capacity in Mexico develop almost exclusively in urban, medium, and large municipalities. Seldom does one find success cases in poor, rural municipalities. The same applies to states—the larger and wealthier the state, the more innovative it tends to be.

At the state level, the Constitution limits the range of taxes that can be levied and in most cases allows only for a supplementary tax to be applied, in effect restricting the states' flexibility. Thus states can add a surcharge such as hotel and payroll taxes, but they often hesitate to do so for fear of penalizing themselves vis-à-vis their neighbors. Most would much prefer to levy taxes in their own right from base level rather than simply having the option of applying an overtax, but the federation continues to resist. Since the late 1990s the federal government has recognized the states' needs for greater resources both by raising local tax opportunities and by giving them greater access to federal tax revenues. For example, from 2004 onwards, while the federation continues to receive revenues from value-added taxes (VAT), a state is allowed to retain any additional VAT that it chooses to levy up to a maximum additional 2 percent. Though these are important steps forward in recasting fiscal federalism in Mexico, and though an increased share of the national budget is managed by the states, the federal government remains paramount.

In the USA, the subnational revenue systems are quite sensitive to overall economic conditions, as in Brazil and Mexico, and periods of fiscal austerity are correlated with downturns of the economy. However, an additional constraint on local spending emerged during a citizens' tax revolt in the 1970s. The tax revolt, never far from the minds of politicians, focused principally on property taxes, the major sources of revenue for local governments. The decline in federal aid, a hostile tax climate, and the recession of 1982 created enormous challenges for state fiscal policy. During the 1980s states increased intergovernmental transfers to local governments, compensating in part for the decline in federal aid. Fiscal health returned by the end of the 1980s but was short-lived, and the fiscal effects of federal mandates on states, particularly on health services (Bowman and Pagano 1990), and the national recession of the early 1990s wreaked havoc with many state budgets (Snell 1991; J. Zimmerman 1994). The cyclical nature of states' fiscal health is well established. Periods of economic growth produce strong state revenues. But during economic downturns, demands for services, especially social services, escalate and place great pressure on state governments. Even in times of growth, two structural elements will continue to pressure state government finance: demands for social services associated with the aging of the population and constraints on federal-state transfers for the foreseeable future.

In the USA, the substantial disparities in local tax bases, across states but especially across local governments within a state, create challenges. One feature of the more decentralized fiscal system is that local governments are increasing own-source revenues to meet the demand for local services. A significant share of federal aid to local governments, after the 1960s, was targeted to low-income areas in order to address, partially, the disparities in tax bases. After the substantial decrease in federal-local government transfers in the 1980s, states slightly increased transfers to local governments (R. Wilson 1993). Reliance on own-source revenues, however, embodies one prominent principle of local governance in the USA: that is, if a community wishes to have a certain level of services, it should be responsible for raising the necessary revenues. This argument, however, ignores the effect of the vast disparity in tax bases among local jurisdictions on disparities in service provision. Only in education policy have states adopted significant equalization efforts, but these have occurred independent of the devolution movement and often under the order of judicial decisions.

Thus the transition to more decentralized public sectors in the three countries encountered difficulties in securing the financial resources that subnational governments needed to fulfill their responsibilities. The levels of resources available to local governments frequently seem well below levels needed to meet the demand for services and infrastructure. Given that federal revenue systems are much more efficient than those available to subnational governments, a tension around fiscal matters appears inherent in decentralization. The cases of Brazil and Mexico are further complicated by the overall level of public debt and targets for macroeconomic policy. In these countries, federal transfers to subnational governments seem particularly unreliable. Enhancement of local revenue systems (expansion of tax bases and more efficient collection systems) seems to be an appropriate strategy, although not a strategy likely to succeed in areas with poor economic performance (Campbell 2003). In the USA high levels of own-source revenue and a diversified revenue base are not a solution to revenue inadequacy, but they do provide a somewhat higher degree of revenue stability. But the additional lesson observed in terms of local government finance in the USA is the need for equalization of tax bases for school finance that can be addressed only by a higher-level government—that is, by state government.

## National and Subnational Tensions and Opportunities

Despite the reshaping of intergovernmental relations, the presence of the federal government remains strong in all three countries' policy making as a result of (1) the constitutional assignment of key functions, as in defining national purpose; (2) practical considerations, such as efficiency in revenue generation; and (3) institutional legacies. Despite the substantial decentralization of policy making and implementation in the three countries, in many instances federal initiative continues to prevail, creating both tensions, if not conflicts, and opportunities in the intergovernmental system.

Federal governments continue to induce action by subnational governments but, in general, through less heavy-handed means. For example, in Brazil, new public policy initiatives have transformed municipalities from being mere administrators of federal programs, but they have yet to become fully autonomous in policy making. The redefinition of competencies and responsibilities in social areas, as in the implementation of the family health program by the municipalities, has allowed municipalities to formulate local policies, provided that federal guidelines are followed. To assume full responsibility for the unified health system (SUS), municipalities must follow strict guidelines defined by the federal government. In basic education, local governments can decide how to allocate educational resources and to design course content based on the characteristics of the local student population (Draibe 1997). However, once again this flexibility is constrained by the federal guidelines. Access to the resources of the Fund for Decentralizing Basic Education (Fundo para o Desenvolvimento da Educação Fundamental, FUNDEF) depends on meeting a series of criteria defined by the federal government. These examples show a federal government stimulating local action by providing incentives and assisting in the decentralization of programs but maintaining political or operational control in management and distribution of resources (Oliveira and Biasoto 1999, 22). That is to say, local initiatives must follow federal guidelines (Arretche 2005).

In Mexico, notwithstanding major sectoral decentralization (in health and education) and some reform to the system of revenue sharing, the incentives for state or local governments' actions remain closely tied to federal fiscal supports and priorities. There has been very little further legislative strengthening of either state or municipal competencies. States, in particular, remain fiscally handicapped, and until very recently municipalities were prevented from contracting external debt (Ward and Rodríguez 1999). For example, both FAISM and FAFM funds (for social infrastructure and municipal support) offered significant additional sources of local funding but were closely supervised and tied to federally mandated programs. Nevertheless, these federal initiatives served as important inducements.

Even though decentralization in the USA was partially a response to the critique that the federal government had overstepped its authority in state government affairs, the federal government continues to act forcefully through the intergovernmental system. But in general the federal government has become less heavy-handed. As the negative impact of welfare reform on health insurance coverage became clear, Congress approved a 1997 budget resolution that provided $24 billion to fund medical coverage for uninsured children. The participation of states was optional, and matching funds had to be provided. The need for national standards and the revenue-raising capabilities of the federal government provided the justification for this effort.

Rural development policy in the USA provides an example of another federal role. The country's agriculture support system that prevailed for most of the last century has been widely viewed as a successful form of federal-state cooperation (Radin et al. 1996). But the role of agriculture in the national economy changed, and reform of this system required a redefinition of rural development and substantial reductions in funding. The federal reforms encouraged collaborative relations among federal, state, and local public officials and private and community interests but without substantial funding. State and local government participation in such federal initiatives is based, not on the level of federal funding, but on common interests of diverse actors.

In one policy area, health regulation, the traditional pattern of federal action to coordinate or influence state actions reemerged. The Health Insurance Portability and Accountability Act of 1996 replaced a system of authority divided between state and federal governments with a system in which federal authority provides a framework for state action (Ladenheim 1997, 33–51). Even though a case of preemption, federal action was viewed as necessary to protect insurance holders from negative impacts of the variation among state regulatory policies. It represents one of the first significant federal intrusions into state government authority to regulate insurance, a domain where state authority has remained largely intact.

Tensions in intergovernmental relations can originate in a lack of federal leadership or unwanted federal leadership. In the former, states and municipalities must take action in areas where the federal government was the primary actor in an earlier period. For example, in Brazil, to enhance revenues and reduce expenditures, the federal government has adopted a defensive posture and attempted to relinquish responsibilities by "a pure and simple elimination of projects and programs" (Silva and Costa, 1995, 270, cited in Oliveira and Biasoto 1999). In the case of housing policy, the share of federal funding for housing declined from 61 percent to 20 percent between 1980 and 1990 (Medici and Maciel, 1996), reflecting, in part, the closing of the National Housing Bank (Banco Nacional da Habitação–BNH) in 1986. Given this institutional vacuum in such areas as housing, states and municipalities are pressured to replace these federal initiatives.

In the USA, in the field of immigration policy, particularly with respect to the impact of public service demand from illegal immigration, states expect federal leadership. States most acutely affected by illegal immigration argue that the federal government is not fulfilling its responsibilities and that it is thereby imposing substantial costs on local governments. With the important exception of fair housing and discrimination issues, housing policy has been largely displaced as a federal concern in the USA (Bockmeyer 2003). The absence of federal leadership on the issue of homelessness is perhaps the extreme case. The continuing controversy around health insurance coverage, patient privacy, and rising health costs suggests that health will remain a prominent national issue, but one that imposes significant costs upon local governments, which often incur health costs for uninsured individuals. Although state governments may take initiatives on their own, the severity of the problem may well lead to action by the federal government at some point.

In spite of the broad commitment to decentralization, the federal government in the USA preempts states and local governments in some areas, including the regulation of business. The Telecommunications Act of 1996 left many unanswered questions, and in implementing the act the Federal Communications Commission attempted to preempt state and local authority in such areas as control of public rights-of-way and local franchise fees (Tabin 1998). Congress has considered the Internet Tax Freedom Act proposal that would prohibit state and local government collection of tax revenues from business transactions over the Internet. In the area of crime and medical privacy, the U.S. Congress appears anxious to act, if not preempting states, certainly expanding the federal role in areas previously under state and local jurisdiction (Schram and Weissert 1999, 7). The tragic and highly publicized shootings in schools in recent years and the growing influence of the gun control movement contribute to congressional interest in overriding state and local gun control laws. Congress considered legislation that would remove product liability for firms producing firearms, thereby eliminating a legal avenue available to cities to exert a measure of gun control. Although these issues may be controversial, the federal government may believe that federal action should preempt state and local actions on issues of national importance.

## Conflicts and Challenges

Given the size and complexity of the governmental systems and the range of policy responsibilities discussed in this chapter, it can hardly be surprising that a quite complex pattern of change, with at times inconsistent tendencies, has emerged. Decentralization has generated three areas of conflict among governments: (1) ambiguous roles and bureaucratic resistance to change; (2) fiscal federalism and the management of state debt; and (3) unintended impacts of decentralization on state-local government relations. But examples of collaboration and even innovation in intergovernmental relations can also be observed. This section, after discussing findings concerning sources of conflict and cooperation, identifies several challenges to decentralization in the three countries.

Ambiguous definitions of roles and responsibilities, at times exacerbated by resistance from bureaucratic officials at higher levels, can generate conflict. In Mexico decentralization, even though federally mandated and containing a serious commitment to devolve responsibilities to the states, encountered major resistance. In education, for example, there was little ambiguity in the blueprint and legislative guidelines. But fears about possible resource withholding by central government, resistance from teachers' unions over implementation and effective control of hiring practices, and the anomalies arising from an existing dual system (federal and state) in some states all emerged as important constraints to implementation. Nevertheless, the program is now firmly in place. This type of conflict, arising from uncertainties generated by changes in large, complex systems, may be transitory.

Other sources of tensions regarding decentralization between the respective actors at all three levels may not be temporary. At the federal level, arguments to slow the pace of effective devolution persist: subnational governments, both states and municipalities, are ill prepared to assume the tasks of decentralized authority, often lacking the capacity to do so. Also, there is a fear that the federal government may lose control to local warlords or *caciques*—at least in more remote rural regions. And as discussed in the previous chapter, state assemblies are ever more eager to play a more genuine legislative role, and they welcome greater authority to undertake state mandates. But they, too, often deeply resent the apparent lack of "sovereignty"; they complain that they are little more than a monitoring and review body and that the Congress limits their discretion excessively by heavily earmarked funding. Several of the constitutional controversy appeals to the Supreme Court have been made by states' congresses about undue federal interference in their affairs, but these appeals are rarely successful, such is the power that the Constitution continues to guarantee to the federation.

In Brazil, similar tensions among the actors have emerged. On one side, the federal government and its bureaucracies have attempted to maintain political and financial control over services, transferring responsibilities without a clear model of coordinated federalism. On the other side, governors and mayors have attempted to secure greater transfers without specification of spending priorities by taking advantage of the ambiguous definitions of intergovernmental responsibilities (Abrucio and Costa 1998; Arretche 2002). And in the USA, with its long history of shared policy responsibilities, moments of shifting intergovernmental responsibilities frequently generate tensions, but these tend to be resolved within the implementation structures themselves (Scheberle 2005; Hoornbeek 2005). Governors and congressional oversight can be helpful in resolving such tensions. But tensions between federal and state agencies may emerge around regulatory issues. For example, in 2004 the federal Environmental Protection Agency withdrew its support, previously undertaken in cooperation with several state governments, from a legal process against power plants in the Midwest whose discharges were creating air pollution in states in the Northeast. As a result, state governments in the Northeast felt that their efforts to protect the environment were undermined by the federal government.

Intergovernmental fiscal relations are a common source of tension in the three countries. In Brazil and Mexico in the 1990s, a reduction of federal transfers to subnational governments affected their ability to fulfill their responsibilities. In Mexico, the federal treasury remains resistant, notwithstanding the decade-long arguments from state finance secretaries for more equitable revenue sharing and a larger share of the total. Nor did the victory of the PAN at the national level and the greater distribution of non-PRI parties across the thirty-two entities appear to reduce the Treasury's resolve. Since the federal fiscal reform project takes precedence and any devolution to the states would weaken that authority, this result might be expected. Also President Fox did not choose a militant PANista to head the Treasury Department but chose, instead, a well-respected former Treasury undersecretary from the previous administration. In general, state executives (governors) would like more authority, but they are reluctant to assume the responsibilities without the guarantee of additional funding. For them, in several respects, devolution is a poisoned chalice from which they would dearly love to drink but dare not.

In Brazil, state government debt increased in the 1990s and the federal government started to demand more favorable terms from states during renegotiations. States attempted to transfer their financial difficulties to the federal government through a strategy intended to maintain the financial protection provided by the federal government in previous periods. In practice, the states attempted to extend indefinitely debt payment to the federal government without substantially altering state fiscal policy through reducing expenditures or increasing revenues.

In the USA, one prominent issue of the decentralization debates of the early 1990s was the imposition of federal laws on state and local governments that carry financial implications but no, or inadequate, federal funding. Congress approved the Unfunded Mandates Act of 1995 to protect local governments from financial burdens imposed by federal legislation, but its impact is disputed (Posner 1997, 53–71). Proposals for improving the quality of assessing the impact of federal programs on state and local government, encouraging more deference to state and local laws and procedures, and increasing state flexibility to respond to cuts or caps on entitlement programs continue to be circulated.

The very process of decentralization has generated conflicts among subnational governments in the three countries. In Mexico, the frontline local executive officers (the municipal presidents) are invariably strapped for resources, and while they have considerable opportunity—in the case of cities—to raise local revenues, they resent the tight oversight functions that state assemblies have over them. They, too, rarely win cases brought before the Supreme Court. Even in the famous constitutional controversy brought by Puebla city authorities against the decision by the state congress to alter the formula in the State Fiscal Coordination Law in ways that the city believed was penalizing them for partisan political reasons, the Supreme Court found that the state congress was acting within its rights. In Mexico, unlike Brazil, municipalities are not federal entities, and although they are "autonomous and free" they are represented within the federalist pact under the authority of the state congress. As noted earlier, in the USA, the reauthorization of the Intermodal Surface Transportation Efficiency Act's transportation planning initiative in 1998 revealed tensions between state and city officials. Many state officials wanted to raise the level of earmarking of funds for highways, while larger cities wanted to maintain funding available for transit systems.

Unintended consequences of devolution, in which actions in one policy area affect other local delivery systems, have also emerged. In the USA, welfare reform under the Personal Responsibility and Work Opportunity Reconciliation Act required that local training systems place a high priority on job placement, in some states sidetracking ongoing efforts to reform training systems in order to meet the demand for highly skilled workers. The federal imperative of welfare-to-work has forced supportive systems, such as child care, to refocus. In other areas, the deinstitutionalization of the mentally ill and the absence of federal homelessness policy have placed burdens on cities. Reductions in the school lunch program impose problems on schools with large numbers of poor children. The burdens resulting in shifts, if not increases, in responsibilities, due to devolution, among service delivery systems at the local level appear to be substantial, and the ability of these systems to respond adequately is uncertain.

Intergovernmental conflict during the recent process of decentralization does not represent a new phenomenon in these three countries. As discussed in chapter 2, federalist systems can be conceived as political systems designed to address inherent tensions in large, regionally diverse countries (Eaton 2004b). Today, however, the size of the implementation systems, as in health and education, along with well-developed interests among the constituencies in these systems, implies that any systemwide change will be difficult. Furthermore, fiscal constraints, especially in Brazil and Mexico but also in the USA, mean that not all demands for financial resources can be met, further complicating the potential effectiveness of decentralized delivery systems (Almeida 2005b; Kugelmas and Sola 1999). Even though the higher level of federal-subnational transfers and federal budget constraints found in Brazil and Mexico helps explain conflictual relations, the U.S. case clearly indicates that even a well-developed subnational revenue system will not resolve all of the inherent tensions of fiscal federalism and tax base disparities.

### Explaining Cooperation and Innovation

Decentralization and greater subnational autonomy have also led to cooperative and innovative initiatives. A pattern of cooperation and innovation in federal-subnational government policy making in the USA has existed for many decades in a variety of policy arenas. Some examples rely on provisions in the U.S. Constitution, and others result from incentives or requirements in federal legislation. This is also becoming increasingly common in Mexico and, especially, in Brazil. In general, the degree of cooperation and coordination is greater when (1) the policy issue has significant spatial externalities crossing multiple jurisdictions; (2) an appropriate incentive structure is embedded in federal policy; and (3) local governments have inadequate resources to meet needs. But in decentralized systems where local leadership and policy initiative are not found universally, these structural explanations of cooperation must be supplemented. Innovative collaborative policy was found in the form of local governmental actions enhancing the effectiveness of federal initiatives and of local innovative initiatives being adopted by a higher level of government. In the latter, local governments are effectively experimenting with new approaches to policy challenges.

Natural ecological systems, such as river basins or estuary systems, that cross state jurisdictions may require the collaboration of state governments for effective management of the resource. In the USA, compacts, one form of collaboration, establish a contractual relationship between the signatory parties (Florestano 1994). Compacts for river basin management have historically been the most common form, but since 1980 newly formed compacts have been most concerned with environmental matters, especially low-level radioactive wastes (Weissert and Hill 1994), followed by compacts on transportation (Florestano 1994). The Appalachian Regional Commission exemplifies a collaboration of several state governments based on common economic and social problems. The formation of a compact requires voluntary action by states (enabled by the U.S. Constitution). If interests of states coincide and a regional vision is created, the compact strengthens the regional interests in negotiations with the federal government. In Brazil, river basin management has also provided the impetus for collaboration among local governments. During the 1990s, the Union and most states recognized the importance of water management systems. A 1997 law sanctioned important innovations. An integrated, decentralized, and participative management structure was adopted, with the water basin as the territorial unity to implement the national policy. The institutional architecture is based on public management of the water basins, with technical negotiations among state, municipal, and civil society representatives in water basin committees.

Incentive structures embedded in implementation strategies of federal policy can create the conditions for multiple interests at the subnational level to collaborate in innovative and productive ways. In the Mexican social policy arena, opportunities for cooperation are substantial, but they are articulated through carefully circumscribed mechanisms such as the FAISM and the FAFM, which mandate approved areas of possible funding and collaboration. Elsewhere, cooperation occurs in the decentralized federal agency the local PROGRESA or SEDESOL offices, for example. In matters relating to health and child welfare since the 1970s, the nationwide Desarrollo Integral de la Familia (Family Integration Development, DIF) has linked municipal DIFs operated by the municipal president's spouse. But this too has been hierarchically organized from the top down through the spouse of the national president and the spouses of the state governors, respectively.

Few attempts to "municipalize" public education exist in Mexico. Generally, decentralization has gone no further than the state level, and neither municipalities nor parents are effectively engaged. However, certain states such as Guanajuato and Aguascalientes have successfully created specialized teams for educational administration and planning, and this has occasionally encouraged the adoption of novel approaches by state and local organizations (Arnaut 1994). Generally, though, in Mexico unmandated cooperation remains the exception that proves the rule.

In the USA, President George Bush signed the Intermodal Surface Transportation Efficiency Act into law in 1991, as discussed above. In an effort to incorporate environmental measures into federal transportation policy and to shift spending priorities (McCann and Vance 2001), the governance systems of transportation planning were modified and metropolitan planning organizations were granted much greater authority in determining priorities. Public involvement is a formal requirement, and local officials have enhanced standing in transportation and land use planning. This governance structure has been highly effective in creating decision-making forums with multiple governmental and nongovernmental interests present. Federal environmental policies often create the opportunity for subnational collaboration. The implementation of the many environmental programs adopted in the 1960s and 1970s required state and local government agencies to cooperate in both the design of plans and their implementation (Burchell, Listokin, and Galley 2000). The availability of federal funding or assistance may lead to collaboration of local governments that might not otherwise occur.

In some cases, vertical cooperation originates in local initiatives to confront obstacles that can be overcome only through collaboration with other levels of government. In Brazil some local sustainable development programs integrate both rural development and environmental questions with technical assistance provided by federal and state agencies. The technical competence in the Brazilian Agency for Agriculture Research (Empresa Brasileira de Pesquisa Agropecuária—EMBRAPA), which in the earlier period was politically insulated, is now being mobilized and utilized by the local governments.[3] The need for assistance from some municipal initiatives has led to renewal and a sense of purpose for federal agencies that had been in decline since the 1980s (Farah and Barbosa 2000; Farah 2000b).

The approval of federally funded housing programs in a municipality illustrates the challenge and benefits of coordination. The necessary coordination among local, state, and federal agencies is quite difficult, and the approval of a single project may require two years. The Technical Cooperation Agreement established between the special secretary for urban development (Secretaria Especial de Desenvolvimento Urbano) in the President's Office, the secretary of housing of the State of São Paulo, the secretary of housing of the Municipality of São Paulo, and the Federal Savings Bank (Caixa Econômica Federal) attempts to make the access to popular housing less bureaucratic and more flexible by requiring integrative action of the various levels of government and other entities (Cherkezian 2001). Similarly in Mexico, state housing agencies have generally been quite successful in leveraging funds from national housing funds like the National Workers Housing Fund Institute (Instituto Nacional para el Fomento de la Vivienda de los Trabajadores, INFONAVIT) and the National Fund for Low-Income Housing (Fideicomiso Fondo

Nacional de Habitaciones Populares, FONHAPO) as the latter have become increasingly intermediary or "second-line" funding agencies, delegating decision making to the subnational level so long as broad funding guidelines are met. States, too, have become more effective in leveraging funding for housing and urban development from private sector housing actors who are given incentives to provide submarket interest rate loans to state and local housing agencies.

The actions of local governments can enhance the effectiveness of federal policies, as illustrated by a rural credit program in Brazil. The National Program for Development of the Family Farmer (Programa Nacional de Fortalecimento da Agricultura Familiar—PRONAF) was created to expand access to national credit for rural development programs. In response to rules of the federal program that effectively excluded many small farmers from access to this credit, several municipalities sought mechanisms to overcome this barrier (Farah and Barbosa 2000). Creative local action, as distinct from mere administration of federal policies, illustrates how intergovernmental cooperation overcame obstacles faced by the federal government due to inadequate knowledge of local conditions (Farah 2000b).

In the USA, the participation of local governments can also be crucial to the effectiveness of federal policies. In the 1960s the federal government in the USA encouraged the formation of Councils of Governments (COGs) throughout the country. The councils, consisting of representatives of local government in a particular geographical area, were given the responsibility for coordinating the expenditure of federal funds in a region as well as monitoring other federal initiatives. Commitment of local public officers is required for the councils to succeed as venues for regional collaboration. The reform of rural development policy initiated by the federal government, as discussed above, encouraged collaborative relations among federal, state, and local public officials and private and community interests, but without substantial funding (Radin et al. 1996). State and local government participation in such federal initiatives is based not on the level of federal funding but on common interests of diverse actors; but without the participation of local governments the federal policy would fail. These cases reflect the trend of increasing use of networks of policy actors to design and implement policy at the local level (Agranoff and McGuire 1999).

An encouraging outcome of greater local government autonomy has been many examples of local innovation that become models for policy at higher levels of government or for policy of other governments at the same level. In the USA, this phenomenon was recognized and appreciated in terms of state-level initiatives in the early 1900s, when state governments were leaders in social welfare, workers' compensation, vocational education, minimum wage policy, and administrative efficiency (Robertson and Judd 1989, 35–53). In 1932, Supreme Court Justice Louis D. Brandeis wrote, "It is one of the happy incidents of the federal system that a single courageous state may, if its citizens choose, serve as a laboratory, and try novel social and economic experiments."[4] Recent decentralized policy making has again encouraged innovation at the state level, and in a few instances these innovations were adopted at the federal level. The National Performance Review, which is concerned with efficiency in public service delivery, was modeled on an effort first tested in the state of Texas.

In Brazil, inspired by the pioneering example in the city of Niteroi in 1992, the Family Doctor Program (Médico de Família) was implemented initially in a few municipalities as a local initiative, a result of the proposals of health workers and social movements. In the mid-1990s, the Family Doctor Program was adopted as a federal policy and implemented in a decentralized manner under guidelines of the Ministry of Health in most municipalities. Similarly, Bolsa Escola, a program that encourages children to attend school by providing a small stipend to families, was first implemented by municipalities and later incorporated in federal policy and a national program.

Decentralization in each of the three countries has stimulated numerous examples of new or reformed policies and programs that have led to greater cooperation between federal agencies and subnational units. While proper program design and adequate administrative capacity are important for cooperation, the various initiatives for vertical cooperation—whether originating at the federal government level or at the subnational—also presuppose sufficient discretion in subnational government to act autonomously. Given that a certain level of autonomy is required to avoid mere subordination to federal programs, the role of leadership becomes critical. Without effective leadership, cooperative ventures are not likely to emerge. State governments play very different roles across the three countries. In Mexico, where the federal government has not encouraged decentralization within states, only a few states have pursued municipalization of education. In Brazil, through both constitutional provisions and specified federal policy, municipalities have substantial independence from state government. To date, the record of vertical collaboration in the three countries is encouraging, but the critical dependence on local capacity almost ensures that the potential benefits will not be realized in all local governments.

## Relationships among States and Local Governments

An important feature of any federalist system is the degree of collaboration and cooperation among states or among local governments. The U.S. Constitution, for example, includes provisions for governing several types of relationships among states (J. Zimmerman 1994, 1–11). States can cooperate through interstate compacts, uniform laws, and reciprocity statutes, but they are subject to constitutional prohibitions against participation in state alliances and the formation of confederations and treaties. But federalist systems can also vary by the degree to which they generate competition among states and localities (Melo 1996b).

A critical structural element conditioning relations among subnational governments is the degree of their autonomy, and the varying levels of autonomy afforded to local governments in each of the three countries generate quite distinct contexts. For example, jurisdictional boundaries of municipalities established in federal law may be inflexible, eliminating the opportunity for their institutional reconsolidation in a larger jurisdiction. In contrast, in the USA, boundaries of local governments are subject to state laws, and in many states cities have substantial powers to incorporate, to annex land, and even to consolidate with adjacent jurisdictions. Further complicating the comparison of subnational collaboration in the three countries is a significant difference in the nature of local government. Brazil and Mexico have only one kind of local sphere of government—the municipality—whereas the USA has a wide range of local units of government. In all three countries, beyond constitutional restrictions, relationships among states and localities are shaped by political and other extraconstitutional considerations.

The relations across states and localities oscillate between two poles: competition and cooperation. Collaboration among governments can be attractive for both programmatic activities, such as the provision of a particular service, and political action. These forms of collaboration are voluntary, and consequently choices are made by government leaders. As a result, both the nature of the problem or issue and political leadership are critical dimensions of collaboration. But federalist structures can also create ample opportunities for competition among governments, especially for resources and economic investments.

## Competition

In Brazil, recent changes in the federalist system have been accompanied by an increase in competition among state governments and municipalities, as well as by a change in the nature of competition. Prior to the broad pattern of decentralization of the 1980s and 1990s, competition appeared in the political arena and consisted of disputes over privileged access to highly concentrated power and to resources of the federal government. This competition occurred through a clientelistic political game based on the exchange of favors with the federal government. With the decentralization of resources and competencies to subnational governments, the competition was redefined. Facing severe fiscal limitations, state governments could ally themselves with other states for commonly funded programs to attract investments (opting for cooperation) or directly compete with other states, taking advantage of the flexibility afforded to states in the reformed tax system. States and municipalities frequently adopt noncooperative practices in attempting to attract new economic investment and construction through tax abatements and subsidies. This competition, especially among states, can be characterized as a fiscal war, described by some as a predatory competition (Abrucio and Costa 1998). Some states, particularly those losing in the competition, have sought redress in federal courts and in Congress, but without any success.

In Mexico the traditional forms of competition continue to rule. Although states (especially) and municipalities are heavily dependent upon the central government for revenue sharing and complain bitterly about their respective shares, with certain notable exceptions they almost never band together and act in concert. State governments are reluctant to institute surcharges and surtaxes over the federal rate for fear that their neighbors will take advantage of the differential. However, there are clear indications that this is beginning to change: since 2003 CONAGO has met regularly, and governors are beginning to band together—even across party lines—to present a united front to the federal government. In the North, plans are being enacted between three states to collaborate in order to coordinate and develop economic relations with Texas (González Parás 2003).

In the USA competition among governments dominates the field of economic development. The federal government has the constitutional authority to prohibit interstate tariffs, and a state cannot erect barriers or restrict imports from other states that would provide unfair advantage to local firms. Nevertheless, states have a variety of policy instruments for attracting investment. Since the 1930s, Mississippi has utilized a program of tax incentives to attract low-wage manufacturing firms to the state. In the 1970s and 1980s, the competition expanded beyond low-wage manufacturing to sectors such as automobile production, high-tech manufacturing, corporate headquarters, research laboratories, professional sports teams, and transportation facilities (R. Wilson 1993). States compete with each other by providing incentives, especially tax abatements, to make a state more attractive. Often this competition involves additional incentives from local governments. Although the cost-benefit ratio of these activities is widely disputed, elected officials feel compelled to enter the competition.

In the field of economic development, the federalist structure, especially the assignment of revenue bases among governments and discretion in setting rates, shapes the competitive environment differently in the three countries. In all three, federal law prohibits taxes on interstate exports and imports, eliminating this potential instrument of competition. However, the lack of competition around tax incentives in Mexico results from the fact that state and local governments are severely constrained in setting tax rates by federal rules. In Brazil, competition across states has emerged exactly as states and, to a lesser extent, municipalities have gained flexibility in setting tax rates. In the USA, tax incentives for attracting investment are quite varied and substantial in amount as a result of the high degree of autonomy that states have in creating state and local tax systems.

In recent decades new forms of economic competition have emerged in the USA and Brazil (R. Wilson 1993, 2001). For a firm, the attractiveness of an area may depend not only on the tax structure but also on the quality of public services and the quality of the labor force. Governmental jurisdictions that become known as efficient, with a sound economic infrastructure and a well-educated labor force, will become more attractive to firms that value these factors. As the critical information and high-technology sectors grow in all three countries, investment priorities shift to the quality of the labor force and scientific and technological infrastructure, thus providing subnational governments with new instruments for establishing competitiveness. In Brazil the state of São Paulo, in Mexico the state of Nuevo León, and in the USA the state of California are well known for their long-term commitment to higher education, research, and extension services. Funded in large part by state resources, these state government investments have had an extraordinary impact on economic growth.

Competition among states is not a new phenomenon in the three countries, although the forms of competition have changed. Decentralization provides subnational governments a wider range of instruments that can be used to promote development. But the new economy has shifted the basis of competition and created a new economic geography. Old industrial areas in all three countries have been superseded by manufacturing growth in other areas, and the advanced technology service sectors have a relatively dispersed location pattern (R. Wilson 1993). Subnational governments have an opportunity to redefine local economic conditions to a degree unprecedented for many decades.

## Collaboration

Although competition among states and localities prevails in many fields, the enhanced autonomy in policy making of subnational governments creates opportunities for cooperation and joint action. Instances of horizontal collaboration are very new in Mexico and, paradoxically, only began as a result of the political opening that began in the 1990s. (One would have imagined that cooperation between governments coming from the same all-powerful single party would have been the norm, but it never was: PRIístas fought PRIístas as much as they fought members of other parties.) However, as more states and municipalities across the country fell into the hands of the PAN and the PRD, new mechanisms of communication emerged both vertically and horizontally. While the vertical dimension is dominated by conflict, the horizontal dimension offers better prospects for collaboration between governments from the same party and, more recently still, between state executives from all parties.

The organizations built around these efforts at horizontal collaboration vary from informal mechanisms to formal associations. Municipalities have been at the vanguard of the formation of formal associations, such as the Association of Mexican Municipalities (Asociación de Municipios de México, AMMAC, 1994), the Local Authorities Association of Mexico (Asociación de Autoridades Locales de México, AALMAC, 1997), and the Mexican Federation of Municipalities (Federacion Nacional de Ajedrez de México, FENAM, 1998), all with a very strong partisan orientation. The first is composed of municipal governments of the PAN; the second, the PRD; and the third, the PRI. Although they have very clear partisan orientations, these associations have been firm in sharing common goals and also have been critical for placing municipalities on a firmer footing vis-à-vis the federal government and the states. In May 2001 the three associations signed an integration agreement that will further strengthen their presence. There are also important NGO attempts to provide municipal support services (training, information, best practices dissemination, etc.), but, as mentioned above, these have tended to be driven by partisan motives, namely to provide a linkage party to municipal government.

At the state level, collaboration has taken a different shape. While formal associations (akin to the National Governors' Association in the USA, discussed below) were until recently anathema, governors are now becoming increasingly effective in influencing policy decisions by presenting a united front. Once again, governors, primarily those of the opposition who united to confront the almighty federal executive in the 1990s, have taken the initiative (e.g., to demand a larger share of revenue, an effort led by the first PANista governor, of Baja California). After the election of Vicente Fox, governors have become even stronger. In 2001, there was a major debate surrounding a new fiscal policy proposed by Fox, which was eventually rejected by the Congress—an outcome almost unprecedented for a major executive initiative. But far more unprecedented was the fact that governors of all three parties united to resist Fox's proposal and collectively presented an alternative proposal. It was the first time in modern Mexican history that such an event had occurred. Subsequently, there have been a series of national meetings of governors to discuss policy collectively, and this has led to the creation of a standing conference of governors (CONAGO). These meetings, very much like mayors' meetings in municipal associations, provide opportunities to discuss common experiences and problems, share information, and discuss administrative and technological matters. Without question, governors—collectively—are developing a much stronger position in relation to both the federal government and the municipalities. Thus, this case of horizontal collaboration also has important implications for the more problematic vertical collaboration.

In Brazil, associations of municipalities first emerged in the 1940s with the principal purpose of defending the interests of municipalities in negotiations with other levels of government, especially the federal government.[5] Equivalent entities with similar objectives have more recently been formed at the state level. Governors associating in formal or informal ways have been very powerful in influencing policy decisions on the national level. A recent example is the collective position taken by the governors in the debate in the federal legislature in 2003 concerning the reforms of the national welfare system *(reforma previdenciária)* and the tributary system *(reforma tributária)*. These two systems are important for state governments, and the position of the governors influenced the policy reforms.

As the 1988 Constitution reinforced the importance of state and local government, the number of cooperative subnational associations increased. Today, national, regional, and state associations of municipalities and of sector-specific municipal secretaries exist. These entities tend to act in two areas: (1) to register collective positions and pressure the federal and state governments and (2) to provide technical assistance to municipalities to enhance their performance capacity. State associations pursue similar purposes and define joint objectives and strategies in their relation to the federal government. Thus these associations, as in the Mexican case, also affect the vertical dimension of intergovernmental relations.

In the USA, collaboration among state officials notably increased in the 1980s. As the federal government pursued more decentralized policies in the 1970s and 1980s, governors became more assertive, utilizing the National Governors' Association (NGA) as a forum to address common concerns and, most importantly, making it a vehicle for placing state issues on the national policy agenda (Sabato 1983). Established in 1906, the NGA enhanced its policy analysis and lobbying capabilities in the 1970s and 1980s, and its location, in Washington, D.C., acknowledges the continued importance of federal actions on the states. Although governors from the Republican and Democratic parties each had a party caucus, the common interests of governors and the demands for pragmatic solutions reduced the importance of partisanship in federal-state relations. The NGA has been particularly prominent in recent decades, but other national associations of state government officials (the Council of State Governments and the National Association of State Legislatures), associations of local government officials (mayors, city councils, city managers, and county governments), and many professional associations are important forums for the exchange of ideas on policy issues and professional development. These organizations frequently participate in policy discussions at the federal level. An association of western governors, for example, often presents common positions to the federal government on the management of federal lands.

States also collaborate on specific policy and institutional initiatives. Under the U.S. Constitution, interstate compacts can be formed for specific purposes. But in the 1990s, states also became involved in multistate legal actions and adopted uniform state laws (Bowman 2004). This type of cooperation leads to administrative networks outside traditional structures.

The presence of associations of state and local government officials to a certain extent reflects the vitality and maturity of decentralization. As subnational governments become less dependent on rigid systems of federal leadership, one should expect other forms of political activity and association to emerge. Even though such associations may have a strong partisan orientation, they nevertheless reflect the emergence or existence of new centers of political power. In this sense, such associations represent one element of a properly structured federalist system in which strong subnational governments constitute a counterweight to the power of federal government.

*Successful Collaborative Experiences in Brazil: Municipal Consortia*
*and Intersectoral Cooperation*

In Brazil, horizontal cooperation at the local level has led to an interesting innovation with institutional implications: the intermunicipal consortium. Generally composed of small and middle-sized municipalities within a region, intermunicipal consortia have addressed common problems and jointly defined policies and programs (Cruz 2001). Besides jointly formulated policies and programs, the consortia are developing a new model of public management of social policies in microregions, increasing the levels of provision of public services. Consortia can make more efficient use of equipment, have greater flexibility in the purchase of equipment and personnel management, can provide technical cooperation, can undertake joint public works, and can provide either temporary or permanent services (Cruz 2001).

The increase in the competencies of municipal governments in the 1988 Constitution and a July 1998 constitutional amendment authorizing joint management of public services and establishing regulatory procedures for cooperative accords between governmental entities contributed to the rapid emergence of consortia (R. Cunha 2004). The pace of formation of intermunicipal consortia has varied across regions because of the aggressiveness of some state governments in utilizing consortia as policy instruments for the regionalization of services. The frequency of horizontal collaboration also varies by policy area, with consortia most commonly formed in the areas of health (almost 30 percent of all municipalities) and environmental policy (Cruz 2001; Levy 2002, 175–95; Jacobi 2000).

The greater presence of consortia in the field of health reflects the process of reform of health policy pursued by social movements under the leadership of health professionals (Jacobi 2000). These consortia represent a strategy of shared management, one of the principal instruments of the country's new health model, which attempts to replace the previous curative and exclusive orientation of health care provision (Cruz 1992). Partnerships among local governments, as in the Health Consortium of Penapolis, generally involving small and middle-sized municipalities, guarantee the availability of medical specialists and more advanced services. These consortia represent the principal form of regionalization of public services and have proven successful in terms of management and finance and of securing participation of community organizations in planning processes. The case of cooperation and coordination at the local level in health policy departs from the prevailing logic of political fragmentation resulting from partisan and electoral conflicts. The increased presence of intermunicipal consortia in health reflects, in part, the fact that this approach has been incorporated in federal guidelines for the reform of the sector and thereby stimulates collaboration.

Municipal consortia have also organized around environmental concerns. Many environmental issues—such as preservation of hydrological resources, recuperation of native vegetation, agriculture practices of environmental conservation, sewage treatment, water disposal, soil erosion, and garbage systems—require common action of local governments, since the problems cross municipal jurisdictions.[6] The preservation of hydrological resources through municipal consortia became federal policy with the implementation of the National Policy for Hydrological Resources in 1997 and the creation of the National System of Hydrological Resources. This policy encouraged an integrated, participatory, and decentralized management approach. With a water basin as the unit for planning and management, this policy uses consortia and municipal associations as its central instrument and thereby constitutes a qualitative advance in enhancing governance capacity. Today, basin committees are functioning in almost all regions of Brazil, although their scope of responsibilities remains limited due to the difficulty of achieving consistency between the goals of the committees and other public policies affecting hydrological resources (Jacobi 2005; Teixeira and Spink 2005).

Cooperative initiatives are also found in agriculture, rural supply, and agricultural and (especially) forestry production, as well as shared information systems (Centro de Estudos e Pesquisas em Administração Municipal [CEPAM] 2001). In social assistance, even though legislation explicitly refers to consortia, formation of this type of consortium had not been reported in the literature as of 2002. This example suggests that legislation to stimulate the formation of consortia will be most successful in policy areas where some experience has already accumulated, as in the health and environmental fields.

One of the principal challenges to intergovernmental cooperation is found in the metropolitan regions, formal governmental entities introduced in Brazil in 1973. Until 1988, the legal framework of the 1967 Constitution assigned to the federal government the prerogative of creating the metropolitan region entity and to state governments the responsibility of creating the institutions needed to provide common services and to coordinate the various agencies involved in these services. Although representation of the relevant municipalities in advisory councils was prescribed, meaningful participation of local governments was not forthcoming, and the councils served only to ratify decisions of state government (Alves 1998; Montoro 1984). Under the centralized model of metropolitan governance that prevailed until the 1980s, effective horizontal collaboration was not realized, even though municipalities were present on the councils. In terms of vertical relations, despite occasional advances in metropolitan policies, decisions tended to be made by state agencies, with municipalities in a subordinated position.

The Constitution of 1988, however, introduced important changes to the governance structure of the metropolitan regions that allowed greater collaboration among municipalities within the metropolitan regions. First, the Constitution transferred the power to create metropolitan regions from the federal government to state governments, as an element of the broader decentralization policy pursued at that time. Second, these regions were formally recognized as relevant to the "structural-organizational interest of the Brazilian State" (Alves 1998). Several state constitutions contain provisions for co-management of planning and implementation of public functions of common interest rather than assigning sole competency to either state or municipal governments, thereby requiring a coordinated and shared management of services.

Although promising constitutional provisions exist, effective shared management in the metropolitan regions has yet to emerge in practice. The reformed management structure has not produced significant advances in terms of effective responses to the metropolitan problems or in terms of open and participatory governance. The actions of the metropolitan regions tend to be sectoral, especially in transportation policy, and do not incorporate participation of all the municipalities within the region.

In contrast to the limited achievement of the formal metropolitan regions, in recent years some municipalities within metropolitan areas have entered into coordinated, multisector initiatives with neighboring municipalities, using the consortium model. These initiatives tend to emphasize local development led by the public sector and have stimulated new forms of cooperation among public entities, among public and private entities, and among private entities. The initiatives attempt to address several dimensions of current urban crises, including unemployment, social exclusion, urban conviviality, public safety, and socioenvironmental sustainability.

In response to the ineffectiveness of the metropolitan policy system, seven municipalities in metropolitan São Paulo formed a consortium to address urgent regional problems, including industrial disinvestments and rapid growth in unemployment (Fujiwara, Alessio, and Farah 1999). The consortium represented the municipalities on issues of common interest in negotiations with private and public sector entities in country and abroad. The consortium was authorized to plan, adopt, and execute projects intended to promote, improve, or control the water supply, waste treatment and disposal, and physical infrastructure in the region. The mechanisms for this regional planning included acquisition of consulting services, sponsorship of studies, and implementation and monitoring of activities. The principal focus, however, was the development of a regional identity and actions of interest to the member municipalities. The consortium changed the prevailing practice of local politics, breaking the cycle of clientelistic practices and exchange of favors among governments, and improved the interactions of the group with other government and social actors.

This consortium evolved into the Council of the Greater ABC, a forum composed of the seven municipalities and representatives of the state legislature, state executive, and civil society. The council provides an example of innovative institutional engineering in response to the challenges of regional governance that protects the specific characteristics of participating municipalities. This cooperation addresses multiple objectives, including the reconstruction of public space, preservation of natural resources, and improvement of the region's competitiveness. In this and other experiences, local political leadership has been fundamental to success. But this example also illustrates the limited success in resolving metropolitan questions in Brazil and the precarious nature of intergovernmental collaboration in these regions. In spite of the council, no government entity effectively addresses the problems of the greater metropolitan São Paulo and its more than eighteen million inhabitants. The council includes only seven of the thirty-nine municipalities in the metropolitan area; for the others, no structure for metropolitan governance exists.

### Intermunicipal Collaboration in Mexico: Early Days

As stated earlier, in Mexico consortia of municipal governments do not exist, although there are recent efforts—partisan and nonpartisan—to encourage collaboration in information sharing, training programs, and organized lobbying. But formal intergovernmental executive collaboration is anathema. Even where several municipalities make up a single metropolitan area—as in Guadalajara and Monterrey—the opportunities and incentives to collaborate are virtually nil, even among governments of the same party, and sometimes especially among them. In terms of executive cooperation, there are no municipal consortia in Mexico: *municipio libre* (autonomy) almost always means freedom to go it alone, not to work in concert.

It is at the metropolitan level in Mexico that some discussion of cooperation has begun to emerge. While the National Human Settlements Law provides for planning cooperation in conurbation areas (usually metropolitan), executive authority for such spatial regional entities does not exist—these bodies are primarily consultative. Metropolitan cooperation has been taken the furthest in Mexico City (Ward 1998). Here, governance for a metropolitan area of over twenty million people is almost equally divided between two federal entities—the State of Mexico and the Federal District—each with its elected governor or equivalent (*jefe de gobierno* in the Federal District). The latter is further subdivided into sixteen elected subunits, while the metropolitan area corresponding to the State of Mexico comprises no less than twenty-eight separate municipalities, which make up a raft of governments led by all three major parties and which have little or nothing to do with each other.

However, the imperative of planning and governing a city of this size across two major federal jurisdictions and almost fifty local ones has begun to generate discussion and debate (Ward 1998; Aguilar and Ward

2003). The dilemma is a classical federal one: namely, how to create an empowered single executive metropolitan authority within a federalist system (Ward 1998). Arguments for a single superstate of the metropolitan area are politically unacceptable, since its adoption would dramatically reduce the powers of the State of Mexico and create a major political imbalance. Attempts to collaborate through municipal consortia have failed, as have various levels and degrees of metropolitan consultation and collaboration. If planning and metropolitan cooperation are ultimately to be achieved in Mexico City, they will probably require the following: (1) an identification of principal areas of metropolitan collaboration (transportation, environment, infrastructure, and policing); (2) integrated executive planning at the highest levels of State of Mexico governors and the *jefe de gobierno* in the Federal District; and (3) legislative approval of collaborative plans by the respective congresses (the Mexico State Congress and the D.F. Legislative Assembly, respectively). If this can be achieved in places like Mexico City and other large metropolitan areas, then the federal mold may have been partially broken, but in a way that is flexible and empowered and that sits relatively comfortably within the Mexican federal tradition.

Within the metropolitan area there is also need for decentralization as well as collaboration between constituent governments to avoid a balkanization of local authorities. Perhaps here the concept of subsidiarity is helpful. Normally conceived as the desire to pass as many functions as possible down to the local level that can best be resolved at that level, in fact the philosophy of subsidiarity works the other way around: namely, that all functions of government should be local, and only those that can best be achieved at a higher level should be passed *up* the hierarchy to a higher level. In the context of Mexican federalism the latter conceptualization is unlikely, even though it is essentially a Catholic tradition that was embraced by PANista philosophers at the party's inception in the 1940s. If subsidiarity and cooperation between local governments are to occur in metropolitan areas, they will probably have to happen through constitutional change or through the general realization of the imperatives of collaboration to survive. But Mexico is not there yet.

### Fragmentation Forces Collaboration: The Case of the USA

In 2000, the USA had over eighty thousand local governments, including cities, counties, townships, school districts, and other forms of special districts, in which officials of the jurisdictions were elected and had the power to levy taxes. This highly fragmented system generates the need for collaboration among governmental entities, and the country has a rich and diverse history of collaboration. Cities may cooperate on major infrastructure projects of mutual interest. For example, the Dallas–Fort Worth airport was constructed and is now operated through an agreement of two cities whose history was largely one of rivalry. Collaboration is common between cities and counties through consolidated or co-managed service systems for health, emergency medical services, social services, fire services, and others. In spite of the incentive for competition in the field of economic development, examples of cooperation can be observed where neighboring cities or the county and special districts collaborate with chambers of commerce, public-private partnerships, utility companies, foundations, and other local NGOs. These relations may be formal, as when binding agreements to plan or share in the delivery of service are established, or they can be more informal interactions among partners (Agranoff and McGuire 1999, 352). Although many specialists argue that even further collaboration is needed in such a highly fragmented system of local government, collaboration appears most frequently as a pragmatic response to a specific problem. Since these arrangements are voluntary, trust and political leadership are essential for their creation.

In the major metropolitan areas, because of geographical proximity, the challenge of multiple fragmented governmental jurisdictions is most acute (Altshuler et al. 1999; Weir 1996; Swanstrom 2001). In Houston over four hundred governmental entities have elected officials with the power to tax. Among the challenges to governance being faced in metropolitan regions are rising disparities in both fiscal and socioeconomic conditions between central cities and surrounding suburban jurisdictions; increased global competition, which threatens the economic base of inner cities and inner suburbs; and urban sprawl, which is increasingly threatening the sustainability of the physical environment of urban communities (Mitchell-Weaver and Miller 2000, 851). Transportation planning in metropolitan areas is quite common, having emerged under requirements and funding inducements of the federal government. Similarly, the Air Quality Control Board of Southern California has substantial power to force cooperation among the multitude of local governments. The lack of attainment of federal environmental standards led to the formation of this body.

Despite some few exceptions, examples of metropolitan coordination and cooperation are surprisingly rare. A few metropolitan areas have adopted forms of metropolitan government (Sawitch and Vogel 1996). Others have adopted more narrow forms of collaboration such as metropolitan revenue sharing, "smart growth" strategies, and the matching of job training, housing, and transportation needs to trends of employment expansion. But with the lack of success in resolving these lingering policy issues, which may well become more intense in the future, more creative responses to metropolitan challenges may appear. In the field of growth management, for example, a number of states, under leadership of governors from both the Democratic and Republican parties, have adopted growth management policies that encourage the cooperation of local governments (R. Wilson and Paterson 2003).

New forms of intergovernmental relations are emerging between subnational governments in the USA and Mexico. Border issues, long the domain of national foreign services, are increasingly being addressed by state or local governments along the border. The management of the Rio Grande basin involves a binational commission with great autonomy. But common problems of pollution, transportation, employment mobility, and health services have led to subnational government collaboration across the national boundary. NAFTA has had a substantial effect on encouraging cooperation of local governments on both the Mexican and the Canadian borders.

## Conclusions: New Patterns of Intergovernmental Relations

### A New Federalist Pact for Policy Making?

This chapter has documented major recent changes in intergovernmental systems in Brazil, Mexico, and to a lesser extent the USA. In spite of quite different historical legacies and starting points, the last two decades of the twentieth century witnessed parallel processes of decentralization. The relations between the different levels of governments vary markedly and need to be understood against the backdrop of the particulars and differences within each country and often within different policy areas. For example, decentralization in the USA has focused largely on federal-state relations, with virtually no attention given to federal-local relations. In Brazil and Mexico, in contrast, greater emphasis has been placed on strengthening the role of the municipalities. In each of the three countries, however, processes of decentralization and resulting changes in intergovernmental relations have contributed to a strengthening of subnational governments. In spite of the notable differences among the countries, innovative initiatives have emerged in many fields of public policy. In the USA and Brazil and, to a lesser extent, in Mexico, state or municipal governments have found new ways to address economic and social challenges.

The policy perspective adopted in this research provides a unique view on change in the federalist system, especially in terms of intergovernmental relations. In most policy areas discussed in this chapter, federal governments and subnational governments share responsibilities—if not in policy formulation, certainly in policy implementation. In Brazil and Mexico, the broad use of federal-state transfers and the legacy of national delivery systems mean that intergovernmental relations will be key to decentralization of public policy. But even in the USA, where there is less dependence on federal transfers, public policy is a shared responsibility. The variation in the nature of federal-subnational relations in specific policy areas, across countries and even within countries, results largely from pragmatic political and administrative considerations rather than ideological ones. In addition, at the subnational level, many instances have been observed where governments respond to policy demands in light of inaction by other levels of government. The consortia of municipalities in Brazil reflect the same pragmatic approach to responding to needs given inadequate resources. Although many promising instances of such initiatives have been identified, it is clear that not all subnational governments will necessarily have the will or capacity to engage in innovation.

From a policy perspective, an important difference in the three countries relates to the set of principal policy actors influencing federal-subnational relations. In Mexico decentralization has come largely from an initiative of the executive to "loosen" the reins of power, in combination with a rise in democratically elected subnational governments from a range of parties, whereas in the USA a range of actors have been important. In some policy arenas, such as economic development, governors have acted in response to inaction at the federal level. However, in social policy, Congress has played the central role, though sometimes nudged into action by the executive—as under Reagan's New Federalism and Clinton's New *(sic)* Federalism. Further efforts by the U.S. Congress and the executive branch to decentralize federal-state relations are unlikely, although the Supreme Court may become a venue for the fight for stronger states' rights. In Brazil, the governors had a central role in the 1980s as leaders of reform. More recently, the mayors have also assumed an important role as both democratically elected officials and chief executives of increasingly important service delivery systems now found in municipal government. State caucuses of deputies and senators, representing state interests in the national congress, can affect the vertical relationship between federal and subnational governments and provide another degree of subnational independence (Gibson 2004).

Notwithstanding the trend toward enhanced roles for subnational governments, federal governments continue to assume critical policy functions in all three countries. National standards and guidelines in areas such as environmental and labor laws and federal revenue-sharing programs are at the heart of subnational government infrastructure and social programs, especially in Mexico and Brazil. Many policy sectors continue to be characterized by a very strong federal presence in formulating policies and programs, controlling funds, establishing performance requirements, and coordinating the action of the subnational units.

While in the USA federal government interference is more constrained and firmly resisted by states, in Brazil and Mexico it is the pattern, being present in almost every area of public policy. This difference between the USA and the other two case studies is a by-product of the *status quo ante,* namely the federalist model that preceded the recent drive toward decentralization. The federalist system in the USA has traditionally been highly decentralized, at least compared to Brazil and Mexico, with the states having a great amount of autonomy since the birth of the country. In the USA, to decentralize is to further enhance the relative autonomy of the subnational governments, and the term *devolution* is often used, suggesting a process of returning to the states a level of autonomy they held in the past. In contrast, the term *devolution* is inappropriate in the very centralized federal systems that purposively evolved in Brazil and Mexico to establish the political control necessary for industrialization and development. On the other hand, decentralization is a new process that demands institution building as well as the consolidation of new practices. These different traditions explain the more extensive presence of regulatory federalism in Brazil and Mexico than in the USA.

In Brazil, provisions in the 1988 Constitution created a framework of substantial decentralization in several policy areas. In large part, these provisions have been implemented. Resources and responsibilities have been decentralized, primarily to municipalities, with a lesser role for state-level policy making. In some areas, states have acted aggressively in taking advantage of new autonomy, as demonstrated in the fiscal incentives competition. An impressive expansion of collaboration among municipalities has occurred, especially on health and environmental issues. Despite disputes over the adequacy of federal transfers to local governments, the subnational state in Brazil has become more capable. Nevertheless the challenge remains daunting given that the county has over 5,500 municipalities and strong regional differences.

Decentralization in intergovernmental relations in Mexico has progressed less than in Brazil, limited by a variety of constitutional provisions and by the historical weakness and incapacity of municipalities. Although the bureaucratic practices and traditional politics fostered by a hegemonic party are an important legacy to be addressed in the current situation, these should further weaken as competitive politics at the subnational level intensifies. Incentives for local government action remain highly dependent on federal fiscal supports and priorities. Of the three countries, subnational governments in Mexico have the most limited level of autonomy in policy making and revenue generation, a situation exacerbated by fiscal austerity in the 1990s.

At the beginning of the new century, the policy-making and implementation function of federalism in the USA is more decentralized than at any point since the 1950s (Bowman and Krause 2003; for the 1990s, see Cho and Wright 2004). Decentralization has focused largely on federal-state relations and the result of federal action (both executive and congressional), as well as on activist governors. Federal transfers to local government declined substantially in the 1980s, and subnational governments have had to expand their revenue-generating capabilities. The pendulum, however, seems to be changing its direction, if not moving to greater centralization, at least in some policy areas. The consensus around decentralization in Congress is increasingly subject to intraparty disputes, and the attempt to seek federal support for fiscal difficulties of states and localities during the early years of the new century was not successful (Krane 2003, 2004). The homeland defense policy (Kettl 2004) and federal requirements for educational testing (McGuinn 2005) demonstrate the movement toward a more aggressive federal role. State-local intergovernmental relations have followed a distinct trajectory. A deep and long-held tradition of local control in the public sector is widespread, and state governments set the powers and responsibilities of local governments. During the more recent phase of decentralization, state-local government relations have not been significantly modified. Adjustments in these relations continue in school finance equalization, where state governments must ameliorate the effects of tax base disparities in school systems, and growth management, where states are becoming increasingly disposed to force cooperation of local governments.

The U.S. system expects local governments and populations to bear directly a large share of the expense of providing governmental services. Brazil seems to be pursuing this goal, at least at the municipal level. In Mexico, the fiscal element of decentralized systems remains relatively undeveloped. Although arguments about efficiency of redistribution in federal revenue systems to overcome disparities in local tax bases are not irrelevant, shades of difference in fiscal decentralization in the three countries appear in the attitudes toward generation of local revenues. Even though the subnational state in Brazil is consolidating its fiscal capacity as the result of both automatic federal transfers, unlike the previously negotiated transfers of the centralized system, and increases in own-source revenues, local governments remain constrained by the imposition of federal priorities and guidelines that accompany the federal transfers. In the USA, recent shifts in federal transfers have had the effect of shifting focus from relations between federal and local governments to relations between state and local governments. In Mexico, regular federal aid transfers support municipal governments, but a high dependency on these transfers has resulted in slow progress in development of own-source revenues, thereby limiting local autonomy.

## Performance: Innovation and Constraints

In Brazil, increased efficiency and efficacy of public policies, administrative reform of social policies, and reductions in public spending were among the principal state reform objectives that the Cardoso government announced in 1995. Although not fully implemented, the proposed changes in social policy depended directly on the restructuring of intergovernmental relations and the creation of a federal system of cooperation and coordination (Afonso, Rodrigues, and Araújo 2000; Neves 2000; Arretche and Rodrigues 1999). The venue for local decision making, defined by the Constitution of 1988, creates the opportunity for cooperative actions among levels of government and state agencies that are less asymmetrical than they were in the system of social policy existing prior to the 1980s. This constitutes an important dimension of recent change in intergovernmental relations. Although the Lula administration remains committed to many of the same social policies, the restructuring remains incomplete and has progressed unevenly, subject to systematic restrictions in social spending related to the priority assigned to macroeconomic stability.

The subordination of local governments to federal guidelines in Brazil has been interpreted as an indication of a managed decentralization process that violates the spirit of collaboration and cooperation. But the action of the federal government can also be understood as an effort to coordinate the process, which otherwise would be highly fragmented and would incur the risk of increasing existing regional inequalities and the great differences in financial, technical, and political capacities among municipalities. Decentralization in Brazil is ongoing, but in spite of its different rhythm in different sectors and regions it has already contributed significantly to the policy-making process. On the other hand, its limits and challenges are today more visible and explicit than in the years immediately following democratization, when the ideological climate associated decentralization with democracy and policy effectiveness. Today the need for some coordination from the higher levels of government to overcome excessive fragmentation and substantial inequalities between regions is recognized. It is also evident that the consolidation of democracy and autonomous government at the local level requires a long process of political and technical capacity building among segments of civil society as well as public officials to avoid capture of political processes by the old clientelistic mechanisms.

The pace of decentralization in Mexico has been somewhat slower than in Brazil, and as a result changes in governmental performance resulting from shifts in intergovernmental relations are hard to assess, even in those areas that have gone furthest, such as education and health (Robles 2006; Homedes and Ugalde 2006b). On some measures subnational government has clearly been strengthened, but continuing resistance in federal agencies and slowly developing local governmental capacity, especially in terms of financial resources, still render an assessment of performance premature. A recent study of some thirty municipalities asked whether government performance in Mexico is being shaped most systematically by (1) competitive elections; (2) entrepreneurial leadership; (3) state modernization; or (4) pressures from civil society. It found that all were closely interrelated but that the leadership of public officials appeared to be crucial in explaining how municipalities adjusted to the newfound responsibilities; this leadership and entrepreneurship was given meaning through competitive elections and, iteratively, further spurred modernization of the state apparatus (Grindle 2007, 171–72). The study found that, at least in part, local entrepreneurship was able to thrive because of the relative weakness of state institutional structures. State modernization was demand driven by local officials rather than being supply driven.

It appears safe to conclude, however, that in Mexico, in contrast to Brazil, the changes to date have not generated the same level of enthusiasm and commitment to decentralized policy making, especially among state executives suspicious that they must, in effect, do more with less. Whether this is a reflection of inflexible laws and rules or bureaucratic and political culture, the pace of change is slow.

In the USA, one of the criticisms raised against decentralization in the 1980s was that decentralized systems would generate competition among states, resulting in poor policy decisions, the so-called "race to the bottom," and that disparities in tax bases would result in inadequate service provision in some states. As one might expect in a large federalist system, instances where these fears were realized can be found. However, in large measure, states and local governments have performed well. One study of welfare reform, environmental regulation, and state competition for corporate charters concluded that "states can do better than the federal government as creators, managers, and financiers of certain programs" (Lorch 1998, 159). A recent study of local implementation of reform found that effectiveness can be improved if the local network of professionals have the right set of expertise and entrepreneurial instincts and if increased authority is actually devolved to the implementation networks (Cho et al. 2005). Although the performance of decentralized systems in the USA will continue to be disputed, the opportunity afforded by decentralized systems for state and local governments to serve as laboratories for public policy experimentation and to adapt to local circumstances is a quite positive feature. Nevertheless, it has become clear in the USA that a federal presence, if not federal leadership, is needed even in decentralized systems. The federal government can prevent the more pernicious race-to-the-bottom outcomes and ensure that issues of national importance are addressed in a coordinated fashion.

In all three countries we have found that the issue of very-large-city (metropolitan) governance and policy is an unresolved challenge and a shortcoming of decentralized federalist systems. The nature of infrastructure and natural systems (water and air), especially the geography of these systems, does not follow the jurisdictional boundaries of local governments in the large metropolises. Furthermore, the incentive structure for collaboration among local governments appears inadequate. Given continued urbanization, metropolitan governance will be a challenge not just in the great metropolises—Mexico City, New York, São Paulo—but increasingly in second-tier cities. Local governmental jurisdictions are ill designed and produce governance structures that are ill prepared to respond adequately given the multi-jurisdictional nature of many service delivery systems, such as water supply and transportation. Decentralization in the three countries may in fact be aggravating the problems faced in metropolitan areas. While it is still early days in terms of academic analysis, the effects on New Orleans and the surrounding coastal areas of Hurricane Katrina in August 2005 demonstrated how quickly these different overlapping linkages—or the "mild chaos" of intergovernmental relations, as Deil Wright (2005) described it—can break down disastrously, such that chaos loses its mild character.

### Explaining Change in Intergovernmental Relations and Policy Making

Subnational governments in the three countries have become empowered largely as result of actions taken by their respective federal governments. In other words, the "levers" (constitutional, fiscal, regulatory) to change relationships are held largely by federal governments. A number of pressures were being brought to bear on national leaders and decision makers for decentralization, but in broad terms formal national-level decisions have been decisive in structuring the decentralized systems. Even in the case of permissive federalism, as found in the USA, the lack of federal action has encouraged state governments to take initiative in several policy areas. However, in the three countries, relatively few instances of subnational governments acting in a truly autonomous manner were found.

The ability of governments to adapt to changes in federal-subnational relations is, in part, shaped by historical legacies. In the USA, the historical legacy of strong state governments throughout the nineteenth and early twentieth centuries and the expanded state government role in the implementation of federal policy in the 1950s and 1960s have made recent decentralization relatively easy to accommodate. In Mexico, the legacy of centralization works in opposite direction, with subnational governments lacking the capability to expand policy-making functions. In Brazil, the historical legacy of federalism is more complex. In spite of centralizing tendencies since the 1950s and especially after 1964, preexisting capacity in the subnational state, at least in more prosperous states and cities, has provided a foundation for a fairly rapid improvement in capacity needed to meet new responsibilities. An example of this incipient structure is found in the public health sector, where professionals from all levels of government and from the nongovernment sectors worked toward decentralization for several decades.

This variation in the nature of the federal-subnational relations in specific policy areas, across countries and even within countries, results largely from pragmatic political and administrative considerations rather than ideological ones (Almeida 2005a, 2005b). In addition, at the subnational level, many instances have been observed where governments respond to policy demands in light of inaction by other levels of government. The development of intermunicipal consortia in Brazil reflects the same pragmatic approach to responding to needs given inadequate resources. Although many promising instances of such initiatives have been identified, it is clear that not all subnational governments will necessarily have the will or capacity to engage in innovation.

In terms of changes in intergovernmental fiscal systems, the levels and regularity of federal transfers have strengthened subnational governments in Mexico and, especially, Brazil. The substantial discretion afforded to subnational governments in the USA in the application of several programmatic federal transfers is not common in Brazil and Mexico. In addition, the level of self-finance of subnational government in the USA is much higher than in Brazil and Mexico. One result of the variation is the degree of competition through tax incentives, which are much more extensively used in the USA.

The relations across states and local governments in Brazil, Mexico, and the USA demonstrate both competitive and cooperative dimensions. The frequency and intensity of both competition and collaboration among subnational governments in Mexico, however, are significantly lower than in the other two countries, a phenomenon explained in part by the historical legacy of past PRI domination and a less-than-conducive legal framework. Competitive strategies and practices occur most frequently in economic development policy and have become more frequently adopted with decentralization. In Brazil, the fiscal incentive war, principally among states but also among municipalities, became a matter of federal concern in the 1990s.

Collaboration occurs in associations of state or local governments intent on political negotiation with higher levels of government and in programmatic consortia where several localities unite to address common problems. Although states cooperate politically to negotiate with the federal government, the number of programmatic collaborations is low except in the USA, where collaboration has been encouraged by a number of federal initiatives. Programmatic collaborations among localities, however, are numerous in Brazil and the USA. Inadequate resources in a single local government contribute to this form of collaboration. Furthermore, the nature of the problem can be a crucial factor in collaboration: some issues, such as the management of hydrological resources in a water basin or the prevention of air pollution, cannot be solved by a locality by itself. In Brazil and the USA, the extent of local cooperation varies among states, suggesting that state government plays a role in stimulating such activity. There is also variation between sectors, reflecting the differing importance of cooperation in the agenda of each public policy arena. The legal framework constitutes an additional stimulus that can induce cooperation. Finally, since subnational collaboration is largely voluntary, and thus fragile, political leadership is a critical stimulus.

# Government and Citizens

*The Changing Nature of Civil Society*

## Peter K. Spink, Victoria E. Rodríguez, Peter M. Ward, and Robert H. Wilson

The nature and quality of governmental action in a democracy depend critically on the relationship between citizens and government, which in turn depends on the mechanisms available for interaction, the organizational capacity of citizens to voice their concerns and wishes, and the willingness of governments to listen. In viewing the state as a set of institutions and social relations, most of which are sanctioned and supported by a legal system that controls a spatial territory, Guillermo O'Donnell (2005) argues for the need to take account of three dimensions: first, the state as a set of bureaucracies and agencies with responsibilities to achieve or protect some aspect of the public or general good; second, the state as a legal system that along with the bureaucracy is the ultimate guarantor of the predictability of the greater public good; and third, the state as seeking to be a focus of collective identity for all or most of the inhabitants. Modern democracies grew up within this notion of a nation-state and not outside it. The socially constructed notion of *citizenship* is a consequence of this process and not a precursor; it is both an expression of rights and at the same time an ascriptive reminder of the nonvoluntary nature of territoriality. How far any state has gone in advancing along these three dimensions will vary considerably, and, as O'Donnell (2005) rightly concluded:

In Latin America, we can confidently, albeit sadly, assert that we are dealing with states that in most cases score low in these three dimensions. The poor efficacy of their bureaucracies has been amply documented. The scarce and biased penetration of their legal system has been less noted, although I and more recently other authors have registered it. However the most ignored of these deficiencies is the third: the low, and often decreasing, credibility of these states as true enactors of the common good for their nations. (26)

The (re)turn to civil society in the development literature of the 1990s was in part a response to this same concern and its implicit question: Who, then, speaks and acts for the common good, and how can state credibility and performance be improved? As we have noted elsewhere in this volume, there is a common (if rather "rosy") assumption that decentralization improves government-citizen relations by bringing government closer to the day-to-day issues that constitute the territorially rooted features of collective life and that the government is by nature good and seeks to serve in the widest public interest. Of course, even a moment's reflection should suggest that this is not necessarily the case and that particular issues, actors, and moments in history can combine in very uncertain ways, especially within the federal model. Would the U.S. civil rights movement have been better off in the South if it had not been able to count on centralized federal support but instead had depended upon local state policy makers? Would Brazil's indigenous population have made any progress in land demarcation if the issue had been left to state and municipal policy makers? And would Mexico's decentralization process have occurred from the bottom up without federal executive leadership to pursue an overhaul of article 123 of the Constitution? We doubt it. On the other hand, in some areas of action decentralization has clearly facilitated the voicing of concerns and progress on issues that address the general good.

In the same way, the assumption that "civil society" offers some a priori leadership in these processes must also be considered with caution. Does democracy strengthen civil society or does civil society strengthen democracy, and what role does decentralization play in shaping the relationship? Or are they independent of each other? Indeed, we might ask, what *is* civil society in our different countries, and *whose* civil society is it? In this chapter we examine these issues in relation to two broad questions. First, given the current trend of decentralization and democratic opening, what is happening to subnational civil society? Second, is civil society a leader or a laggard in relation to decentralization? As we will show, the situation is rather different in each country.

We begin with a brief discussion of civil society, citizenship, and rights to identify some of the aforementioned differences across our three case study countries, which will partly be reflected in the empirical data presented on the existence and activities of different types of associations and interest groups. This is followed by observations on forums and movements that are emerging from within civil society itself. The chapter concludes with some observations on political culture and party membership. We conclude that overall there is some call for optimism regarding civil society's presence within the different arenas and action spaces of the subnational state, but that many doubts remain, especially regarding the effective institutionalizing of broad public spheres of participation and civic action.

## Civil Society: Framing the Discussion

Civil society is not a social given. Rather, at least in Western societies, it is the result of the slow and many-stranded historical construction of the idea itself: that of spaces and places for public discussion of the common good, which have taken such varying forms over time as premedieval monasteries, early scholastic centers and universities, the guilds, merchant associations, and city leagues of the medieval period, and the discussion clubs and literary and scientific societies of the nineteenth century.

In the early nineteenth century civil society was defined in terms of collective values and civility (Ferguson [1767] 1969). A strong civil society, represented in those days by those who had land or professions, was seen as a necessary counterweight to the central power, usually vested in the monarch or latterly in the republican state. For Marxist social reformers at the end of the nineteenth century, the state was seen as a reflection of the violence that existed within civil society, and the end of the state could be achieved only by the reabsorption of political society into a transformed civil society. For Antonio Gramsci, writing in the journal *Ordine Nuevo* in 1917 about the factory occupations and the workers' committees in Turin, civil society was *the* privileged place within which to fight for political rights, mobilization, active education, and the transformation of conditions (Gramsci 1994). Time and time again, throughout his prison reflections in the 1930s, he returned to the theme of the organic capacity for organization, leadership, and intellectual development that emerges within civil society and of the battle for hegemony over the matrix of ideological and cultural relations in and around the organizations and institutions involved in the transmission of dominant values (Gramsci 1971). In a similar vein, a new generation of trade union leaders in Brazil would, toward the end of the military period, "take over" the state-regulated trade union structure and use it as a voice for industrial negotiations and later as the basis for a new political party.

By the latter part of the twentieth century, a new concept of civil society was emerging, influenced by democratization events in Eastern Europe and Latin America, the growing presence of issue-based social movements, the rise of NGOs, the emergence and modernization of demographic giants such as China and India, and the intensification of religious fundamentalism. This version recognized conflict but for the most part also recognized the negotiated order of modern democracy (Jean Cohen and Arato 1992; Keane 1998; Hall 1995). It focused on the autonomous organization of society and envisioned a public sphere of intermediate level association that would be independent of the state, political society, and economic society; could be created through self-constitution and self mobilization; would include family, associations, social movements, and forms of public communication; and would be institutionalized through law, thereby allowing association and the existence of collective rights and customs. As Jürgen Habermas (1996) so aptly put it, "The core of civil society comprises a network of associations that institutionalize problem-solving discourse on questions of general interest inside the framework of organized public spheres. These discursive designs have an egalitarian, open form of organization that mirrors essential features of the kind of communication around which they crystallize and to which they lend continuity and permanence" (367).

In the practice of everyday governance, echoes of all concepts of civil society make themselves present—drawn on in different ways by different groups of actors at different moments (Ehrenberg 1999; Edwards 2002). For example, civil society organizations and associations have been a central element in U.S. democracy throughout the country's history, as de Tocqueville ([1835] 1969) enthusiastically noted. The existence of "conflicting factions," as they were called in the Federalist Papers (no. 10), was a key concern at the Constitutional Convention. Equally, the importance of community solidarity and individual civil disobedience expressed by such authors as Thoreau ([1849] 1967) left little doubt about the need for checks and balances between the state and civil society.

If the nature of civil society in the USA has traditionally been both broad and deep, in Latin America all too often—at least until relatively recently—it has been severely circumscribed by a lack of democratic and human rights, as well as by direct acts of repression. Organizations and associations can be bombed, their leaders threatened, and the law used to make it difficult for them to receive financing and support. In general the situation has been worse in rural areas than in the larger towns and cities. This situation has changed since the late 1970s as societies began the slow shift from militarized bureaucratic authoritarianism to the beginning of more open and participatory democracies. It has been consistently argued that the democracies present in Latin America before the widespread militarization of the mid-1960s to mid-1980s were characterized, not by any clear and independent public space, but by what Philip Oxhorn (1995) has called *controlled inclusion*. In Brazil, such inclusion was achieved by the incorporation of different groups into the state apparatus to avoid independent action that might threaten the state— Getulio Vargas's labor laws and state-supported trade unions are a case in point. It was the state that determined who would be the social actors and how they would be included (Avritzer 1994). Mexico, too, although not a military regime, was widely recognized as "inclusionary authoritarian" insofar as the PRI, dominant for more than seventy years, was able to elaborate an hierarchical and often authoritarian structure of control and mobilization that included almost all major labor groups and popular organizations. In effect, therefore, while the public space remained open, it was carefully controlled, with little need for overt repression by the state.

In both Brazil and Mexico democratization was marked by the emergence of a variety of social organizations within a more independent social space: these included more autonomous professional bodies and trade unions and new political parties; NGOs; and social movements, which in Brazil often had their roots in the Catholic Church's *comunidades eclesiais de base* (CEBs). Throughout the dictatorship, within the institutional and physical sanctuary of the church, these small and local rural and urban social organizations had met regularly to talk about social conditions from the perspective of liberation theology (Gutiérrez 1975) and were perhaps, along with a few universities, the only significant part of the public sphere to counter the oppression of the dictatorship. At their peak they numbered some eighty thousand separate groups, but the cost was also high. It is estimated that by 1979, 122 religious and 273 lay workers had been imprisoned—and usually tortured—and four priests had been murdered (Rocha 1997). Among these emerging issue-based movements were several linked to rural questions, out of which would emerge the Landless Rural Workers' Movement (Movimento dos Trabalhadores Rurais Sem Terra, MST) (Scherer-Warren and Krischke 1987; Sader 1998; Fernandes 1994; Alvarez, Dagnino, and Escobar 1998; Stedile and Fernandes 1999; Branford and Rocha 2002). The CEBs lost some of their focus as a result of efforts to involve them in the 1988 constitutional process, but they would emerge again with the antipoverty committees that exploded on the national scene in the early 1990s (Gohn 2000).[1]

The consolidation in the postauthoritarian period of a civil society in Brazil and of an increasingly democratic Mexico seems to be primarily associated with three factors: (1) the emergence of modern and democratic social actors; (2) the dissemination by these actors of the idea of free association within the relation between the state and society, supported by a relatively unfettered press; and (3) the formation of new legal, political, and public structures capable of providing institutional support for the sociocultural concerns of civil society. But, as might be expected, this development has also been a process in which those better placed to represent would at times extend their existing roles, often to the detriment of other unheard voices. The resultant pushing and shoving reflects the "creative chaos" that Ralf Dahrendorf (1996) describes as a feature of civil society:

> Civil society describes the associations in which we conduct our lives, and which owe their existence to our needs and initiative rather than to the State. Some of these associations are highly deliberative and sometimes short-lived, like sports clubs or political parties. Others are founded in history and have a very long life, like churches or universities. Still others are the place in which we work and live—enterprises, local communities. The family is an element of civil society. The criss-crossing network of such associations—their creative chaos as one might be tempted to say—make up the reality of civil society. It is a precious reality, far from universal, itself the result of a long civilizing process; yet it is often threatened by authoritarian rulers or by the forces of globalization. (237)

If the initial picture in Brazil and Mexico is one of the consolidation of civil society, in the USA voices have been raised about civil society's potential fragmentation (Sennett 1977; Putnam 2000). However, civil society cannot be considered as a given or as a unidirectional social process. It is also by no means homogeneous, and while the "crisscrossing network of associations" can lead to overarching consensus on certain issues at certain times, this should never be taken to imply that there is a single voice of civil society or that it can be "represented." We are therefore using the term as an analytic shorthand for a diverse, plural, and conflictive set of places, spaces, associations, and possibilities of connection ranging from sports clubs, political parties, neighborhood groups, and church groups through professional bodies of lawyers and doctors, to associations such as the Rotary and youth groups of all kinds, as well as a vast array of philanthropic bodies, voluntary service providers, activists, and advisory agencies. What makes any attempt at classifying them difficult—apart from their sheer and continuous variety—is that they may frequently change their aims, since they are the social products of people in action. Philanthropic bodies can change from being concerned with service provision to taking a very active role with regard to a specific social issue. However, all these groups in different ways express and reflect parts of the concerns that are present in the wider moral commonwealth. In the following discussion we have tried to separate out some of these different arenas of association so as to provide a broad picture of the diversity of civil society and the different processes that are in place, but we make no assumptions that the separations have any theoretical validity: for example, we follow Dahrendorf (1996) in including political parties because of their associational aspects. In day-to-day life, while some of these associations and organizations may devote part of their energy to supporting activities that help to articulate the different crisscrossing networks, and others are more concerned with specific activities and services, still others are concerned with specific issues, with policy areas, and in different ways with citizenship and rights, a theme to which we turn first.

### Citizenship and Rights

Recent years have seen a tremendous growth in discussion about citizenship and rights in both the developing and the developed world, coupled with a complex debate on inclusion, exclusion, marginality, and civic inclusion.[2] The concern with citizenship and rights is often the driving force behind many civil society organizations, as well as behind government initiatives to build new relations with a wider community of interests, especially with those that are only marginally included, or even totally excluded, from the public arena. Citizenship has become an everyday, taken for granted concept for discussing rights and vice versa, reflecting the widespread explicative presence of the Western democratic model and the corresponding "age of rights" (Dahl 1998; Bobbio 1996). Yet the use of the term *citizenship* as a primary concept in the discussion of living conditions, social inclusion, and democracy is quite recent. Indeed, as Roberts (2005) has shown, during the 1960s the term can hardly be found in the English-, Spanish-, and Portuguese-language academic literature other than in the area of law, whereas in the 1990s it shows an upsurge in popularity of usage.

In Western democracy, to use the arguments of T. H. Marshall (1950), equalities in relation to rights and duties are balanced with a minimum tolerance of certain inequalities in terms of degrees of economic and cultural capital. Western societies are class societies that, rather than giving allegiance to a static hereditary system, are a result of a constant process of tension, conflict, and negotiation. The rise of the Western welfare state is part of this process of continued attempts to consolidate redistribution and social guarantees. Part of its slowly negotiated conception involves, as Marshall argued, the interweaving of three different strands of rights: civil rights—those of freedom of speech, thought, faith, property, and the right to justice; political rights—the right to participate actively in the polis, whether as elector or as elected; and social rights—varying from the right to a modicum of social welfare, to the right to share in the wider social heritage of education and culture and to live the life of a civilized being with dignity. While there is much debate about whether Marshall's model can deal effectively with the variety of today's world, in which there are also notions of identity rights and of collective (diffuse) rights that transcend territoriality and the nation-state, most would agree that it offers a useful starting point (Isin and Wood 1999).

Marshall proposed that at least in the northern European democracies (and specifically the postwar United Kingdom that he was analyzing), the different strands of rights followed a specific order of historical con-solidation, with civil rights leading, followed by political rights and fi-nally social rights. The consolidation and coming together of the three sets of rights in the 1950s was, as he saw it, a key characteristic of con-temporary society. This, however, was not the situation in most, if not all, Latin American countries. In Brazil, as Murilo de Carvalho (2001) has ar-gued, constant authoritarian interventions and regime changes led to in-stability of political rights, and the generalized lack of access to justice— the right to have rights—considerably undermined any notion of civil rights. At the same time, populist regimes and social interventions prac-ticed by such authoritarian social reformers as Vargas left a legacy within which certain expectations came to be built around social rights (such as pensions and other so-called *acquired* rights introduced by Vargas's labor laws). The result was that

> [t]he chronology and the logic of the sequence described by Marshall were inverted in Brazil. Here first came the social rights, implanted in a period in which political rights were suppressed and civil rights re-duced by a dictator who became popular. After this came the political rights, also in a bizarre manner. The greatest expansion of voting rights took place in another dictatorial period, in which the organs of po-

litical representation were transformed into decorative pieces of the regime. Finally, still today many civil rights, the base of Marshall's sequence, continue inaccessible to the majority of the population. The pyramid of rights was turned upside down. (Murilo de Carvalho 2001, 220–21)

In Mexico the picture is different. While civil rights have often remained unfulfilled, and social rights are being eroded by privatization and neoliberal orthodoxy, the last decade has seen a resurgence of recognition of indigenous rights and civil liberties. Moreover, the electoral reform process started in the early 1990s has galvanized authentic political rights and the opportunities to exercise representative democratic rights. In the USA, amendments to the Constitution in the 1960s solidified civil rights, particularly for minority populations. Enforcement of these rights has been protected in following decades by many court cases and institutional policies, but also by NGOs that play an important role as watchdogs. Recent welfare and immigration reform measures, however, are creating differential and often segmented social rights and access to services.

A growing proportion of people in all three countries are today prepared to identify themselves as part of an indigenous population or as being of indigenous descent. In the USA, links are being made in a number of regions between members of tribes living on tribal lands and those living in mixed cities and towns, bringing very different resources to aid economic and social development. In Brazil what was in 1991 an estimated indigenous population of 294,000 spread over some two hundred ethnic groups and with some three hundred different indigenous organizations, including the intertribal, has suddenly become, in the ten years between the 1991 and the 2000 censuses, 734,000. The increase of nearly 150 percent is attributed by the Brazilian Institute of Geography and Statistics (Instituto Brasileiro de Geografia e Estatística [IBGE]) to changes in the pattern of self-classification by urban indigenous peoples and descendants. In Mexico, where almost 9 percent of the population speak an indigenous language, from the 1970s onwards the recognition of indigenous groups and rights has become more widely embraced, in contrast to earlier periods when indigenous characteristics and culture were ignored and indigenous rights were systematically denied (Mattiace 2003).

Today's recognition and development of indigenous rights under indigenous law precede the Chiapas uprising of 1994 and are connected to the broader indigenous rights movements and intercultural social policy trends found in most parts of Latin America, but, for Mexico at least, Chiapas was an important turning point.

The question of indigenous peoples and tribal rights—many of which are collective—has further opened up the discussion of citizenship and civil society. Esteva and Prakash (1998), for example, discuss a Oaxaca leader saying: "Westerners represent justice with a blindfolded woman. We want her with her eyes well open, to fully appreciate what is happening. Instead of neutrality or impartiality we want compassion. The person committing a crime needs to be understood, rather than submitted to a trial" (111). In both Mexico and Brazil, the question of indigenous peoples' independent authority over their own territories and the right to adopt their own models of governance is still relatively new, if not in principle, certainly in practice. In the USA the picture is somewhat clearer in legal terms, even though there is considerable discussion of the institutional logic of their relation to the federalist state and much questioning over service provision.

The language of rights, whether through the social imaginary of bills, universal declarations, laws, historical precedents, or assumed natural conditions, is present throughout our three countries. With different accents and dialects it provides a way in which people define themselves as citizens and discuss their relationship with the state. It is not surprising therefore, to find that this also provides the *moral high ground* to which social movements and advocacy groups appeal in seeking leverage over policy initiatives and in influencing agendas. Yet the ways they have done so have varied considerably. For example, slavery and the forced relocation of people from various African nations were features of both the USA and Brazil, yet the various human rights movements of descendants of Africans in the USA were hallmarks of the 1950s and 1960s, while in Brazil militant groups have only recently gained more visibility on issues regarding the rural territories occupied by escaped slaves and on urban ethnic exclusion. In Mexico, women's political rights of suffrage were not finally acknowledged until 1953, and once that challenge was met, the debate about rights (until recently at least, when indigenous rights came more into the foreground) related primarily to the ways corporatist labor groups were to be included in the "revolutionary pact" with the governing political elite—essentially through workers' corporative federations and unions. This began to change only when new "democratic" and independent unions emerged in the 1970s and began to link themselves to more broad-based (largely urban) social movements whose demands concerned claims on land and services for informal housing settlements. In the USA, after more than half a century of struggle, women's political rights were acknowledged in 1920 through a constitutional amendment (DuBois 1998). Race then became the key issue around which civil rights challenges were articulated from the 1950s onwards. Judicial decisions finally ruled the unconstitutionality of the "separate but equal" provision of public services in southern states, and constitutional amendments in the mid-1960s guaranteed that civil and political rights could not be abridged by race (Branch 1988, 1998). The language of rights remains central to political action around such issues as sexuality, immigration, and abortion.

Thus civil society is as diverse and multifaceted as its bases of mobilization: it may be about neighborhood organization, leisure, child care, or education, yet it is through these overlapping networks that issues circulate, movements form, and opinions change. In the sections that follow we first explore different types of associations and interest groups to describe similarities and differences across countries. Then we seek to identify those elements that seem most central to the subnational arena. Finally, we look at the causal relationship between decentralization and democratic opening and civil society.

## Associations and Local Interest Groups

Interest groups and associations have been a distinctive characteristic of the civic architecture in the USA since its founding. Alexis de Tocqueville ([1835] 1969) noted how

Americans of all ages, all conditions and all dispositions constantly form associations. . . . The Americans make associations to give entertainment, to found seminaries, to build inns, to construct churches, to diffuse books, to send missionaries to the antipodes; in this manner

they found hospitals, prisons and schools. If it is proposed to incul-
cate some truth or to foster some feeling by the encouragement of
a great example, they form a society. Wherever at the head of some
new undertaking you see the government in France, or a man of rank
in England, in the United States you will be sure to find an association. (106)

These associations and groups, still common in the USA and increasingly present in Brazil and Mexico, reflect an important element of civil
society. However, measuring association as a social practice is not an easy
task in a comparative setting, especially given cultural and political differences in registration. For example, data may be available from local
government or state registries of organizations formally constituted but
will not include those that, for a number of reasons, have not registered.
The result is a jigsaw puzzle based on different extrapolations.

For example, in Brazil Queiroz and Merege (2000) profiled in depth
a mixed agricultural and commercial municipality in the interior of the
state of São Paulo and identified ninety-one different public interest organizations (including associations and local interest groups) among its
sixty-five thousand inhabitants; of these, 18 percent were informal. A second study (Merege 2005), carried out in the metropolitan region of Belém
in the northern state of Pará, identified 2,181 organizations among the
population of some 1,300,000, of which 22 percent were informal. Interestingly, the ratio of number of organizations to population is not dissimilar: one organization per seven hundred inhabitants in the first case and
one per six hundred inhabitants in the second case. For the country as a
whole, recent aggregated data that certainly exclude many local groups
and all nonregistered organizations have placed the number of associations at some 275,000, this being a 150 percent increase from 1996
(Rezende and Tafner 2005), and again close to the ratio of one organization per six hundred inhabitants. The variety of organizations and associations present in these studies provides further confirmation for the
findings presented in chapter 4 about the diversity of organizations that
can be involved in policy implementation.

A recent study by Mendonça and Alves (2006) provides a good example of such involvement and points also to the way in which civil
society and the state may be interacting. The research focus was Brazil's

semiarid region, covering a significant part of eleven states with 1,448 municipalities and 28 million inhabitants. This is an area in which infant mortality rates are much higher than the national average and in which salaries and the human development index are much lower. Comparing matched municipalities in terms of significant examples of innovative public action, the authors found that while some kind of collaboration with community organizations, local associations, and national and international agencies was present in a number of municipalities, those with more significant reported levels of innovation tended to have more community-based organizations and local university links. The authors' conclusions suggest that despite the institutional fragility that has led to a certain pessimism about effective decentralization and municipal strengthening (Baqueiro 2001; C. Souza 2004), local government and civil society are actually stimulating each other, and improvements are taking place in both, not because of a theory about the good society, but because of real and immediate needs.

While the presence of a substantive number of organizations and associations is an indicator for an active civil society that shows support for many day-to-day activities and the potential for engagement in wider social issues, it is difficult to accurately gauge participation and membership in these organizations. A recent study allows us to compare varying propensities for participation in the USA and Mexico, as well as to allow for some disaggregation by region.[3] The data are interesting and show that more people in the USA than in Mexico declare themselves to be active in formal associations. Only participation in sports and religious activities is significant in Mexico, but even here it is lower than in the USA, where levels are generally twice as high, three times in the Bible Belt regions of the South and Midwest (table 5.1). In both countries men participate more than women, except in religious associations. (See also Instituto Nacional de Estadística Geografía e Informática [INEGI] and Secretaría de Gobernación 2003.)

Amateur sports is a major feature of associational life in the USA, in terms of both active participation and organization. Youth athletics, for example, frequently draws in parents to organize weekend events, and bowling leagues still remain an active feature of everyday life, despite warnings of their decline (Putnam 2000). Fraternal organizations, possibly a carryover from college life, abound in local chapters of Lions,

Table 5.1  Membership in Organizations, USA and Mexico (in Percentages)

|  | Sports | Religious | Unions | Neighborhood | Political | Parent Teacher |
|---|---|---|---|---|---|---|
| **MEXICO** | | | | | | |
| Border | 26 | 20 | 9 | 10 | 8 | 18 |
| Urban | 25 | 36 | 11 | 10 | 7 | 16 |
| Rural | 20 | 37 | 6 | 9 | 4 | 17 |
| **Mexico by Region** | | | | | | |
| North | 27 | 23 | 9 | 10 | 8 | 19 |
| South | 39 | 42 | 13 | 14 | 11 | 17 |
| Center | 27 | 34 | 10 | 11 | 7 | 18 |
| East | 12 | 36 | 9 | 7 | 4 | 12 |
| West | 26 | 55 | 11 | 9 | 1 | 10 |
| **USA** | | | | | | |
| West | 43 | 64 | 31 | 49 | 32 | 34 |
| Midwest | 46 | 71 | 33 | 52 | 20 | 37 |
| Northeast | 40 | 61 | 37 | 49 | 28 | 32 |
| South | 42 | 79 | 19 | 53 | 28 | 50 |

Source: Ward, Rodríguez, and Robles (2003).

Elks, Moose, Shriners, and the internationally influential Rotary, all of which can be found engaged in local social and civic activities. Interest groups, however, can also take on a distinctive ideological turn, as in the case of the National Rifle Association (on the right) or the AARP (on the left), to the point of significantly influencing elections and policy decisions (Furlong 1997, 325–48).

In Brazil, the limited data available about participation in associations are either collected through a small number of local direct survey studies or derived from the various census activities conducted by IBGE. For example, in 1988, IBGE's annual National Survey of a Sample of Households (Pesquisa Nacional por Amostra de Domicílios, PNAD) showed 12 percent of adults linked to some kind of trade union, 14 percent to a community organization, and 3 percent to a political party—almost certainly underestimates, as noted above for Mexico. While the results showed that those with higher levels of income were more likely to be involved in associations such as trade unions, a more detailed study by Queiroz Ribeiro and Santos (1996) points to the significant presence of community associations within very-low-income and excluded groups. Their own analysis of the municipality of Rio de Janeiro was able to identify some 273 *associações de favela* and 396 *associações de moradores* in the municipality, plus some 400 welfare and philanthropic organizations, nearly 2,500 churches, and at least 50 activist NGOs, not forgetting 57 *escolas de samba* and many other forms of cultural association. The authors suggest that much of the growth in civil associations is recent, with some 65 percent of associations of all types in Rio de Janeiro and São Paulo being formed between 1970 and 1986, during military rule and the return to democracy, including 90 percent of all community organizations. This corroborates the idea that civil society has an important role in democratic transition and the consolidation of democracy. Finally, a study by Neri (2001) using microdata time-series information from the monthly IBGE survey of employment trends in the six largest metropolitan areas, disaggregated into two groups (poor and nonpoor), has shown that whereas participation in community level associations is reported at a lower rate by the poor than by the nonpoor, the difference (14.6 percent vs. 11.6 percent) is small enough to support the conclusions of the Rio study.

### Trade Unions

A key, historically rooted element of civil society is trade unionism, particularly union activity that is independent of government control. Klesner (2007), for example, has shown how involvement in nonpolitical organizations leads to greater participation in explicitly political activities, and of the organizations he studied, labor unions were the most important mobilizers (Inter-American Development Bank [IADB] 2006). Certainly anyone who has followed the broad sweep of U.S. and Latin American politics will be aware of the often dramatic role that these have played in both urban and rural affairs. At the same time, globalization and new forms of economic association have brought considerable and abrupt changes.

Over the last twelve years, for example, the Brazilian trade unions have been feeling the impact of the concentrated application of market-oriented and neoliberal policies largely focused on deregulation coupled with considerable changes in production methods brought about by global markets. Nearly two million jobs have been lost, and those that have been created are largely temporary, with few social benefits. An economy in which 60 percent of all jobs were in the formal sector and 40 percent in the informal sector has inverted to one in which 40 percent of jobs are in the formal sector and 60 percent are informal. A consequence is a decline of about 90 percent in the number of strikes over the 1990s in relation to the 1980s, largely as a result of the lack of capacity to mobilize (Portes and Hoffman 2003; Roberts and Portes 2006). At the same time, the data from Neri's (2001) study on the metropolitan regions show that some 23.6 percent of the low-income population who are working are members of trade unions, a figure that rises to 38.3 percent among the nonpoor. However, any optimism suggested by these numbers needs to be tempered by the fact that only some 3 to 6 percent declare that they attend meetings (at least one a year). Data from a recent IADB study (Stein et al. 2006) place 29 percent of Brazil's economically active population in trade unions. (The corresponding level for Mexico is 13.5 percent.) IBGE (2001) suggests a value closer to 23 percent of the economically active population, although that study alerts us to the difference between being registered in a trade union and being an active, dues-paying member. Both categories of participation are valid, and the second will always enroll fewer people than the first. Of the 19.5 million people registered in trade unions and other professional associations in 2001, only some 10.8 million were regular monthly contributors, bringing the level closer to that of Mexico (IBGE 2001).

In the current Brazilian setting, the more authentic trade unions have been rethinking their roles and adding to their traditional activities in the areas of representation and negotiation, the wider discussion of social policy and action in relation to job creation, and the setting up of employment exchanges and job shops at the local level, either independently or with municipal governments for whom job creation and employment are also an agenda concern. In the rural areas, the Agricultural Workers'

Union has become an active spokesperson for family-based agriculture and local sustainable development. Given that the annual negotiations of the minimum salary affect all low-income Brazilians since the *minimo* is used to set salary levels in the public sphere, the industrial sphere, and the domestic sphere and is also the minimum pension, this wider interest has maintained the unions, and especially their overarching forums and *centrais,* on the front stage of national social policy, thus recovering some of their loss in image and power due to industrial restructuring. All three of the autonomous *centrais sindicais,* which are modeled on the French and Spanish federations—the Unified Workers' Central (Central Unico dos Trabalhadores [CUT], a major supporter of the PT), the General Confederation of Workers (Confederação Geral dos Trabalhadores, CGT), and Union Power (Força Sindical)—have developed social programs open to both union and nonunion members. The presence of women among the executive members of the CUT has increased impressively, from none (out of thirty-two seats) in 1991 to twelve in 2000. The presence of women as delegates at the CUT national congress increased from 18.4 percent of 1,546 delegates in 1991 to 31.3 percent of 2,309 delegates in 2000. The proportion of urban versus rural workers in the trade unions has remained a constant fifty-fifty, demonstrating the key role that the trade unions have outside the urban areas, where they are frequently not only trade unions but also major civic associations and local community organizers.

Like the Mexican government born under PRI rule, the modern Mexican labor movement has its roots in the Mexican Revolution. The participation of worker-organized forces—the "Red Battalions"—against Porfirio Díaz's authoritarian regime marked the emergence of urban and industrial workers as potential political allies. The right to unionize and to strike was written into the 1917 Constitution as a statement to the burgeoning working class of their place in "the ideology of the Mexican Revolution," an ideology that in theory emphasized nationalism, participation, economic redistribution, and social justice (Middlebrook 1991, 3–5). In the 1920s and 1930s, the government provided subsidies to fledgling labor movements.

Since then—and until very recently—the government was generally successful in cultivating patron-client relationships with labor organizations by making available financial and political subsidies, including material support for union activities and access to elective positions in the

PRI for pro-government labor leaders (Middlebrook 1991, 9). In return, the "kept" labor movement helped maintain political control. Because it could be mobilized on a national scale, labor participated in everything from mass demonstrations in support of government policies to voter registration drives.

Labor unions suffered economically and politically from the economic crisis of 1982, and the labor movement in general continued to be debilitated by structural and political weakness. Both the de la Madrid (1982–88) and Salinas (1988–94) administrations maintained a hard-line approach to their economic stabilization measures, refusing labor demands and breaking wildcat strikes (Middlebrook 1991, 15). Labor leaders, fearful of losing any more political leverage, never officially mobilized workers to openly challenge the new economic and political liberalization policies; instead, they offered their overall support for the economic stabilization measures. The years following 1982 marked a significant shift in state-labor relations as the erosion of labor's political bargaining power began to expose the constraints inherent within labor's unbalanced alliance with the state (Whitehead 1991).

The 1990s posed new challenges to the labor movement in Mexico. NAFTA has increased the number of employers resistant to unionization. Also, the stress experienced by new industries characterized by employment instability (*maquiladoras* and tourism) has exacerbated problems for an already weak and fractionalized labor movement. Political liberalization policies implemented by Salinas and continued under his successor, Ernesto Zedillo, threatened the traditionally anti-opposition labor movement that equated the rise in opposition movements with a reduction in labor's own political leverage. As Whitehead suggested in 1991, the principal obstacle to the renegotiation of Mexico's long-standing labor-state alliance was not only current and future economic difficulties but also the shift in official attitudes concerning the appropriate place for organized labor in the Mexican regime (80–82). The new labor movement in Mexico has become more versatile and dynamic, with several new politically independent unions.

Outside the labor organizations, Mexico has a long history of urban social movements seeking redress and improvement in urban services, access to housing, and so forth, although a few have also pressed for more radical structural changes (Ramírez Sáiz 1986; Montaño 1976; Gilbert and Ward 1985; Haber 2006). Usually the level of engagement for these local movements has been at the subnational level, only occasionally spilling over into national prominence, as in 1992 when Salvador Nava's supporters marched on Mexico City to protest electoral fraud in San Luis Potosí, and the Zapatista uprising of 1994 in Chiapas. More recently (in 2006) a civil society crisis emerged in the southern state of Oaxaca that amply demonstrates how labor and civil society conflicts at the subnational level can generate national pressures and even constitutional crisis. In Oaxaca the statewide section (no. 22) of the all-powerful Teachers' Union (Sindicato Nacional de Trabajadores de la Educación, SNTE) had long-standing tensions with the national union leadership, tensions that were exacerbated after decentralization to the states from 1993 onward (Cabrero Mendoza 1999). Decentralization placed firmly at the state level negotiations about salaries, benefits, and control over teacher appointments and promotions. Early in 2006 an unpopular PRI governor, upcoming highly contested national federal elections (in July), conflicts and tensions within the union leadership and between state and national union leaders, and political mishandling by the state authorities provoked serious social unrest and street rioting that caused a number of deaths in October and November. The teachers' strike of several months was joined by other groups in a new movement called the Popular Assembly of the People of Oaxaca (Asamblea Popular del Pueblo de Oaxaca, APPO), which sought to oust the governor, and the political crisis intensified after the very close and highly contested presidential elections of July 2. The rioting, the disturbances, and the demand that the PRI governor resign were widely publicized nationally and internationally, thereby creating a federal constitutional crisis: How to identify the point at which a state had become ungovernable, and, once it was identified, how to achieve a political solution? The PANista federal government was reluctant to send in troops to defend the beleaguered governor, preferring instead that he step down voluntarily (as he steadfastly refused to do). Constitutionally it fell to the Senate to declare an "absence of powers," but an investigatory Senate committee found that the three branches of government in Oaxaca were functioning. Eventually the government was obliged to send in the federal police, causing an escalation of civil unrest and a major problem for incoming President Felipe Calderón to address. This example demonstrates three important aspects of subnational civil society in Mexico's incipient democracy. First, civil society mobilization takes on different hues and forms at the subnational level—in this case, the Teachers' Union supported by other organizations melded into the APPO. Second, subnational events and processes can become conflated with national ones: in the Oaxaca case specifically, internecine struggles between the central union's hierarchy and that of the state union leaders were further complicated by a close-fought presidential election, political partisanship, and political opportunism. Third, challenges by civil society at the subnational level can expose the weaknesses and shortcomings of an emerging democracy, creating a constitutional crisis at the national level, which in this case was about how to find a political solution in a society that was no longer characterized by a strong presidency with substantial metaconstitutional powers (see chapter 3).

Union activity in the USA dates from the period of national independence, but the industrial unionization movement emerged in the post–Civil War period (Craver 1993; Brady 1993). The struggle for institutional and organizational representation in labor evolved from trade unions, with a largely workplace focus, to broader industrial unionism in the 1930s (Brady 2005; Robertson 2000). Significant pieces of national legislation, including the National Labor Relations Act of 1935 (the Wagner Act), established the legal infrastructure for collective bargaining. But unions in the USA, in contrast with those of Brazil and Mexico, have never formally been under the control of the state. Although some scholars and union officials argue that the legal framework favors employers over organizing efforts of workers, the history of state-union relations in the USA differs greatly from that of Brazil or Mexico. The independence of unions has enhanced their role in politics. They have had traditionally close links with the Democratic Party, but some unions have at times supported Republican efforts. After reaching their zenith of political power in the 1960s, they underwent a steady decline that became more precipitous in the 1980s in response to a widespread reduction in manufacturing employment in the country (Chaison 2006). Attempts to organize migrant agricultural workers in South Texas and in California in the 1960s and 1970s had some effect on the politicization of Hispanic populations in these regions but little lasting effect on the lives of workers. During this period, the Reagan presidency adopted a very effective antiunion posture. Although there has been some success in unionization in the rapidly growing service sectors, a number of state laws outlawing compulsory membership and other similar wide-ranging measures, including attempts to restrict political contributions, have in general reduced the influence of labor in the political life of the country both nationally and subnationally.

### Philanthropic Bodies, Nonprofit Organizations, and Nongovernmental Organizations

In Mexico, the decline of the PRI and its sectors since 1994 and the associated rise of opposition parties no longer wedded to corporatist organizations have systematically undermined the union arenas of formal or semiformal participation. In their place, however, new forms of civic involvement have emerged, derived in part from the broadening and opening of civil society since the early 1990s. NGOs, also, have increased dramatically since the 1980s. A key event catalyzing the emergence of NGOs was the earthquake that devastated parts of Mexico City in 1985. Many informal organizations mobilized to help the government rescue teams, as well as to collect food and medicines and channel them to affected people. Then, as the government proved incapable of responding effectively, more organizations emerged and began to participate in the reconstruction of the city. While NGOs and community groups had existed before 1985, the government had invariably viewed them with ambivalence. The 1985 catastrophe and the response of civil society through NGOs was a turning point in mobilization and government acceptance in Mexico (Eckstein 1990). Following this, the "political earthquake" of the 1988 elections—widely seen as fraudulent—and the later emergence of the new left-of-center party the PRD have accelerated the political opening and the proliferation of local and subnational organizations. The PRD's strength remains largely vested in the Federal District, as indicated by its victories there in 1997 and 2000, but with the rise of its leader López Obrador it is gaining ground more widely. At the beginning of the 1990s, some 2,300 NGOs were formally recognized by the Mexican government. That figure almost doubled between 1994 and 1998, and by 2000 it had reached 5,202 (INEGI and Secretaría de Gobernación 2001).

There is no general register of nonprofit organizations in Brazil that enables distinctions to be made among different types of nonprofit activity. Indeed, the nonprofit status is used for a wide range of activities, ranging from the more expected types of social activity to sports clubs, schools, specialist associations such as private hospitals, and even "quasi-for-profit" activities in education and welfare. The Brazilian Association of NGOs (Associação Brasileira de Organizações Não Governamentais, ABONG), a highly effective advocacy network of some 270 organizations that is responsible to a great extent for the early success of the World Social Forum, places the number of organizations effectively concerned with issues of development and rights at some 8,600 in 2002, a significant increase since 1996, when the number was around 2,800. Many Brazilians are involved at some point in voluntary activities, an estimated one-fifth of the population between fifteen and sixty years of age. Some twenty million people ("Guia para fazer o bem" 2001) were said to have been active during the 2002 UN "Year of the Volunteer." Voluntary activities are almost exclusively local in focus, even when they are part of a nationwide campaign such as that against hunger led by the Brazilian Institute for Social and Economic Analysis (Instituto Brasileiro de Análises Sociais e Econômicas, IBASE), a Rio de Janeiro—based NGO (see n. 1). While some NGOs can generate partial leadership at the national level, the general pattern is for a local or at most a subregional expression. Most of the ABONG member organizations are small, based in major capital or provincial centers where they can maintain links with universities and other research groups. Even though it is difficult to get precise data, most are considerably vulnerable in financial terms and remain dependent on international nonprofit and bilateral donor support.

Some of Brazil's philanthropic organizations have existed virtually from the arrival of the Portuguese in 1500. In 1543, for example, the Irmandade de Misericórdia (Sisterhood of Mercy) was founded in São Vicente on the coast of São Paulo State only eleven years after the municipality—Brazil's first—had itself been created. Today the various Irmandades das Santas Casas de Misericordia hospitals can still be found in many areas of the country, playing a vital role in public health provision and managed by voluntary directors drawn from the professional community. Equally important are the various "pastoral" organizations of the Catholic Church that promote action on a number of key issues such as those of street dwellers, rural workers, and the landless. The Pastoral da Criança, the Catholic Church's mission for children, mobilizes some 150,000 volunteers, mainly women, in the poorest areas of the country to provide coverage to over one million families in nearly thirty-three thousand communities in 3,555 municipalities. Their highly effective process of weekly follow-up visits with data analysis and discussion has not only saved the lives of thousands of children in vulnerable situations but also made a significant impact on community development and empowerment of both the local coordinators and their neighborhoods.

Following Landim's pioneering 1993 study on the philanthropic sector, interest has grown in trying to identify the different types of organizations actively present within the nonprofit sector. In their recent study for the Institute of Applied Economic Research (Instituto de Pesquisa Econômica Aplicada, IPEA), Fernando Rezende and Paulo Tafner (2005) have gathered information from the general registry of organizations—which, as we have commented earlier, will always be an underestimate—for the period 1996–2002, which, again as already stated, saw an increase of some 150 percent in the number of private foundations and nonprofit associations. It is interesting that while in the health area growth was considerably less (only 50 percent), perhaps demonstrating the beginnings of the consolidation of the decentralized health service, the areas of environment and animal protection and of development and the defense of rights showed an increase of some 300 percent. In absolute terms, environmental associations and bodies represent a small part of the total (0.6 percent in 2002), but development and rights associations represent a healthy 16.4 percent of all foundations and nonprofits. In fairness, it is necessary to add that most of these are very small organizations with either few or no paid staff (only 1.85 percent employ more than five people). Observations such as a 48 percent increase in jobs over the 1996–2002 period, or estimates in newspaper reports about careers in the third sector, where there are some 1.5 million jobs, may be accurate but also tend to be misleading and are largely due to (ab)use of the nonprofit legislation by hospitals and universities, which together represent only 1 percent of all nonprofit organizations yet employ over a million people. The picture is therefore mixed, but since most of the smaller organizations are active locally and since we are finding, as reported elsewhere (Spink 2006), that there is no slowdown in local-level government innovation, the results on balance are positive.

While the community as a whole may be leading the growth of philanthropic and volunteer activities, the business sector in Brazil is lagging behind. The type of large-scale philanthropic support, either directly by business or through charitable trusts and foundations, that is common in the USA does not occur in Brazil. A study of business social activity by the University of São Paulo's Third Sector Center (Fischer and Falconer 1999), the first of its kind at a national level, showed that while 56 percent of firms that replied to a survey (and were therefore more likely to be involved in social activities) did support social programs, 43 percent were quite prepared to state that they did not! Among those that did, support tended to be through financial donations rather than active engagement. Where support was given, it was more likely to be for activities concerning the education of children and adolescents (47 percent of support) and was very unlikely to be for human rights, ethnic minorities, people with drug dependency, street dwellers, and people living with HIV/ AIDS. This pattern was confirmed recently in a study that used a leading association's database to identify effective business support for poverty reduction activities. Children and education were again the most favored focus areas (Camarotti and Spink 2003). Business is becoming slowly more active, but there is no sign of the creation of large independent foundations that has marked the philanthropic history of the USA. A recent overview of all published work on partnerships in social policy implementation from the business side (Aliança Capoava 2005) shows that businesses are still more likely to support—either financially or through volunteer activities—organizations that individual firms have themselves created and not other civil society organizations.

In the USA, with a broader tradition of independent associations and nonprofit organizations, the position is less clear, as is the distinction between associations, interest groups, and NGOs. In everyday action these are often superimposed and, for this reason, will be dealt with together. Here, for more than two decades, a debate has raged concerning the health of the country's democracy. Citizen anger over a perceived decline in public sector performance and declining voter turnout have suggested an erosion of democratic participation in governance. Further, it has been argued that participation of citizens in the organizations and associations of civil society, upon which the richness of public life depends at the local level, has also decreased (Putnam 2000).

While questions can be raised about how general these trends are (Barber 1984; Wuthnow 1998), research continues to suggest that there is a wide range of opportunities for citizens to consider public issues and to act on them in concert with others, although the numbers of people actually participating regularly remain limited. Although table 5.1 shows considerable civic participation in the USA, especially in sports and religious activities, participation in politics is uniformly much lower. Moreover, during the last two decades, the nature of interest group politics has changed dramatically (Cigler and Loomis 2002; Advisory Commission on Intergovernmental Relations [ACIR] 1986; Kincaid 1990). Business groups, for example, have proliferated as a result of the increasing complexity and diversity of the economy. While there are several broad national business interest group representatives, such as the U.S. Chamber of Commerce and the National Association of Manufacturers, scores of other organizations represent specific industries, small businesses, major corporations, public utilities, and minority businesses, among others. Although these organizations focus principally on federal policies that affect their industries, the effects of state and local government policies on specific industries contribute to the need for locally based business associations. Virtually all cities have chambers of commerce concerned with local public policies affecting business conditions. Since telecommunications, energy, and insurance companies, among others, are significantly affected by state government policy, especially regulatory policy, statewide associations in these industries are common (R. Wilson 1993). The emergence of new economic sectors, market segmentation, and the expansion of international markets have diversified the economic interests of firms. In 1989, it was estimated that 70 percent of the interest groups present in Washington, D.C. represented business interests (Tierney and Scholozman 1989). Occupational groups—teachers, public sector employees, unions, medical and health care workers—have formed interest groups, some of which are very influential. As with state- and local-level business organizations, to the extent that state and local governments affect these occupational categories, subnational organizations are formed to represent their interests. For example, the Consumers Union is a national organization with several regional offices that address state-level issues.

The new communications and information technology has permitted more actors to gain access to information critical to public policy making and to mobilize affected constituents. A modern form of a faction is the broad-based group membership organization, typically an organization of the middle class. Members pay dues that are used to support educational and lobbying campaigns conducted by a permanent staff.

Public interest groups have multiplied; there were 2,500 in 1986, with supporting memberships of forty million and budgets that totaled more than $4 billion (Shaiko 1991). Citizen groups, environmental groups, and single-issue groups have become adept at forming coalitions and are now significant factors in policy making. Thomas Anton (1988) argues that the control of federal policy making by the *iron triangle*—an alliance among congressional subcommittees, federal agencies, and affected client groups—has been weakened as these new actors have begun participating in coalitions to affect policy outcomes.

The proliferation of groups has occurred at the state level as well. In 1973, the forty-six states that required lobbyists to register reported 12,188 individuals and organizations registered; in 1991 the fifty states reported more than 29,000 individuals and organizations (Mollison 1991). National interest groups will frequently have state affiliates, as mentioned above. State-level business organizations have specialized and proliferated (Thomas and Hrebenar 1991; ACIR 1986, 238–41). Interest groups have become increasingly professional as the old-boy network method of state lobbying has faded (Gray and Lowery 1999, 256–67). The increasing sophistication of state legislators and state executive officers and the legal restrictions placed on lobbying activity are requiring increasing competence on the part of lobbyists. While business interest groups have always had the resources to develop and present technical and empirical data to bolster their recommendations, other interest groups have also developed this capacity, frequently drawing upon national organizations or groups in other states.

Interest groups have proliferated and their active participation in politics has increased as the influence of the two major political parties has declined. It has been argued that the shift from candidate-centered to interest group-centered elections, especially at the state and federal levels, results from the strength of interest groups and that these are assuming functions traditionally found in parties (Rozell and Wilcox 1999). Neither party has been entirely successful in capturing fully the interests and political expressions of minorities, women, taxpayers, environmentalists, consumers, community groups, and others (Herbers 1998). These various publics are aggressively exercising their preferences, frequently outside the party structure and even outside the legislative process, as seen in the increased use of initiatives and referenda.

The recent proliferation of interest groups, especially in Washington, D.C. but also in state capitals, has been broadly criticized on several grounds. Some argue that the large number of groups makes it difficult to build consensus and reach policy compromises, gives minority interests (i.e., single-issue groups) too much power, and consequently undermines political parties and the policy-making process. In addition, if interest groups significantly influence policy making, those groups in society unable to organize and express themselves politically will not be part of the political process. One solution is to create surrogates, such as an office of public counsel in state regulatory commissions. Also citizens' groups, such as the Consumers Union and the AARP, may assume positions that reflect the interests of low-income constituents. This pattern has clearly been established at the national level, but state-level organizations, at times affiliated with national organizations, are increasingly common in larger states (ACIR 1986, 208–21). Public education, an issue of great importance to low-income populations, often attracts business groups to policy debates and deliberations. Elements of the business community have also participated in policy discussions concerning social programs, particularly education (ACIR 1986, 208–21).

The role and presence of interest groups that are so distinctive of the USA are not as apparent in Mexico, at least not in the formal sense. In Mexico, at least until the rise of the opposition parties and the victory of the PAN in 2000, the majority of workers and of popular organizations were cultivated and contained within the three corporatist sectors of the PRI, each of which was organized at state and local levels. These included blue-collar workers in the CTM, farmworkers in the CNC, and service workers, the self-employed, and working-class resident associations in the National Confederation of Popular Organizations (Confederación Nacional de Organizaciones Populares, CNOP). So well articulated and sophisticated was this inclusion that many people were unaware that they formally belonged to these associations. Controlled by the national confederation leadership, subnational chapters and municipal *secciones* had considerable local force and were crucial in channeling support upwards through the confederation (and therefore the PRI) and for (de)mobilizing citizen demands (Cornelius 1975; Gilbert and Ward 1985). Since the entry and rise of non-PRI parties into government, these old-style corporatist structures have often been disassembled at the local level, with new opportunities for civil society groups to engage with local authorities more directly. In the past, at least, though the majority of the population was included (albeit often unwittingly), surveys about participation rates in resident associations and trade union activities, petitioning and public protest, tend to suggest negligible involvement. For example, the data in table 5.2 that measure and compare civic and political activism in the USA and in Mexico show very low percentage participation rates in Mexico: among urban populations, 8 percent participated in political demonstrations, only 2 percent were willing to join unofficial strikes, and 8 percent reported having asked a politician for a favor. In rural areas participation was even lower (Ward, Rodríguez, and Robles 2003; see also Camp 2003; Klesner 2003). Thus, even though empirical research and observation suggest that many more people do engage in these activities in Mexico, the point is that they do not see this as formal participation. Interestingly, in the USA reporting rates for these same dimensions of political participation were usually at least twice as high, and in the case of "signing a protest letter" the participation rate ranged from almost one-third in the South to one-half in the Northeast (table 5.2).

While it often goes unmeasured, an important dimension of local and everyday civil society participation in the Americas is church group participation. As we saw in table 5.1 comparing the political and civic cultures of Mexico and the USA, a significant proportion of the population in both countries participated in church-based activities, and this accurately reflects the high church-based participation that exists in the USA. Both Brazil and Mexico are strongly religious (Catholic), and a significant proportion of the population attend church regularly, yet their declared participation in religious association meetings tends to be much lower than in the USA. Whether this reflects a difference in perception, such that people in Mexico and Brazil see going to church or being associated with the church as a regular part of their lives and therefore take it for granted instead of reporting it as a formal association, or whether this reflects a real absence of de facto association as it is conceived in the USA is difficult to say. Given that these links can be, and are, activated in times of emergency, forming part of the basic matrix of social resources, it is

Table 5.2  Participation in Civic Political Activism by Region, Mexico and
the USA Compared (in Percentages)

| | Ask a Favor of a Politician | Sign a Protest Letter | Attend a Demonstration | Join an Unofficial Strike | Participate in a Boycott |
|---|---|---|---|---|---|
| **MEXICO** | | | | | |
| Border | 9 | 8 | 7 | 2 | 2 |
| Urban | 8 | 6 | 8 | 2 | 0 |
| Rural | 9 | 4 | 4 | 1 | 0 |
| **Mexico by Region** | | | | | |
| North | 8 | 8 | 7 | 2 | 2 |
| South | 10 | 5 | 10 | 3 | 0 |
| Center | 9 | 5 | 9 | 2 | 0 |
| East | 11 | 3 | 4 | 2 | 0 |
| West | 5 | 3 | 1 | 0 | 0 |
| **USA** | | | | | |
| West | 10 | 42 | 21 | 11 | 20 |
| Midwest | 16 | 38 | 14 | 10 | 20 |
| Northeast | 15 | 49 | 22 | 8 | 26 |
| South | 10 | 30 | 15 | 9 | 14 |

likely that in all three countries church associations are an important, if
underestimated, form of potential civic activity.

As we have commented, the term *nonprofit organization* in the USA
covers a wide range of citizen-based service organizations, voluntary organizations, and local philanthropic groups as well as the more recent activist and advocacy organizations that are more and more being referred
to as NGOs and the major philanthropic foundations active at both national and local levels. Community-based organizations, formed at the
local level, are yet another type of civil society organization that has appeared and proliferated in the USA since the 1960s (S. Smith 1999). These

organizations can serve a variety of functions, from attempting to influence public policy in such areas as social services and economic development to actually delivering public services. In the late 1940s and early 1950s, the federal government began using community-based organizations in the delivery of services, including public and mental health, education, and other services. Federal support and later state government support provided incentives for the expansion of nonprofits, including many faith-based organizations, whose role at the local level was thereby enhanced. The cutbacks in federal social spending in the 1980s did not diminish the numbers or importance of these organizations; rather, state governments made up for the losses in funding, and NGO service provision continued to expand. In fact, under reforms aimed at "reinventing government," service provision by NGOs often became the preferred strategy (Osborne and Gaebler 1992). The number of tax-exempt charitable organizations increased from 322,000 in 1982 to 546,000 in 1992 (S. Smith 1999, 134). At the national level, both Republican and Democratic presidents encouraged volunteerism as an alternative to the provision of services by the public sector. Even though many questions have been raised about the destiny of public policy in this setting (S. Smith and Lipsky 1993), there is no doubt that, at least in relation to civil society and the matrix of social resources that are increasingly being referred to as social capital, the emphasis on volunteerism and the expansion of community-based nonprofits represent an important dimension of subnational civil society in the USA.

## Movements and Forums Created by Civil Society and the Construction of Social Capital

Disenfranchised low-income populations have on occasion acquired power and gained access to policy making through political organizing. In doing so they have both drawn on existing resources that are available to them, including the mobilizing force of their own identity, and constructed new organizational resources out of networks, links, and learning about power. The expression *construction of social capital* is being used in this broader sense to refer to the development of new social and organizational resources, linkages, and local institutions that can strengthen civil society.[4]

One historically important empowerment strategy for relatively powerless organizations has been the protest movement (see especially Lipsky 1969). But protest generally becomes an effective strategy in policy making only if the protesting groups are able to gain the attention and support of so-called reference groups—as we observed earlier for the case of Oaxaca, Mexico. The strategy can be employed around local or national policy issues. Media attention on the protest is an important way in which grievances are articulated and mobilize nonaffected groups (the reference publics that have some political power), who in turn force public officials to respond (Hughes 2006). Relatively weak or powerless groups can thereby indirectly affect policy making by instigating third parties to act on their behalf. This strategy was employed in South Texas to bring attention to substandard housing conditions. Activist groups were successful in attracting national media attention to motivate state government officials to take action (R. Wilson 1997; Ward 1999a).

Frances Fox Piven and Richard Cloward (1977) provide another perspective on the protest strategy. Their analysis of four major protest movements in the USA—movements of the unemployed and union movements during the 1930s, and the civil rights and welfare rights movements during the 1960s—led them to the conclusion that these protests succeeded because of their disruptive potential to the power elites, not because of the ability of the disadvantaged to organize themselves. Political power of the poor depends as much on the fears of the powerful as on the historic windows of opportunity.

Both perspectives suggest significant limitations to the strategy of protest: it is difficult to sustain over time and does not, in itself, allow the powerless group to acquire power. In the USA, Saul Alinsky developed an alternative strategy in the 1930s through his community organizing work in Chicago (Alinsky 1969; Horwitt 1989). Although the original Alinsky model adopted a confrontational approach, it differed in its limited geographical scale and its departure from the ideological emphasis of protest movements. While protest activists from unionists to civil rightists tended to cast politics in a moral vocabulary of right versus wrong, Alinsky organizers recognized that the average citizen's concerns were more pragmatic personal and community problems (Boyte 1990). Alinsky organized around specific issues such as jobs and community infrastructure, rather than broad ideological themes of rights and freedom. The vehicles for organizing became small group meetings and person-to-person discussions through Parent Teacher Associations (PTAs) and churches instead of marches and demonstrations. The tactics used by Alinsky organizers remained confrontational, however, and were aimed at disrupting and annoying local power establishments.

This model became an important foundation for later community work with the poor. Indeed, scholars have traced the parallel evolution of paradigms of organizing in the United States and the political-economic context of the country (Fisher 1994; Boyte 1980). The populist movements toward the end of the nineteenth century were efforts to organize an agriculturally based disenfranchised population against the impending political threat of industrialization. The labor movements of the 1930s were class-based organizing efforts to protect the working poor. As class-based ideology diminished in political significance, so the organized protests of the 1960s became more issue oriented, evolving from the broader-based civil rights movements to women's rights, welfare rights, gay rights, and so on.

Against this historical backdrop, the Alinsky model's central tenets of *neighborhood* organizing became all the more appealing as the public at large, and low-income communities in particular, developed a sense of alienation from electoral politics and mistrust of governmental institutions in the 1970s and 1980s. Modern-day community organizing groups emphasize the use of mediating structures close to the life of the people— churches, schools, and neighborhood groups—as rallying points to pursue issues of economic and political interest to the local communities. This citizen-based version of political participation ascribes to low-income outsider groups a role that is in direct contrast to the electoral-based version upon which both the elitist and pluralist models of advocacy, discussed below, were predicated.

Neighborhood organizing in low-income communities is by no means the only tradition of what Harry Boyte (1980, 7) calls citizen advocacy. Other U.S. traditions of citizen advocacy that transcend neighborhoods include public interest advocacy, represented by Ralph Nader, the Consumers Union, and the Public Interest Research Campaign. In addition, constituency advocacy for specific groups such as migrant farmworkers or the elderly (e.g., through the Gray Panthers) is common (Boyte and Riessman 1986). Nor has the Alinsky model remained unchanged through the last few decades (Reitzes and Reitzes 1987; Rogers 1991). An important development in the evolution of this model is the shift from the initial emphasis on issue organizing to a more contemporary emphasis on political education and indigenous leadership development.

An examination of six local government cases in Texas in which NGOs played critical roles in policy formation revealed several significant findings (R. Wilson 1997). Voting was an important mechanism for groups in these cases to gain legitimacy and standing. The creation of organizations through which individuals could express themselves politically provided a successful mechanism for inducing participation of large numbers of people. In other words, these organizations constituted successful political intermediaries and, as such, represent an interesting substitute for a role played formerly by political parties. But their emergence is all the more striking in that they represent the interests of low- and moderate-income populations, groups that historically have had very little power. None of the groups were formed as a result of government initiatives, but they did take advantage of avenues for participation created by federal policy, such as the Voting Rights Act and community participation provisions of the Community Development Block Grant program of the U.S. Department of Housing. The inclusion of representatives of low-income populations in blue ribbon commissions to examine education and indigent health care provided opportunities for influence. Forums with broad participation also provide an opportunity for contention and debate, another principle of democratic practice. These examples reinforce a widely held belief in policy studies: that the design of effective policy processes should incorporate a broad range of interests and that to be effective these interest groups should come to policy discussions with their own technical expertise and analysis.

Social movements have also been an important feature of Mexican civil society, especially between 1968 and the late 1980s to mid-1990s, when alternative forms of civil society mobilization began to make them, if not redundant, less necessary. Social movements have a checkered history theoretically as well as empirically (Castells 1983). In Mexico, broadly speaking, as outlined above, they have shifted from being clientelistic and heavily co-opted organizations in the 1970s, to being more genuinely representative and independent during the late 1970s and 1980s (Montaño 1976; Gilbert and Ward 1985), to being more reflective of so-called postindustrial society, embracing new social movements and dimensions of mobilization (human rights, reproductive rights, sexuality, cultural defense, etc.).[5] These movements converged in the post-1988 elections as civil society was galvanized into electoral reforms, forming a number of civic organizations to defend the vote, to defend human rights, and so on.

In Brazil, where civil society is a far more recent development and where many basic civil rights are not yet broadly accessible, it is not surprising to find that autonomous forums where various social movements and pressure groups can gather are still at an early stage. There are notable exceptions, such as the MST (Branford and Rocha 2002) and a number of urban equivalents, especially in the area of health and housing. In the case of the MST, the results of some twenty years of dedicated and highly focused pressure are considerable: there are currently some 1,300 settlements in different parts of the country involving about half a million families, of which 80 percent have their own schools, and some 470 different forms of cooperatives and associations deal with the distribution and sale of agricultural products. The impact of the MST has illustrated a number of features of Brazil's federalism that have been touched on elsewhere. As a movement it has targeted federal and state governments in terms of land reform and has had to negotiate its day-to-day presence with municipal governments. An early sign of a pending land occupation is usually a long line of homemade black plastic tents camped out alongside a major arterial road. Both the Catholic and the Protestant churches have specialist priests working with the movement, which has a distinctive Alinsky style of remaining independent of government yet at the same time playing different levels off each other. The MST has made considerable progress in guaranteeing the effective occupation of previously unused land, but it is under constant threat, since land, to invoke the title of Eduardo Galeano's 1976 book, is one of Latin America's open veins of conflict.

While the MST is perhaps the most visible movement, dating from the 1980s and earlier, it has already spawned more radical offshoots and helped to provide identity for urban equivalents, including organizations of the homeless, or, to use their expression, the roofless (sem teto). A number of these movements have learned how to make use of the openings provided by other more statutory bodies and councils that have been set up as a result of the 1988 Constitution. In different ways, the many councils, forums, participative budgeting experiences, and other forms of association, though often initiated by local government (executive or legislative), are helping to create a new kind of "public space" that is bringing together very different social actors to debate the direction of public action (Dagnino 2002). Space is, as Lefebvre pointed out (1991), a social product and not a given, and progress toward the relative autonomy of civil society actors in such forums is still at its beginning. In a recent quantitative study of the characteristics of participation in the city of São Paulo, where social movements are active, Houtzager, Lavalle, and Acharya (2003) showed that those most likely to be participating in constituted forums and policy councils were those with previous ties to political parties and the state. Contrary to expectations, members of advocacy groups were no more likely to participate than others.

Although there is some movement to create space in formally constituted forums, the next stage of organization (that of organizations of organizations, to use the Alinsky model) is less common. Apart from the trade union movement, with its three autonomous *centrais,* and the various forums supported by the NGO movement (such as the National Urban Reform Forum, the Forum for Popular Participation, the National Health Conference, and Waste and Citizenship), the forums that can be identified have more to do with specific local questions or foci, and there is still a great tendency, especially in the larger urban areas, for many different organizations to be working in the same place without any effective interorganizational linkage. Brazil has twenty-five metropolitan regions in which forty million people are crammed into 2 percent of the country's territory, yet apart from very few and usually monothematic instances there is hardly any effective metropolis-wide social movement or overarching civil society forum. Here the absence also of effective metropolitan government perhaps suggests support for the mutual-pushing-and-shoving model that we have seen elsewhere. Two important exceptions are first, the various regional forums and confederations of the indigenous peoples, who have begun to be very effective in relation to their own principal concerns of territorial demarcation, bilingual schooling, and economic development, seeking to place themselves as regional confederations across a mix of state and municipal jurisdictions. Second, mention should be made of the Brazilian Semiarid Joint Endeavor (Articulação no Semi-Árido Brasileiro, ASA), an umbrella organization that has brought together over eight hundred associations, trade unions, NGOs, and governmental and international agencies working in the semiarid region of Brazil to lobby for effective regional policies and for simple but effective solutions to water storage and management. Here the process of linkage has been a complex one in which social movements and certain international agencies have played a key role. While there is some cause for optimism in Brazil, there are significant exceptions, especially with regard to the vast community of descendants of Africans (Berquó, Pinho, and de Souza 1998), for many of whom Brazil's social apartheid is also one of racial intolerance and discrimination, or, to be more explicit, of racial exclusion (F. Gomes and Paixão 2006). Black NGOs and social movements are gathering strength, but very few state and local governments have begun to move ahead with affirmative action programs, all of which are still in their infancy.

In Mexico there is also cause for optimism with strengthening of beliefs in democracy and a greater participation in both representative and participatory activities. This has led to a more fertile and less antagonistic environment for minority groups to articulate their interests (gay and lesbian rights, for example), as well as to an opening of the public space in terms of civic participation in local governance, as we discussed in chapter 3. Also, greater transparency of information, better media coverage, and the protection afforded citizens by the implementation of slander and libel laws have leveled, considerably, the playing field of power relations at the subnational and local levels. In the USA, the situation is more diverse: the broad-based movements of the 1960s and 1970s have given way to more specifically focused groups and coalitions (Castells 1983) among previously active political movements such as the civil rights movement, cultural movements such as gay rights, and the ever more significant Hispanic population.

### Political Culture and Electoral Turnout

Political parties can be an active part of civil society, serving not only as parties but also as spaces for discussion and debate and for the organization of events and other social activities. In each of the three countries, parties, elections, and opportunities for plebiscites, such as referenda and political consultations, form different sets of relations between the state and civil society. This is not the place to provide a full-fledged discussion of the political structures that make for representative democracy in the countries or the principal differences between structures that were discussed in chapter 3. However, it is useful to recall that subnational governments are formed in all three cases by citizen-based elections, albeit for different time periods and with different opportunities for reelection and requirements for voting and being voted into office. In the USA, all elections at national and state level are through the parties and by direct majority for specified constituencies. In contrast, at the local level they are frequently nonpartisan: that is, they are truly civic elections.[6] In contrast, in both Brazil and Mexico direct election and partial proportional representation take place through parties at all levels, resulting in the presence of a number of minority parties but at the same time making the independent type of civic participation difficult. Thus, in the previously mentioned study by Neri (2001) using data from the monthly metropolitan regions survey on employment trends (IBGE's Monthly Survey of Employment [Pesquisa Mensal de Emprego, PME]), some 3.3 percent of the low-income population and 5.5 percent of the nonpoor declared effective membership in political parties, and of these, 43 percent of the poor and 37 percent of the nonpoor said that they participated in party activities.

In Mexico, the number of parties is relatively limited (three major parties and a handful of satellite parties, most notably the Green Party), whereas in Brazil there are many parties, the relative strength of which can vary over time. Mexico, for decades riddled with electoral fraud and ballot rigging, now has a credible electoral system that has led to a much greater plurality of party representation in subnational government. The fact that the vote now actually does count for something has galvanized the emergence of an active political culture and reduced the cynicism of what was formerly referred to as the *cultura de sospecha*. But because of the closeness of the 2006 presidential elections, the mass mobilizations, and the refusal of the PRD's Lopez Obrador to accept the result, setting up instead a "legitimate presidency" and "legitimate cabinet" has posed a major challenge to electoral institutions and processes that, for the previous decade or so, had become the poster child of how to conduct elections in the Americas.

The data in table 5.3 provide an interesting comparative picture of political culture in the USA and Mexico and point to some aspects of regional variation not previously discussed. Briefly, U.S. citizens have a much greater belief in democratic practices than do their Mexican counterparts (notwithstanding the PAN victory in 2000, which actually predates the survey). Interestingly, when respondents were asked about what democracy meant, those in the USA were twice as likely (over 50 percent) to relate it to some concept of liberty and freedom, whereas in Mexico it was far more heavily embedded in ideas of equality of opportunity and equity (Ward, Rodríguez, and Robles 2003; Camp 2003). In part these affirmations reflect national cultural and ideological constructions in each country, especially insofar as these are reinforced in public education, but they also underscore the important relationship between national ideology, belief systems, and political participation. When respondents were asked about what was required for democracy to work well, those in Mexico emphasized the importance of a good presidency (cf. U.S. respondents, who emphasized the role of Congress). When they were asked about action-specific tasks of democracy, those in Mexico emphasized combating crime (including corruption) and inequity, whereas those in the USA were more likely to show a pragmatic orientation and emphasize electing officials.

Also important in activating participation in political culture is whether voting is mandatory. In the USA voting is optional, while in Brazil and Mexico it is obligatory, with voting taking place either on a Sunday or on a formal electoral holiday. In Brazil, proof of voting is required for a number of activities, such as the issue of a passport. Turnout in Brazil is relatively high (75–85 percent), and the number of spoiled ballots or empty votes is currently around 5 to 10 percent.[7] In Mexico rates have become meaningful only since the early 1990s, once the electoral system gained greater credibility and accurate vote counting came of age. Before then the vote was largely rigged, and voting was inflated to disguise the rate of abstentions. The level of actual participation varies depending on whether the election is a federal election where the presidential race is being contested alongside congressional positions, as it is every six years, or whether it is a midterm election. Thus presidential elections in 1994, 2000, and 2006 have participation rates of between 64 and 74 percent, whereas midterm participation ranges between 42 and 66 percent. In

Table 5.3  Perceptions of Democracy and Its Tasks among Mexican and U.S. Populations (in Percentages)

| | Country Democratic? Yes, Very [= Very or Somewhat] | What Is Important for Democracy to Work Well? | | | | Main Tasks of Democracy? | | | Satisfied with the Way Democracy Works? | | |
| --- | --- | --- | --- | --- | --- | --- | --- | --- | --- | --- | --- |
| | | Good Pres. | Good Legisl. | Good Judges | Combat Crime | Elect Officials | Protect Minorities | Redist. Wealth | Very | Somewhat | Neither Satisfied nor Dissat. |
| **MEXICO** | | | | | | | | | | | |
| North | 8 | 34 | 13 | 26 | 25 | 26 | 19 | 22 | 2 | 27 | 26 |
| South | 27 | 42 | 9 | 17 | 28 | 15 | 21 | 18 | 6 | 23 | 10 |
| Center | 16 | 38 | 12 | 15 | 28 | 22 | 19 | 22 | 6 | 24 | 5 |
| East | 26 | 53 | 15 | 16 | 36 | 30 | 7 | 18 | 11 | 31 | 3 |
| West | 7 | 36 | 7 | 8 | 15 | 31 | 11 | 26 | 5 | 21 | 28 |
| **USA** | | | | | | | | | | | |
| West | 35 | 19 | 30 | 9 | 19 | 38 | 15 | 11 | 22 | 37 | 7 |
| Midwest | 41 | 16 | 36 | 7 | 21 | 35 | 13 | 13 | 22 | 43 | 5 |
| Northeast | 44 | 14 | 46 | 10 | 14 | 47 | 12 | 12 | 22 | 47 | 2 |
| South | 44 | 20 | 31 | 11 | 18 | 33 | 26 | 9 | 19 | 37 | 6 |

Source: Ward, Rodríguez, and Robles (2003).

both cases, however, the trend is one of decline since 1991; indeed, it appears that participation was especially marked when clean elections were a relative novelty and has declined as elections have been less problematic. These same patterns are replicated at the subnational level.

The USA continues to be a predominantly two-party nation of Democrats and Republicans; rarely do independents or other parties accede to power. Both Brazil and Mexico, in contrast, have been characterized in the last twenty years by the slow but steady rise of a number of political parties with strong links to different sectors of society but on opposing sides of the political center (with the center being represented in Mexico by the PRI and in Brazil by the PMDB). In Mexico the older PAN, founded in 1939, has become the strongest party on the right and the PRD, founded in 1989, the strongest party on the left, while in Brazil the main force on the right is the PFL, now renamed as the Democratas, and on the left the PT, growing steadily since 1982 and winning the national presidential elections in 2002 and 2006. In several respects the PT has, since the beginning, been viewed as an exception among Brazilian parties, whose general and distinctive features, as Scott Mainwaring (1995, 354) described, "are their fragility, their ephemeral character, their weak roots in society, and the autonomy politicians of the catch-all parties enjoy with respect to their parties." However, in the long run-up to the 2006 Brazilian elections, the PT was rocked by a number of voting bribery scandals and other charges of using the party machine for dirty tricks. Probably due to the stronger personality and increased populism of the incumbent president, plus the positive effects of the family grant program in the poorer parts of the country, the Lula administration was able to win a second term of office, but not without being forced into a second-round run-off election. In general terms, with the possible exception of a weakened PT, there is relatively little connection between voters and their parties (Samuels 2003), and, as Jeffrey Rubin (2006) has suggested, most activists adopt a two-pronged strategy of working within the institutional framework and mobilizing outside it at the same time.

The Family Grant Program in Brazil, put together from a series of previous grants and allowances at state, municipal, and federal levels, provides an income supplement of between the equivalent of US$14–56 per month (R$30–95) to families whose per capita monthly income is below US$56 (R$120). It has created a direct link between the federal government and the individual family, bypassing the state government and leaving the municipality with the role of including or excluding families. The scheme has attracted considerable attention for its impact on the poorest sectors of the population and is generally supported by all parties and sectors of the population; arguments about it have more to do with what is now needed to extend the basic safety net. Yet perhaps few realized the extent of its influence in the 2006 elections. The emergence of a direct symbolic link between president and poorer voters became clear when it was seen that the highest percentages of votes for the incumbent president were to be found in municipalities and regions that concentrated the highest percentages of grant-receiving families. There is still much to be analyzed, including the program's effect on former powerful state-level oligarchies and on the different sides of the three-way federalist pact.

Given that in the USA voting is not compulsory, actual participation in elections serves as a useful indicator for civil society mobilization, at least from the institutional perspective. (Compulsory voting in Brazil and Mexico makes such an analysis impossible.) The share of eligible voters in the USA who vote (the voter turnout ratio) fell into long-term decline in the 1960s. Presidential election turnout dropped from 65 percent in 1960 to 50 percent by 1996 (Jewell and Morehouse 2001, 276). The turnout for nonpresidential elections of U.S. House candidates dropped from 47 percent to 36 percent during this same period. Possible explanations of the decline include disengagement from political life, changes in the way political parties interact with members, restrictions in election and voter registration laws, and complacency. A variety of efforts to increase voter turnout have been pursued, including campaign finance reform and the National Voter Registration Act of 1993, which was intended to ease registration (Weber and Brace 1999, 16).

Thus, somewhat paradoxically, although the provision of opportunities for citizen engagement in governance is mandated in the USA, formal participation in voting is low, especially among minorities. The low voter turnout among the Hispanic population is particularly noteworthy given that the size of the Hispanic population now exceeds that of the African American population.

The politics of local elections differs from that of state elections in quite distinct ways. In large cities, the success of the neighborhood movement, the black power movement, unions' participation in the public sector in the 1960s, and the passage of the Voting Rights Act in 1965, with its imposition of single-member districts, dramatically transformed urban politics (Davidson and Grofman 1994; Jones-Correa 2001), particularly by greatly increasing the number of minority city council members and mayors (Bullock 1999, 232–40). The increasing racial diversity of the country's major cities has meant that politics are very competitive and conflictive. Rarely can consensus be formed on issues, and underrepresented groups must organize and express themselves politically for concerns to be placed on the public agenda.

Voter turnout in municipal elections typically ranges from 25 to 35 percent. Cities with nonpartisan elections average around 25 percent, while cities with partisan elections average over 35 percent (Dye 1997, 318–19). A distinctive feature of local political participation and local politics is a fairly systematic variation according to size and location of the city. Suburbanization has produced relatively homogeneous local government jurisdictions of fifty thousand to one hundred thousand people adjacent to large central cities, and these jurisdictions produce a quite different pattern of local participation (Oliver 2001). The probability of participating in elections declines with the size and the wealth of the community as well as with the size of the metropolitan area where the city is located (Oliver 2001, 220). The somewhat surprising result with respect to wealth in the community is related to another determining factor: socioeconomic and racial/ethnic homogeneity produces less interest in politics and lower voter turnout. This tendency to reduce political contestation is also reflected in the lower voter turnout in cities with a council-manager form of government than in cities with a mayor-council form.

## Conclusions: The Emerging Patchworks of Subnational Civil Society

Table 5.4 draws together the observations made in this chapter and provides a broad perspective of the qualitative changes that we believe are taking place. The five categories reflect whether a particular aspect of civil society suggests "growth," suggests "decline," is the current status quo "characteristic," is incipient (at an "early stage"), or is "absent." While it is important to avoid any suggestion of a continuum about who

Table 5.4   Civil Society across the Three Countries

|  | Brazil | Mexico | USA |
|---|---|---|---|
| Community-based organizations | Growth | Growth | Characteristic |
| Independent forums | Early stage | Early stage | Characteristic |
| Interest groups | Growth | Growth | Growth |
| Voluntary/philanthropic organizations (& base level) | Growth (low) | Growth (low) | Growth (high) |
| Independent workers' trade unions | Growth | Growth | Decline |
| Political parties | Mixed | Early stage | Mixed |
| Electoral involvement | Mixed | Growth | Decline |
| Plebiscites/referenda Single issue voting | Absent | Early stage | Growth |
| Civil society impact on state level | Early stage | Early stage | Characteristic |
| Civil society impact on municipal/town level | Growth | Early stage | Characteristic |
| Civic inclusion of low-income population | Early stage | Early stage | Early stage |
| (Government mechanisms for participation)* | (Growth) | (Growth) | (Characteristic) |

(*) Included to help interpretation of impact descriptors.

Key:   Absent—does not exist or is not provided for.
Early stage—is visible but not yet consolidated in terms of clear growth.
Growth—still developing and increasing.
Decline—clear signs of a falloff in importance or activity.
Characteristic—a constant presence and part of the everyday scene.
Mixed—variable and contradictory trends.

is where in the pecking order, or to imply an autonomous theory of civil society development—for indeed, as the Marxist analysis would suggest, state and civil society mirror each other—it does appear that the situation in the USA is characterized more by stability, that of Brazil by already established processes of change, and that of Mexico by the beginning of such processes.

Our examination of the relationship between civil society and governments in our three societies reveals conflicting and contradictory trends, not least in the USA. Here, despite the structural breadth and depth of democratic practice, including the opportunity for participation in free and fair elections, U.S. democracy seems to be suffering a qualitative decline, not least at the subnational level. Although voter turnout is trending downward, partisan competitiveness at the national and state levels has clearly increased. Competitiveness at the local government level varies according to the pattern of urban and suburban development. Local jurisdictions with homogeneous populations tend to have less competitive politics, and the political parties themselves seem to be less important in terms of agenda setting.

Through participation in elections and in civil society organizations, citizens affect public policy but rarely as individuals. Political power is exercised through organized groups. Economically disadvantaged groups are the most vulnerable in the U.S. political system, since their ability to mobilize and sustain political action is constrained. In a Texas study by Robert Wilson (1997), community-based organizations successfully influenced policy, but the outcomes did not lead to dramatic improvement. However, in these cases, when subnational governments were presented with legitimate problems, the policy process did provide reasonable outcomes that were responsive to the interests and needs of low-income communities. Changing laws and political culture were enabling, but the mobilization of citizens provided the critical element affecting policy outcomes.

Decentralization in the USA has generated more opportunities for citizen participation in state and local policy making. The formal context of political practice, such as the Voting Rights Act as well as open meetings and open records initiatives, also expands the opportunities for a broader range of citizens to participate in government. Despite the disengagement of many citizens from electoral politics, subnational policy making does incorporate a wider range of interests and perspectives than in decades past. The representation, if not the direct participation, in the policy process of groups heretofore excluded from policy making can help redefine elements of the public policy agenda in the state and enrich public life. But as more civil society organizations become engaged, policy making becomes more contested, presenting a challenge to decision-making bodies. Decentralization and other forces have provided the states with greater responsibility and more capacity, and states have produced better policy. The same generalization, however, cannot be made about local government, especially in metropolitan areas. The variation in civil society organization and engagement, and the disparities generated in tax bases among local jurisdictions in metropolitan and other urban areas, constrain the potential performance of local governments on a wide range of issues, as observed in chapter 4. The prospects that civil organizations will emerge to address metropolis-wide issues are bleak, since there is no equivalent governmental jurisdiction for addressing the issues raised.

In Brazil and Mexico, we suggest that significant moves are under way to enhance civil society participation in governance, *especially at the sub-national level*, and in ways that are not followed at the national level. These are stimulated by many factors, not least of which are the construction of democracy itself and the growing concern within the population over the huge differences in income levels and service access, along with the very real associated problems of social exclusion that such disparities bring to the foreground in local affairs. Whether this concern will also produce a real consolidation of civil society in the near future is an open question. The number of Brazilians and Mexicans engaged in volunteer actions appears to be much higher than many previously imagined, and more and more linkages and partnerships are being formed between public and civil society organizations, especially in the more progressive municipalities and states. However, even though associational life is present in a wide variety of different organizations and associations, few political parties have clear links to social organizations and specific electoral communities; indeed, more often than not, they appear to be actively discouraged from creating close constituency ties, as the case of Mexico amply demonstrates. Governments, especially the subnational and municipal, are exploring ways and means to encourage participation, as discussed earlier in chapter 3, and in Brazil the participative budgeting model for financial planning has already crossed its original party boundary of the PT and is now found beyond its left-wing origins in over 150 different municipalities (Avritzer and Navarro 2003).

The extent to which these relations and changes can be seen as consequences of decentralization is difficult to judge. If anything, they are themselves pressure points for change in relation to central government specifically and to government and society more generally. There seems little doubt that the subnational arena is undergoing a significant process of reconfiguration in Brazil and Mexico, but it is one in which a historically rooted and municipalist ideology, present in local oligarchies and clientelist relations as well as strong immigrant traditions of local control (as is also very much the case in the USA), may have as much of a role to play as any developmentalist theory of democracy. Given that the same square meter of land is, at the same time, under the jurisdictions of federal, state, municipal, and, in the USA, multiple local governments, as well as "public" interest practices such as *usos y custumbres* in Mexico, it is perhaps inevitable that the changes that we describe are open to different interpretations depending on which particular angle the observer takes. There is no doubt that in both Mexico and Brazil a number of recent arrivals on the field of public action have received somewhat exaggerated praise in claims of breakthroughs being created by social responsibility and third-sector partnerships within an enhanced civil society. But bottom-up community-based organizations have also been learning how to go beyond the reactive defense of hard-won benefits or the offers of those who speak on their behalf and have begun to take advantage of emerging opportunities in local policy arenas.

There has been much pushing and pulling and even some embracing in the different relationships observed between subnational state and civil society, such that it is perhaps better to talk about mutual reinforcement of the processes rather than a causal chain. Decentralization has brought problems and opportunities, democratic opening has produced a conducive climate in Brazil and Mexico, and a heterogeneous civil society has done its part. Yet even the most preliminary look at the impact of globalization on job and work requirements in the USA is enough to halt accelerated optimism. As Ehrenberg (1999) has commented, "[T]here seems to be plenty of work, but the replacement of stable government and unionized manufacturing labor, by nonunion, low-wage service and retail jobs has had a profoundly destructive impact on civil society" (246). Stable jobs within a stable environment may not produce civil society, but unstable jobs within an unstable environment can quickly rupture the criss-crossing networks and the previous arrangements with which we began this chapter. Thus cautious optimism is perhaps the appropriate conclusion.

Of specific interest to this chapter is the strengthening of the broad matrix of community organizations and their growing capacity to act politically, along with their reminder to the "state" that not all that is "public" belongs to the "government." Given the size of the three countries and their democratic openness, it is perhaps understandable why engagement with national governments has become increasingly a question for the "lobby" model of public influence. At the same time, however, the richness of the different approaches that we observe developing at the subnational level suggests that national governments may have a lot to learn from what is taking place elsewhere within their own federalist arrangements, where different nongovernmental actors appear to be learning how to play three-dimensional federal policy checkers. Certainly, de Tocqueville would still have plenty to write about if he were to take a trip around the American continent today.

# The Past, Present, and Future of Subnational Governments and Federalism

## Peter K. Spink, Peter M. Ward, and Robert H. Wilson

The principal question posed in this study has been the effect of decentralization and of changes in democratic practice on the efficacy of subnational policy making: that is, the ability and readiness of subnational governments to respond to the issues and concerns of the moral commonwealth. In this final chapter our intention is not to revisit directly the specific conclusions reached in each of the previous chapters; rather, we wish to draw back and look at some of the key themes that have emerged across the experiences of the three countries. First, we discuss the tensions created by decentralization and the recasting of federalism. Second, we offer an overview of what the newfound practices and responsibilities of subnational government mean for the nature and efficacy of policy making. This is where we also return to our opening question about the relative efficacy of subnational policy making. Third, having examined past and present experiences of federalism and subnational governments, we look to the future and ask: Whither federalism? How are the structures and processes that we have described in this book likely to evolve as these subnational governments become ever more embedded within a globalized political system—albeit often within discrete regional and hemispheric blocs?

## Tensions of Centralization and Decentralization

The decentralization debate is affecting many countries, not only those with a federalist model. For example, the new institutional architecture of the confederation of nation-states in the European Union is built around a bottom-up governance structure predicated upon the concept of subsidiarity: retaining as much governance and policy implementation as possible at the local and subregional levels and passing upwards only those functions that, perforce, can best be managed at that higher level. But change and the implementation of new dimensions of representation and participation invoke tensions and create resistances. Our overview of the evolution of federalism in the three countries over two centuries (see chapter 2) underscored those tensions and dynamics, alerting us to the danger of assuming that decentralization is a linear process or that there is a single dynamic or pattern of its implementation. Seen from afar, the dynamic of decentralization—to use a different metaphor—resembles a pendulum that may appear to have been swinging from centralized to decentralized government structures. But closer up, at the level of our three countries, we observe quite marked differences in swing: closer still, within each country, we can see many different pendulums swinging in different ways across different policy areas.

Our "pendulum" metaphor points to certain tensions created as different actors promote or resist the processes of decentralization and devolution. Such tensions are an inevitable part of this process and should not be viewed as negative or as peculiar to federal systems of government. All systems of governance are likely to demonstrate tensions and volatility, and these are an outcome of a number of overarching changes, as we point out above. Some pressures are unidirectional and derive from increasing globalization, but even here there is debate about whether they produce an overall convergence of political and socioeconomic outcomes across countries (Ritzer 2004) or, as we tend to view it, they have more regionally and locally differentiated impacts as global processes intersect with local ones. Other pressures are bidirectional between levels and branches of governments. These can have both positive and negative impacts on policy making depending in large part upon the "elasticity" that governments demonstrate to accommodate change and adjust.

Our historical overview found that the colonial legacies in each of the three countries have significantly influenced the specific evolution of federalism. The creation of a central government followed independence from colonial powers in the three countries. In Brazil and the USA, the consolidation of a nation was far from automatic, and the regional nature of economic interests and political power has influenced the evolution of governmental structure. Although a centralizing authority, dating from the colonial period, was more prominent in the Mexican case, Mexico too has had to address the challenge of core-periphery relations in its governmental structure. Of course, an important part of the history of the three countries lies within their different legal traditions: common law in the USA and the civil code in Brazil and Mexico have created rather different roles for the judiciary in the three governmental systems.

In both Brazil and Mexico, which have had highly centralized federalist systems until recently, decentralization has faced broader challenges than in the USA. The centralized systems limited, if they did not diminish, the capacity of subnational governments to participate effectively in the design of policy, although in both countries subnational governments had a role in implementing federal initiatives. In contrast, subnational governments in the USA were generally better prepared for their new responsibilities and the decline in federal resources available to them, in part because of the historical commitment to local control in the country's governmental structure.

### Tensions Born of Globalization Pressures

Time-space compression, the increasing flexibility of production systems, technological advances, and improved communication systems have all meant that most subnational governments, including many local governments, are, in different ways, linked to global patterns. In the past, outside media and telecommunications, such activities were largely the prerogative of national governmental institutions and occasionally of strategic states (although here, too, they were subject to national priorities). This chapter is not the place to engage in the many complex debates about globalization's contribution to cultural and economic convergence; to a loss of autonomy and freedom of maneuver, as described by Saskia Sassen in *Losing Control?* (1996); or to an ever-growing sense of superficiality, as suggested in George Ritzer's *The Globalization of Nothing* (2004). Suffice it to say that we doubt the veracity of such arguments.[1] However, there is no doubt that globalization processes are pervasive and that such processes—for example, the very strong promotion of decentralization as international conventional wisdom—are creating new and additional challenges for the public sector in general, as well as for the institutional development of subnational governments.

Although we have not analyzed the impact of globalization specifically, logic and observation confirm that it is having an influence and generating tensions for intergovernmental relations. For example, while many regional governments and large cities in Brazil and Mexico have always had external dependent or interdependent international links, these were often mediated by the national government. Increasingly, however, states and cities in these countries, like their counterparts in the USA, are locked into globalized trading and information exchanges and linkages. Many states in Mexico, for example, now have their own trade delegation offices in the USA and elsewhere, and cities are contracting into "sister" city relationships. Before the 1990s, in the relatively closed and PRI-dominated Mexico, such direct relationships would have been actively discouraged, whereas today they are part and parcel of subnational development. It is not uncommon for the larger Brazilian cities to have special departments for international relations. States in the USA are similarly collaborating not only with particular states but also with the federal governments of other countries. For over a decade Texas has enjoyed close relations and special status with many federal agencies in Mexico, even though, strictly speaking, these interactions should be conducted between federal governments (Lyndon B. Johnson School 2000). The drive toward these international relationships and linkages often reflects new tensions and a new competitiveness between subnational governments.

For similar reasons, the creation of trading blocs—NAFTA in the case of Mexico and the USA and MERCOSUR in the case of Brazil, with the likelihood of a Free Trade of the Americas Alliance in the future—has stayed on national and subnational agendas. Such arrangements may lead to a "supranational" tier of government organization, although still nothing on the scale of the European Union's confederation. This level of integration engenders its own tensions between national and subnational governments. To the extent that subnational and local governments expect to participate in and to benefit directly from such trading arrangements, their institutional architecture and calculus are likely to be affected both by governmental restructuring to make participation possible (raising efficiency and accountability, for example) and by the "backwash" effects imposed on subnational governments (e.g., compliance with supranational labor practices).

Other tensions derive from enhanced connectivity and communications systems that facilitate access to and exchange of information between the local and the global. For example, we observe a quickening of experimentation and dissemination of governance best practices. While these sometimes come to be viewed as international conventional wisdom, many alternative approaches and best practices are emerging from subnational experiences—the much-lauded practice of participatory budgeting in Brazil is just one example—and are being disseminated among these governments without the imprimatur of multilateral organizations. Within the growing culture of information exchange, more and more local governments (especially the larger cities and towns) are likely to find their performance being judged against international standards, and many others are being called to task through national, state, and local comparisons.

### Spatial and Temporal Variations

In all three countries there has been an ongoing tension about how far, how fast, and precisely what government activities should be decentralized. There are considerable spatial and temporal variations in the speed of decentralization and in fluctuation between decentralizing and recentralizing trends. In the USA, despite the call for a highly decentralized model in the original federalist pact, there have been many periods when either the federation or the states have held the upper hand. Equally, in the international arena, decentralization has enjoyed periods when it has been in and out of favor as orthodoxy. Prior to the early 1990s, although a number of Latin American countries espoused decentralization, it was invariably nominal and in reality consisted of "deconcentration" of certain (usually nonstrategic) government activities, largely as a token political response to demands from the periphery that the center redress spatial inequalities (Morris and Lowder 1992; Rodríguez 1997). From the 1990s onwards, however, the imperatives of democratization and the relative strengthening of regional interest groups and governments, the growing diseconomies and negative externalities associated with excessive centralism, a growing political pragmatism on the part of national leaders, and an active promotion of decentralization orthodoxy by international organizations such as the World Bank all combined to move the agenda from nominal deconcentration to a genuine, even though at times chaotic, devolution (Almeida 1996; C. Souza 1996; O'Neill 2005). In the words of one author, decentralization became the "Quiet Revolution of Latin America" (Campbell 2003).

Nevertheless, recasting intergovernmental relations and empowering subnational governments have not occurred without opposition, albeit different in each country. In the USA, this opposition was directed against unfunded mandates, the federal government's requirement that subnational governments assume responsibility for policy implementation without being given the necessary resources. In such cases states have resisted the federal imposition. In Mexico, opposition to decentralization was largely centered in the federal bureaucracy, which, to retain political control, deliberately sought to constrain the autonomy of subnational actors. This changed only when free elections brought an independent legitimacy to those actors and when the (then PRI) federal government realized that the best chance to hold onto overall power was to partially concede powers to subnational governments through decentralization (Rodríguez 1997). In Brazil, initial opposition to decentralization was relatively weak given that postmilitary democratization and decentralization had tended to go hand in hand and that a long tradition of *municipalismo* provided a ready environment for expanded local autonomy (Melo 1993).

Our study has drawn attention to the obvious differences between the USA compared with Brazil and Mexico, but we have also observed considerable variation in the period and extent of decentralization in each country, the relative strengths of subnational and local governments, and the functioning of intergovernmental relations between levels. In policy we have observed major differences in the extent of revenue sharing and subnational responsibility and control, ranging from a high degree of state and local government control in the USA to lesser levels of effective decentralization in Brazil and Mexico, in that order (Díaz Cayeros 2006). But in the latter two countries the rate of change is much faster and generally is, we argue, quite impressive. Even in the USA, while there is less flux, national and subnational governments constantly fine-tune and sometimes reshape patterns of federal-state-local governance within specific policy arenas.

Subnationally at a regional level, tensions also arise, since it has proven easier to decentralize and modernize in some policy areas than in others. Poverty, level of development, urbanization, political culture, and relative remoteness from or, in the case of Mexico, closeness to the United States all tend to shape receptiveness and resistance to policies that devolve power from the center. Some regional economic or metropolitan power-houses, especially those tied to strategic development priority sectors and activities, appear to be more willing and able to ratchet up their politico-administrative capacity. These regions are the likely leaders in innovation and modernization. Locally one observes parallel tensions about devolving functions and responsibilities to lower-order centers and levels: to boroughs within a metropolitan area, and even within a municipality from the primary urban government seat (the *cabecera*) to outlying areas. In short, decentralization and subnational government innovation and strengthening invoke a number of spatial tensions, and the decentralization clock has many different pendulums.

As with any pendulum action, there are swings in the opposite direction. Just as in the USA, with its recent instances of recentralization of certain functions and powers, we are beginning to observe a partial counter-reaction in Latin America. However, it is not yet altogether clear whether this shows that these countries overdecentralized in the first place and are now pulling back to redress imbalances or whether this is a policy accommodation to emerging challenges that allows for a more efficient reordering of responsibilities and activities. But as would be consistent with our foregoing argument about tensions, we expect that it probably represents a bit of both, depending upon the country and the particular sector of activity. Several authors have already noted a recentralization trend in parts of Latin America (Eaton and Dickovick 2004), and while none of the countries show a strong swing in that direction, all three have had some areas where such readjustments are apparent (national security in the USA, education in Mexico, and fiscal federalism in

Brazil), leading a number of observers to comment on the coexistence of decentralizing and centralizing forces and thus supporting the multiple-pendulum perspective (Almeida 2005b; C. Souza 2005a; Robles 2006; Díaz Cayeros 2006).

### Sectoral Variations

To continue this theme, there are many sectoral variations in the speed of decentralization and in counter-reactions to decentralization. While all sectors do not lend themselves equally to decentralization, there seems little intrinsic reason why any one sector should be excluded—with the exception of foreign policy and national defense policy, perhaps. In this context the concept of subsidiarity may be useful: de facto decentralization of most activities to the lowest level with exceptions for those that by consensus may be better managed at the higher levels and should thus be passed up the hierarchy for management by supralocal governments. In the USA, the historical preference for local control embraces the spirit of subsidiarity, but to date such an ordering has found little support in Latin America, and the direction from which decentralization has been imposed has been firmly down the governmental hierarchy instead of up. Thus we expect to find—and do find—tensions and differences between different sectors: fiscal decentralization is most strongly resisted, while education and health are less strongly contested once a national commitment and consensus to move in that direction has developed. At the same time such consensus does not necessarily imply subservience to federal policy directives: in a number of policy areas in our three countries, we have found that policy directives that might appear highly restrictive offer, at the local level, many more options. Indeed, one of the skills of more entrepreneurial—in the broad development sense—local public sector leaders appears to be their ability to interpret and adapt such programs to local requirements. The result is characteristically efforts that "draw in support and programs from below" instead of "pushing them down from above."

Precisely how far down the hierarchy of subnational government these responsibilities are passed is another source of tension. Primary and secondary education in the USA has a legacy of local action in the tradition of independent school districts, whereas in Mexico the states are reluctant to pass down or to share many functions with local-level leaders or organizations, whether these are municipal authorities or parent-teacher organizations. Brazil, on the contrary, has witnessed considerable relocation of education to the municipal level, supported by both constitutional requirements for educational spending and the Federal Education Development Fund, which has provided much-needed support for staff and other vital resources. The result has been a number of innovations, such as the school grant (Bolsa Escola), now part of the federal family grant support; more effective recognition of the different demands of rural and urban education; and even the early signs of a willingness to recognize the bicultural dimensions of Brazil's original peoples and the descendants of escaped slaves *(quilombos)*.

But while there are sometimes increased imperatives for a subregional tier of government, particularly in large cities and metropolitan areas that embrace multiple jurisdictions—at least for certain strategic activities such as planning, transportation, and environmental policy—we have yet to find any example of a concerted effort to create a new, intermediate tier of executive and legislative authority at the regional or metropolitan level. We do find a number of joint planning bodies, and a disposition on the part of local executives to consult with and sometimes to form municipal consortia, but never a full recasting of government structures. In the USA the need for regional or metropolitan coordination is partially addressed through the capacity to annex neighboring areas, but a patchwork of counties and administrative units remains common. Of course, major regional authority initiatives such as the Tennessee River Valley Authority in the USA and river basin management in Mexico and Brazil are exceptions, but they also prove the rule.

It is possible that, in the future, some degree of recentralization of formerly decentralized activities will emerge as part of an overall adjustment process aimed at improving governmental efficiency. It seems likely, too, that some level of regional authority for metropolitan areas will eventually have to be contemplated, but this will probably emerge as a pragmatic accommodation to the need for negotiation within existing federalist structures rather than by constitutional reform to create new federalist levels between state and municipal government or between entities at similar levels (states and municipalities). If constitutional changes occur, they are more likely to concern the accommodation of indigenous populations, in order to reconcile claims of autonomy and sovereignty over spatial entities, than to involve any revision of the intergovernmental relations hierarchy.

### Intragovernmental Tensions and Fragilities Born of Co-governance

This book has highlighted horizontal decentralization, understood as the (growing) political space between the executive, legislative, and judicial branches of government and the distribution of more co-governance responsibility, with the aim of governing more effectively. Here, too, there is no single pendulum dynamic, and in a series of figures (figs. 3.1–3.3) we have contrasted the differences between the three countries regarding the relative power of the three branches of government at different levels and the direction of changes. In the USA the pattern is one of a real and long-term separation of powers embodying an effective system of checks and balances; in Brazil and Mexico, the pattern is only relatively recently changing toward a genuine balance among the branches. Mexico, a relative laggard compared to Brazil, is also making considerable strides in developing its legislative branch as a counterweight to the executive. The pressures generating these "tipping points" are similar to those outlined earlier in this chapter, although the endogenous variables of political pragmatism, electoral reform, and career path development within politics (reelection possibilities) are likely to be rather more important than the exogenous ones of globalization, international orthodoxy, and so forth, with the exception, perhaps, of the increasing international attention given to independent judiciaries. But as before, the trend toward decentralization and opening between the branches creates its own tensions and potential fragilities.

Tensions arise from the historical specificities of transitions. Each country's constitution represents the outcome of debates and tensions from early on—well exemplified in the case of the USA by the divisions between federalists and antifederalists—over how to create a structure in which no one power or level would dominate and, in particular, the executive would be constrained. All of the constitutions offer variations on the theme in theory, but in Brazil and Mexico in practice the relations between the branches have remained unbalanced and have favored the executive branch. Nor have these been the only tensions. In the USA there have been ongoing tensions between the federal and subnational governments as well as between the branches, although no one branch has ever gained dominance over another. In Brazil and Mexico too, these tensions have existed throughout both countries' long federal history, although the relationship between the branches has been in greater flux. In both countries, however, it is the tensions of the relatively recent past that are important: in Brazil, operationalization of the post-1988 Constitution and increased democratization, and in Mexico, democratic opening, also since 1988, have, generally speaking, led to increasing constraints on the role of the executives at the state and local levels by the other two powers. Notwithstanding the decline in executive powers relative to the local congress, governors continue to be key actors, albeit for different reasons in each case. To the extent that executives are more constrained today, paradoxically in some ways they are also more powerful. Modernization of the executive branch, and the heightened expectation that development can be managed more effectively at the local and subnational levels (rather than managed from on high or driven by patronage and cronyism), have provided executives with stronger individual mandates to exercise greater responsibility, although under greater congressional and public scrutiny.

In this book we have seen also how the structure of the respective branches, their relative power, and their institutionalization vary among the three countries. The structure embodies a number of tensions and potential fragilities. State congresses in the USA are generally bicameral, are highly institutionalized and stable, and possess strong traditions of incumbency resulting from unrestricted reelection (a practice that is under intense scrutiny in some states). Thus relatively few tensions and fragilities are associated with the process of elections and the way local congresses are formed and voted into office; the only doubts revolve around who wins control and the size of the majority. And as elected representatives come and go, the rules of turnover are predictable, and the process of renewal is fairly stable and secure. Moreover, the advantages of incumbency make for low turnover and invest the congress with strong traditions of experience and seniority. Not so in Brazil and Mexico, where, for different reasons, the formation of state congresses and local councils is much more unstable and therefore more intrinsically fragile. There is total turnover in Mexico every three years because of the no-reelection rule, and turnover is also high in Brazil, though more because of the movement of political actors around the different levels and branches, so that in Brazil, unlike the USA, the possibilities for the creation of a more permanent cadre of experienced legislators in the subnational congresses are severely hampered.

The absence of a second house in subnational congresses probably further weakens the role of this branch, although we do not think that creating a second chamber is in itself either a necessary or a desirable step toward legislative strengthening. It does seem, however, that the inclusion of a degree of proportional representation to select deputies in Brazil and Mexico makes for multiple-party representation and a greater likelihood of smaller majorities and divided (plural) government. But while these fragilities and tensions remain in the USA and Brazil, and are beginning to be observed in Mexico, it would be wrong to see congresses as toothless institutions: they never have been so in the USA; and in Brazil and even in Mexico, whether by design or by practice, they are playing an important role in contemporary policy making and oversight.

Another aspect of co-governance fragility in Mexico and Brazil, in both the executive and legislative arenas, concerns the poorly developed systems of partisanship and discipline and the relatively weak tradition of co-governance. In Brazil, party identification and discipline have been viewed as relatively weak, except possibly in the case of the PT, and individual leader-follower alliances have been seen as more predominant, although this view has recently been contested. In Mexico, too, the linkage between party and policy platforms and ideology remains generally weak, so that, in contrast to the Westminster model, there is little consistency between the party in power and the policies pursued. Even in the USA, constituency interests and parties' relatively weak impact on local officials in terms of articulating policy make it difficult to predict policy outcomes from ideology and partisanship and place a higher value on governmental (bureaucratic) effectiveness.

Sometimes, too, partisanship does not extend to certain areas of local government. In the USA, for example, local (city and county) governments and public officials are commonly elected on nonpartisan grounds. Moreover, many functions, such as water provision, parks, and policing, are perceived to be nonpolitical, and effectiveness is therefore emphasized instead. But in Mexico (especially) and in Brazil, most politics is party politics, albeit often tied to individual career trajectories, and partisanship is more likely to directly shape the calculus of local governance.

We have also observed intrinsic fragilities that derive from a lack of clarity about how to include civil society in effective co-governance. In the USA the problem is largely one of sustaining engagement, and while it is mandated that multiple opportunities be mandated for civic participation, only a relatively small fraction of citizens actually participate. Elections are not compulsory, and local election turnouts are low. Organized interest-group articulation is high, however, and lobbying tends to substitute for widespread or generalized political participation. Whether this is a fragility of the USA's system we cannot say, but it is a notable and ongoing feature. Brazil and Mexico have compulsory voting, which leads to higher turnout in elections. But here there is considerable fragility and lack of clarity about how best to achieve effective participation in co-governance. For different historical reasons, such as repression in Brazil and cooptation and corporatist control in Mexico, any tradition of genuine participation in subnational and local governance has been heavily circumscribed. Thus, today, local governments are seeking institutionalized ways to encourage participation (such as plebiscites, referenda, and popular initiatives), but the idea of direct and continued participation of citizens in civics remains poorly developed. Nor do formal interest groups and lobbies offer a strong substitute. While they exist, their role in co-governance is limited. NGOs offer an alternative and have become increasingly visible actors in subnational policy making, sometimes directly as the whittled-down state devolves greater responsibilities to them or to quasi-NGOs. However, in our view they still lack clout, especially in Brazil and Mexico, and their activities are a far cry from civic participation.

Little is fragile about the constitutional role played by the judicial branch in the United States: it is powerful and has great institutional breadth and depth nationally—features that are replicated subnationally. In contrast, we have suggested that the judiciary resembles a twig (rather than a branch) in Mexico and remains a fragile element in subnational government. In contrast, in Brazil the judiciary is much stronger, but in the past its poor level of administrative organization and unevenness across the country made for relative weakness. However, as we observed in chapter 3, through statewide accounting tribunals the judiciary is becoming more active in overseeing the government bureaucracy and policy implantation, reinforced by the Public Prosecutor's Office (Ministerio Público). This office, drawing strength from the 1988 Constitution, has assumed an active role in relation to collective rights, and its independent, open-access competition and career structure are attracting a new generation of civically oriented lawyers.

Identifying these aforementioned tensions and fragilities is important, not least because it allows us to assess whether the overall changes in subnational and local government performance—generally moving in a direction for the better, we would argue—are also vulnerable to sudden reverses. While many of the tensions identified above are likely to be present to a certain degree and will inevitably create counter-reactions and adjustments, we are generally confident that the advances observed in Brazil and Mexico will be difficult to undo. But many aspects of their institutionalization are still undeveloped and sometimes precarious, and much remains to be done. Later in this chapter we will return to the future of federalism in the three countries, but we first turn to some of the specific policy outcomes that derive from decentralization and from the changing nature of subnational governments.

## The Performance of Subnational Governments

### Reshaping Capacity in Subnational Policy Making

Intergovernmental relations are crucial for the development and implementation of public policies. Moreover, they are increasingly complex. Although the Brazilian and Mexican traditions have not embraced a multiple-sovereignty system of separate and distinct sets of responsibilities (federal, state, and, in the case of Brazil, local) to the extent found in the USA, in all three countries intergovernmental relations today do help shape the ability of subnational governments to fulfill their responsibilities.

For this reason assessing capacity in policy making has been a core issue of our discussion of the subnational state. The effectiveness of decentralization of the public sector inherently depends on the capacity of the subnational state to effectively make and implement policy. We have observed in the three countries instances of inadequate capacity, but we have also observed the development of new capabilities and innovative approaches to new responsibilities.

In policy making, *capacity* is generally understood to refer to the executive branch and, more specifically, to human and material resources and to service delivery systems. The decentralization of urban infrastructure provision—for example, the distribution of water—will succeed only if local government has engineers, construction facilities, financing mechanisms, and land acquisition authority, among other elements, and the ability to coordinate them. If a government does not have the necessary resources, then the question becomes whether they can be developed or mobilized. Thus increasing revenues to meet the demands of decentralized policy making has become an important issue in all three countries. On this element, the USA is quite different from Brazil and Mexico. In the USA's system, subnational governments generate much of their own revenue and rely less on transfers. To that extent, therefore, they are more autonomous in setting and implementing their policy agendas. Brazil and Mexico, on the other hand, are more reliant on federally mandated transfers for funding. But one significant change in both the Brazilian and Mexican systems has been the increased use of automatic transfers. This provision has substantially diminished the ability of the federal government to use transfers for political patronage (especially in Brazil), thus enhancing transparency but also facilitating budgetary and service provision planning. In addition, notable improvements in the capacity of subregional and local governments to generate home-grown resources have occurred, and this greater fiscal capacity is a driving element in the enhanced ability of state and local governments to develop their programs. In the USA, local control of government has always been predicated upon relatively high levels of local revenue generation, thus directly linking governmental capacity to local policy preferences and resources. In one policy area, public education, transfers from state government significantly supplement locally generated revenues to compensate for tax base disparities within a state. In Brazil, while certainly the relation to federal program funding does require municipalities to follow overall guidelines—for example, in health and education—suggesting a lack of autonomy (C. Souza 2005b), there is, as we remarked above, space for interpretation that, in the case of some municipalities, provides opportunities for significant innovation and—for all intents and purposes—local policy formation (Jacobi and Pinho 2006).

Our study suggests that the traditional understanding of capacity in subnational policy making needs to be extended in two directions. First, co-governance has become a critical element, especially in Brazil and Mexico. Both countries have a tradition of strong executive branches, particularly at the federal level but also at the state and local levels. In fact, in these two countries *government* is all too often (mis)perceived as referring exclusively to the executive branch. We have emphasized that government actually embraces a process of co-governance and involves the collaboration of all three branches in policy making. The strengthening of this process is relatively new in Mexico and Brazil and will need to be sustained and intensified. The USA differs quite substantially, since it has a long tradition of effective co-governance, at least at the state if not the local level.

Second, we believe that the participation of citizens and civil society associations in subnational policy making must be understood to be an important element of policy-making capacity. Beyond the democratic imperative that citizens elect public officials in fair and free elections, citizens have been observed to play meaningful roles in setting policy agendas by identifying and defining issues and also proposing solutions. Here, however, despite the presence of new forms of consultation and even institutional innovations of the participatory budgeting type that are moving across national boundaries, it is still early days in Brazil and Mexico, especially in relation to the effective self-representation of those facing poverty and other forms of defacto exclusion. In the USA, with a longer tradition, similar issues are emerging in relation to urban marginalization. Civil society is certainly on the move, but, as we noted in chapter 5, it too is in process.

Decentralization also implies a new role for the federal government vis-à-vis the states. Instead of being the principal provider of goods and services or intergovernmental transfers, it becomes increasingly the guarantor or regulator of actions taken by subnational governments. Although regulatory agencies have a long history in relation to national governments, their new regulatory role in terms of policy making is somewhat different, at least in Brazil and Mexico. How specific a policy should be, and how directive the national directives should be, are we suggest, important issues that mark the beginning of a new chapter in national-local government relations. The need for sensitivity in policy leadership is not easy to meet, especially by those used to more centralized forms of policy implementation.

### Promising Developments in Improving Subnational Government Capacity: A General Assessment

Our survey of policy making in subnational governments in the three countries has found many positive developments, and, despite some un-evenness in the pace of change, progress has been quite widespread. As discussed earlier in this chapter, the pace of change varies substantially across countries and among different policy areas within countries. Again, we find many pendulums at different cyclical phases. But notable progress has been achieved in several areas. First, institutional capacity (both the creation of new structures and institutions and the reform and improvement of existing ones) has developed to offer an expanded range of venues for discussions of public policy. These range from the strengthening of the powers of legislatures and participation in co-governance to new forums for citizens and to the emergence of a wide variety of associations of governments.

Second, decentralization has placed an emphasis on the modernization of subnational government and the development of new resources. The generation of local resources in the USA has always been the norm, but substantial progress may also be observed in Brazil and, to a lesser extent, Mexico. Capacity is being significantly improved by advances in the modernization of bureaucracy performance, including the adoption of new or innovative techniques.

A third area of promising development is the participation of civil society in policy making at the subnational level. Competitive elections are a key element of effective democratic practice, and on this score developments at the subnational level in Brazil and Mexico are unambiguously positive. But it is also useful in this context to recall Dahl's (1989) notion of polyarchy, his claim that the ability of groups of people, or civil society associations, to articulate and promote effectively their interests is one indicator of democracy. Promising trends emerge in Brazil and Mexico, while somewhat inconsistent patterns emerge for the USA. Although the latter has a rich history of civil society associations, the decline of participation in electoral politics is striking and quite unlike the new vitality found in subnational political life in Brazil and Mexico. Although we could interpret this trend in the USA as apathy or dissatisfaction among the electorate, one also finds increasing levels and effectiveness of participation involving a broader range of socioeconomic groups and of civil society entities in subnational policy making. Despite the widespread criticism of the powerful influence of special interests and, in the USA, the decline of the effectiveness of political parties to capture citizen preferences, greater competition in the public space should generate better government practice, though not necessarily with less contention. Expanded participation can make consensus building on policy even more difficult. Nevertheless, the success of decentralization will depend in part upon ensuring that adequate opportunities exist for participation of citizens, especially those who are less able to express themselves. On this point, our study has found much to suggest at least a certain level of optimism.

A fourth area of promise is that of bringing policy making and implementation closer to the people, since this usually improves the quality of policies by ensuring that they are more closely in tune with people's needs and with local priorities—or at least so decentralization theory suggests. Locally generated programs also cultivate a greater sense of ownership that can be important for program maintenance and cost recovery. Good examples are the local health programs in Brazil and the Intermodal Surface Transportation Efficiency Act in the USA, which was widely praised for broadening decision-making authority of local officials in metropolitan transportation planning.

Finally, even though we recognize the inherent dangers of generalization, we should pause to ask: Has it all been worth it? Is decentralization—coupled in the case of Brazil and Mexico with ongoing democratization—responding adequately to the need for advancing the general democratic well-being of the moral commonwealth, as we termed it in chapter 1? Here, too, depending on the specific arena or pendulum considered, our answer would seem to be: so far, so good.

In the key areas of social policy delivery (health care and education) in both Brazil and Mexico, decentralization certainly appears to be helping and moving access in the right direction. In Brazil the broad alliance that has emerged to support health reform has established new expectations for health delivery. The alliance itself was a key lever for democracy, thus showing how care needs to be taken in discussing decentralization and democracy simultaneously. In contrast, in Mexico the decentralization of both health care in the 1980s and public education from 1992 onwards was firmly promoted from the top down by federal government initiative rather than broad political or civic alliance. In both countries nearly all children are attending primary school, and the problem of educational quality has come to the fore, with much to be done to improve the moderate performance indicators relating to functional literacy, on-time graduation rates, and quality of technical training. Similar preoccupations over quality and its measurement may be observed at the subnational level in the USA. In fact, the issue of quality has been taken up by the federal government, which has established a system of national testing clearly infringing upon local control of public education. In Brazil and Mexico public school student access to the free federal and state universities remains at embarrassingly low levels. Moreover, whereas in the USA local governments (cities especially) have been able to develop reasonable to good levels of infrastructure for social policy delivery, aided by state and federal transfers, municipalities in Brazil and Mexico invariably remain strapped for resources and must collaborate with state and federal authorities, though they are doing so with increasing success. And while resource constraints are considerable, local governments are becoming more aware of the need to broaden and deepen their engagement in social policy by developing local programs for adolescents and the elderly, thereby reducing social inclusion. This is a far cry from what was once almost total dependency upon upper-level tiers of government.

However, employment and income generation are *the* major concerns of the large part of Brazil and Mexico's population living around or below minimum income levels. Even in the USA, persistent poverty and large numbers of the near-poor and the uninsured remain unresolved problems. In all countries targeted federal government programs are seeking to supplement family subsistence and human capital development (health and family grant programs to families in Brazil and Mexico and an earned income tax credit in the USA, for example), but fiscal constraints limit the extent to which state and especially local governments can add much substantively. When it comes to job creation, there is relatively little that subnational governments in Brazil and Mexico can reasonably be expected to achieve, and major financial investments are simply not yet a part of their mandate. In Brazil, while a number of municipalities have created employment departments and local development has returned to the agenda, the first Lula administration was unable to develop any kind of effective federal policy to kick-start local development and job creation. In the USA, with greater independence of action on the part of state government, promoting economic development is a key political concern, and local governments have traditionally been important in promoting the creation of the physical and service infrastructure that will attract new employment opportunities. But even here individual states remain substantially constrained by national economic conditions. Much of the recent expansion of employment opportunities has consisted of low-paying jobs, heralding a growing national debate about immigration, labor needs, and citizenship. Though the issue is nationally debated, state and local legislation and policy making have produced the major initiatives to advance or to cut back access to work, social services, and participation in daily life. This differentiation between the formal and informal (unregulated) sectors and the social exclusion of migrant workers—long a feature of daily life in Mexico and Brazil—has recently become a key issue centered upon immigrant groups living in the USA. How it plays out will depend ultimately and in large part upon the deliberations and policies adopted by federal government. But meanwhile the state and especially the local governments where these new populations reside and work are the entities facing the policy-making demands that will determine immigrants' capacity to contribute to and be a part of the nation's daily life.

A third major concern—and sometimes the primary concern—of local government is that of public security. In Brazil and Mexico a rising tide of violence is a key preoccupation given the state's incapacity to protect its citizens. In the USA, too, public security is a growing concern, less from day-to-day threats of criminal violence than from international (or national) terrorist threats.

Generally speaking, with some variation across the three countries, decentralization has been positive in its effects on the provision of education, health, and other social services at the state and local levels. On the negative side, however, there are major concerns and questions regarding its effects on job creation and development, and its effects on public security are somewhere in the middle. Decentralization has helped to the extent that it has drawn attention to the different roles and responsibilities of the three principal levels within the federal system, but equally important will be the extent to which the respective branches can lend their weight and influence through effective co-governance in lagging arenas.

### Decentralization—A Downside?

Although decentralization has been found in this study to produce a number of promising if not positive outcomes—at least when it is accompanied by the governance improvements that we have documented—several potential problems are well known. This section gives examples of these problems and discusses some of the practical solutions that have been found. First, decentralization in the face of major disparities between jurisdictions in tax base and capacity for resource generation may accentuate regional differences and promote divergence in policy outcomes unless there are countervailing forces to ensure some level of resource equalization. For example, in the three countries, fiscal equalization in education finance helps redress imbalances among states and localities. In the USA, state governments hold principal responsibility for equalization, but several federal programs also target low-income school districts. In Mexico funding is provided principally through the federal budget (Ramo 33), complemented by federally driven compensatory programs, while in Brazil through FUNDEF federal governments have adopted systems for addressing tax base disparities. But outside the field of education, mechanisms to address tax base disparities in specific policy arenas are less common, if not absent. This reinforces the point made above about the continuing need for a federal (or state) role in revenue equalization within any program of decentralization and devolution.

A second potential disadvantage of decentralizing a particular activity is the result of a loss of economies of scale or greater transaction costs. There may be a positive side to this—as we observed in chapter 4, the absence of such economies in smaller or poorer municipalities has led in Brazil to the extensive growth of consortia or *mancomunidad* (commonwealth) relationships in service provision—but substantial costs are involved. In metropolitan areas in the USA, the extensive use of interlocal agreements reflects a solution to inefficiencies in service delivery resulting from incongruities of scale in demand within existing jurisdictional boundaries and in production systems. Despite the compelling logic, creating such arrangements is far from easy and is, in fact, still far from common in all three countries.

Third, a frequent argument against devolution is that subnational and local governments are not yet ready, and do not have the capacity, to take on such new and expanded responsibilities. Increasingly, as our study has shown, this argument fails to recognize the convincing evidence of the enhanced capacity of subnational governments to deliver high-quality service. There are problems with the distribution of service providers, and there is plenty of space for improved capacity, including a role for higher levels of government to assist lower levels in capacity development (Campbell and Fuhr 2004). The question, however, is whether the public will recognize slow but steady improvement or call for recentralization in the face of inadequate outcomes.

Fourth, and closely related, is the argument that decentralization will not necessarily generate better democratic practice and that it can even strengthen the role of local oligarchs who will abuse their powers for personal gain (Hutchcroft 2001). In the USA, among those arguing for the return to the constitutionally defined dual-sovereignty form of federalism were southern segregationists unhappy with the federal government's intervention regarding state laws on racial segregation (i.e., the separate-but-equal provision of public services) and protection of voting rights. In Mexico and Brazil, the power of nondemocratic spatially based political oligarchs has sometimes been enhanced. But in many areas, both rural and urban, free elections and political competition have reduced the influence of such traditional political power, and the likely trend is that this will decline further in the future. "Brown zones" (O'Donnell 1994), where the state's writ is limited, may emerge, but they are unlikely to last unless the macro-level trend of democratic opening is thrown into reverse. To the extent that the rule of law is applied, and local democracy is working so that people can vote their government officials and representatives in (and out) of office, our evidence tends to be that learning does take place.

## Strategies for Enhancing Capacity

This study has revealed that Brazil, Mexico, and the USA are all making significant efforts to improve subnational policy making, guided by the recognition that such improvements will add to the positive impacts already achieved. The need to strengthen the legislative branches at the subnational level is clearly a recognized priority in Brazil and Mexico. Numerous examples of the need for enlightened political leadership have also been observed, and the practice in Brazil and Mexico of political leaders moving across the career tracks of the executive and legislative branches may prove beneficial as a new cadre of leaders, with a broader range of views, emerges. Moreover, numerous strategies for modernizing government are being developed. On the other hand, the "no reelection" rule in Mexico severely reduces performance incentives and inhibits the development of capacity, especially given the lack of any well-developed career civil service to provide continuity.

The role of political parties across the three countries in policy making is quite varied. The success of opposition parties in Mexico and Brazil has expanded the range of voices and positions that are incorporated in policy discussions and decisions. Even though increased competition in local politics can complicate decision making and produce inefficiencies when a newly elected party overturns the priorities of a previous administration, one should expect that in the long term the competition will encourage parties to seek citizen support by pursuing policies responsive to their needs and with reasonable levels of efficiency and appropriate assignment of costs. In the negative case, politicians and affiliated parties will lose credibility if they are ineffective when holding executive power. While political parties in Brazil and Mexico are gaining experience in subnational partisan competition, contemporary practices in local government in the USA are focused primarily on the personalities of candidates and not on the coherent and consistent policy agendas that one might expect of parties. Although parties are very important at the state level in the USA, they serve principally as electoral vehicles rather than as mediating agents to help citizens understand policy challenges.

We have found that federalist systems that afford subnational governments some degree of discretion and autonomy will be more supportive of innovation than those that seek to be directive. This pragmatic rather than normative conclusion is based on the observation that such innovation will take place with or without federal intervention. Subnational governments are becoming increasingly skilled in the art of interpreting federal wishes in their own interests, repeating at the local government level what Michael Lipsky's lower-order bureaucrats learned to do on the streets (Lipsky 1980). For example, subnational levels of government are forming associations, some of which focus on training, lobbying, and disseminating best practices. Such associations have long been important in the USA, especially during the 1970s and 1980s, while in Brazil associations are only now beginning to proliferate, and even in Mexico since 2002 we have observed a strengthening of collaboration among state executives (through CONAGO).

### Challenges of Decentralization

Decentralization continues to face a number of challenges, not least of which are the growing complexity of society and the rising demand for public services. Service delivery is a question not only of policy but also of administrative competence (Keck and Abers 2006). Most issues of public policy are also complex and frequently subject to conflicting values. This increasing complexity imposes challenges not only to government but also to citizens, who must, in the end, judge whether governmental action is effective. As citizens become more involved in co-governance, they, too, must be better informed and have adequate access to information, which in turn influences and changes demands.

Political leadership is also required, and leaders need to be willing to take risks and learn to share power responsibly and, within a context of partisanship, fulfill their co-governance roles. But this involves a process of adjustment to enhance co-governance relations and power sharing; and political leadership and risk taking, particularly from the executive branch, are crucial. Given that most legislative bodies are only now developing capacity for policy analysis and debates in Brazil and Mexico, the executive branch continues to be stronger. Enhanced partisan competition in local elections in Brazil and Mexico further constrains the victors of local elections, particularly if the victors are from an opposition party. Over time, and with changes in the governing political party, the practice of co-governance and sharing of decision-making power between the legislative and executive branch should become more acceptable and even expected. But since this implies a fairly fundamental change in political culture and practice, the period of transition is likely to be long and subject to setbacks.

We have already made the point that federal governments will continue to be central to the government structure in spite of decentralization. In addition to their role in fiscal federalism and defense of national citizenship, federal governments must still be the venue for establishing national priorities (Díaz Cayeros 2006). If a decentralized system gives greater weight to regional actors, one can expect the formation of consensus on national goals to become even more contested. From historical practice, certainly in the USA but also in Brazil and Mexico, national priorities can sometimes come into conflict with local priorities and values. In fact, examples of a return to centralization, if not preemption, have already appeared in the USA (national security), in Brazil (the fiscal responsibility law), and in Mexico (compensatory programs in public education).

Confronting disparities is a major challenge, whether in resources, tax base potential, human resources, or even capacities of subnational governments. The ability of wealthy regions such as the state of São Paulo, Nuevo León (Monterrey), and the state of California to pursue innovative policies of long-term impact has historically depended on their local economies to generate the underlying wealth and knowledge. In a decentralized system, relatively poor regions remain at a distinct disadvantage. This observation does not necessarily mean that recentralization is the only means to reduce such inequalities, but certainly such inequalities are unlikely to disappear without special actions by higher-level, especially national, governments. The European Union, for example, has addressed the problems of the relatively lesser-developed regions through its structural funds program and very significant transfers to infrastructure development.

### Interstate and Regional Relations

There are a number of signs that countries are beginning to tackle the challenge and opportunities of creating not just regional alliances between state governments but also corresponding levels of citizen involvement through participation. Initial government studies (2003) to reestablish Northeast Brazil's SUDENE (Superintendencia do Nordeste), a former major development agency of the 1960s–70s modeled on the Tennessee Valley Authority, have proposed that, in addition to the presence of the region's governors on the agency's board, provision should be made to guarantee representation of civil society organizations. The

Amazon basin region is another area that could well see proposals for regional integration, and similar questions are being raised in southern Mexico (Puebla-Panama) and even by some governors in three relatively well-off states in northern Mexico, with the possible participation of Texas (González Parás 2003). Again, we find that the overall federal framework, as a conceptual device for thinking about governance in relation to territoriality, not only allows considerable elasticity but also can be a stimulus for innovation.

### The Metropolis

The enormous range in size and scale of the urban systems of each of the three countries that we studied itself creates challenges, and there can be no single template for effective governance in metropolitan areas (Paiva 2003). A significant number of the world's largest megacities lie within our focus countries, concentrating huge populations in often complex dynamics of urban poverty and inequality. Metropolitan São Paulo and Mexico City, each with around twenty million residents, exemplify many of the problems: some thirty-nine and sixty-three different municipalities respectively, in each case constituting a single urban area with hardly any linked arrangements, let alone governance institutions of the kind that can be found, for example, in London. Yet in each case there are anomalies associated with adequate representation, so that in municipal São Paulo a handful of elected representatives (fifty-five) struggle to represent adequately nearly ten million people, while in Mexico's Federal District only sixty-six individuals make up the legislative assembly. This problem of metropolitan fragmentation and representation is also present in the USA. In Harris County, where the city of Houston is located, and where there is a population of about 3.5 million residents, over five hundred independent or semi-independent governmental units operate, including thirty-five municipalities, twenty-three independent school districts, and over four hundred municipal utility districts. In the city of Los Angeles, a city council of fifteen representatives must respond to a constituency that totals around four million residents. However, as yet we have not observed any significant support for a metropolitan tier of government in these three countries, and the problems of social disparities, political representation, and inefficiencies in service delivery in metropolitan areas are not a visible element of the policy agenda of any government.

### Whither Federalism?

Brazil, Mexico, and the USA share geographical and historical similarities while being different on a number of cultural dimensions. They are also part of what has been at times referred to as the "Western World" and, as such, are both products and producers of broader views of state and governance expressed both in international orthodoxies and in their countermovements. It is perhaps significant that the same continent that produced the territorial reference in the name of the leading international orthodoxy of the 1980s (the so-called Washington Consensus) should also be the place where its principal nongovernmental countermovement also took on an international perspective (World Social Forum).

Even though the actual number of federal governments around the world is relatively small (twenty-five), they represent a significant proportion of the world's population (40 percent), and three of the larger ones form our study. Federalism, as an approach to the design of institutional governance, is growing in importance, especially as an approach to difference. Thus, as Juan Linz and Alfred Stepan (1996) point out, federalist-type models can be found among those countries in southern Europe that emerged from dictatorships; those in Latin America that threw over "bureaucratic authoritarian regimes"; and those of the post-communist former Soviet Union. While, as in the case of our three countries, federalism may be the product of a bottom-up or a top-down institutional design history, it has been societally interpreted as carrying an assumption of the relative independence of the subnational territorial parts, with constitutionally based authority, that is not found within the unitary state approach, independently of any difference in legislative-executive relations. In principle, and as we have found, to different degrees, municipalities and states see themselves as different from each other and from the general whole. Constitutional specialists and lawyers may argue that Latin America's federalist countries are federalist "on paper" but not in practice, but our analysis from the policy perspective suggests otherwise: that is, that subnational governments have found the federal approach convenient for their own desires for identity and independence (Stepan 1997). To follow Paul Pierson's (1995) argument, different actors have learned to bring interests to arenas that are more favorable for them. Brazil's indigenous populations, for example, have no interest whatsoever in letting their territorial and development agenda be assumed by subnational governments; on the contrary, their concern is firmly focused on the federal government. The U.S. civil rights movement attacked practices concerning electoral rights and public accommodation in southern states that violated federal laws, anticipating federal intervention in defense of the rights of African Americans.

In the subnational arenas of the three countries we can see numerous movements and changes taking place, many of them specific to national questions. But a number of broader issues also surround both federalism and the nation-state model, and these too make themselves present in the various subnational contexts. The answer to the question "Whither federalism?" will be a consequence of these external and internal pressures and counterpressures. To what degree each will play a part is beyond the scope of our research competence, but we can draw attention to some of the pressures and counterpressures that we have noted during the study and sketch how these might shape federalism in the future.

The first set of pressures, especially strong in the context of our three countries, are those global issues that reinforce overall national boundaries at the expense of subnational autonomy. The increase in concern with international terrorism after the September 11 attack on the World Trade Center in New York, the increased need for health and sanitary controls following recent epidemics of SARS and mad cow disease, and the overall concern with international drug activity and money laundering have all led to a centralization of coordination and regulation. At the same time, in other areas, a number of towns, cities, and states that share similar problems may find themselves gathering together to share information and seek common answers on issues such as housing, poverty reduction, health management, and economic development. Significant here has been the recent amalgamation of the two leading city and town associations, the International Union of Local Authorities and the World Federation of United Cities (IULA-FMCU), at the second World Assembly of Cities and Local Authorities (2001), with Barcelona as the headquarters of the international secretariat.

In the same vein, with different consequences for their own members and their areas of interest (which certainly include Latin America), are the institutional changes being introduced slowly but steadily by the European Community, itself always a potential model for regional integration (given Latin America's symbolic links with Europe) in opposition to the more restricted ALCA/FTAA set of propositions. Given the variety of institutional designs present in the individual European countries, it is inevitable that the search for a more integrative model will provide international leadership for thinking not just about regionalism between and within nations but also about questions that combine the two, as in the case of natural resources like water. In the case of the Americas, the IADB and the Organization of American States will also be key forums for discussion, and it is possible that the pressures and counterpressures emerging around the World Trade Organization will be an increasing feature of subnational relations, especially with state governors and municipal mayors attempting to play a more active part in job creation by attracting employment opportunities and protecting their economic interests.

While we doubt that there will be any specific cataclysmic future moments of "recasting the federal pacts" (indeed, in the case of Brazil and Mexico the term *pact* is still something of an overstatement), we also have no doubt that the pressures we have mentioned, and others, could lead to a process of significant stepwise incremental adjustment; indeed, we think it is already under way. Eaton (2004b) has argued that subnational institutional design is not unique to the late twentieth century. It will probably be necessary for federalism to develop greater flexibility as it seeks to occupy new institutional territories and architectures (de Figueiredo and Weingast 2005; Wibbels 2005). In Brazil, as chapter 4 has shown, full-scale municipalization of health has strengthened the use of a subsidiarity approach within the different tiers of public service provision; equally we can point to changes in education in Mexico (from federal to state control), and in the USA both the Environmental Protection Agency and the Intermodal Surface Transportation Act have produced important consequences for federal, state, and local relations. All of these developments, and the many others cited throughout this book, are responses to specific concerns of policy and—simultaneously—carry implications for the general institutional frame. Perhaps one of the most striking conclusions that we can make about federalism as a reference model for organizing institutional discussion is its elastic capacity to *enable*, in the sense of providing a symbolic justification for multiple actions to take place in different directions without generating an overall institutional crisis.

That said, we expect a broadening of the options available for federalist interorganizational design as its institutional and social architects go about their day-to-day problem solving in their different thematic areas. Some of the newer structural options that are emerging may have taken a number of years to mature, but once they have reached a certain visibility their use can accelerate rapidly. One such example is the intermunicipal consortia in Brazil, which can now be found all over the country targeting a variety of thematic concerns. Rather like participative budgeting, which forged a new kind of relationship between local governments and citizens over planning and budgeting in a way that had not been foreseen by law, the intermunicipal consortia have provided a new angle on regional institutional relations.

In the USA, single-purpose issue-related governments are common and are a strong feature of local education, with its model of independent school districts. Even though these districts are closely tied to state governments and, indeed, are created under state government authority, democratically elected governing bodies, as we have commented elsewhere, not only manage local education but also help raise taxes and assume debt on behalf of their member populations. In international comparisons, the limited role of the federal government in public education makes the USA an outlier. Independent school districts are not a product of decentralization—indeed, they are a product of a much earlier process of service provision—but they offer a thought-provoking approach to government, for it is not axiomatic that within a federal model one should automatically expect a single tier of government to assume a large number of different responsibilities.

Mexico also is currently the proving ground for several institutional ideas that create new public spaces for the indigenous populations of what, after Columbus, we call the Americas. While in the USA the territories of the indigenous tribal peoples are currently more clearly marked (since they were artificially constructed and imposed as reservations), in all three countries the presence of a significant number of different indigenous peoples with their own models of government and territorial organization has presented a design challenge to future federalist arrangements. By constitutional definition, in the USA and Mexico the federal members are states, while in Brazil the federal members are states and municipalities, yet in all three countries substantial areas are under varied forms of tribal jurisdiction. One form of broadening access is the election of indigenous mayors within municipalities that have a significant indigenous population; but this can be considered only the beginning of a process that will involve state or interstate dimensions, for the designers of state boundaries are more concerned with questions of rivers, mountains, and other physical markers than with the roaming areas of the many different indigenous populations. Thus an important emergent issue is the capacity of federalism to accommodate the growing number of indigenous, ethnic, and cultural identities. Here Mexico, with its acceptance of the superseding of municipal rights by *usos y costumbres,* offers a potential for the concept of "federacies" as a means of recognizing spatial patchworks corresponding to ethnic, cultural, and language rights and groupings (Elazar 1987b).

A general concern with rights and the growing presence of self-identified tribal and indigenous peoples has fast-forwarded the emergence of new actors on the regional and national stage in Latin America. While indigenous rights were largely ignored in the past, today they have salience in many countries throughout the region (Birnir 2006; Van Cott 2005; Yashar 2005; Mattiace 2003). In Brazil through its 1988 Constitution, the indigenous peoples' own organizations are recognized as the legitimate representatives of their interests, thus ending a long battle for the right to voice but starting a new battle for multilingual education, culturally appropriate health services, economic opportunities, and land demarcation. In Mexico the trajectory is similar, and the constitutional changes throughout the 1990s will formally recognize the legitimacy of the indigenous peoples' own organizations and their rights to cultural differentiation and cultural preservation (Mattiace 2003). In both cases, at least at the formal institutional level, the various indigenous peoples have begun to exercise this institutional right to representation in the subnational arena, along with its accompanying questions of territorial relations. Although the USA has advanced further—despite an extremely troubled past—the tribal nations still face serious problems with education; only in the state of New Mexico, with a large and varied tribal population, has a specific department been created to serve as a liaison office with the tribal governments.

Identity rights (Isin and Wood 1999) is a theme that affects many people in different ways, and given the potential of federalism to offer multiple access points to affect public policy and to leverage rights, many new issues are emerging. For example, to the extent that accessing certain rights is determined by state and local governments in the USA, gay marriage has become a feature of everyday life long before its acceptance by federal authorities. Other issues may follow similar paths.

In Brazil (increasingly) and in Mexico (especially) there is a growing intersection between the local and the transnational as hometown populations maintain close ties with their kinsmen and *paisanos* residing and working in the USA, a relationship articulated both through remittances and more formally through hometown associations. These linkages create a whole new arena of civic participation that is being mobilized by state and local governments in states such as Zacatecas, Michoacán, and Oaxaca as they reach out to hometown associations in the USA (Fox and Rivera Salgado 2004; Stephen 2006). Moreover, these states are exploring ways in which migrant populations may be effectively enfranchised (by voting in local elections) and represented (by having a state deputy or even a mayor) who is a migrant living in two places (Mexico and the USA). Thus, for many migrants and their origin populations today, the subnational and local space extends beyond the formally drawn boundaries, and to the extent that such relationships are likely to intensify we should probably be open to the apparent contradictory idea that transnational space has a subnational and local component. More research is needed to understand better how such spaces and actors perceive, shape, and intersect with the moral commonwealth of "hometowns" and "home states." Although there is only an incipient literature at present, the role of transnational civics within the subnational civil society, together with another concept, that of federacies, is likely to be an increasingly important area of research and praxis, and not just in Mexico and the USA.

These comments—extending as they do our observations into present and future research possibilities—lead us to recognize that any attempt to conclude this volume with a single conception of federalism as a common normative model would be doomed to failure. In fact, as we have found constantly in our research, the various trends along the continuum of centralization to decentralization are taking place in the creative chaos brought about by differences that range from the demographic to the cultural and from the regionally geographical to the international and global, and especially by the different practical theories that people have about governance (the mechanisms that organizations, communities, and societies develop to steer themselves). In these processes, new institutional forms are being created to offer specific solutions to specific questions, and this elasticity—as we have come to call it—is perhaps the strength of the federalist approach. In the USA and especially more recently in Brazil and Mexico, it is the subnational dimension of the federalist approach that is being exercised and tested. It has been said that while ancient Greece was able to devise the confederate model of territorial aggregation, it was not until the American Revolution that polities could move onwards to federalism. So "Whither federalism?" Onwards, outwards, upwards, downwards, and from side to side, at least until we discover the limits of its conceptual elasticity and efficacy.

# Notes

ONE Decentralization and the Subnational State

1. Defined as where "[a] larger power and smaller polity are linked asymmetrically in a federal relationship in which the latter has substantial autonomy and in return has a minimal role in governance of the larger power. Resembling a federation, the relationship between them can only be resolved by mutual agreement" (Cameron and Falleti 2005, 262). Examples of federacies are Greenland (relative to Denmark), the Isle of Man and the Channel Islands (relative to the United Kingdom), and the Northern Marianas (USA). But such arrangements may become increasingly significant to regional, ethnic, linguistic, and religious entities as an alternative to full sovereignty.

2. We wish to acknowledge the exceptionally insightful and useful comments from the referees. As well as providing the usual critique of argumentation, quality of evidence, and other matters, the commentators—through their engagement with the substantive issues raised—offered insights and suggestions that the authors had not previously recognized. To the best of our ability we have sought to address their criticisms in the subsequent revisions. Naturally, the usual disclaimers apply.

3. It was also agreed that the names of the authors of the overall book should be listed in reverse alphabetical order so as both to reflect the effective coauthorship and also to credit the role that Robert Wilson played in bringing the research team together in the first place.

4. In a major review article, "The New Separation of Powers," Bruce Ackerman (2000) discusses the shortcomings of the U.S. presidentialist system and its export to other nations (especially in Latin America) and argues that a "constrained parliamentarianism" offers a more promising path to constitutional development than the American model and that it can provide for a variety of institutional strategies that will enhance a modern doctrine of separation of powers. See also Linz (1994) and Cameron and Falleti (2005).

5. It should be noted, however, that most of the literature on decentralization focuses on administrative decentralization. Since the 1980s, with the "devolution revolution" in the USA, there has been a growing discussion of devolution in the USA.

6. See Wolman (1990, 30) for a discussion of the public choice justification for decentralization.

7. This section relies heavily on and sometimes reproduces Victoria Rodríguez's discussion "Participation, Representation and Democracy," taken from ch. 1 of her book *Women in Contemporary Mexican Politics* (2003).

8. See Pateman's (1970) succinct summary of what a democratic system entails: "In the theory, 'democracy' refers to a political method or set of institutional arrangements at national level. The characteristically democratic element in the method is the competition of leaders (elites) for the votes of the people at periodic, free elections. Elections are crucial to the democratic method for it is primarily through elections that the majority can exercise control over their leaders. Responsiveness of leaders to non-elite demands, or 'control' over leaders, is ensured primarily through the sanction of loss of office at elections; the decisions of leaders can also be influenced by active groups bringing pressure to bear during inter-election periods. 'Political equality' in the theory refers to universal suffrage and to the existence of equality of opportunity of access to channels of influence over leaders. Finally, 'participation,' so far as the majority is concerned, is participation in the choice of decision makers. Therefore, the function of participation in the theory is solely a protective one; the protection of the individual from arbitrary decisions by elected leaders and the protection of his private interests" (14).

THREE    The Changing Institutional Capacity of Subnational Government

1. Sometimes *decentralization* has also been used to refer to the transfer of activities from government to business or social organizations, usually in relation to the implementation of policies, but as S. Smith and Lipsky (1993) have pointed out, this can also have policy implications.

2. Other systems—both unitary and federal—often give greater aegis to the executive branch of government (the "one-and-a-half house structure," as Ackerman [2000] calls it) through their specific design of the allocation and separation of powers, even though there may also be greater opportunities to remove the executive in those structures (through a vote of no confidence, realignment of coalitions, recall votes, etc.).

3. Some states accord the governor considerable powers, although in Texas, for example, as in other states, the lieutenant governor (the independently elected leader of the state congress who is the legal substitute for the governor) exercises greater influence by virtue of having more direct control over the legislative pro-

cess and over congressional committee assignments. In the USA not all state congresses are bicameral, and this also shapes the relative strength of the local congress and the relations between the branches.

4. As one governor cogently expressed it more than thirty years ago, "The federal government screws me; and I screw the municipality" (Ugalde, quoted in Fagen and Tuohy 1972, 22).

5. Formal impeachment by the state congress was never an issue in Mexico, since a governor or municipal president could, in effect, informally be removed from office if he incurred the president's displeasure. But as such opportunities for summary dismissals ended, the legislature has been obliged to exercise its constitutional role of impeachment of the governor or the removal of a congress representative's parliamentary immunity. The point, here, is one of *activation* of previously dormant constitutional roles.

6. While the Brazilian Ministério Público (Public Prosecutor's Office) is independent and separate from the judiciary—seen by some commentators as a fourth power—it is considered in the Constitution as an integral part of the judicial function of the state.

7. Although this is not the case in all states. In North Carolina, for example, the governor has no veto power.

8. A simple list of their identification letters is sufficient to understand the problems raised: PMDB, PFL, PSDB, PDS, PDC, PST, PTR, PP, PPR, PPB, PTB, PDT, PT, PL, PSB, PPS, PMN, PV, PcdoB, PSC, PST, PSL, PSD, and PRONA.

9. That is, coalitions that are always in a quasi-unstable state and subject to change at any moment.

10. Indeed, until 2002 incumbents did not even have to battle for renomination, since they were considered "birthright candidates" *(candidatos natos)* whose names automatically went forward to the next election. As we discuss earlier in the chapter, surprisingly Brazil shows a high legislative turnover (over 50 percent) compared to the low level in the USA (Samuels 2003, 1–2).

11. It is not unknown in Mexico for the outgoing majority party, facing as it may an incoming governor or a change in majority-party control of Congress, to hurry through changes that are deliberately designed to constrain the newcomers, seeking to tie their hands or to embarrass them into passing reversal legislation (Rodríguez and Ward 1994; Aziz 1996; Morales Barud 2003).

12. The permanent home page of the National Conference of State Legislatures can be found at www.ncsl.org/, and electoral and other data that are considered here may be found at that location. They are regularly updated.

13. In Brazil, the impeachment of President Collor led to a rash of similar actions at the local level.

14. The Senate blocked two of President Clinton's nominees latterly during his presidency. The average period between nomination and confirmation increased dramatically under his administration from 54 to 115 days (Rynders 2003, 41), and more and more vacancies are unfilled due to congressional grid-

lock. Interesting, too, is the growing antipathy toward so-called "activist" justices (i.e., those who seek to recast law rather than simply abide by precedent [*stare decisis*] decisions, whether conservative or radical). President Bush came out heavily against activist judges, who, he said, should not seek to legislate from the bench. This preoccupation, rhetorical or not, indicates the substantial powers of the judicial branch in U.S. national and subnational governments.

15. In a few states, such as Massachusetts, the governor appoints judges (Friedman 1984). States also use a mixed approach whereby vacancies for judges are filled by appointment but only for a limited term, after which time voters elect to retain or dismiss the sitting judge.

16. One of these electoral victories was a recent breakthrough, that of Amalia García in Zacatecas in 2004.

17. Led by the (then) minister of administration and state reform, Bresser Perreira (see Bresser Pereira and Spink 1998). For a critical evaluation, see Paes de Paulo (2005), and for a recent overview of its wider effects, see the texts assembled by Levy and Drago (2005).

18. This can be seen in the entries to the annual awards of the Public Management and Citizenship Program, where the area of administration (that is, actions to improve administration independent of specific policy areas) has contributed 9 percent of all applicants and the general area of public services some 47 percent (Spink 2006). Other evidence comes from state governments, such as that of Minas Gerais, which recently introduced its "management shock" program of administrative modernization, or that of Ceará, which figured prominently in Judith Tendler's *Good Government in the Tropics* (1997). Abrucio (2005), reporting on the results of a countrywide study carried out by the Federal Planning Ministry with support from the IADB as part of the National Program to Support the Modernization of State-Level Management and Planning, points to important transformations taking place especially in information management and planning, which are "administrative aspects essential for the improvement of public policies."

19. If we use the Public Management and Citizenship Program as an approximate guide, entries by municipal and state legislative powers during the first eight award cycles (1996–2003) resulted in a total of only seventeen applications, but in the ninth and tenth cycles a further twenty-one entries were received, more than 100 percent over the previous period—a significant though small improvement.

20. *Ejidos* are social collectives created as part of Mexico's agrarian reform program.

21. An example is the federal government's education program to supplement teacher pay and aid decentralized educational development, which requires the municipality to create an educational planning council. A similar council has to be created for school meal support.

22. Data results are from a survey carried out by the Popular Participation Forum, which polled all municipalities during the 1997–2000 period, and data from a Ford Foundation sponsored study currently under way.

FOUR   Intergovernmental Relations and the Subnational State

1. Ministerio da Saude, "Annuário Estatistico de Saúde do Brasil, 2001," 2001, http://portal.sauda.gov.br/portal/aplicacors/anvario2001/index.cfm (accessed June 21, 2007).

2. Brazil's municipalities continue to grow in number as a result of the division of existing jurisdictions, a process referred to as *emancipation*. The number 5,562 represents the number of municipalities taking part in the 2005 local elections (Brenacker 2004).

3. Two initiatives identified in the Public Management and Citizenship Program's annual awards provide clear illustrations of this approach: the Consórcio Intermunicipal de Produção e Abastecimento in Maranhão and the Processo de Desenvolvimento Sustentável in Urupema, Santa Catarina (Farah and Barbosa 2000; Programa Gestao Pública e Cidadania 1999).

4. *New York State Ice Co. v. Liebman,* 295 U.S. 262 (1932), n.p.

5. Interviews with Maria do Carmo Meirelles Toledo Cruz and Ana Thereza Junqueira, from Fundação Prefeito Faria Lima and CEPAM, in São Paulo, March 6, 2001.

6. The first initiative of this type, the Intermunicipal Consortium of the Piracicaba River Watershed, was formed in the early 1990s and by 2002 included forty-two municipalities (Comitê das Bacias Hidrográficas 2005). Its principal purpose is the recovery and preservation of water resources.

FIVE   Government and Citizens

1. Ação da Cidadania contra a Miséria e Pela Vida was officially created on March 8, 1993, as an initiative of multiple actors, including the Workers' Party, the government, and the Catholic Church, organized around the figure of Herbert de Souza of the Brazilian Institute for Social and Economic Analysis (Instituto Brasileiro de Análises Sociais e Econômicas, IBASE), a Rio de Janeiro–based NGO. By October of the same year over three thousand committees had been established around the country. Another contributing factor to their success was, no doubt, the impeachment of President Collor, which had itself generated widespread social action.

2. For example, see the work of Zygmunt Bauman (1998), Robert Castel (1995), John Friedmann (1992), and Amartya Sen (1999).

3. See the unpublished paper by Ward, Rodríguez, and Robles (2003), written as part of the "Democracy through U.S. and Mexican Lenses" William and Flora Hewlett Foundation Grant No. 2000-4406, Roderic Ai Camp (principal investigator), Miguel Basáñez, Rodolfo de la Garza, Joseph Klesner, Chappell Lawson, Alejandro Moreno, Pablo Parás, Victoria Rodríguez, and Peter Ward (Camp 2003). See also IADB (2006).

4. In doing so we avoid both entering the debate sparked by Robert Putnam's (1993) study of the historical underpinnings of associative resources in Italy (see Sabetti 1996) and joining the wave of those who see social capital as the latest pivotal concept (www.worldbank.org/socialcapital).

5. See Castells (1983); Ramírez Saíz (1986).

6. Partisan elections still mark cities such as New York and Chicago, where political machines once ruled.

7. In Brazil the introduction of the electronic voting method in 1998 (partially) and 2002 (totally) brought about a significant drop in the number of spoilt ballots.

SIX   The Past, Present, and Future of Subnational Governments and Federalism

1. See Aguilar and Ward (2003), Cox (1997), and Swyngedouw (1997) for further critiques.

# Bibliography

Abrucio, Fernando Luis. 1998. *Os barões da Federação: Os governadores e a redemocratização brasileira*. São Paulo: Departamento da Ciência Política, Universidade de São Paulo.

———. 2005. "Reforma do estado no federalismo brasileiro." *Revista de Administração Pública* 39, no. 2:401–20.

Abrucio, Fernando Luis, and Valeriano Mendes Ferreira Costa. 1998. *Reforma do estado e o contexto federativo brasileiro*. Série Pesquisas 12. São Paulo: Fundação Konrad-Adenauer-Stiftung.

Ackerman, Bruce. 2000. "The New Separation of Powers." *Harvard Law Review* 113, no. 3:634–729.

Acuña, Carlos, and Mariano Tommasi. 1999. "Some Reflections on the Institutional Reforms Required for Latin America." Working Paper 20, Centro de Estudios para el Desarrollo Institucional and Yale University Center for International and Area Studies.

Adams, John. 2000. "Letter to John Penn." In *The Political Writings of John Adams*, edited by George W. Carey, 491–97. Washington, DC: Regnery.

Advisory Commission on Intergovernmental Relations. 1984. *Regulatory Federalism: Policy, Process, Impact and Reform*. Washington, DC: Advisory Commission on Intergovernmental Relations.

———. 1986. *The Transformation in American Politics: Implications for Federalism*. Washington, DC: Advisory Commission on Intergovernmental Relations.

Afonso, José, Roberto Rodrigues, and Érika Amorim Araújo. 2000. "A capacidade de gastos dos municípios brasileiros: Arrecadação própria e receita disponível." *Cadernos Adenauer* 1 (June): 35–57.

Agranoff, Robert, and Michael McGuire. 1999. "Expanding Intergovernmental Management's Hidden Dimensions." *American Review of Public Administration* 29, no. 4:352–69.

———. 2003. *Collaborative Public Management: New Strategies for Local Governments*. Washington, DC: Georgetown University Press.

Aguilar, Adrian, and Peter Ward. 2003. "Globalization, Regional Development, and Mega-city Expansion in Latin America: Analyzing Mexico City's Peri-urban Hinterland." *Cities* 20, no. 1:3–21.

Aliança Capoava. 2005. *Alianças e parecerias: Mapeamento das publicações brasileiras sobre alianças e parcerias entre organizações da sociedade civil e empresas.* São Paulo: Imprensa Oficial do Estado de São Paulo.

Alinsky, Saul D. 1969. *Reveille for Radicals.* New York: Vintage Books.

Almeida, Maria Hermínia Tavares de. 1996. "Federalismo e políticas sociais." In *Descentralização e políticas sociais,* edited by Rui de Britto Álvares Affonso and Pedro Luiz Barros Silva. São Paulo: Fundação do Desenvolvimento Administrativo.

———. 2005a. "Federalismo e políticas sociais." *Revista Brasileira de Ciências Sociais* 28, no. 10:88–108.

———. 2005b. "Recentralizando a federação." *Revista de Sociologia e Política* 24:29–40.

Altshuler, Alan, William Morrill, Harold Wolman, and Faith Mitchell, eds. 1999. *Governance and Opportunity in Metropolitan America.* Washington, DC: National Academy Press.

Alvarez, S. E., E. Dagnino, and A. Escobar, eds. 1998. *Cultures of Politics/Politics of Cultures: Revisioning Latin American Social Movements.* Boulder, CO: Westview Press.

Alves, Alaôr Caffé. 1998. *Saneamento básico: Concessões permissões e convênios públicos.* São Paulo: Edipro.

Anton, Thomas J. 1984. "Intergovernmental Change in the United States: An Assessment of the Literature." In *Public Sector Performance: A Conceptual Turning Point,* edited by Trudi Miller. Baltimore: Johns Hopkins University Press.

———. 1988. *American Federalism and Public Policy: How the System Works.* New York: Temple University Press.

Apud, Salvador. 2003. "The Implications of Culture in the Study of Public Management Reform and Change." PhD diss. proposal and ongoing research, Lyndon B. Johnson School of Public Affairs, University of Texas, Austin.

Arantes, Rogério B. 2002. *Ministerio público e política no Brasil.* São Paulo: Fundação de Amparo à Pesquisa do Estado de São Paulo/EDUC.

———. 2005. "Constitutionalism, the Expansion of Justice and the Judicialization of Politics in Brazil." In *The Judicialization of Politics in Latin America,* edited by Rachel Sieder, Line Schjolden, and Alan Angell, 231–62. New York: Palgrave.

Arantes, Rogério B., Fernando L. Abrucio, and Marco A. C. Teixeira. 2005. "A imagem dos tribunais de contas subnacionais." *Revista do Serviço Público* 56, no. 1:57–84.

Arnaut, Alberto. 1994. "La federalización de la educación básica y normal, 1978–1994." *Política y Gobierno* 1, no. 2:237–74.

Arrellano Gault, D. 2004. "Porque un servicio profesional de carrera es importante para una democracia?" *Servicio Profesional de CARRERA* 1, no. 1:59–64.

Arretche, Marta T. S. 1999. "Políticas sociais no Brasil: Descentralização em um estado federativo." *Revista Brasileira de Ciências Sociais* 14 (June): 112–41.

———. 2000. *Estado federativo e políticas sociais: Determinantes da descentralização.* Rio de Janeiro: Fundação de Amparo à Pesquisa do Estado de São Paulo.

———. 2002. "Federalismo e relações intergovernamentais no Brasil: A reforma de programas sociais." *Dados* 45, no. 3:431–58.

———. 2004. "Toward a Unified and More Equitable System: Health Reform in Brazil." In *Crucial Needs, Weak Incentives: Social Sector Reform, Democratization, and Globalization in Latin America,* edited by Robert R. Kaufman and Joan Nelson. Washington, DC: Woodrow Wilson Center Press.

———. 2005. "Quem taxa e quem gasta: A barganha federativa na federação brasileira." *Revista de Sociologia e Política* 24:69–85.

Arretche, Marta, and Vicente Rodrigues, eds. 1999. *Descentralização das políticas sociais no Brasil.* São Paulo: Fundação do Desenvolvimento Administrativo and Fundação de Amparo à Pesquisa do Estado de São Paulo.

Avelar, Lúcia. 2001. *Mulheres na elite política brasileira.* São Paulo: Fundação Konrad Adenauer and Editora Universidade Estadual Paulista.

Avritzer, Leonardo. 1994. *Sociedade civil e democratização.* Belo Horizonte: Editora Del Rey.

Avritzer, Leonardo, and Zander Navarro, eds. 2003. *A inovação democrática no Brasil: O orçamento participativo.* São Paulo: Cortez.

Aziz Nassif, Alberto. 1996. *Territorios de alternancia: El primer gobierno de oposición en Chihuahua.* Mexico City: Triana Editores.

Baqueiro, Marcelo. 2001. Cultura política participativa e desconsolidação democrática: Reflexões sobre o Brasil contemporânea. *São Paulo em Perspectiva* 15, no. 4:98–104.

Barber, Benjamin R. 1984. *Strong Democracy: Participatory Politics for a New Age.* Berkeley: University of California Press.

Barfield, Claude E. 1981. *Rethinking Federalism: Block Grants and Federal, State, and Local Responsibilities.* Washington, DC: American Enterprise Institute for Public Policy Research.

Barrón, Luis F. 2001. *Economic Regions, Fueros and Political Integration in México (1821–1824).* División de Historia, Documento de Trabajo No. 06. Mexico City: Centro de Investigación y Docencia Económicas. www.cide.edu.

Bauman, Zygmunt. 1998. *Work, Consumerism and the New Poor.* Buckingham: Open University Press.

Beard, Charles A. 1952. *American Government and Politics.* 7th ed. New York: Macmillan.

Beato, Claudio. 1999. "Social Theory and the Violence Question: Explanation and Analysis of Rising Crime Rates in Latin America." Paper presented at the International Conference on Rising Violence and Criminal Justice Response in Latin America, University of Texas at Austin, May 6–9. http://lanic.utexas.edu/project/etext/violence/memoria.

Bebbington, A. 1997. "New States, New NGOs? Crisis and Transition among Rural Development NGOs in the Andean Region." *World Development* 25, no. 11:1755–65.

Bednar, Jenna, William N. Eskridge, and John Ferejohn. 1996. "A Political Theory of Federalism." Mimeo. Stanford University.

Beer, Caroline. 2001. "Assessing the Consequences of Electoral Democracy: Subnational Legislative Change in Mexico." *Comparative Politics* 33 (July): 421–40.

———. 2003. *Electoral Competition and Institutional Change in Mexico*. Notre Dame: University of Notre Dame Press.

———. 2004. "Democracy and Human Rights in the Mexican States: Elections or Social Capital?" *International Studies Quarterly* 48, no. 2:293–312.

Benevides, M. V. de M. 1991. *A cidadania ativa*. São Paulo: Editora Atica.

Benson, Nettie Lee. 1992. *La diputación provincial y el federalismo mexicano*. Mexico City: Colegio de México and Universidad Nacional Autónoma de México.

Berquó, E., M. D. G. Pinho, and V. C. de Souza, eds. 1998. *População Negro em Destaque*. São Paulo: Centro Brasileiro de Análise e Planejamento.

Berruecos, Susana. 2002. "Electoral Justice in Mexico: The Role of the Electoral Tribina under New Federalism." *Journal of Latin American Studies* 35: 801–25.

Berry, Jeffrey M., Kent E. Portney, and Ken Thomson. 1993. *The Rebirth of Urban Democracy*. Washington, DC: Brookings Institution.

Besley, Timothy, and Stephen Coate. 1998. "Sources of Inefficiency in a Representative Democracy: A Dynamic Analysis." *American Economic Review* 88 (March): 139–56.

Bird, Richard. 1999. "Intergovernmental Fiscal Relations in Latin America: Policy Designs and Policy Outcomes." Mimeo. Inter-American Development Bank, Washington, DC.

Bird, Richard M., and François Vaillancourt. 1998. "Fiscal Decentralization in Developing Countries: An Overview." In *Fiscal Decentralization in Developing Countries*, edited by Richard M. Bird and François Vaillancourt. New York: Cambridge University Press.

———, eds. 2000. *Fiscal Federalism in Developing Countries*. Cambridge: Cambridge University Press.

Birnir, Jóhanna K. 2006. *Ethnicity and Electoral Politics*. New York: Cambridge University Press.

Birnir, Jóhanna K., and Donna Lee Van Cott. 2007. "Disunity in Diversity: Party System Fragmentation and the Dynamic Effect of Ethnic Heterogeneity on Latin American Legislatures." *Latin American Research Review* 42, no. 1: 99–125.

Bobbio, N. 1996. *The Age of Rights*. Cambridge: Polity Press.

Bockmeyer, Janice L. 2003. "Devolution and the Transformation of Community Housing Activism." *Social Science Journal* 40, no. 2:175–88.

Borba, Angela, Nalu Faria, and Tatau Godinho. 1998. *Mulher e política: Gênero e feminismo no Partido dos Trabalhadores*. São Paulo: Fundação Perseu Abramo.

Borja, Jordi, Calderón Fernando, María Grossi, and Peñalva Sussana. 1989. *Descentralización y democracia: Gobiernos locales en América Latina*. Santiago de Chile: Consejo Latinoamericano de Ciencias Sociales.

Bowling, Cynthia J., and Deil S. Wright. 1998. "Change and Continuity in State Administration: Administrative Leadership across Four Decades." *Public Administration Review* 58 (September–October): 429–44.

Bowman, Ann O'M. 2004. "Horizontal Federalism: Exploring Interstate Interactions." *Journal of Public Administration Research and Theory* 14 (October): 535–46.

Bowman, Ann O'M., and George Krause. 2003. "A Power Shift: Measuring Policy Centralization in U.S. Intergovernmental Relations, 1947–1998." *American Politics Research* 31, no. 3:301–25.

Bowman, Ann O'M., and Michael A. Pagano. 1990. "The State of American Federalism: 1990–1991." *Publius: The Journal of Federalism* 20 (Summer): 1–25.

Boyte, Harry C. 1980. *The Backyard Revolution: Understanding the New Citizens' Movement*. Philadelphia: Temple University Press.

———. 1990. "The Growth of Citizen Politics: Stages in Local Community Organizing." *Dissent* 37, no. 4:513–18.

———. 2004. *Everyday Politics: Reconnecting Citizens and Public Life*. Philadelphia: University of Pennsylvania Press.

Boyte, Harry C., and Frank Riessman, eds. 1986. *The New Populism: The Politics of Empowerment*. Philadelphia: Temple University Press.

Brady, David. 1993. *In Labor's Cause: Main Themes on the History of the American Worker*. New York: Oxford University Press.

———. 2005. *Labor Embattled: History, Power, Rights*. Urbana: University of Illinois Press.

Branch, Taylor. 1988. *Parting the Waters: America in the King Years, 1954–63*. New York: Simon and Schuster.

———. 1998. *Pillar of Fire: America in the King Years, 1963–65*. New York: Simon and Schuster.

Branford, Sue, and Jan Rocha. 2002. *Cutting the Wire: The Story of the Landless Movement in Brazil*. London: Latin American Bureau.

Brenacker, Francois E. J. de. 2004. *IBAM, 52 anos: Perfil dos prefeitos brasileiros*. Rio de Janeiro: Instituto Brasileiro de Administracao Municipal.

Bresser Pereira, L. C. 2001. "New Public Management Reform: Now in the Latin American Agenda, and Yet . . ." *International Journal of Political Studies* 9:117–48.

Bresser Pereira, L. C., and Peter K. Spink, eds. 1998. *Reforma do estado e administração públicca gerencial*. Rio de Janeiro, Editora da Fundação Getulio Vargas. Translated as *Reforming the State: Managerial Public Administration in Latin America* (Boulder, CO: Lynne Rienner, 1999).

Bruhn, Kathleen. 1997. *Taking on Goliath: The Emergence of a New Left Party and the Struggle for Democracy in Mexico.* University Park: Pennsylvania State University Press.

———. 1999. "PRD Local Governments in Michoacán: Implications for Mexico's Democratization Process." In *Subnational Politics and Democratization in Mexico,* edited by Wayne Cornelius, Todd Eisenstadt, and Jane Hindley, 19–48. Contemporary Perspectives Series 13. San Diego: Center for U.S.-Mexican Studies.

Bullock, Charles S., III. 1999. "The Opening Up of State and Local Election Processes." In *American State and Local Politics: Directions for the 21st Century,* edited by Ronald E. Weber and Paul Brace, 232–40. New York: Seven Bridges Press.

Burchell, Robert, David Listokin, and Catherine C. Galley. 2000. "Smart Growth: More Than a Ghost of Urban Policy Past, Less Than a Bold New Horizon." *Housing Policy Debate* 11, no. 4:821–79.

Cabrero Mendoza, E., ed. 1996. *Los dilemas de la modernización municipal: Estudios sobre la gestión hacendaría en municipios urbanos de México.* Mexico City: Grupo Editorial Miguel Ángel Porrúa.

———. 1998. *Las políticas descentralizadoras en México (1983–1993): Logros y desencantos.* Mexico City: Grupo Editorial Miguel Ángel Porrúa.

———. 1999. "Education: The Cutting Edge of New Federalism." Ch. 6 in *New Federalism and State Government in Mexico: Bringing the States Back In,* Peter M. Ward and Victoria E. Rodríguez, 127–57. U.S.-Mexican Policy Report 9. Austin: Lyndon B. Johnson School of Public Affairs, University of Texas at Austin.

Caixeta, Nely. 2002. "Educação." In *A era FHC: Um balanço,* edited by Bolívar Lamounier and Rubens Figuerdo. São Paulo: Cultura Editores Associados.

Camarotti, Ilka, and Peter Spink. 2003. *O que as empresas podem fazer para a redução da pobreza.* São Paulo: Instituto Ethos.

Cameron, Maxwell A., and Tulia G. Falleti. 2005. "Federalism and the Subnational Separation of Powers." *Publius: The Journal of Federalism* 35 (Spring): 245–71.

Camp, Roderic Ai. 1998. "Women and Men, Men and Women: Gender Patterns in Mexican Politics." In *Women's Participation in Mexican Political Life,* edited by Victoria E. Rodríguez, 167–78. Boulder, CO: Westview Press.

———. 2003. "Learning Democracy in Mexico and the U.S." *Mexican Studies/ Estudios Mexicanos* 19, no. 1:3–27.

———. 2006. *Politics in Mexico: The Democratic Consolodation.* 5th ed. New York: Oxford University Press.

Campbell, Tim. 2003. *The Quiet Revolution: Decentralization and the Rise of Political Participation in Latin American Cities.* Pittsburgh: University of Pittsburgh Press.

Campbell, Tim, and Harald Fuhr, eds. 2004. *Leadership and Innovation in Subnational Government: Case Studies from Latin America.* Washington, DC: World Bank.

Carey, John M., Richard G. Niemi, and Lynda W. Powell. 2000. *Term Limits in State Legislatures.* Ann Arbor: University of Michigan Press.

Carey, John, and Matthew Shugart, eds. 1998. *Executive Degree Authority.* New York: Cambridge University Press.

Carmagnani, Marcello, ed. 1993. *Federalismos latinoamericanos: México/Brasil/ Argentina.* Mexico City: Colegio de México and Fondo de Cultura Económica.

Carneiro, José Mario Brasiliense. 2000. "O município e as relações intergovernamentais no cotidiano da base federativa." *Cadernos Adenauer* 1 (June): 57–80.

Carpizo, Jorge. 1978. *El presidencialismo mexicano.* Mexico City: Siglo XXI Editores.

Carroll, T. F. 1992. *Intermediary NGOs: The Supporting Link in Grassroots Development.* West Hartford, CT: Kumarian Press.

Castel, Robert. 1995. *Les métamorphoses de la question sociale.* Paris: Libraire Arthème Fayard.

Castells, Manuel. 1983. *The City and the Grassroots: Cross-Cultural Theory of Urban Social Movements.* Berkeley: University of California Press.

Centeno, M. A. 1994. *Democracy within Reason: Technocratic Revolution in Mexico.* University Park: Pennsylvania State University Press.

Center for American Women and Politics. 2007. "Women Officeholders: Historical." www.rci.rutgers.edu/~cawp/Facts2.html. Accessed June 21, 2007.

Centro de Estudos e Pesquisas em Administração Municipal. 2001. "Consórcio: Uma forma de cooperação intermunicipal." *Informativa CEPAM* 1:2.

Centro Feminista de Estudos Assessoria. 2007. "Poder e política: Dados estatísticos." www.cfemea.org.br/tcmascdados/temasedados.asp?IDArea=6&Tipo=D ados+Estat%EDsticos. Accessed June 21, 2007.

Centro Latinoamericano de Administración para el Desarollo. 1998. *A New Public Management for Latin America.* Caracas: Centro Latinoamericano de Administración para el Desarollo.

Chaison, Gary. 2006. *Unions in America.* Thousand Oaks, CA: Sage Publications.

Cherkezian, Henri. 2001. "Acordo de cooperação técnica." Paper presented at the conference "São Paulo, minha cidade," São Paulo, Sindicato das Empresas de Compra, Venda, Locação, Administração de Imóveis (SECOVI), June 28.

Cho, Chung-Lae, Christine A. Kelleher, Deil S. Wright, and Susan Yackee Webb. 2005. "Translating National Policy Objectives into Local Achievements across Planes of Governance and among Multiple Actors: Second-Order Devolution and Welfare Reform Implementation." *Journal of Public Administration Research and Theory* 15:31–54.

Cho, Chung-Lae, and Deil S. Wright. 2004. "The Devolution Revolution in Intergovernmental Relations in the 1990s: Changes in Cooperative and Coercive State–National Relations as Perceived by State Administrators." *Journal of Public Administration Research and Theory* 14:447–68.

Christopher, Howard, Michael Lipsky, and Dale Roger Marshall. 1994. "Citizen Participation in Urban Politics: Rise and Routinization." In *Big-City Politics, Governance, and Fiscal Constraints,* edited by George E. Peterson, 153–78. Washington, DC: Urban Institute Press.

Cigler, Allan J., and Burdett A. Loomis. 2002. *Interest Group Politics.* 6th ed. Washington, DC: Congressional Quarterly Press.

Cleary, Matthew, and Susan Stokes. 2006. *Democracy and the Culture of Skepticism: Political Trust in Argentina and Mexico.* New York: Russell Sage Foundation.

Clemente, Roberta Aguilar dos Santos. 2000. "A evolução histórica das regras do jogo parlamentar em uma casa legislativa: O caso da assembléia legislativa do Estado de São Paulo." Master's thesis, Escola de Administração de Empresas de São Paulo, Fundação Getulio Vargas.

Cohen, Jean, and Andrew Arato. 1992. *Civil Society and Political Theory.* Cambridge, MA: MIT Press.

Cohen, John M., and Stephen B. Peterson. 1999. *Administrative Decentralization: Strategies for Developing Countries.* West Hartford, CT: Kumarian Press.

Cohen, Stephen S., John Dyckman, Erica Schoenberger, and Charles R. Downs. 1981. *Decentralization: A Framework for Policy Analysis.* Berkeley: Project on Managing Decentralization, Institute of International Studies, University of California.

Cole, Richard L. 1974. *Citizen Participation and the Urban Policy Process.* Lexington, MA: Lexington Books.

Coleman, James S. 1990. *Foundations of Social Theory.* Cambridge, MA: Harvard University Press.

Collis, Maurice. 1943. *The Land of the Great Image, Being Experiences of Friar Manrique in Arakan.* New York: Alfred A. Knopf.

Comitê das Bacias Hidrográficas dos Rios Piracicaba, Capivari e Jundaí, Compania de Saneamento Basico do Estado de Sao Paulo. 2005. "Minuta do Relatório Final." March 15. www.comitepsj.sp.gov.br/PlanoBacias/PB-MRF-V3_15-03-05.pdf.

Commission of Intergovernmental Relations. 1955. *A Report to the President for Transmittal to the Congress.* Washington, DC: Government Printing Office.

Conlan, Timothy. 1988. *New Federalism: Intergovernmental Reform from Nixon to Reagan.* Washington, DC: Brookings Institution.

Contreras, Oscar F., and Vivienne Bennett. 1994. "National Solidarity in the Northern Borderlands: Social Participation and Community Leadership." In *Transforming State-Society Relations in Mexico: The National Solidarity Strategy,* edited by Wayne Cornelius, Ann L. Craig, and Jonathan Fox. La Jolla: Center for U.S.-Mexican Studies, University of California, San Diego.

Cooter, Robert. 2002. "Constitutional Consequentialism: Bargain Democracy versus Media Democracy." *Theoretical Inquiries in Law* 3, no. 1:1–20.

Cornelius, Wayne. 1975. *Politics and the Migrant Poor in Mexico.* Stanford: Stanford University Press.

———. 1996. *Mexican Politics in Transition: The Breakdown of a One-Party-Dominant Regime.* Monograph Series 41. La Jolla: Center for U.S.-Mexican Studies, University of California, San Diego.

Cornelius, Wayne, and Ann Craig. 1991. *The Mexican Political System in Transition.* Monograph Series 31. La Jolla: Center for U.S.-Mexican Studies, University of California, San Diego.

Cornelius, Wayne, Todd Eisenstadt, and Jane Hindley, eds. 1999. *Subnational Politics and Democratization in Mexico.* Contemporary Perspectives Series 13. La Jolla: Center for U.S.-Mexican Studies, University of California, San Diego.

Cortes Conde, Roberto. 1989. *Dinero, deuda y crisis.* Buenos Aires: Sudamericana.

Costa, Nilson do R., Pedro Luís B. Silva, and José M. A. Ribeiro. 1998. "Descentralização do sistema de saúde no Brasil." *Revista do Serviço Público 50* (July–September): 32–55.

Council of State Governments. 1949. *Federal Grants-in-Aid: Report of the Committee on Federal Grants-in-Aid.* Chicago: Council of State Governments.

Cox, Kevin R., ed. 1997. *Spaces of Globalization: Reasserting the Power of the Local.* New York: Guilford Press.

Cramer, Reid. 1998. "Local Economic Development Planning in Low-Income Urban America: The Implementation of the Empowerment Zone and Enterprise Community Initiative." PhD diss., University of Texas at Austin.

Craske, Nikki. 1998. "Mexican Women's Inclusion into Political Life: A Latin American Perspective." In *Women's Participation in Mexican Political Life,* edited by Victoria E. Rodríguez, 41–62. Boulder, CO: Westview Press.

Craver, Charles B. 1993. *Can Unions Survive? The Rejuvenation of the American Labor Movement.* New York: NYU Press.

Cruz, Maria do Carmo Meirelles T. 1992. "O consórcio intermunicipal de saúde da microrregião de Penápolis como instrumento de viabilização dos sistemas locais de saúde." Master's thesis, São Paulo, Escola de Administração de Empresas de São Paulo, Fundação Getulio Vargas.

———. 2001. *Consórcios intermunicipais.* São Paulo: Pólis, Programa Gestão Pública e Cidadania, Escola de Administração de Empresas de São Paulo, Fundação Getulio Vargas.

Cunha, Euclides da. 1957. *Rebellion in the Backlands (Os Sertões).* Translated by Samuel Putnam. Chicago: University of Chicago Press.

Cunha, Rosani Evangelista da. 2004. "Federalismo e relações intergovernamentais: Os consórcios públicos como instrumento de cooperação federativa." *Revista do Serviço Público 55* (July–September): 5–37.

Dagnino, E., ed. 2002. *Sociedade civil e espaços públicos no Brasil.* Rio de Janeiro: Paz e Terra.

Dahl, Robert A. 1956. *A Preface to Democratic Theory.* Chicago: University of Chicago Press.

————. 1986. "Federalism and the Democratic Process." In *Democracy, Identity and Equality*, edited by Robert A. Dahl, 114–26. Oslo: Norwegian University Press.

————. 1989. *Democracy and Its Critics*. New Haven: Yale University Press.

————. 1998. *On Democracy*. New Haven: Yale University Press.

Dahrendorf, Ralf. 1996. "Economic Opportunity, Civil Society and Political Liberty." *Development and Change* 27, no. 2:229–49.

Davidson, Chandler, and Bernard Grofman, eds. 1994. *Quiet Revolution in the South: The Impact of the Voting Rights Act, 1965–1990*. Princeton: Princeton University Press.

Davis, Norman. 1996. *Europe: A History*. Translated by Arther Brakel. London: Random House.

de Figueiredo, Rui J. P., Jr., and Barry R. Weingast. 2005. "Self-Enforcing Federalism." *Journal of Law, Economics, and Organization* 21 (April): 103–35.

Derthick, Martha. 1987. "American Federalism: Madison's Middle Ground in the 1980s." *Public Administration Review* 47 (January/February): 67–74.

Desposato, S., and D. Samuels. 2003. "The Search for Party Discipline in the Brazilian Chamber of Deputies and Implications for Comparative Research." Paper presented at the 2003 meeting of the Latin American Studies Association, Dallas, Texas, March 26–29.

Diamond, Larry. 1996. "Toward Democratic Consolidation." In *The Global Resurgence of Democracy*, 2nd ed., edited by Larry Diamond and Marc F. Plattner, 227–40. Baltimore: Johns Hopkins University Press.

Diamond, Larry, and Marc F. Plattner, eds. 1996. *The Global Resurgence of Democracy*. 2nd ed. Baltimore: Johns Hopkins University Press.

Díaz Cayeros, Alberto. 1995. *Desarrollo económico e inequidad regional*. Mexico City: Grupo Editorial Miguel Ángel Porrúa.

————. 2006. *Federalism, Fiscal Authority and Centralization in Latin America*. Cambridge: Cambridge University Press.

Díaz Rivera, G. 1988. "Poder político y pacto ideológico en Mexico." In *Mexico: Estabilidad y luchas por la democracia 1900–1982*, edited by Octavio Rodríguez Araujo. Mexico City: Centro de Investigación y Docencia Económicas and El Caballito.

Diniz, Eli. 1996. "Governabilidade, governance e reforma do estado: Considerações sobre o novo paradigma." *Revista do Serviço Público* 120 (May–August): 5–23.

————. 1999. *Crise, reforma do estado e governabilidade*. Rio de Janeiro: Editora Fundação Getulio Vargas.

Domingo, Pilar. 1999. "Judicial Independence and Judicial Reform in Latin America." In *The Self-Restraining State: Power and Accountability in New Democracies*, edited by Andreas Schedler, Larry Diamond, and Marc F. Plattner, 151–76. Boulder, CO: Lynne Rienner.

———. 2005. "Judicialization of Politics: The Changing Political Role of the Judiciary in Mexico." In *The Judicialization of Politics in Latin America*, edited by Rachel Sieder, Line Schjolden, and Alan Angell, 21–46. New York: Palgrave.

Domínguez, Jorge I., and Abraham F. Lowenthal, eds. 1996. *Constructing Democratic Governance: Latin America and the Caribbean in the 1990s*. Baltimore: Johns Hopkins University Press.

Domínguez, Jorge I., and Michael Shifter. 2003. *Constructing Democratic Governance in Latin America*. 2nd ed. Baltimore: Johns Hopkins University Press.

Draibe, Sônia Miriam. 1997. "Uma nova institucionalidade das políticas sociais? Reflexões a propósito da experiência latino-americana recente de reformas e programas sociais." *São Paulo em Perspectiva* 11 (October–December): 3–15.

———. 2004. "Federal Leverage in a Decentralized System: Education Reform in Brazil." In *Crucial Needs, Weak Incentives: Social Sector Reform, Democratization, and Globalization in Latin America*, edited by Robert R. Kaufman and Joan Nelson. Washington, DC: Woodrow Wilson Center Press.

Dresang, Dennis, and James J. Gosling. 1989. *Politics, Policy, and Management in the American States*. New York: Longman.

DuBois, Ellen Carol. 1998. *Woman Suffrage and Women's Rights*. New York: NYU Press.

Dye, Thomas R. 1997. *Politics in States and Communities*. 9th ed. Upper Saddle River, NJ: Prentice Hall.

Eaton, Kent. 2004a. "The Link between Political and Fiscal Decentralization in South America." In *Decentralization and Democracy in Latin America*, edited by Alfred P. Montero and David J. Samuels. Notre Dame: University of Notre Dame Press.

———. 2004b. *Politics beyond the Capital: The Design of Subnational Institutions in South America*. Stanford: Stanford University Press.

Eaton, Kent, and Tyler Dickovick. 2004. "The Politics of Re-Centralization in Argentina and Brazil." *Latin American Research Review* 39, no. 1:90–122.

Eckstein, Harry. 1966. "A Theory of Stable Democracy." Appendix B of *Division and Cohesion in Democracy*. Princeton: Princeton University Press.

Eckstein, Susan. 1990. "Poor People versus the State and Capital: Anatomy of a Successful Community Mobilization for Housing in Mexico City." *International Journal of Urban and Regional Research* 14:274–96.

Edwards, Michael. 2002. *Civil Society*. Cambridge: Polity Press.

Ehrenberg, John. 1999. *Civil Society: The Critical History of an Idea*. New York: NYU Press.

Eisenstadt, Todd A. 1999. "Off the Streets and into the Courtrooms: Resolving Postelectoral Conflicts in Mexico." In *The Self-Restraining State: Power and Accountability in New Democracies*, edited by Andreas Schedler, Larry Diamond, and Marc F. Plattner, 83–104. Boulder, CO: Lynne Rienner.

Elazar, Daniel J. 1987a. *Exploring Federalism.* Tuscaloosa: University of Alabama Press.

———. 1987b. "Our Thoroughly Federal Constitution." In *How Federal Is the Constitution?* edited by Robert A. Goldwin and William A. Schambra. Washington, DC: American Enterprise Institute for Public Policy Research.

Esler, Michael. 1998. "Federalism and Environmental Policy." Book review. *Publius: The Journal of Federalism* 28 (Winter): 263–65.

Esteva, G., and M. S. Prakash. 1998. *Grass Roots Post-modernism.* London: Zed Books.

Fagen, Richard R., and William S. Tuohy. 1972. *Politics and Privilege in a Mexican City.* Stanford: Stanford University Press.

Falleti, Tulia G. 2004. "A Sequential Theory of Decentralization and Its Effects on Intergovernmental Balance of Power: Latin American Cases in Comparative Perspective." Working Paper No. 314, Kellogg Institute, University of Notre Dame, July.

Farah, Marta Ferreira Santos. 2000a. "Governo local, políticas públicas e novas formas de gestão pública no Brasil." *Organizações e Sociedade* 7 (January–April): 59–86.

———. 2000b. "Inovações em governos locais no Brasil." Paper presented at the Seminário Internacional, "Federalismo nas Américas," Fundação Getulio Vargas de São Paulo, September 21–22.

———. 2001. "Parcerias, novos arranjos institucionais e políticas públicas no nível local de governo." *Revista de Administração Pública* 35 (January–February): 119–45.

Farah, Marta Ferreira Santos, and Helio Batista Barbosa. 2000. *Novas experiências de gestão pública e cidadania.* Rio de Janeiro: Editora da Fundação Getulio Vargas.

Fausto, Boris. 1999. *A Concise History of Brazil.* New York: Cambridge University Press.

Ferguson, Adam. [1767] 1969. *An Essay on the History of Civil Society.* London: Gregg International.

Fernandes, R. C. 1994. *Privado porem público: O terceiro setor na America latina.* Rio de Janeiro: Relume Dumará.

Figueiredo, Angelina Cheibub. 2003. "The Role of Congress as an Agency of Horizontal Accountability: Lessons from the Brazilian Experience." In *Democratic Accountability in Latin America,* edited by Scott Mainwaring and Christopher Welna, 170–98. New York: Oxford University Press.

Fischer, R., and A. Falconer. 1999. *Estratégias de empresas no Brasil: Atuação social e voluntariado.* São Paulo: Centro de Estudos em Administração do Terceiro Setor, Universidade de São Paulo.

Fisher, Robert. 1994. *Let the People Decide: Neighborhood Organizing in America.* New York: Twayne.

Flamand, Laura. 2004. "The Vertical Dimension of Government: Democratization and Federalism in Mexico." PhD diss., Department of Political Science, University of Rochester, New York.

Florestano, Patricia. 1994. "Past and Present Utilization of Interstate Compacts in the United States." *Publius: The Journal of Federalism* 24 (Fall): 13–25.

Foweraker, Joe, Todd Landmann, and Neil Harvey. 2003. *Governing Latin America*. Cambridge: Polity Press.

Fox, Jonathan, and Gaspar Rivera Salgado. 2004. *Indigenous Mexican Migrants in the United States*. La Jolla: Center for U.S.-Mexican Studies, University of California, San Diego, Center for Comparative Immigration Studies.

Fox Piven, Frances, and Richard A. Cloward. 1977. *Poor People's Movements: Why They Succeed, How They Fail*. New York: Pantheon Books.

Friedman, Lawrence M. 1984. *American Law: An Introduction*. New York: W. W. Norton.

Friedmann, John. 1992. *Empowerment: The Politics of Alternative Development*. Oxford: Blackwell Books.

Fujiwara, Luiz Mario, Nelson Luiz Nouvel Alessio, and Marta Ferreira Santos Farah, eds. 1999. *20 experiências de gestão pública e cidadania: Ciclo de Premiação 1998*. São Paulo: Programa Gestão Pública e Cidadania.

Fullinwider, Robert, ed. 1999. *Civil Society, Democracy, and Civic Renewal*. Lanham, MD: Rowman and Littlefield.

Furlong, Scott R. 1997. "Interest Group Influence on Rule Making." *Administration and Society* 29, no. 3:325–48.

Galeano, Eduardo. 1976. *Las venas abiertas de américa latina*. Buenos Aires: Siglo Veintiuno Editores.

Genro, T., and U. de Souza. 1997. *Orçamento participativo: A experiência de Porto Alegre*. São Paulo: Editora Fundação Perseu Abramo.

Gibson, Edward L., ed. 2004. *Federalism and Democracy in Latin America*. Baltimore: Johns Hopkins University Press.

Gilbert, Alan, and Peter Ward. 1985. *Housing, the State and the Poor: Policy and Practice in Three Latin American Cities*. Cambridge: Cambridge University Press.

Gohn, Maria da Glória M. 2000. *Os sem-terra, ONGs e cidadania: A sociedade civil brasileira na era da globalização*. São Paulo: Cortez.

Gomes, Flavio, and Marcelo Paixão. 2006. "Exclusão racial, uma questão política e moral." *Teoria e Debate* 67 (August–September): 30–36.

González Casanova, Pablo. 1981. *El estado y los partidos políticos en México: Ensayos*. Mexico City: Era.

González Oropeza, Manuel. 1983. *La intervención federal en la desaparición de poderes*. Mexico City: Universidad Nacional Autónoma de México.

———. 1996a. "La irresponsibilidad de los gobernadores." In *New Federalism, State and Local Government in Mexico: Memoria of the Bi-national*

*Conference,* edited by Victoria Rodríguez and Peter Ward. Austin: Mexican Center of the Institute of Latin American Studies, University of Texas at Austin.

———. 1996b. "Justice by Challenge: The Administration of Justice and the Rule of Law in Mexico." Unpublished paper.

———. 2003. *Los orígines del control jurisdiccional de la Constitución y de los derechos humanos.* Mexico City: Comisión Nacional de Derechos Humanos.

González Parás, Natividad. 2003. *Una nueva visión de la política.* Mexico City: Oceano.

González y González, Luis. 1995. "The Period of Formation." In *A Compact History of Mexico,* 3rd ed., edited by Daniel Cosío Villegas et al., 65–102. Mexico City: Colegio de México.

Graham, Lawrence S. 1990. *The State and Policy Outcomes in Latin America.* New York: Praeger.

———. 2006. *The Politics of Governing: A Comparative Introduction.* Washington, DC: Congressional Quarterly Press.

Graham, Lawrence S., and Pedro Jacobi. 2002. "São Paulo: Tensions between Clientelism and Participatory Democracy." In *Capital City Politics in Latin America: Democratization and Empowerment,* edited by David J. Myers and Henry A. Dietz, 297–324. Boulder, CO: Lynne Rienner.

Gramsci, Antonio. 1971. *Selections from the Prison Notebooks of Antonio Gramsci.* Edited by Quintin Hoare and Geoffrey Nowell Smith. New York: International Publishers.

———. 1994. *Pre-prison Writings.* Edited by Richard Bellamy. Translated by Virginia Cox. New York: Cambridge University Press.

Gray, Virginia, and David Lowery. 1999. "Interest Group Representation in the States." In *American State and Local Politics: Directions for the 21st Century,* edited by Ronald E. Weber and Paul Brace, 256–67. New York: Seven Bridges Press.

Grindle, Merilee M. 2000. *Audacious Reforms: Institutional Invention and Democracy in Latin America.* Baltimore: Johns Hopkins University Press.

———. 2004. *Despite the Odds: The Contentious Politics of Education Reform.* Princeton: Princeton University Press.

———. 2007. *Going Local: Decentralization, Democratization, and the Promise of Good Governance.* Princeton: Princeton University Press.

Grodzin, Morton. 1963. "Centralization and Decentralization in the American Federal System." In *A Nation of States: Essays on the American Federal System,* edited by Robert A. Goldwin. Chicago: Rand McNally.

"Guia para fazer o bem." 2001. *Veja* (São Paulo) 34 (December): 14.

Guillén López, Tonatiuh. 1993. *Baja California 1989–92: Balance de la transición democrática.* Tijuana: Colegio de la Frontera Norte and Universidad Nacional Autónoma de México.

————. 1995. *Municipios en transición: Actores sociales y nuevas políticas de gobierno.* Mexico City: Friedrich Ebert Stiftung Foundation and Ford Foundation.

————. 1996. *Gobiernos municipales en México: Entre la modernización y la tradición política.* Mexico City: Colegio de la Frontera Norte and Miguel Ángel Porrúa.

————. 1998. "Política municipal y partidos: Una relación difícil." In *Desarrollo municipal: Retos y posibilidades,* edited by Carlos Garrocho and Jaime Sobrino, 299–314. Toluca: Colegio Mexiquense.

————. 2000. "El federalismo en México: Una historia en construcción." Unpublished paper, Colegio de la Frontera Norte.

Gutiérrez, G. 1975. *Teologia da libertação.* Petropolis, Rio de Janeiro: Vozes.

Haber, Paul Lawrence. 2006. *Power from Experience: Urban Popular Movements in Late Twentieth-Centure Mexico.* University Park: Penn State University Press.

Habermas, Jürgen. 1996. *Between Facts and Norms.* Cambridge, MA: MIT Press.

Haggard, Stephen, and Steven B. Webb. 2004. "Political Incentives and Intergovernmental Fiscal Relations." In *Decentralization and Democracy in Latin America,* edited by Alfred P. Montero and David J. Samuels. Notre Dame: University of Notre Dame Press.

Hagiopan, Frances, and Scott P. Mainwaring, eds. 2005. *The Third Wave of Democratization in Latin America: Advances and Setbacks.* New York: Cambridge University Press.

Hall, John, ed. 1995. *Civil Society.* Cambridge: Polity Press.

Hansen, Roger D. 1971. *The Politics of Mexican Development.* Baltimore: Johns Hopkins University Press.

Hedge, David M. 1998. *Governance and the Changing American States.* Boulder, CO: Westview Press.

Herbers, John. 1998. "It's the New Activism as Business Primes the Government's Pump." *Governing* 10, no. 1:32–38.

Hernández Chávez, Alicia. 1993. "Federalismo y gobernabilidad en México." In *Federalismos latinoamericanos: México/Brasil/Argentina,* edited by Marcello Carmagnani, 263–99. Mexico City: Colegio de México and Fondo de Cultura Económica.

————. 1996. *¿Hacia un nuevo federalismo?* Mexico City: Colegio de México and Fondo de Cultura Económica.

Hernández Valdez, Alfonso. 1998. "Definiciones y teorías sobre el federalismo: Una revisión de la literatura." *Política y Gobierno* 5, no 1:225–60.

Hiskey, Jonathan T. 2005a. "Local Context and Democratization in Mexico." *American Journal of Political Science* 49 (January): 57–71.

————. 2005b. "The Political Economy of Subnational Economic Recovery in Mexico." *Latin American Research Review* 40, no. 1:30–55.

Hiskey, Jonathan T., and Mitchell A. Seligson. 2003. "Pitfalls of Power to the People: Decentralization, Local Government Performance, and System Support in Bolivia." *Studies in Comparative International Development* 37 (Winter): 64–88.

Homedes, Núria, and Antonio Ugalde, eds. 2006a. *Decentralizing Health Services in Mexico: A Case Study in State Reform.* La Jolla: Center for U.S.-Mexican Studies, University of California, San Diego.

———. 2006b. "Decentralization of Health Services in Mexico: A Historical Review." In *Decentralizing Health Services in Mexico: A Case Study in State Reform,* edited by Núria Homedes and Antonio Ugalde, 45–94. La Jolla: Center for U.S.-Mexican Studies, University of California, San Diego.

Hoornbeek, John A. 2005. "The Promises and Pitfalls of Devolution: Water Pollution Policies in the American States." *Publius: The Journal of Federalism* 35 (Winter): 87–114.

Horwitt, Sanford D. 1989. *Let Them Call Me Rebel: Saul Alinsky, His Life and Legacy.* New York: Knopf.

Houtzager, Peter P., Adrián Gurza Lavalle, and Arnab Acharya. 2003. "Who Participates? Civil Society and the New Democratic Politics in São Paulo, Brazil." Working Paper No. 210, Institute of Development Studies, Brighton.

Huber, John D., and Charles Shipan. 2002. *Deliberate Discretion?* Cambridge: Cambridge University Press.

———. 2004. "Politics, Delegation and Bureaucracy." In *The Oxford Handbook of Political Economy,* edited by Barry Weingast and Donald Wittman. New York: Oxford University Press.

Hughes, Sallie. 2006. *Newsrooms in Conflict: Journalism and the Democratization of Mexico.* Pittsburgh: University of Pittsburgh Press.

Huntington, Samuel P. 1991. *The Third Wave: Democratization in the Late Twentieth Century.* Norman: University of Oklahoma Press.

———. 1996. "Democracy's Third Wave." In *The Global Resurgence of Democracy,* 2nd ed., edited by Larry Diamond and Marc F. Plattner, 3–25. Baltimore: Johns Hopkins University Press.

Hutchcroft, Paul. 2001. "Centralization and Decentralization in Administration and Politics: Assessing Territorial Dimensions of Authority and Power." *Governance* 14 (January): 23.

Iaryczower, Matías, Sebastián Saiegh, and Mariano Tommasi. n.d. "Coming Together: The Industrial Organization of Federalism." Working Paper No. 30, Centro de Estudios para el Desarrollo Institucional, Fundación Gobierno y Sociedad, and the Universidad de San Andrés.

Instituto Brasileiro de Geografia e Estatística. 2001. *Indicadores sociais, 2001.* Rio de Janeiro: Instituto Brasileiro de Geografia e Estatística.

Instituto Nacional de Estadística Geografía e Informática and Secretaría de Gobernación. 2001. *Encuesta Nacional sobre Cultura Política y Prácticas Ciudadanas 2001.* Mexico City: Encuesta Nacional sobre Cultura Política y Prácticas Ciudadanas.

———. 2003. *Encuesta Nacional sobre Cultura Política y Prácticas Ciudadanas 2003*. Mexico City: Encuesta Nacional sobre Cultura Política y Prácticas Ciudadanas.

Instituto Universitário de Pesquisas do Rio de Janeiro. 2006. "Banco de dados eleitorais do Brasil (1982–2006)." http://jaironicolau.iuperj.br/dados%20eleitorais%20do%20Brasil%201982-2004.html. Accessed June 21, 2007.

Inter-American Development Bank. 2006. *The Politics of Policies: Economic and Social Progress in Latin America, 2006 Report*. Cambridge, MA: Inter-American Development Bank and David Rockefeller Center for Latin American Studies, Harvard University.

Isin, Engin F., and P. K. Wood. 1999. *Citizenship and Identity*. Thousand Oaks, CA: Sage Publications.

Jacobi, Pedro. 2000. *Políticas sociais e ampliação da cidadania*. Rio de Janeiro: Editora da Fundação Getúlio Vargas.

———. 2005. "Comitês de bacias hidrográficas: O que está em jogo na gestão compartilhada e participativa." In *Administrando a água como se fosse importante*, edited by L. Dowbor and R. A. Tagnin, 81–88. São Paulo: Editora SENAC.

Jacobi, Pedro, and José Antonio Pinho, eds. 2006. *Inovação no campo da gestão pública local*. Rio de Janeiro: Editora Fundação Getulio Vargas.

Janda, Kenneth, Jeffrey M. Berry, and Jerry Goldman. 1989. *The Challenge of Democracy: Government in America*. 2nd ed. Boston: Houghton Mifflin.

Jaquette, Jane S., and Sharon L. Wolchik, eds. 1991. *Women and Democracy: Latin America and Central and Eastern Europe*. Baltimore: Johns Hopkins University Press.

Jewell, Malcolm E., and Sarah M. Morehouse. 2001. *Political Parties and Elections in American States*. 4th ed. Washington, DC: Congressional Quarterly Press.

Joint Federal-State Action Committee. 1960. *Final Report of the Joint Federal-State Action Committee to the President of the United States and to the Chairman of the Governor's Conference*. Washington, DC: Government Printing Office.

Jones-Correa, Michael. 2001. *Governing American Cities: Inter-ethnic Coalitions, Competition, and Conflict*. New York: Russell Sage Foundation.

Junqueira, Ana Thereza Machado, Maria do Carmo Toledo Cruz, and Maria Teresinha de Resenes Marcon. 2002. *Cooperação intermunicipal na federação brasileira: Os consórcios intermunicipais e as associações de municípios*. Série Documenta: Leituras de interesse local e regional No. 1, May. São Paulo: Fundação Konrad-Adenauer-Stiftung.

Kaufman, Robert R., and Joan M. Nelson, eds. 2004. *Crucial Needs, Weak Incentives: Social Sector Reform, Democratization, and Globalization in Latin America*. Washington, DC: Woodrow Wilson Center Press.

Keane, John. 1998. *Civil Society: Old Images, New Visions*. Cambridge: Polity Press.

Keck, Margaret, E., and Rebecca N. Abers. 2006. "Civil Society and State-Building in Latin America." *LASA Forum* 37, no. 1:30–32.

Kenyon, Daphne A., and John Kincaid, eds. 1991. *Competition among States and Local Governments: Efficiency and Equity in American Federalism.* Washington, DC: Urban Institute.

Kettl, Donald F. 2004. *System under Stress: Homeland Security and American Politics.* Washington, DC: Congressional Quarterly Press.

Khair, Amir A., and Francisco H. Vignoli. 2001. *Gestão fiscal responsável.* Brasilia: Ministério de Planejamento, Fundação Getulio Vargas.

Kincaid, John. 1990. "Federalism and Community in the American Context." *Publius: The Journal of Federalism* 20 (Winter): 69–87.

Klesner, Joseph. 2003. "Political Attitudes, Social Capital and Political Participation: The US and Mexico Compared." *Mexican Studies/Estudios Mexicanos* 19, no. 1:29–63.

———. 2007. "Social Capital and Political Participation in Latin America." *Latin American Research Review* 42, no. 2.:3–32.

Kliksberg, Bernardo. 1997. *O desafio da exclusão: Para um gestão social eficiente.* São Paulo: Edições Fundap.

———. 2001. *Towards an Intelligent State.* International Institute of Administrative Science Monograph 15. Washington, DC: IOS Press.

Krane, Dale. 2003. "The State of American Federalism, 2002–2003: Division Replaces Unity." *Publius: The Journal of Federalism* 33 (Summer): 1–44.

———. 2004. "The State of American Federalism, 2003–2004: Polarized Politics and Federalist Principles." *Publius: The Journal of Federalism* 34 (Summer): 1–53.

Krane, Dale, Carol Ebdon, and John Battle. 2004. "Devolution, Fiscal Federalism, and Changing Patterns of Municipal Revenues: The Mismatch between Theory and Reality." *Journal of Public Administration Research and Theory* 14 (October): 512–33.

Krane, Dale, and Heidi Koenig. 2005. "The State of American Federalism, 2004: Is Federalism Still a Core Value?" *Publius: The Journal of Federalism* 35 (Winter): 1–40.

Kugelmas, Eduardo, and Lourdes Sola. 1999. "Recentralização/descentralização: Dinâmica do regime federativo no Brasil dos anos 90." *Tempo Social: Revista de Sociología da USP* 11, no. 2:63–83.

Ladenheim, Kala. 1997. "Health Insurance in Transition: The Health Insurance Portability and Accountability Act of 1996." *Publius: The Journal of Federalism* 27 (Spring): 33–51.

Landim, L. 1993. *Para além do mercado e do estado? Filantropia e cidadania no Brasil.* Rio de Janeiro: Instituto de Estudos da Religião.

Landman, Todd. 2006. "Violence and Democracy in Latin America." Paper presented at the panel "Violent Democracies of Latin America: Towards an Interdisciplinary Reconceptualization," Congress of Latin American Studies Association, San Juan, Puerto Rico, March 15–18.

Langton, Stuart, ed. 1978. *Citizen Participation in America*. Lexington, MA: Lexington Books.

Lawson, Chappell. 2002. *Building the Fourth Estate: Democratization and the Rise of a Free Press in Mexico*. Berkeley: University of California Press.

Lefebvre, Henri. 1991. *The Production of Space*. Oxford: Blackwell.

Lemaresquier, T. 1980. "Beyond Infant Feeding: The Case for Another Relationship between NGOs and the United Nations System." *Development Dialogue* 1:120–25.

Levy, Evelyn. 2002. "Ganhar e ganhar: Estratégias de negociação bern sucedidas entre os municípios, os estados e a União." In *Novos contornos da gestão local: Conceitos em construção*, ed. Peter Spink et al., 175–95. São Paulo: Institute Polis/Programa de Gestão Pública e Cidadania, Getulio Vargas Foundation.

Levy, Evelyn, and Pedro Drago, eds. 2005. *Gestão pública no Brasil contemporâneo*. São Paulo: Edições Fundação do Desenvolvimento Administrativo.

Linz, Juan J. 1994. "Presidential or Parliamentary Democracy: Does It Make a Difference?" In *The Failure of Presidential Democracy*, edited by Juan J. Linz and Arturo Valenzuela. Baltimore: Johns Hopkins University Press.

Linz, Juan J., and Alfred Stepan. 1996. *Problems of Democratic Transition and Consolidation: Southern Europe, South America and Post-Communist Europe*. Baltimore: Johns Hopkins University Press.

Lipsky, Michael. 1969. *Protest in City Politics: Rent Strikes, Housing, and the Power of the Poor*. Chicago: Rand McNally.

———. 1980. *Street-Level Bureaucracy: Dilemmas of the Individual in Public Services*. New York: Russell Sage Foundation.

Litvack, Jennie, Junaid Ahmad, and Richard Bird. 1998. *Rethinking Decentralization in Developing Countries*. Washington, DC: World Bank.

Lorch, Robert S. 1998. "The New Federalism: Can the States Be Trusted?" Book review. *Publius: The Journal of Federalism* 28, no. 2:159–61.

Love, Joseph L. 1993. "Federalismo y regional en Brasíl, 1889–1937." In *Federalismos latinoamericanos: México/Brasil/Argentina*, edited by Marcello Carmangani, 263–99. Mexico City: Colegio de México and Fondo de Cultura Económico.

Lujambio, Alonso. 1995. *Federalismo y Congreso en el cambio político de México*. Mexico City: Instituto de Investigación Jurídicas, Universidad Nacional Autónoma de México.

———. 1998. *Federalismo y Congreso*. Mexico City: Instituto de Investigación Jurídicas, Universidad Nacional Autónoma de México.

Lyndon B. Johnson School of Public Affairs. 2000. *Reaching across the Border: Intergovernmental Relations between Texas and Mexico*. Policy Research Project Report No. 134. Austin: University of Texas at Austin, Lyndon B. Johnson School of Public Affairs.

Madrid, Raúl. 2005a. "Ethnic Cleavages and Electoral Volatility in Latin America." *Comparative Politics* 38 (October): 1–20.

————. 2005b. "Indigenous Voters and Party System Fragmentation in Latin America." *Electoral Studies* 24, no. 4:689–707.

————. 2006. "Electoral Volatility and Indigenous Voters in Latin America." *Comparative Politics* 31, no. 1:23–42.

Magaloni, Beatriz. 2003. "Authoritarianism, Democracy and the Supreme Court: Horizontal Exchange and the Rule of Law in Mexico." In *Democratic Accountability in Latin America*, edited by Scott Mainwaring and Christopher Welna, 266–306. New York: Oxford University Press.

Mainwaring, Scott. 1995. "Brazil: Weak Parties, Feckless Democracy." In *Building Democratic Institutions: Party Systems in Latin America*, edited by Scott Mainwaring and Timothy R. Scully, 354–98. Stanford: Stanford University Press.

————. 1997. "Multipartism, Robust Federalism, Presidentialism in Brazil." In *Presidentialism and Democracy in Latin America*, edited by Scott Mainwaring and Matthew Soberg Shugart, 55–109. Cambridge: Cambridge University Press.

Mainwaring, Scott, and Timothy R. Scully, eds. 1995. *Building Democratic Institutions: Party Systems in Latin America*. Stanford: Stanford University Press.

Mainwaring, Scott, and Matthew Soberg Shugart. 1997. *Presidentialism and Democracy in Latin America*. New York: Cambridge University Press.

Mainwaring, Scott, and Christopher Welna, eds. 2003. *Democratic Accountability in Latin America*. Oxford: Oxford University Press.

Marcelino, Gileno F. 2003. "Em busca da flexibilidade do Estado: O desafio das reformas planejadas no Brasil." *Revista de Administração Pública* 37, no. 3:641–59.

Marshall, Thomas Humphrey. 1950. *Citizenship and Social Class*. Cambridge: Cambridge University Press.

Marván Laborde, Ignacio. 1997. *¿Y después del presidencialismo? Reflexiones para la formación de un nuevo régimen*. Mexico City: Océano.

Mattiace, Shannan L. 2003. *To See with Two Eyes: Peasant Activism and Indian Autonomy in Chiapas, Mexico*. Albuquerque: University of New Mexico Press.

Mattoso, Jorge. 2001–2. "Relações internacionais e poder local: O caso de São Paulo." *Política Externa* 10, no. 3:113–20.

McCann, Barbara, and Stephanie Vance. 2001. "Ten Years of Progress." Surface Transportation Policy Project. www.transact.org. Accessed March 5, 2002.

McCarthy, Kathleen. 2003. *American Creed: Philanthropy and the Rise of Civil Society, 1700–1865*. Chicago: University of Chicago Press.

McCullough, David G. 2001. *John Adams*. New York: Simon and Schuster.

McDowell, Bruce D. 2003. "Wildfires Create New Intergovernmental Challenges." *Publius: The Journal of Federalism* 33 (Summer): 45–61.

McGuinn, Patrick. 2005. "The National Schoolmarm: No Child Left Behind and the New Educational Federalism." *Publius: The Journal of Federalism* 35 (Winter): 41–68.

Medici, André Cezar, and Marco Cícero M. P. Maciel. 1996. "A dinâmica do gasto social nas três esferas de governo: 1980–1992." In *Descentralização e políticas sociais,* edited by Rui de Britto Álvares Affonso and Pedro Luiz Barros Silva. São Paulo: Fundação do Desenvolvimento Administrativo.

Melo, Marcus. 1993. "Municipalismo, nation building e a modernização do estado no Brasil." *Revista Brasileira de Ciências Sociais* 23, no. 8:85–100.

———. 1996a. "Crise federativa, guerra fiscal e hobesianismo municipal: Efeitos perversos da descentralização?" *Revista São Paulo em Perspectiva* 10, no. 3: 1–14.

———. 1996b. "*Governance* e reforma do estado: O paradigma agente x principal." *Revista do Serviço Público* 120 (January–April): 67–82.

Mendonça, Patricia, and Mario Aquino Alves. 2006. "Institutional Environment, Society and Public Management at the Semi-Arid of Brazil." Paper presented at the 22nd European Group for Organizational Studies Colloquium, Bergen, Norway, July.

Merege, Luiz Carlos. 2005. *Censo do terceiro setor do estado do Pará: Região metropolitana de Belém.* February. Belém: Relatorio.

Merino, Mauricio. 1998. *Gobierno local, poder nacional: La contienda por la formación del estado mexicano.* Mexico City: Colegio de México.

Middlebrook, Kevin, ed. 1991. *Unions, Workers, and the State in Mexico.* La Jolla: Center for U.S.-Mexican Studies, University of California, San Diego.

Mill, John Stuart. [1861] 1958. *Considerations on Representative Government.* Edited by Currin V. Shields. New York: Liberal Arts Press.

———. 1962. *Essays on Politics and Culture,* edited by G. Himmelfarb. New York: Doubleday.

Mitchell-Weaver, David Clyde, and Ronald Miller Jr. 2000. "Multilevel Governance and Metropolitan Regionalism in the USA." *Urban Studies* 37 (May): 851–76.

Mizrahi, Yemile. 1994a. "Entrepreneurs in the Opposition: Modes of Political Participation in Chihuahua." In *Opposition Government in Mexico,* edited by Victoria Rodríguez and Peter Ward, 81–96. Albuquerque: University of New Mexico Press.

———. 1994b. "Rebels without a Cause? The Politics of Entrepreneurs in Chihuahua." *Journal of Latin American Studies* 26, no. 1:137–58.

———. 2003. *From Martyrdom to Power: The Partido de Acción Nacional in Mexico.* Notre Dame: University of Notre Dame Press.

Mollison, Andrew. 1991. "State-Level Lobbyists Doubled since '73." *Austin American-Statesman,* October 27, A11.

Montaño, Jorge. 1976. *Los pobres de la ciudad de México en los asentamientos espontáneos.* Mexico City: Siglo XXI Editores.

Montero, Alfred P., and David J. Samuels, eds. 2004a. *Decentralization and Democracy in Latin America.* Notre Dame: University of Notre Dame Press.

———. 2004b. "The Political Logic of Decentralization in Brazil." In *Decentralization and Democracy in Latin America,* edited by Alfred P. Montero and David J. Samuels. Notre Dame: University of Notre Dame Press.

Montoro, Eugênio Augusto Franco. 1984. *A implantação das regiões metropolitanas*. Relatório de Pesquisa No. 32. São Paulo: Núcleo de Pesquisas e Publicações da Escola de Administração de Empresas de São Paulo.

Moog, Clodomir Vianna. 1983. *Bandeirantes e pioneiros: Paralelo entre duas culturas*. 14th ed. Rio de Janeiro: Civilização Brasileira.

Morales Barud, Jorge. 2003. "Executive-Legislative Relations in Sub-national Government in Mexico: Legislative Plurality, *Alternancia*, and the Policy-Making Process." PhD diss. proposal and ongoing research, Teresa Lozano Long Institute of Latin American Studies, University of Texas at Austin.

Moreno, Carlos Luis. 2005. "Decentralization, Electoral Competition and Local Government Performance in Mexico." PhD diss., Lyndon B. Johnson School of Public Affairs, University of Texas at Austin.

———. 2007. "Do Competitive Elections Produce Better-Quality Governments? Evidence from Mexican Municipalities, 1990–2000." *Latin American Research Review* 42, no. 2:139–56.

Moreno Toscano, Alejandra. 1995. "The Viceroyalty." In *A Compact History of Mexico*, 3rd ed., edited by Daniel Cosío Villegas et al., 45–64. Mexico City: Colegio de México.

Morgenstern, Scott. 2002. "U.S. Models and Latin American Legislatures." In *Legislative Politics in Latin America*, edited by Scott Morgenstern and Benito Nacif. New York: Cambridge University Press.

Morgenstern, Scott, and Luigi Manzetti. 2003. "Legislative Oversight: Interests and Institutions in the United States and Argentina." In *Democratic Accountability in Latin America*, edited by Scott Mainwaring and Christopher Welna, 132–69. New York: Oxford University Press.

———. 2004. *Patterns of Legislative Politics: Roll-Call Voting in Latin America and the United Status*. New York: Cambridge University Press.

Morris, Arthur, and Stella Lowder, eds. 1992. *Decentralization in Latin America*. New York: Praeger.

Murilo de Carvalho, José. 1993. "Federalismo y centralización en el imperio brasileño: Historia y argumento." In *Federalismos latinoamericanos: México, Brasil, Argentina*, edited by Marcello Carmangani, 51–80. Mexico City: Colegio de México and Fondo de Cultura Económica.

———. 2001. *Cidadania no Brasil*. Rio de Janeiro: Civilização Brasileira.

Nathan, Richard P. 2005. "Federalism and Health Policy." *Health Affairs* 24 (November/December): 1458–66.

Navarro, Zander. 1998. "Democracia y controle social de fundos publicos: El caso del 'presupuesto participativo' de Porto Alegre." In *Lo publico no estatal en el reforma del estado*, edited by Luiz Carlos Bresser Perreira and Nuria Cunill Grau, 291–332. Buenos Aires: Editora Paidós.

Neri, M. 2001. *Mapa de Ativos: Combate sustentável à pobreza (conceitos e propostas)*. Rio de Janeiro: Fundação Getulio Vargas.

Neves, Gleisi Heisler. 2000. "O município no Brasil: Marco de referência e principais desafios." *Cadernos Adenauer* 1 (June): 9–34.

Nickson, R. A. 1995. *Local Government in Latin America.* Boulder, CO: Lynne Rienner.

Nicolau, Jairo Marconi. 1995. *Multipartidarismo e democracia.* Rio de Janeiro: Editora da Fundação Getulio Vargas.

Nylen, William. 2003. *Participatory Democracy versus Elitist Democracy: Lessons from Brazil.* New York: Palgrave Macmillan.

Oates, Wallace. 1990. "Decentralization of the Public Sector: An Overview." In *Decentralization, Local Governments and Markets: Towards a Post-welfare Agenda,* edited by Robert J. Bennett, 43–58. Oxford: Oxford University Press.

———. 2005. "Towards a Second Generation Theory of Fiscal Federalism." *International Tax and Public Finance* 12:349–73.

O'Donnell, Guillermo. 1994. "The State, Democratization, and Some Conceptual Problems: A Latin American View with Glances at Some Post-community Countries." In *Latin American Political Economy in the Age of Neoliberal Reform: Theoretical and Comparative Perspectives for the 1990s,* edited by William Smith et al., 157–80. Miami: North South Center.

———. 1999. "Horizontal Accountability in New Democracies." In *The Self-Restraining State: Power and Accountability in New Democracies,* edited by Andreas Schedler, Larry Diamond, and Marc F. Plattner, 29–52. Boulder, CO: Lynne Rienner.

———. 2003. "Horizontal Accountability: The Legal Institutionalization of Mistrust." In *Democratic Accountability in Latin America,* edited by Scott Mainwaring and Christopher Welna, 34–54. New York: Oxford University Press.

———. 2005. "State, Regime, Government and Nation." In "Public Action for Social Purpose: Evolving Ideas about the Role of the State," unpublished report from the Ford Foundation Learning Circle on the Changing State, New York, March.

O'Donnell, Guillermo, Jorge Vargas Cullell, and Osvaldo M. Iazzetta, eds. 2004. *The Quality of Democracy: Theory and Applications.* Notre Dame: University of Notre Dame Press.

O'Donnell, Guillermo, Philippe C. Schmitter, and Laurence Whitehead, eds. 1986. *Transitions from Authoritarian Rule: Prospects for Democracy.* Baltimore: Johns Hopkins University Press.

Oliveira, Fabrício Augusto de Oliveira, and Geraldo Biasoto Jr. 1999. "Descentralização das políticas sociais no Brasil." In *Descentralização das políticas sociais no Brasil,* edited by Marta Arretche and Vicente Rodrigues. São Paulo: Fundação do Desenvolvimento Administrativo; Fundação de Amparo à Pesquisa do Estado de São Paulo.

Oliver, J. Eric. 2001. *Democracy in Suburbia.* Princeton: Princeton University Press.

Olloqui, José Juan de. 1983. "La descentralización del gobierno federal: Un punto de vista." *Trimestre Económico* 50:401–18.

O'Neill, Kathleen. 2003. "Decentralization as an Electoral Strategy." *Comparative Political Studies* 36 (November): 1068–91.

———. 2005. *Decentralizing the State: Elections, Parties, and Local Power in the Andes*. New York: Cambridge University Press.

Osborne, David, and Ted Gaebler. 1992. *Reinventing Government: How the Entrepreneurial Spirit Is Transforming the Public Sector*. Reading, MA: Addison-Wesley.

Oxhorn, Philip. 1995. "From Controlled Inclusion to Coerced Marginalization: The Struggle for Civil Society in Latin America." In *Civil Society: Theory, History and Comparison*, edited by John A. Hall, 250–77. Cambridge: Polity Press.

Oxhorn, Philip, Joseph S. Tulchin, and Andrew D. Selee, eds. 2004. *Decentralization, Democratic Governance, and Civil Society in Comparative Perspective: Africa, Asia, and Latin America*. Washington, DC: Woodrow Wilson Center Press.

Paes de Paulo, Ana P. 2005. *Por uma nova gestão pública*. Rio de Janeiro: Editora da Fundação Getulio Vargas.

Pagano, Michael A., and Ann O'M. Bowman. 1989. "The State of American Federalism: 1988–1989." *Publius: The Journal of Federalism* 19 (Summer): 1–17.

Paiva, Antonio. 2003. *Relevance of Metropolitan Government in Latin American Cities: Inter-institutional Coordination in Caracas, Venezuela and Monterrey, Mexico*. Delft: Eburon.

Panizza, Francisco. 2000. "Is Brazil Becoming a 'Boring' Country?" *Bulletin of Latin American Research* 19:501–25.

Pardo, María del Carmen, ed. 1998. *Aprendizajes y dilemas de la federalización educativa*. Mexico City: El Colegio de México.

Parry, G., and G. Moyser. 1994. "More Participation, More Democracy?" In *Defining and Measuring Democracy*, edited by David Beetham. Thousand Oaks, CA: Sage Publications.

Pateman, Carole. 1970. *Participation and Democratic Theory*. Cambridge: Cambridge University Press.

Payne, Stanley G. 1973. *A History of Spain and Portugal*. Vol. 2. Madison: University of Wisconsin Press.

Pereira, C., E. Leoni, and L. Rennó. 2004. "Political Survival Strategies: Political Career Decisions in the Brazilian Chamber of Deputies." *Journal of Latin American Studies* 36:109–30.

Pereyra, Carlos. 1990. *Sobre la democracia*. Mexico City: Cal y Arena.

Pierson, Paul. 1995. "Fragmented Welfare States: Federal Institutions and Development of Social Policy." *Governance* 8 (October): 449–78.

Pitkin, Hanna. 1967. *The Concept of Representation*. Berkeley: University of California Press.

———. 1969. *Representation*. New York: Atherton Press.

Portes, Alejandro, and Kelly Hoffman. 2003. "Latin American Class Structures: Their Composition and Change during the Neoliberal Era." *Latin American Research Review* 38, no. 1:268–86.

Posner, Paul. 1997. "Unfunded Mandates Reform Act: 1996 and Beyond." *Publius: The Journal of Federalism* 27 (Spring): 53–71.

Programa Gestão Pública e Cidadania. 1999. *Descobrindo o Brasil cidadão—1999*. São Paulo: Programa Gestão Pública e Cidadania.

Prud'homme, Remy. 1995. "On the Dangers of Decentralization." *World Bank Research Observer*, 10, no. 2:201–20.

Putnam, Robert D. 1993. *Making Democracy Work: Civic Traditions in Modern Italy*. Princeton: Princeton University Press.

———. 2000. *Bowling Alone: The Collapse and Revival of American Community*. New York: Simon and Schuster.

Queiroz, Adele, and Luiz Carlos Merege. 2000. "Profiling the Third Sector in Local Communities in Brazil." *Cadernos do III Setor* (Centro de Estudos do Terceiro Setor, Fundação Getulio Vargas, São Paulo) 7 (December): 1–29.

Queiroz Ribeiro, Luiz Cesar de, and Orlando Alves dos Santos Jr. 1996. *Associ ativismo e participação popular: Tendências da organização popular no Rio de Janeiro*. Rio de Janeiro: Instituto de Pesquisa e Planejamento Urbano e Regional, Federação de Órgãos para Assistência Social e Educacional, Observatório de Políticas Urbanas e Gestão Municipal.

Radin, Beryl, et al. 1996. *New Governance for Rural America: Creating Intergovernmental Partnerships*. Lawrence: University Press of Kansas.

Ramírez Sáiz, Juan Manuel. 1986. *El movimiento popular en México*. Mexico City: Siglo XXI Editores.

Reagan, Michael. 1972. *The New Federalism*. New York: Oxford University Press.

Reitzes, Donald C., and Dietrich C. Reitzes. 1987. *The Alinsky Legacy: Alive and Kicking*. Greenwich, CT: JAI Press.

Renault, Sergio R. T. 2005. "A reforma do poder judiciario sób a ótica do Governo Federal." *Revista do Serviço Público* 56, no. 2:127–36.

Rezende, Fernando, and Paulo Tafner, eds. 2005. *Brasil: O estado de uma nação*. Rio de Janeiro: Editora Instituto de Pesquisa Econômica Aplicada.

Ritzer, George. 2004. *The Globalization of Nothing*. Thousand Oaks, CA: Pine Forge Press.

Roberts, Bryan. 2005. "Citizenship, the State and Social Policy." In *Rethinking Development in Latin America*, edited by Charles H. Wood and Bryan Roberts. University Park: Pennsylvania State University Press.

Roberts, Bryan, and Alejandro Portes. 2006. "Coping with the Free Market City: Collective Action in Six Latin American Cities at the End of the Twentieth Century." *Latin American Research Review* 41, no. 2:57–83.

Robertson, David Brian. 2000. *Capital, Labor, and State: The Battle for American Labor Markets from the Civil War to the New Deal*. Lanham, MD: Rowman and Littlefield.

Robertson, David Brian, and Dennis R. Judd. 1989. *The Development of American Public Policy: The Structure of Policy Restraint*. Glenview, IL: Scott, Foresman.

Robinson, Mark. 1998. "Democracy, Participation, and Public Policy." In *The Democratic Developmental State: Politics and Institutional Design*, edited by Mark Robinson and Gordon White, 150–68. New York: Oxford University Press.

Robles Peiro, Héctor. 2006. "Better Settings for Better Education: Does Decentralization Work?" PhD diss., Lyndon B. Johnson School of Public Affairs, University of Texas at Austin.

Rocha, Jan. 1997. *Brazil: A Guide to the People, Politics and Culture*. London: Latin American Bureau.

Rodden, Jonathan. 2005. "Federalismo e descentralização em perspectiva comparada: Sobre significados e medidas." *Revista de Sociologia e Politica* 24 (June): 9–26.

Rodin, Judith, and Stephen P. Steinberg, eds. 2003. *Public Discourse in America: Conversation and Community in the Twenty-first Century*. Philadelphia: University of Pennsylvania Press.

Rodrigues, Horácio Wanderlei. 2002. "O poder judiciário no Brasil." *Cadernos Adenauer* 3, no. 6:13–54.

Rodrigues, Horácio W., Gláucio F. M. Gonçalves, Christian E. C. Lynch, Alexandre Veronese, and Rogério D. dos Santos, eds. 2002. *O terceiro poder em crise: Impasses e saídas*. Special issue, *Cadernos Adenhauer* 3, no. 6.

Rodríguez, Victoria E. 1995. "Municipal Autonomy and the Politics of Intergovernmental Finance: Is It Different for the Opposition?" In *Opposition Government in Mexico*, edited by Victoria Rodríguez and Peter Ward, 153–72. Albuquerque: University of New Mexico Press.

———. 1997. *Decentralization in Mexico: From Reforma Municipal to Solidaridad to Nuevo Federalismo*. Boulder, CO: Westview Press.

———. 1998. "Recasting Federalism in Mexico." *Publius: The Journal of Federalism* 28 (Winter): 235–54.

———. 2003. *Women in Contemporary Mexican Politics*. Austin: University of Texas Press. Revised and translated as *La mujer en la política mexicana* (Mexico City: Fondo de Cultura Económica, 2008).

Rodríguez, Victoria E., Allison Rowland, and Peter M. Ward. 2001. "Decentralization and Sub-national Governments in Mexico and in the U.S." Mexico-U.S. Partnership for Improved Public Administration: Key Issues of Public Policy in Comparative Perspective, Issue No. 2. Paper prepared for the annual meeting of the Partnerships for Improved Public Administration Consortium, Mexico City, January 27–29.

Rodríguez, Victoria E., and Peter M. Ward. 1992. *Policymaking, Politics, and Urban Governance in Chihuahua: The Experience of Recent Panista Governments*. Austin: Lyndon B. Johnson School of Public Affairs, University of Texas at Austin.

———. 1994. *Political Change in Baja California: Democracy in the Making?* Monograph Series 40. La Jolla: Center for U.S.-Mexican Studies, University of California, San Diego.

———, eds. 1995. *Opposition Government in Mexico.* Albuquerque: University of New Mexico Press.

———. 1999. "New Federalism, Intra-governmental Relations, and Co-governance in Mexico." *Journal of Latin American Studies* 31:673–710.

Rogers, Mary Beth. 1991. *Cold Anger: A Story of Faith and Power Politics.* Denton: University of North Texas Press.

Rosenbaum, Walter A. 1978. "Public Involvement as Reform and Ritual." In *Citizen Participation in America,* edited by Stuart Langton. Lexington, MA: Lexington Books.

Rowland, Allison M. 2001. "Population as a Determinant of Variation in Local Outcomes under Decentralization: Cases of Small Municipalities in Bolivia and Mexico." *World Development* 29, no. 8:1373–89.

Rowland, Allison M., and Georgina Caire. 2001. *Federalismo y federalismo fiscal en México: Una introducción.* Departamento de Administración Pública Working Paper No. 95. Mexico City: Centro de Investigación y Docencia Económicas.

Rozell, Mark J., and Clyde Wilcox. 1999. *Interest Groups in American Campaigns: The New Face of Electioneering.* Washington, DC: Congressional Quarterly Press.

Rozell, Mark, Clyde Wilcox, and David Madland. 2006. *Interest Groups in American Campaigns: The New Face of Electioneering.* Rev. 2nd ed. Washington, DC: Congressional Quarterly Press.

Rubin, Jeffrey W. 2006. "In the Streets or in the Institutions." *LASA Forum* 37, no. 1:26–29.

Rynders, Dustin W. 2003. "New Battles over U.S. Appellate Court Nominees: How the Selection Process Will Survive." Master's policy report, Lyndon B. Johnson School of Public Affairs, University of Texas at Austin.

Sabato, Larry. 1983. *Goodbye to Goodtime Charlie: The American Governorship Transformed.* 2nd ed. Washington, DC: Congressional Quarterly Press.

Sabetti, Filippo. 1996. "Path Dependency and Civic Culture: Some Lessons from Italy about Interpreting Social Experiments." *Politics and Society* 24, no. 1:19–44.

Sachs, Wolfgang, ed. 1992. *The Development Dictionary: A Guide to Knowledge as Power.* Atlantic Highlands, NJ: Zed Books.

Sadek, Maria Tereza, ed. 2000. *Justiça e cidadania no Brasil.* São Paulo: Editora Sumaré.

———. 2001. *Reforma do judiciario.* São Paulo: Fundação Konrad Adenauer.

Sader, E. 1988. *Quando novos personagens entraram em cena.* Rio de Janeiro: Paz e Terra.

Saffell, David C. 1987. *State and Local Government.* 3rd ed. New York: Random House.

Samuels, David. 1998. "Political Ambition in Brazil, 1945–95: Theory and Evidence." Paper presented at the Annual Conference of the Latin American Studies Association, Chicago, September 24–26.

———. 2003. *Ambition, Federalism, and Legislative Politics in Brazil.* New York: Cambridge University Press.

Samuels, David, and Scott Mainwaring. 2004. "Strong Federalism, Constraints on the Central Government, and Economic Reform in Brazil." In *Federalism and Democracy in Latin America*, edited by Edward L. Gibson. Baltimore: Johns Hopkins University Press.

Samuels, David, and Al Montero. 2004. *Decentralization and Democracy in Latin America.* Notre Dame: University of Notre Dame Press.

Sartori, Giovanni. 1962. *Democratic Theory.* Detroit: Wayne State University Press.

Sassen, Saskia. 1996. *Losing Control? Sovereignty in an Age of Globalization.* New York: Columbia University Press.

———. 2000. *Cities in a World Economy.* 2nd ed. Thousand Oaks, CA: Pine Forge Press.

Sawitch, H. V., and Ronald K. Vogel. 1996. *Regional Politics: Politics in the Post-city Age.* Thousand Oaks, CA: Sage Publications.

Scheberle, Denise. 2005. "The Evolving Matrix of Environmental Federalism and Intergovernmental Relationships." *Publius: The Journal of Federalism* 35 (Winter): 69–86.

Schedler, Andreas. 1998. "What Is Democratic Consolidation?" *Journal of Democracy* 9, no. 2:91–107.

Scherer-Warren, I., and P. J. Krischke, eds. 1987. *Uma revolução no cotidiano? Os novos movimentos sociais na América latina.* São Paulo: Brasiliense.

Schmitter, Phillipe C., and Terry Karl. 1993. "What Democracy Is . . . and Is Not." In *The Global Resurgence of Democracy*, edited by Larry Diamond and Marc F. Plattner, 49–62. Baltimore: Johns Hopkins University Press.

Schneider, Jo Anne. 2006. *Social Capital and Welfare Reform: Organizations, Congregations, and Communities.* New York: Columbia University Press.

Schneider, Ronald M. 1971. *The Political System of Brazil: Emergence of a "Modernizing Authoritarian" Regime, 1964–1970.* New York: Columbia University Press.

Schneider, Saundra K. 1997. "Medicaid Section 1115 Waivers: Shifting Health Care Reform to the States." *Publius: The Journal of Federalism* 27, no. 2: 89–109.

———. 2005. "Administrative Breakdowns in the Governmental Response to Hurricane Katrina." *Public Administration Review* 65 (September): 515–17.

Schram, Sanford F., and Carol S. Weissert. 1999. "The State of U.S. Federalism: 1998–1999." *Publius: The Journal of Federalism* 29 (Spring): 1–34.

Schumpeter, Joseph A. 1943. *Capitalism, Socialism and Democracy.* London: Allen and Unwin.

Schuurman, Frans J. 1998. "The Decentralisation Discourse: Post-Fordist Paradigm or Neo-Liberal Cul-de-Sac?" In *Globalisation, Competitiveness, and Human Security*, edited by Cristobal Kay. London: Frank Cass.

Sempere, J., and H. Sobarzo. 1996. *Federalismo fiscal en México*. CEE-DT 96/IV. Mexico City: Colegio de México.

Sen, Amartya. 1999. *Development as Freedom*. Oxford: Oxford University Press.

Sennett, Richard. 1977. *The Fall of Public Man*. Cambridge: Cambridge University Press.

Sernau, S. 1997. "Economies of Exclusion: Economic Change and the Global Underclass." In *At the Crossroads of Development: Transnational Challenges to Developed and Developing Societies*, edited by Joseph E. Behar and Alfred G. Cuzan. New York: E. J. Brill.

Serra, José, and José Roberto Rodrigues Afonso. 1999. "Federalismo fiscal à brasileira: Algumas reflexões." *Revista do BNDES* (Rio de Janeiro) 6, no. 12: 3–30.

Setzler, Mark H. 2002. "Democratizing Urban Brazil: Voters, Reformers, and the Pursuit of Political Accountability." PhD diss., University of Texas, Austin.

Shaiko, Ronald G. 1991. "More Bank for the Buck: The New Era of Full-Service Public Interest Organizations." In *Interest Group Politics*, 3rd ed., edited by Allan J. Cigler and Burdett A. Loomis, 109–10. Washington, DC: Congressional Quarterly Press.

———. 2004. *The Interest Group Connection: Electioneering, Lobbying, and Policymaking in Washington*. 2nd ed. Washington, DC: Congressional Quarterly Press.

Shugart, Matthew, and Martin Wattenberg. 1992. *Presidents and Assemblies: Constitutional Design and Electoral Dynamics*. Cambridge: Cambridge University Press.

———, eds. 2001. *Mixed-Member Electoral Systems: The Best of Both Worlds?* Oxford: Oxford University Press.

Sieder, Rachel, Line Schjolden, and Alan Angell, eds. 2005. *The Judicialization of Politics in Latin America*. New York: Palgrave Macmillan.

Sistare, Christine, ed. 2004. *Civility and Its Discontents: Essays on Civic Virtue, Toleration, and Cultural Fragmentation*. Lawrence: University Press of Kansas.

Skocpol, Theda. 1985. "Bringing the State Back In: Strategies of Analysis in Current Research." In *Bringing the State Back In*, edited by Peter Evans, Dietrich Rueschemeyer, and Theda Skocpol, 3–37. Cambridge: Cambridge University Press.

———. 2003. *Diminished Democracy: From Membership to Management in American Civic Life*. Norman: University of Oklahoma Press.

Smillie, Ian, and Henny Helmich, eds. 1993. *Non-governmental Organisations and Governments: Stakeholders for Development*. Paris: Development Centre of the Organisation for Economic Co-operation and Development.

Smith, Brian C. 1985. *Decentralization: The Territorial Dimension of the State*. Boston: Allen and Unwin.

———. 1988. *Bureaucracy and Political Power*. Brighton: Wheatsheaf Books.

Smith, Peter H. 2005. *Democracy in Latin America: Political Change in Comparative Perspective*. Oxford: Oxford University Press.

Smith, Steven Rathgeb. 1999. "Civic Infrastructure in America: The Interrelationships between Government and the Voluntary Sector." In *Civil Society, Democracy, and Civic Renewal*, edited by Robert Fullinwider, ch. 5. Lanham, MD: Rowman and Littlefield.

Smith, Steven Rathgeb, and Michael Lipsky. 1993. *Nonprofits for Hire: The Welfare State in the Age of Contracting*. Cambridge, MA: Harvard University Press.

Smulovitz, Catalina, and Enrique Peruzzoti. 2003. "Societal and Horizontal Control: Two Cases of a Fruitful Relationship." In *Democratic Accountability in Latin America*, edited by Scott Mainwaring and Christopher Welna, 309–32. Oxford: Oxford University Press.

Snell, Ronald K. 1991. "Deep Weeds: Dismal Outlook for 1991." *State Legislatures*, February, 15–18.

Snyder, Richard. 2001a. *Politics after Neoliberalism: Reregulation in Mexico*. New York: Cambridge University Press.

———. 2001b. "Scaling Down: The Subnational Comparative Method. (Regimes and Democracy in Latin America)." *Studies in Comparative International Development* 36 (Spring): 93–110.

Solt, Frederick. 2004. "Electoral Competition, Legislative Pluralism, and Institutional Development: Evidence from Mexico's States." *Latin American Research Review* 39, no. 1:155–67.

Souza, Celina. 1996. "Redemocratization and Decentralization in Brazil: The Strength of the Member States." *Development and Change* 27, no. 3:529–55.

———. 1998. "Federalismo, descentralização e desigualdades regionais no Brasil." Paper presented at the XXII Encontro Anual da Anpocs, Caxambu, October 27–31.

———. 2001. "Federalismo e gasto social no Brasil: Tensões e tendências." *Revista Lua Nova* 52:5–19.

———. 2002. "Brazil: The Prospects of a Center-Constraining Federation in a Fragmented Polity." *Publius: The Journal of Federalism* 32, no. 2:23–48.

———. 2003. "Federalismo e conflitos distributivos: Disputa dos estados por recursos orçamentários federais." *Dados* 46, no. 2:345–84.

———. 2004. "Governos locais e gestão de políticas sociais universais." *São Paulo em Perspetiva* 18, no. 2:27–41.

———. 2005a. "Federalismo, desenho constitucional e instituições federativas no Brasil pós-1988." *Revista de Sociologia e Política, Curitiba* 24:105–21.

———. 2005b. "Sistema brasileiro de governança local: Inovações institucionais e sustentabilidade." In *Desenho institucional e participação política: Experiências no brasil contemporâneo*, edited by Catia Lubamba, Denilson B. Coelho, and Marcus Andre Melo. Petropolis, Rio de Janeiro: Editora Vozes.

Souza, Celina, and Inaiá M. M. de Carvalho. 1999. "Reforma do estado, descentralização e desigualdades." *Lua Nova,* no. 48:187–212.

Souza, Renilson, R. de. 2003. "Redução das desigualdades regionais na alocação dos recursos federais para a saúde." *Ciência e Saúde Coletiva* 8, no. 2:449–60.

Spink, Peter Kevin. 2000a. "Gestão municipal faz escola: Aprendendo com os governos locais." *Cadernos Adenauer* 1 (June): 81–98.

———. 2000b. "The Rights Based Approach to Local Public Management: Experiences from Brazil." *Revista de Administração de Empresas* 40, no. 3:45–65.

———. 2002. "Parcerias e alianças com orgaizações não-estatais." In *Novos contornos da gestão local: Conceitos em construção,* edited by Peter K. Spink, S. Caccia Bava, and V. Paulics. São Paulo: Gestão Pública e Cidadania, Polis.

———. 2006. "The Pros and Cons of Learning from Innovation: Educational Policies Seen through the Public Management and Citizenship Program." Paper presented at the Congress of the Latin American Studies Association, San Juan, Puerto Rico.

Spink, Peter, and Roberta Clemente, eds. 1997. *20 experiências de gestão pública e cidadania.* Rio de Janeiro: Fundação Getulio Vargas.

Spink, Peter, Roberta Clemente, and Rosane Keppke. 1999. "Governo local: O mito da descentralização e as novas práticas de governança." *Revista de Administração* (São Paulo) 34, no. 1:61–69.

Spink, Peter, and Fernando Tenorio. 2004. "Parcerias na prática: A experiencia do programa gestão pública e cidadania." Unpublished research report, Center for Public Administration and Government, Escola de Administração de Empresas de São Paulo, Fundação Getulio Vargas.

Staudt, Kathleen. 1998. "Women in Politics: Mexico in Global Perspective." In *Women's Participation in Mexican Political Life,* edited by Victoria Rodríguez, 23–40. Boulder, CO: Westview Press.

Stedile, J. P., and B. M. Fernandes. 1999. *Brava gontoi A trajetória do MST e a luta pela terra no Brasil.* São Paulo: Fundação Perseu Abramo.

Stein, Ernesto, Mariano Tommasi, Koldo Echebarría, Eduardo Lora, and Mark Payne, eds. 2006. *The Politics of Policies: Economic and Social Progress in Latin America.* Report. Washington, DC: Inter-American Development Bank.

Stepan, Alfred. 1997. "Toward a New Comparative Analysis of Democracy and Federalism: Demos Constraining and Demos Enabling Federations." Paper presented at the annual meeting of the International Political Science Association, 17th World Congress, Seoul, Korea, August 17–22.

Stephen, Lynn. 2006. "Some Thoughts on Concepts for Central American Latino/ Latin American Chicano Studies." *LASA Forum* 37 (Winter): 10–12.

Stevens, Donald Fithian. 1991. *Origins of Instability in Early Republican Mexico.* Durham: Duke University Press.

Stivers, C. 1990. "The Public Agency as Polis: Active Citizenship in the Administrative State." *Administration and Society* 22, no. 1:86–105.

Stocker, Gerry. 1998. "Cinq propositions pour une théorie de la gouvernance." *Revue Internationale des Sciences Sociales: La Gouvernance* (UNESCO), no. 155 (March): 19–30.

Stokes, Susan C. 2001. *Mandates and Democracy: Neoliberalism by Surprise in Latin America*. New York: Cambridge University Press.

Swanstrom, Todd. 2001. "What We Argue about When We Argue about Regionalism." *Journal of Urban Affairs* 23, no. 5:479–96.

Swyngedouw, E. 1997. "Neither Global nor Local: 'Glocalization' and the Politics of Scale." In *Spaces of Globalization: Reasserting the Power of the Local*, edited by Kevin R. Cox, 137–66. New York: Guilford Press.

Tabin, Barrie. 1998. "Protecting Cities' Telecom Interests in Broad Battle for NCL." *Nation's Cities Weekly*, February 16, 5.

Tanzi, Vito. 1995. "Fiscal Federalism and Decentralization: A Review of Some Efficiency and Macroeconomic Aspects." In *World Bank Annual Conference on Development Economics*, edited by M. Bruno and B. Pleskovic. Washington, DC: World Bank.

Tatagiba, Luciana. 2002. "Os conselhos gestores e a democratrização das políticas públicas no Brasil." In *Sociedade civil e espaços públicos no Brasil*, edited by Evelina Danigno, 47–103. São Paulo: Paz e Terra.

Teixeira, Marco Antonio, R. Magalhães, L. Antonini, and M. do C. Albuquerque. 2002. "Experiências de orçamento participativo no estado de São Paulo (1997–2000)." Unpublished paper, Instituto Polis, São Paulo.

Teixeira, Marco Antonio, and Peter Spink. 2005. "Gestão de recursos Hídricos, um panorama de experiências exitosas." In *Administrando a água como se fosse importante*, edited by L. Dowbor and R. A. Tagnin, 271–82. São Paulo: Editora SENAC.

Tena Ramírez, Felipe. 1995. *Leyes fundamentales de México, 1808–1995*. Mexico City: Editorial Porrúa.

———. 1997. *Derecho constitucional mexicano*. Mexico City: Editorial Porrúa.

Tendler, Judith. 1997. *Good Government in the Tropics*. Baltimore: Johns Hopkins University Press.

Ter-Minassian, Teresa, ed. 1997. *Fiscal Federalism in Theory and Practice*. Washington, DC: International Monetary Fund.

Teune, Henry. 1982. "Decentralization and Economic Growth." *Annals of the American Academy of Political and Social Science* 459:98–102.

Theodoulou, Stella Z. 2002. *Policy and Politics in Six Nations as a Comparative Perspective on Policy Making*. Upper Saddle River, NJ: Prentice Hall.

Thomas, Clive S., and Ronald J. Hrebenar. 1991. "Nationalization of Interest Groups and Lobbying in the States." In *Interest Group Politics*, edited by Allan J. Cigler and Burdett A. Loomis, 63–80. Washington, DC: Congressional Quarterly Press.

Thoreau, Henry David. [1849] 1967. *The Variorum Civil Disobedience*. New York, Twayne. Originally published under the title *Resistance to Civil Government*.

Tierney, J., and K. Scholozman. 1989. "Congress and Organized Interests." In *Congressional Politics*, edited by C. Deering. Chicago: Dorsey.

Tocqueville, Alexis de. [1835] 1969. *Democracy in America*. Edited by J. P. Mayer. Translated by George Lawrence. New York: Anchor Books.

Topik, Steven. 1988. "The Economic Role of the State in Liberal Regimes: Brazil and Mexico Compared, 1888–1910." In *Guiding the Invisible Hand: Economic Liberalism and the State in Latin America History*, edited by Joseph L. Love and Nils Jacobsen. New York: Praeger.

Townroe, P. M., and D. Keen. 1984. "Polarization Reversal in the State of São Paulo, Brazil." *Regional Studies* 18:45–54. Reprinted In *Differential Urbanization: Integrating Spatial Models*, edited by H. S. Geyer and T. M. Kontuly (New York: Halsted Press, 1996).

Tsebelis, G. 1995. "Decision Making in Political Systems: Veto Players in Presidentialism, Parliamentarism, Multicameralism and Multipartism." *British Journal of Political Science* 25:289–325.

Uchitelle, Louis. 1991. "States and Cities Are Pushing Hard for Higher Taxes." *New York Times*, March 25, A1.

Ugalde, Antonio, and Núria Homedes. 2006. "Decentralization: The Long Road from Theory to Practice." In *Decentralizing Health Services in Mexico: A Case Study in State Reform*, edited by Núria Homedes and Antonio Ugalde, 3–44. La Jolla: Center for U.S.-Mexican Studies, University of California, San Diego.

UN Development Programme. 2003. "Human Development Indicators 2003. 13: Inequality in Income or Consumption." http://hdr.undp.org/reports/global /2003/indicator/indic_126_1_1.html.

UN Human Settlements Programme. 2001. *Cities in a Globalizing World: Global Report on Human Settlements 2001*. London: Earthscan Publications.

UN Statistics Division. 2006. "Millenium Development Goals Indicators: Population below $1 (PPP) per Day Consumption, Percentage." http://mdgs.un.org /unsd/mdg/SeriesDetail.aspx?srid=580&crid=.

U.S. Bureau of Economic Analysis. "Regional Accounts Data." www.bea.gov/bea /regional/data.htm.

U.S. Bureau of the Census. 1997a. *1997 Census of Governments*. Washington, DC: Government Printing Office.

———. 1997b. *Population: 1790 to 1990*. Washington, DC: Government Printing Office.

———. 1999. *Statistical Abstract of the United States*. Washington, DC: Government Printing Office.

———. 2000. *County and City Data Book: 2000*. Washington, DC: Government Printing Office. www.census.gov/statab/ccdb/cit1020r.txt.

———. 2002a. "Census 2000 Tabulation Entity Counts of Counties, County Subdivisions, and Places." www.census.gov/geo/www/tallies/ctytally.html.

———. 2002b. "2002 Census of Governments." www.census.gov/govs/www /cog2002.html.

U.S. Central Intelligence Agency. 2006a. "World Fact Book—Brazil: Geography." www.cia.gov/cia/publications/factbook/geos/br.html. Accessed April 2006.

U.S. Central Intelligence Agency. 2006b. "World Fact Book—Mexico: Geography." http://www.cia.gov/cia/publications/factbook/geos/mx.html. Accessed April 2006.

U.S. Central Intelligence Agency. 2006c. "World Fact Book—United States: Geography." http://www.cia.gov/cia/publications/factbook/geos/us.html. Accessed April 2006.

U.S. General Accounting Office. 2000. *Welfare Reform: Improving State Automated Systems Requires Coordinated Federal Organization.* Washington, DC: Government Printing Office.

Vago, Steven. 1991. *Law and Society.* 3rd ed. Upper Saddle River, NJ: Prentice Hall.

Van Cott, Donna Lee. 2005. *From Movements to Parties in Latin America: The Evolution of Ethnic Politics.* Cambridge: Cambridge University Press.

Vásquez, Josefina Zoraida. 1993. "El federalismo mexicano, 1823–1847." In *Federalismos latinoamericanos: México/Brasil/Argentina,* edited by Marcello Carmagnani, 15–50. Mexico City: Colegio de México and Fondo de Cultura Económica.

Veronese, Alexandre. 2002. "Direito na fronteira ou fronteira do Direito: Experiências de projetos do Programa Nacional Balcões de Direito." *Cadernos Adenauer* 3, no. 6:93–118.

Vignoli, Francisco H., ed. 2002. *A lei de responsabilidade fiscal comentada para municípios.* São Paulo: Escola de Administração de Empresas de São Paulo, Fundação Getulio Vargas.

Villegas, Daniel Cosío, Ignacio Bernal, Alejandra Moreno Toscano, Luis González, Eduardo Blanquel, and Lorenzo Meyer, eds. 1995. *A Compact History of Mexico.* 3rd ed. Mexico City: Colegio de México.

Wagley, Charles. 1964. *An Introduction to Brazil.* New York: Columbia University Press.

Walker, David B. 1991. "American Federalism from Johnson to Bush." *Publius: The Journal of Federalism* 21 (Winter): 105–19.

———. 1995. *The Rebirth of Federalism: Slouching toward Washington.* Chatham, NJ: Chatham House.

Wampler, Brian. 2000. "Private Executives, Legislative Brokers, and Participatory Publics: Building Local Democracy." PhD diss., University of Texas, Austin.

Ward, Peter M. 1998. "From Machine Politics to the Politics of Technocracy: Charting Changes in Governance in the Mexican Municipality." *Bulletin of Latin American Research* 17, no. 3:341–65.

———. 1999a. *Colonias and Public Policy in Texas and Mexico: Urbanization by Stealth.* Austin: University of Texas Press.

———. 1999b. "Creating a Metropolitan Tier of Government in Federal Systems: Getting 'There' from 'Here' in Mexico City and in Other Latin American Megacities." *South Texas Law Review Journal* 40, no. 3:603–23.

Ward, Peter M., and Victoria E. Rodríguez. 1999. *New Federalism and State Government in Mexico: Bringing the States Back In*. U.S.-Mexican Policy Report 9. Austin: Lyndon B. Johnson School of Public Affairs, University of Texas at Austin.

Ward, Peter M., Victoria E. Rodríguez, and Hector Robles. 2003. "Learning Democracy in Mexico and the US: Do Space and Place Matter?" Unpublished paper for "Democracy through U.S. and Mexican Lenses," William and Flora Hewlett Foundation Grant No. 2000-4406, Roderic Ai Camp (principal investigator), Miguel Basáñez, Rodolfo de la Garza, Joseph Klesner, Chappell Lawson, Alejandro Moreno, Pablo Parás, Victoria Rodríguez, and Peter M. Ward.

Waylen, Georgina. 1994. "Women and Democratization: Conceptualizing Gender Relations in Transition Politics." *World Politics* 46:327–54.

———. 2000. "Gender and Democratic Politics: A Comparative Analysis of Consolidation in Argentina and Chile." *Journal of Latin American Studies* 32: 765–93.

Weber, Ronald E., and Paul Brace. 1999. *American State and Local Politics: Directions for the 21st Century*. New York: Seven Bridges Press.

Weingast, Barry R. 1997. "The Political Foundations of Democracy and the Rule of Law." *American Political Science Review* 91 (June): 245–63.

Weir, Margaret, 1996. "Central Cities' Loss of Power in State Politics." *Cityscape: A Journal of Policy Development and Research* 2 (May): 23–39.

Weir, Margaret, Harold Wolman, and Todd Swanstrom. 2005. "The Calculus of Coalitions: Cities, Suburbs, and the Metropolitan Agenda." *Urban Affairs Review* 40, no. 6:730–60.

Weisner, Eduardo. 2003. *Fiscal Federalism in Latin America: From Entitlements to Markets*. Washington, DC: Inter-American Development Bank.

Weissert, Carol S., and Jeffrey S. Hill. 1994. "Low-Level Radioactive Waste Compacts: Lessons Learned from Theory and Practice." *Publius: The Journal of Federalism* 24 (Autumn): 27–43.

Welborn, David M., and Jesse Burkhead. 1989. *Intergovernmental Relations in the American Administrative State: The Johnson Presidency*. Austin: University of Texas Press.

Weldon, Jeffrey. 1997. "Political Sources of Presidencialismo in Mexico." In *Presidentialism and Democracy in Latin America*, edited by Scott Mainwaring and Matthew Soberg Shugart, 225–58. Cambridge: Cambridge University Press.

Weyland, Kurt Gerhard. 2002. *The Politics of Market Reform in Fragile Democracies: Argentina, Brazil, Peru and Venezuela*. Princeton: Princeton University Press.

Whitehead, Laurence. 1991. "Mexico's Economic Prospects: Implications for State-Labour Relations." In *Unions, Workers, and the State in Mexico*, edited by K. Middlebrook, 57–83. San Diego: Center for U.S.-Mexico Studies, University of California, San Diego.

———. 2006. *Latin America: A New Interpretation*. New York: Palgrave Macmillan.

Wibbels, Erik. 1993. "Introduction: Some Insights from Western Social Theory." *World Development* 21, no. 8:1245–61.

———. 2005. *Federalism and the Market: Intergovernmental Conflict and Economic Reform in the Developing World*. New York: Cambridge University Press.

Wilson, Robert H. 1993. *States and the Economy: Policymaking and Decentralization*. Westport, CT: Praeger.

———, ed. 1997. *Public Policy and Community: Activism and Governance in Texas*. Austin: University of Texas Press.

———. 2000. "Understanding Local Governance: An International Perspective." *Revista de Administração de Empresas* 40 (April–June): 51–63.

———. 2001. "Redefining Regional Development: Decentralized Policymaking and International Markets in Brazil." In *Knowledge for Inclusive Development*, edited by Manuel Heitor, David Gibson, and Pedro Conceição. Westport, CT: Quorum.

Wilson, Robert H., and Robert Paterson. 2002. "State and Local Government Initiatives for Growth Management and Open Space Preservation." Research report, Policy Research Project No. 143, Lyndon B. Johnson School of Public Affairs, University of Texas at Austin.

———, eds. 2003. *Innovative Initiatives in Growth Management and Open Space Preservation: A National Study*. Policy Research Project No. 145. Austin: Lyndon B. Johnson School of Public Affairs, University of Texas at Austin.

Wilson, Woodrow. [1887] 1941. "The Study of Public Administration." *Political Science Quarterly* 56 (December): 481–506.

Wolman, Harold. 1990. "Decentralization: What It Is and Why We Should Care." In *Decentralization, Local Governments and Markets: Towards a Post-welfare Agenda*, edited by Robert J. Bennett, 29–42. Oxford: Oxford University Press.

Wood, Gordon S. 1969. *The Creation of the American Republic, 1776–1787*. Chapel Hill: University of North Carolina Press.

Wood, Richard L. 2002. *Faith in Action: Religion, Race, and Democratic Organizing in America*. Chicago: University of Chicago Press.

World Bank. 2006a. "Brazil Data Profile." http://devdata.worldbank.org/external/CPProfile.asp?PTYPE=CP&CCODE=BRA.

———. 2006b. "Mexico Data Profile." http://devdata.worldbank.org/external/CPProfile.asp?PTYPE=CP&CCODE=MEX.

———. 2006c. "United States Data Profile." http://devdata.worldbank.org/external/CPProfile.asp?PTYPE=CP&CCODE=USA.

———. 2006d. "World Development Report 2006: Equity and Development." http://web.worldbank.org/WBSITE/EXTERNAL/EXTDEC/EXTRESEARCH/EXTWDRS/EXTWDR2006/0,,menuPK:477658~pagePK:64167702~piPK:64167676~theSitePK:477642,00.html.

Wright, Deil S. 1982. *Understanding Intergovernmental Relations*. 2nd ed. Pacific Grove, CA: Brooks/Cole.

———. 2005. "How Did Intergovernmental Relations Fail in the USA after Hurricane Katrina?" *Federations* 5, no. 1 (1982): 11–12.

Wuthnow, Robert. 1998. *Loose Connections: Joining Together in America's Fragmented Communities*. Cambridge, MA: Harvard University Press.

Yashar, Deborah. 2005. *Contesting Citizenship in Latin America: Indigenous Movements and the Post-liberal Challenge*. New York: Cambridge University Press.

Zander, Navarro. 1998. "Participation, Democratizing Practices and the Formation of a Modern Polity: The Case of 'Participatory Budgeting' in Porto Alegre, Brazil (1989–98)." *Development* 41, no. 3:68–71.

Zimmerman, Christopher. 1990. "New Federal Budget Means a Bigger Bill for States." *State Legislatures*, November/December, 12–13.

———. 1991. "The Sad State of the States: Monster Deficits are Cutting Local Services and Delaying Recovery." *Business Week*, April 22, 24–26.

Zimmerman, Joseph. 1994. "Introduction: Dimensions of Interstate Relations." *Publius: The Journal of Federalism* 24 (Autumn): 1–11.

———. 2005. *Congressional Preemption: Regulatory Federalism*. Albany: State University of New York Press.

# About the Authors and Collaborators

## Authors

**Victoria E. Rodríguez** is Vice Provost and Dean of Graduate Studies at the University of Texas at Austin, Ashbel Smith Professor, and Professor at the Lyndon B. Johnson School of Public Affairs. A distinguished author and scholar on women in contemporary Mexican politics, her principal works include *Women's Participation in Mexican Political Life* (Westview Press, 1998) and *Women in Contemporary Mexican Politics* (University of Texas Press, 2003; Fondo de Cultura Económica, 2008). She has co-directed with Peter Ward major research projects on politics and governance in Mexico, and she is coauthor of *Policymaking, Politics and Urban Governance in Chihuahua* (Lyndon B. Johnson School of Public Affairs, 1992); *Political Change in Baja California: Democracy in the Making?* (Center for U.S.-Mexican Studies, 1994); *Opposition Government in Mexico* (University of New Mexico Press, 1995); and *New Federalism and State Government in Mexico: Bringing the States Back In* (Lyndon B. Johnson School of Public Affairs, 1999). Among her other works are *Decentralization in Mexico: From Reforma Municipal to Solidaridad to Nuevo Federalismo* (Westview Press, 1997; Fondo de Cultura Económica, 1999). In 2000 she and Peter Ward were honored by the Mexican government with the Ohtli Medal, and in 2007 she was named one of the Twenty Most Influential Hispanics in the USA. She received her PhD in political science from the University of California, Berkeley.

**Peter K. Spink** is Professor of Public Administration and Government in the School of Business Administration, Getulio Vargas Foundation, São Paulo; former academic dean (1991–95) and current head of the Center for Public Administration and Government; and co-director of the Public Management and Citizenship Innovation Program. His areas of interest include subnational government, processes of social innovation, local strategies for poverty reduction, and relationships between government and civil society. Among his many publications are *Reforming the State: Managerial Public Administration in Latin America* (with Luiz Carlos Bresser Pereira; Lynne Rienner, 1999); *Redução da pobreza e dinâmicas locais* (with Ilka Camarotti; Editora da Fundação Getulio Vargas, 2001), and *Governo local e gênero* (with Ilka Camarotti; Annablume Editora, 2003). He has been a Visiting Scholar at the Centre of Latin American Studies and the Faculty of Social and Political Sciences, University of Cambridge, and Philips Visiting Professor at the Lyndon B. Johnson School of Public Affairs. He has a PhD in organizational psychology from the University of London.

**Peter M. Ward** holds the C. B. Smith Sr. Centennial Chair in U.S.-Mexico Relations in the College of Liberal Arts and is Professor in the Department of Sociology and in the Lyndon B. Johnson School of Public Affairs at the University of Texas at Austin. At the University of Texas he served as Director of the Mexican Center of the Teresa Lozano Long Institute of Latin American Studies (LLILAS; 1993–97 and 2001 5). Between 2002 and 2007 he was Editor-in-Chief of the *Latin American Research Review*. Formerly he was a professor of Geography at University College, London, and at the University of Cambridge. His research spans a number of areas: low-income housing, informal land markets, planning and urban development, Mexican politics and governance, and border affairs. He has published over one hundred journal articles and book chapters and among his fourteen sole or coauthored books are *Housing, the State and the Poor: Policy and Practice in Latin American Cities* (with Alan G. Gilbert, Cambridge University Press, 1985); *Welfare Politics in Mexico: Papering Over the Cracks* (Allen and Unwin, 1986); *Mexico City*, 2nd ed. (John Wiley, 1998) (all published in major Spanish editions); and *Colonias and Public Policy in Texas and Mexico* (University of Texas Press,

1999). He is also coauthor with Victoria Rodríguez of a number of books on governance and political change in Mexico. In 2000 he and Victoria Rodríguez were jointly honored by the Mexican government with the Ohtli Medal for their services in the advancement of understanding of Mexican culture and society. He received a PhD from the University of Liverpool in 1976.

**Robert H. Wilson** is Mike Hogg Professor of Urban Policy and Associate Dean of the Lyndon B. Johnson School of Public Affairs at the University of Texas, Austin and is former director of the University of Texas Brazil Center and the Urban Issues Program. His areas of interest include urban and regional policy, public policy in Brazil, and local governance in developing countries. Among his many publications are *Public Policy and Community: Activism and Governance in Texas* (University of Texas Press, 1997), *States and the Economy: Policymaking and Decentralization* (Praeger, 1993), *The Political Economy of Brazil: Public Policies in an Era of Transition* (University of Texas Press, 1990), and over sixty journal articles, book chapters, and policy reports. He served as a Visiting Professor at the Federal University of Pernambuco (Recife, Brazil); held the Visiting International Philips Professorship at the Getulio Vargas Foundation, São Paulo; held the Fulbright/FLAD (Luso American Development Foundation) Chair in Knowledge Management Policies at the Advanced Technical Institute, Lisbon; and was inducted into the Brazilian National Order of the Southern Cross, rank of Commander. He holds a PhD in urban and regional planning from the University of Pennsylvania.

## Collaborators

**Marta Ferreira Santos Farah** is a Professor of Public Policies at the Escola de Administração de Empresas de São Paulo, Fundação Getulio Vargas. She teaches graduate and undergraduate courses in public administration and government and was formerly coordinator of the Master's Program on Public Administration and Government. Since 2004 she has been the Associate Dean for Undergraduate Courses. She serves as the Vice-Director of the Public Management and Citizenship Program, developed with the support of Ford Foundation and the Banco Nacional de Desenvolvimento Econômico e Social (BNDES), which disseminates innovative initiatives from subnational governments. Her areas of interest include social policies, local government, and gender. Her publications include "El Programa Brasileño de Gestión Pública y Ciudadania," in *Gestión y Política Pública* (with Peter Spink; Mexico City, 2004); "Gender and Public Policies," *Estudos Feministas* 1 (2006); and "Dissemination of Innovations: Learning from Sub-national Awards Programs in Brazil," in *Innovations in Governance and Public Administration: Replicating What Works,* edited by Adriana Alberti and Guido Bertucci (UN Department of Economic and Social Affairs, 2006). She holds a PhD in sociology from the University of São Paulo.

**Lawrence S. Graham** is Emeritus Professor of Government at the University of Texas (UT), Austin. His core interests are centered on the Portuguese-speaking world. In this context, he established the Brazil Center in the Teresa Lozano Long Institute of Latin American Studies and was its director from 1995 to 2000, when he took on responsibilities for UT's international activities at large (2000–2004) as Associate Vice President for International Programs. During these years, he was Philips Professor at the Getúlio Vargas Foundation's School of Business Administration in São Paulo, Brazil (fall 1998). Throughout his career, he has combined teaching and research with contract work with national and international organizations in Latin America, southern and eastern Europe, and Africa. His publications (seventeen books and over one hundred articles) have focused on comparative politics and public policy in these world areas. Illustrative of these interests are *The Political Economy of Brazil*, with Robert Wilson (University of Texas Press, 1990), *The Portuguese Military and the State* (Westview Press, 1993), and *The Politics of Governing: A Comparative Introduction* (Congressional Quarterly Press, 2006).

**Pedro Jacobi** is Full Professor at the School of Education and of the Graduate Program of Environmental Science at the University of São Paulo in Brazil. In 2000 he was Tinker Visiting Professor at the Institute of Latin American Studies, University of Texas at Austin, and in 1992 he was Visiting Professor at the Institut d'Hautes Études d'Amerique Latine en Paris, Université de Paris. His areas of interest include environmental policies in metropolitan areas; decentralization and participation in water management in Brazil; theory and methodology of environmental education; and citizens' participation and mobilization in socioenvironmental policies. Since 1997 he has been co-editor of the journal *Ambiente e Sociedade*, a Brazilian review on environment and society. He has published more than sixty articles in national and international journals and book chapters on social movements and public policies, environmental policies in urban areas, water governance and management with social participation in Brazil, socioenvironmental behavior in urban areas, environmental education, institutional innovations in local governments, educational policies and decentralization, and digital inclusion in Brazil. He recently edited *Gestão compartilhada dos resíduos sólidos no Brasil: Inovação com inclusão social* (Annablume Editora, 2006) and *Diálogos em ambiente e sociedade* (Annablume Editora, 2006); authored *Inovação no campo da gestão pública local* (Editora FGV, 2005); and coauthored *Citizens at Risk: From Urban Sanitation to Sustainable Cities* (Earthscan, 2001), *Políticas sociais e ampliação da cidadania* (Editora FGV, 2000), *Cidade e meio ambiente: Percepções e práticas em São Paulo* (Annablume Editora, 1999), and *Ciência ambiental: Os desafios da interdisciplinaridade* (Annablume, 1999).

**Allison M. Rowland** was Catedrático-Investigador in the Department of Public Administration at the Centro de Investigación y Docencia Económicas (CIDE), A.C. in Mexico City between 1997 and 2007, and now serves as Tax and Budget Policy Director at Voices for Utah Children. Her areas of interest include local government and public policy, intergovernmental relations, and crime prevention and control. Recent publications include "Local Responses to Public Insecurity in Mexico: The Policía Comunitaria of the Costa Chica and the Montaña de Guerrero," in *Public Security and Police Reform in Latin America,* edited by John Bailey and Lucia Dammert (University of Pittsburgh Press, 2006); "La seguridad pública local en México: Una agenda sin rumbo," in *Gobiernos municipales en transición,* edited by Enrique Cabrero (Miguel Angel Porrúa, 2003); and "Population as a Determinant of Variation in Local Outcomes under Decentralization: Cases of Small Municipalities in Bolivia and Mexico," *World Development* 29, no. 8 (2001). She received a PhD in policy, planning, and development from the University of Southern California.

# Index